"The best single examination of America's energy problem in print."
—Peter Passell, *The New York Times Book Review*

"*Energy Future* spares no one—least of all economic experts. Conservation and solar energy—those panaceas of impractical reformers and hippies—that's where the hardheaded Business School calculations point. This book cannot be ignored." —Paul A. Samuelson, Institute Professor, M.I.T. Nobel Laureate in Economics

"*Energy Future* adds significantly to the dialogue over our energy options. It should be read by anyone who has a stake in those options—which means everyone." —Robert O. Anderson, Chairman, Atlantic Richfield Company

"The most comprehensive, readable account of our energy situation that anyone has produced." —Michael Sheldrick, *Business Week*

"Splendid . . . the most lucid and balanced appraisal of the general energy situation that has appeared so far." —*The New Yorker*

"By far the best text currently available. . . . a model of what university research and monograph writing on a major question of policy should be." —John Kenneth Galbraith, *The New York Review of Books*

ENERGY FUTURE

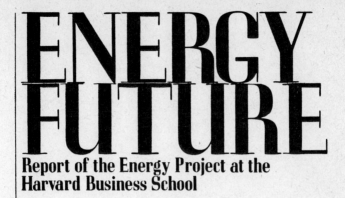

ENERGY FUTURE

Report of the Energy Project at the
Harvard Business School

ROBERT STOBAUGH | DANIEL YERGIN
editors

I. C. BUPP | MEL HORWITCH | SERGIO KOREISHA
MODESTO A. MAIDIQUE | FRANK SCHULLER

new revised third edition

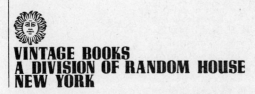

VINTAGE BOOKS
A DIVISION OF RANDOM HOUSE
NEW YORK

First Vintage Books Edition, January 1983

Faculty research at the Harvard Business School is undertaken with the expectation of publication. In such publication the authors responsible for the research
project are also responsible for statements of fact, opinions, and conclusions expressed. Neither the Harvard Business School, its faculty as a whole, nor the
president and fellows of Harvard College reach conclusions or make recommendations as results of faculty research.

Library of Congress Cataloging in Publication Data
Main entry under title:

Energy future.

  Bibliography: p.
  Includes index.
  1. Energy policy—United States. 2. Power
resources—United States. I. Stobaugh, Robert B.
II. Yergin, Daniel. III. Harvard University.
Graduate School of Business Administration.
HD9502.U52E4914 1981   333.79′0973   81-40078
ISBN 0-394-74750-X   AACR2

Manufactured in the United States of America

TO
BEVERLY
AND
ANGELA,
WHO CONTRIBUTED A GREAT DEAL

ACKNOWLEDGMENTS

In the course of researching and writing this book, we two communicated with over three hundred business executives, government officials, labor union leaders, analysts, academics, and other specialists. With some, it was a matter of only a small point. Others gave enormously of their time and attention. Our coauthors had similar exchanges with many hundreds more. Obviously, because of the space required to list a thousand or so names, but also because some spoke to us candidly on condition of anonymity, we do not thank them by name. But we do express our deepest appreciation to all of them. Our undertaking would not have been possible without such assistance.

Fortunately, there are also those we can thank by name. We start not with a person, but with an institution, the Harvard Business School, and in particular its Division of Research and its Associates, which made this entire effort possible in a way that few other institutions could—or would—have. It provided the resources so that we had ample time to explore these complex matters critically and pragmatically. It was Dean Lawrence Fouraker who asked Robert Stobaugh to organize the Energy Project in 1972, and then gave it his continued support; and it was Elmer N. Funkhouser, Jr., the Dean's special assistant, who played a major role in encouraging the research and in raising funds for the

Division of Research. Professor Richard Walton, formerly head of the Division of Research, provided the necessary funding and encouragement for its launching. His successor, former Associate Dean Richard Rosenbloom, supported and encouraged us in a manifold of ways as the research project took shape as a book, and to him all of us have a special and lasting gratitude. Our colleagues in the Production and Operations Management Area at the school were willing to be in the classroom, enabling us to carry on with the required research and writing. For this, we thank them, as well as former Associate Dean Walter Salmon and former Associate Dean (and now Dean) John McArthur, Area Chairmen Wickham Skinner, Robert Hayes, James Healy, and Philip Thurston, all of whom handled the difficult task of working out faculty schedules. We also appreciate the encouragement and support that we have received from John McArthur in his role as Dean, Professor Raymond Corey in his role as Director of Research, and Joanne Segal, in her role as Assistant Dean and Director of Administration for the Division of Research.

As the title of the book suggests, this is a report of a project located at the Harvard Business School, and not a report of the school. And, of course, the conclusions and opinions are those of the authors, for, as the school's policy statement says: "Neither the Harvard Business School [nor] its faculty as a whole . . . reach conclusions or make recommendations as results of faculty research."

We would also like to thank the Center for International Affairs at Harvard, and its directors, Raymond Vernon, Benjamin Brown, and Samuel Huntington, for it was in the Center's International Energy Seminar that important parts of this book took shape. We also appreciate the support of the Energy and Environmental Policy Center at the Kennedy School of Government at Harvard, and its director, William Hogan, and its executive director, Henry Lee.

Nancy Estes served as combination administrative aide and secretary for the Project. Whether scheduling meetings at chaotic moments or typing at the oddest hours, she kept the Project running. Her efforts and skills, plus her kind nature, were invaluable. Nancy Armstrong also kept the project working and was a pleasure to work with. Stacy Miller, as she has for other publications of the Energy Project, spent many hours in the library helping us to find information that did not want to be found. Gay Auerbach and Carmen Vaubel helped a great deal. Leslie Sterling stepped in to maintain order in the Project, and this she did with great skill and patience. Jane Shorall provided the essential administrative and editorial assistance for the second edition. Catherine Judson ably stepped into the role of administrative aide and secretary for this third edition. She organized and coordinated the work with a rare combination of efficiency and pleasantness. Jean Twomey was also very helpful on this revision, and also a pleasure to work with. We thank them all.

On behalf of our coauthors, let us also thank those who worked with them and saw too many drafts of their chapters— Billie Lawrence, Maria Loomis, Rona McCrensky, Elaine Mittell, Mary Day, Muriel Drysdale, Rose Giacobbe, and other members of the Word Processing Center. Peter Thorne and John Ince assisted Modesto A. Maidique in research on solar energy in the first two editions, and John Ince revised the chapter for this third edition.

We speak often in this book of the transition from imported oil to a more balanced energy system. There is also the transition from raw research to a finished book, for what value are years spent researching if the fruits remain unknown? Jason Epstein, editorial director at Random House, saw merit in what we were trying to do, chose to take us on as his authors, encouraged us, but also challenged us many times with tough and blunt questions. His colleague Grant Ujifusa also brought great dedication to this book, and gave it much more time and concern than the rules of publishing allow. As has been written about him when he edited Dan Yergin's *Shattered Peace*, Grant "brought insight, commitment, and patience to this project." Cheryl Merser's dedication and superb abilities made a major contribution to the life of the book. Carolyn Lumsden worked diligently as copy editor. Helen Brann believed that this was an important book that should be published, and made that possible. We thank her deeply for her continuing support, and also express great appreciation to her colleague, John Hartnett.

We twice had the invaluable experience of working with William Bundy, editor of *Foreign Affairs*, who has been editor of some of the truly significant energy articles of the 1970's and early 1980's. We express our appreciation to him and to his thoughtful colleague, James Chace.

Three other people must be mentioned: Sidney Robbins, this time not a coauthor with Robert Stobaugh, provided a careful reading of the entire manuscript. Max Hall provided editorial guidance in the early phases for a number fo us. Herbert Holloman, director of MIT's Center for Policy Alternatives, provided financial support for our earlier studies of nuclear power, a careful reading of several chapters, and moral support for the entire undertaking. In addition, we thank the members of the Resources for the Future Project, "Energy: The Next Twenty Years" (of which Robert Stobaugh was a member), for discussion of our manuscript.

Only those who have participated in this kind of research project know the costs exacted on family life. Taking one away night after night, weekend after weekend, vacation after vacation, the work never ends. Our families deserve special medals for understanding.

As editors, we were extremely fortunate to be working with an unusual group of colleagues, who put aside many other obligations in pursuit of that intangible goal, a first-rate chapter. Strong-willed and determined, they have worked closely with us and with each other, not only on their chapters, but on ours, and never surrendered their independence of judgment. For such a group to be so harmonious throughout this demanding project is a tribute to their abilities and scholarly commitments, and also to their understandings of the frailties of the editors.

Events moved rapidly after the first edition of *Energy Future* was completed, and we and our colleagues subsequently had the opportunity to learn from many more people across the energy spectrum. Thus, when it came time to do a revised edition just a year after the publication of the first, we found ourselves doing a much more extensive revision than we had anticipated.

That has been no less true for this third edition, completed three years after the first. Many factors have changed, many assumptions have shifted, and many energy relationships have been altered. Experience has begun to accumulate about life with $30-plus a barrel oil—a condition that, as late as 1978, was generally not expected until the year 2000. Upheaval has persisted in the Middle East, the breadbasket of world oil production, with the revolution in Iran followed by a protracted war between Iran and Iraq. Mexico has quickly emerged as a major factor in the world oil market; France is the one western nation that has pushed ahead successfully with a major nuclear program. OPEC has faced its own oil crisis—falling demand for its product.

Despite the changes, many basic themes are as pertinent or even more pertinent today than they were at the time of the first edition: the instability surrounding world oil supplies, the uncertainty about the reserves base and the depletion rate of U.S. oil and gas reserves, the immobilization of nuclear energy in the United States, the challenge of building up an expanded coal infrastructure, the potential for conservation. We have sought to integrate the changes with the continuities in order to identify, understand, and explicate the fundamental questions that will be central to the energy future, both for the United States and the entire world, in the rest of this decade and into the next. In other words, our goal is to provide a framework for thinking about the energy future.

As we look through this manuscript, we are reminded of what has occurred to us so often before: The "energy problem" is so fragmented, in so many different pieces. We never doubted the importance of trying to make sense out of those pieces; sometimes we doubted the feasibility. We were willing to forgo much in order to try, for we regarded it as extraordinarily exciting to have the opportunity to try to make sense out of the pieces. It was also a great responsibility. We approached this work in that double spirit.

Robert Stobaugh
Daniel Yergin

Soldiers Field
1982

The names of the individual contributors appear at the heading of each chapter. They are:

I. C. Bupp *(Chapters 3 and 5)*
Mel Horwitch *(Chapter 4)*
Sergio Koreisha *(Appendix)*
Modesto A. Maidique *(Chapter 7)*
Frank Schuller *(Chapter 3)*
Robert Stobaugh *(Chapters 1, 2, 8, 9, and Appendix)*
Daniel Yergin *(Chapters 1, 6, 8, and 9)*

CONTENTS

ENERGY FUTURE

1 THE END OF EASY OIL

ROBERT STOBAUGH
DANIEL YERGIN

In 1968, the State Department sent the word to foreign governments—American oil production would soon reach the limits of its capacity. Friendly governments needed to know that the cushion of the U.S.'s extra capacity, which could be called into production during an emergency, was about to disappear. The end of an era was at hand.

But few people anywhere thought seriously about the implications of losing the cushion, for the industrial world had grown increasingly comfortable using oil to fuel the unprecedented economic growth of the 1950's and 1960's. Western Europe and Japan relied mainly on the Middle East, and the United States also was beginning to import from that region. Middle Eastern oil was the world's favorite fuel—easy to produce in very large volumes (a dime or two a barrel), easy to transport, and easy to burn—certainly easier than coal.

In 1970, some 111 years after the birth of the American oil industry, domestic production peaked and began to decline. But the demand for oil continued to surge, and that demand could be met only by more and more oil from the Middle East, which meant increasing dependence—and increasing vulnerability. The idea that there was something threatening in the growing dependence was an idea better ignored. Even if one recognized a potential problem, what to do about it was hardly clear when the general momentum to use more oil was regarded as unstoppable.

The first oil shock, in late 1973 and early 1974, definitely marked the end of secure and cheap oil. Arab oil producers embargoed the United States and reduced overall output and shipments to other nations. For the first time, OPEC countries stopped negotiating a price with the oil companies; they instead unilaterally set the price on a take-it-or-leave-it basis. The oil buyers had no choice, and they took it, paying the higher price, eight times higher by the end of 1974 than five years earlier.[1] And so the petroleum exporting countries defined a new age for the rest of the world—one of insecure supplies of expensive oil.

The oil crisis of 1973–74 constituted a turning point in postwar history, delivering a powerful economic and political jolt to the entire world. It interrupted or perhaps even permanently slowed postwar economic growth. And it set in motion a drastic shift in world power, in the very substance of international politics. Curiously, however, in the aftermath it became fashionable to discuss the crisis as though it were a unique event, a freak storm that had been weathered.

We have consistently disagreed, viewing it instead as a warning of a fundamental and dangerous disorder, for the basic conditions that allowed the first shock, and then the second, which occurred in 1979–1980 after the fall of the Shah of Iran, have continued to prevail. Indeed notwithstanding the so-called "oil glut" that existed in 1982, higher real oil prices seemed assured over the long run. But as of 1983, no one knows the timing of any price rise. Many expect level or slightly falling real prices for some years prior to a real rise; others expect the real rise to come sooner. Until the recession in the industrialized world ends, it is impossible to sort out how much of the decline in oil consumption has been due to recession and how much to conservation.

Any price increase has immediate, undesirable effects on all oil-importing nations, causing a direct loss in national income. If the price rise is very gradual over a period of many years, thereby allowing the oil-importing nations a gradual adjustment, the direct effects might then be the main ones.

A large, sudden increase in oil prices would have serious

indirect effects. It would exacerbate inflation, place further strains
on the international monetary system, and sharply contract the
demand for goods and services, further reducing national income.
In short, the economic consequences would likely be a major
recession, or possibly even a depression.

The political consequences are potentially no less serious.
Slower economic growth and high inflation intensify conflicts not
only within Western nations, but also among them. As the world's
largest oil importer, the United States would bear much of the
blame for higher oil prices. A bitter competition for oil could
ensue, damaging the Western security and trading systems. Putting aside American relations with the industrialized nations,
greater reliance on Middle East imports would certainly mean that
U.S. foreign policy would be increasingly constrained by its oil
suppliers.

Political instability in the Middle East, supply interruptions,
the extension of Soviet influence—highlighted by the brutal invasion of Afghanistan—such factors only make a very bad situation
much worse. *This point must be underlined.* For the industrial
nations to continue to depend on Middle Eastern oil in the way
current trends indicate means heavy reliance on a region of high
political tension and risk. In the last three decades, the Middle
East has been subjected to a dozen wars, a dozen revolutions, and
innumerable assassinations and territorial disputes. Dependence
reinforces the twin vulnerabilities—interruption of supplies and
major price increases.

In 1975, economic activity, responding to the strains of the
first shock, slowed down, tempering for a time the demand for oil,
and thus postponing the reemergence of a tight petroleum market.
But political and psychological factors were left out of many of the
most prominent forecasts of the international energy scene, for
they could not easily be integrated into economists' equations. It
became quite fashionable to talk complacently of a glut on the
world market.

Beginning in 1977, such factors did begin to make their
influence felt, underscoring how crisis-prone is the current energy
system. Increases in U.S. oil imports helped trigger the sharp
decline of the dollar, which began in 1977 and reached almost

panic proportions by the end of 1978, spilling over into the U.S. stock markets.[2]

Then, in the latter part of 1978 and in early 1979, Iran exploded in revolution, throwing that country—the supplier of 10 percent of the world's oil—into chaos that choked off production and drove the Shah from the Peacock Throne. The interruption in the flow of oil onto the world market helped set the stage for the price leaps of 1979—from $12 to $13 a barrel in late 1978, to the $32–$40 range in 1981. In other words, the world price of oil had about tripled. These increases were fifteen times greater in dollar value than was the price of oil in 1970. The instability produced anxiety nearly everywhere; for one thing, it helped drive the price of gold from $200 to $850 an ounce. With the second oil shock, twenty years of anticipated change had been telescoped into one. The price of oil had risen to levels that many predictions made in 1978 had not anticipated until the year 2000.

Meanwhile, political threats to the world's oil supply that had been discussed as potentially serious five to ten years hence had become realities in 1979.

America's dependence on imported oil poses not only a host of old problems in graver form but at least one new one, the problem of "hostile oil"—potentially decisive proportions of Middle Eastern oil under the actual or prospective control of governments that are politically antagonistic to the United States. Also, the present outlook forces us to consider how, in the 1980's, our country can maintain economic growth with zero energy growth. Moreover, the fact that time had been telescoped means that the difficulty of meeting the challenge is much greater than would have been the case had its gravity become apparent after the first shock. Responses that might have been sufficient between 1974 and 1979 no longer suffice. Indeed, contrary to popular opinion in 1983, the United States—as well as Western Europe, Japan, and all the world's oil importers—are facing a protracted energy problem, now measured in the chilling statistics of the unemployed—an average of 9 million unemployed annually in the industrialized countries prior to the first oil shock, 18 million during the years between the two shocks, and 32 million after the second shock.

Fortunately, the United States has taken some steps to slow oil imports, including the decontrol of oil prices and the partial decontrol of natural gas prices. But, overall, the response still appears insufficient when measured against the scale and urgency of the problem.

Of course, one would hardly expect that it would be easy, even under the most favorable circumstances, to frame a program that could stop the growth of oil imports in a fashion that would not disrupt the economy and society. After all, a wide range of complex engineering and other technical problems is involved, from the difficulties of offshore drilling operations to the way in which electricity is priced. Beyond the technical problems, there is a host of competing economic, political, and regional interests, all of them warring over the allocation of vast resources. To put it bluntly, serious talk about energy involves a very great deal of money. There may never have been so rich a sweepstakes in American history, for the OPEC price revolution of 1973 and 1974 increased the world market value of proved U.S. reserves of oil and gas alone by $800 billion. The second shock increased their value by another trillion dollars.[3] And then, there are uncertainties, which stretch from the revolutionary dreams of some now-unknown Saudi Arabian colonel to the musings of a specialist in photovoltaic technology.

Given these complexities, it is no wonder that people prefer to dream of some simple solution. First it was nuclear power. Then coal. Then fusion. Then Mexican oil. Then shale oil. And then the opening up of public lands. And so on. But none of these is a singular remedy. An easy fix is unlikely to offer itself, and a prudent society does not count on one happening. And the task of policy formation is made even more difficult by the vocal and sometimes quite bitter debates that now becloud the American political process.

The disagreements can be striking. A news article in the *New York Times* was headlined "Oil Report Optimistic"; it reported that a global shortage before the late 1980's was unlikely, and that one before the twenty-first century was only a possibility, "not a probability." Yet elsewhere in the same newspaper on the same day a story warned that the Western world could "face a damaging scramble for oil in the mid-1980s, combined with sharply higher prices."[4] How can governments make reasonable choices when confronted with such uncertainty?

Indeed, making a move away from ever-increasing imports of oil has proved far more difficult than was imagined in 1973 and 1974. And the price of achieving a reduction in 1980–1982 has been horrendously expensive—$300 for every barrel saved via economic recession.

What has gone right? What has gone wrong? We try to answer these questions in this book. We also suggest what else can go right by sorting out some of the basic issues and by setting out in comparative fashion the various sources of energy and potential contribution of each.

We began the book with three premises that framed our entire undertaking. First, we see the crises of 1973–74 and 1979–80 not as isolated phenomena, but rather as part of a major transition for both energy producers and users. Second, we believe that healthy economic growth is essential and that reliance on the free market is the best way to achieve it. Third, we feel that thinking about energy raises important questions about income generation and distribution: What are the total costs and benefits involved in any decision: who profits, and who pays? We believe that some attempt, however rough, has to be made to assess the total "social costs" embedded in the problem.

Our primary focus is the United States. This country is the world's largest producer, consumer, and importer of energy. What happens in the United States, whatever shape it takes, has a profound importance for the rest of the world, both through direct effects and as a model to follow.

Our perspective is what is possible and reasonable in the near and middle term—that is, what can get the United States and other oil importers both in the industrial and the developing world most smoothly through the remainder of the twentieth century. Fundamentally, we discuss the managing of a transition away from a system of recurring heavy reliance on imported oil to a system more balanced. We have therefore tried to apply what might be called a managerial approach, broadly defined. We attempt to assess priority and potential, evaluate costs and risks, compare

returns on different forms of investment, examine how people and
resources can be effectively mobilized, and suggest what can be
done to mediate equitably conflict among competing interests.

We try to explore energy questions pragmatically, from the
bottom up, examining not only the technical and economic obstacles and possibilities, but the political and institutional realities as
well. This means trying to understand the sometimes humble and
often nitty-gritty reality of each energy source. "Coal" to us is not
merely a solidified hydrocarbon that exists in abundance in the
United States, nor is it a simple coefficient in a mathematical
model. "Coal" is in fact a system that involves, among other
things, labor-management strife, uncertain environmental effects,
and the doubts posed by those who make investment decisions for
utilities. Similarly, a serious, not just rhetorical, energy conservation program depends on a set of incentives encouraged by the
government that would satisfy energy users and help create businesses that can "deliver" conservation to the homeowner.

In the chapters that follow, we present our findings and
recommendations. But a quick overview of the book follows.

To begin with, imported oil poses too many risks to be calmly
accepted. Knowing that it would be controversial, we have tried
to put a figure on the "real" cost of a barrel of imported oil. To
compute a price for incremental amounts of imported oil, we have
tried to establish the total "social cost"—that is, market price plus
the costs to the society of future price hikes and economic disruptions that might result from increasing demand. Although in this
calculation we did not include the political and the more dire
economic consequences, our best estimate of the cost still came
out at $65 to $100 a barrel during the second oil shock. To be
conservative, we use $65 a barrel, or about twice the average price
paid in the early 1980's for imported oil. Obviously, this is a very
tentative figure, and the assumptions behind it are explained in
Chapter 2. Yet, the magnitude of the price, $65, is such that the
United States should make a much greater attempt to reduce its
oil imports.

But can the United States do this? There are four conventional sources of domestic energy: oil, natural gas, coal, and
nuclear power. But all four are likely to deliver less energy

than projections by their advocates would lead one to believe.

In the debate about oil, three main domestic oil "solutions" were put forward as alternatives to imported petroleum: break up the industry, decontrol oil prices (and lease more land), and employ unconventional technology. The first two are important and controversial political questions, affecting as they do the distribution of income and power in America. But the "solutions" have little to do with augmenting production. Even with the deregulation of oil prices and regardless of whether the industry is or is not broken up, the physical production of oil from conventional sources in the United States almost surely will continue its long-term decline. And increased output from enhanced recovery and other unconventional means will not be able to keep domestic supplies flowing at current levels. To be sure, outside the United States new oil fields in Mexico and China are important and will augment world supplies, but, claims to the contrary, they are unlikely to make a substantial change in the world oil balance.

Natural gas, which accounts for over a quarter of America's energy needs, has also been entrapped in a great domestic debate: Should it continue to be regulated, with price based on cost of production, or should it be deregulated, with price based on market value? As in the case of oil, the debate is about money and who gets it. But the distributional questions aside, the prudent assumption is that a deregulated price will not enable natural gas production to exceed current levels regardless of the extent of deregulation.

A major goal of the U.S. energy policy in the late 1970's was to foster the substitution of domestically produced coal for imported oil. Given America's great coal reserves, the proposition appears feasible on paper, but in practice it is probably not. For coal to do what had been predicted for it, a traditionally backward industry must be suddenly transformed into a modern, technologically advanced one. Meanwhile, potential users are reluctant to commit themselves to coal, especially because of the uncertainty about meeting environmental requirements. Coal's contribution, in the rest of this century, therefore, is likely to prove more limited than generally thought, although its importance is still likely to grow substantially, particularly for utilities.

Nuclear power is the other conventional alternative in which high hopes were once placed. Yet, even some of the strong nuclear advocates now realize that the further development of nuclear power is stalemated by controversy that has passed beyond the boundaries of the technocratic community to become a substantive matter in the political process. The accident at the Three Mile Island reactor in March 1979 further damaged the prospects of an already troubled industry. Even without a Three Mile Island, however, the problem of what to do with nuclear waste is so confused, and so far from politically acceptable resolution, that it might result in an absolute decline in the energy produced by nuclear power in the years ahead. Moreover, one should remember how limited the potential of atomic power is under the most bullish of circumstances: If nuclear power capacity *doubled* in ten years, it would still provide less than 8 percent of America's total energy.

In short, there is little reason to expect conventional alternatives to make a sizable contribution to reducing our dependence on imported oil. Indeed, it is possible that these energy sources—domestic oil and gas, coal, and nuclear power—as a group may not increase their contribution at all to meeting the nation's additional energy needs over the next decade.

On the other hand, conservation and solar energy, unconventional alternatives that tend to be played down, can make a much greater contribution than is normally assumed. The unconventional as well as the conventional alternatives should be given a fair chance. To date, they have not received anything like that. According to one estimate, conventional energy sources have received more than $120 billion in incentives and subsidies, while the unconventional sources have received virtually nothing by comparison. And some subsidies for producers continue, while subsidies for consumers to use conventional energy sources run into tens of billions of dollars yearly because of controls that keep prices far below replacement costs.[5]

Since 1973 a major reason for the imbalance between conventional and unconventional sources has been the persistent acceptance by policymakers and the media of misleading conclusions drawn from prominent econometric and technological models.

Our work has convinced us that while such models can be valuable, they have been accepted too uncritically. Such models are abstractions and, therefore, simplifications of reality. Too often, the assumptions that govern the models are overlooked. Indeed, we believe that unexamined technicalism has helped to create some of the impasses in U.S. energy policy. Decisions about energy issues ignite intense bargaining and competition for resources, raise major distributive questions, and threaten strongly held values. The world of human institutions in which the real choices have and will be made is in fact a world of power and politics, one not easily captured in mathematical models. Indeed, without acknowledging the genuine distributional problems, and without looking for ways to mediate conflict among competing groups, then stalemate, not coherent energy policies, will persist.[6]

Among the unconventional sources of energy, conservation presents itself as the most immediate opportunity. It should be regarded as a largely untapped source of energy. Indeed, conservation—not coal or nuclear energy—is the major alternative to imported oil. It could perhaps "supply" up to 30 percent of America's current energy usage in addition to what it has already supplied since 1973. Moreover, the evidence suggests that there is much greater flexibility between energy use and economic growth than is generally assumed, and that a conservation strategy could actually spur growth. Conservation does not require technological breakthroughs. But it has been difficult to tap, because a consistent set of signals—price, incentives, and regulations—is not in place. Moreover, the decentralized character of energy consumption means that decisions to conserve, unlike decisions to produce energy, have to be made by millions and millions of often poorly informed people.

It is possible that the range of energy possibilities grouped under the heading of "solar" or "renewables" might—although the uncertainty is much greater than with conservation—meet one-fifth of U.S. energy needs within two decades. This would be more energy in barrels of oil equivalent than we now get from imported oil. But we must stress that this is at the optimistic end of likely outcomes. Like conservation, solar energy faces a problem of decentralized decision-making. Moreover, the lead times for implementation are greater than for conservation, since the most promising near-term solar energy applications, which use existing, relatively simple technologies, are receiving less support than the more uncertain, more distant high-technology solar applications. Low-technology solar energy can make an important contribution, but like conservation, it needs a consistent framework of price, incentive, and regulation, which it does not now have.

Those with a stake in conventional wisdom about conventional energy sources may charge that the conclusions of this book are unrealistic, that we are romantics opposed to economic growth, or that we advocate a fundamental change in the way the society is organized. We are not and we do not. Indeed, we do not side with those romanticists who have a vision of national life decentralized through the vehicle of the energy crisis, giving us something in the end that might be called a post-industrial pastoral society. For we wish to see the system prosper and experience vital economic growth, and this means greater reliance on the free market. Still, we do not subscribe to the views of the other set of even more powerful romanticists—industrial romanticists, who believe that it is possible to return to an era of unlimited production and that production alone can be the nation's salvation. For genuine alternatives for energy policy do exist and we want to contribute to the clarification of the choices. We also believe that it is unwise to ask conventional sources to do more than they really can and by so doing to block the transition to a more balanced energy system. To deny the need for a transition does not prevent change, it only postpones it, ensuring that when change does come, it will cause intense disruption, pain, and conflict.

No easy remedy will solve the energy crisis. Solutions, however, will emerge from a recognition and comparison of benefits and risks, possibilities and obstacles, across a wide range. Political choices are therefore involved, which is why the energy crisis is a crisis of our political system.

Some kind of general clarification and understanding is required if the nation is to move beyond the unacceptable level of progress made to date. We hope that we can, to some degree, redefine the terms in which the American energy debate is being waged. We would not by any means insist that we have all the answers, or that we have correctly assessed all aspects of the many intricately interconnected problems involved. But we believe that we are pointing in the right direction. The easy days of easy and cheap oil are truly over, but there is no need that the process of change and adaptation should prove as difficult as it now appears to be.

We have yet to meet an energy specialist, let alone a generalist, who can keep all the barrels of oil, trillion cubic feet of natural gas, tons of coal, gigawatts of electricity, and quads of energy in his or her head. We certainly can't. In order to keep the energy sources straight, and to make clear the comparisons, we have used barrels of oil per day as our basic unit—though, of course, following convention and common sense as the energy source dictates. Thus, the aim of Table 1-1 is to lay out the equivalences in barrels per day, in addition to showing U.S. energy consumption in 1981.

CONVERSION FACTORS |

One million barrels of oil daily are the equivalent, in rounded numbers, of

OIL: 50 million metric tons per year
NATURAL GAS: 2.1 trillion cubic feet (tcf) per year
COAL: 94 million tons per year
NUCLEAR: 200 billion kilowatt hours (kwh) per year [1 million kwh equal 1 gigawatt hour (GWH)]
HYDRO: 200 billion kilowatt hours (kwh) per year
ELECTRICAL GENERATING CAPACITY AT HISTORICAL OPERATING RATES (ABOUT 50 PERCENT): 50 GW
ANY ENERGY: 2.1 quadrillion (10^{15}) BTUs per year (quads)

TABLE 1·1
U.S. ENERGY CONSUMPTION, 1981

Sources	Millions of Barrels per Day of Oil Equivalent	Percentage of Total	Quantity in Units Commonly Used for Each Source
Petroleum	15.6ᵃ	43%	15.6 million barrels per day
Natural Gas	9.6ᵇ	26	20.0 trillion cubic feet per year
Coal	7.4ᶜ	20	690 million tons per year
Nuclear	1.4	4	273 billion kilowatt hours per year
Renewables	2.4ᵈ	7	510 quadrillion BTU's per year
Total	36.4	100%	

ᵃIncludes imports of 6.0 million barrels per day (mbd) or 38 percent of total oil consumption; excludes 0.6 mbd of exports; and excludes 0.3 mbd of imports for Strategic Petroleum Reserve.

ᵇIncludes imports of 0.4 mbd oil equivalent, or 4 percent of total natural gas.

ᶜExcludes exports of 1.2 mbd oil equivalent.

ᵈIncludes 1.5 mbd hydroelectric and geothermal; 0.2 mbd of this is imported hydroelectricity. Also includes 0.9 mbd biomass. Biomass is not part of statistics published by Department of Energy, Energy Information Administration.

Source (except for renewables): Department of Energy, Energy Information Administration, *Monthly Energy Review* (Washington, D.C.: Government Printing Office). Data on renewables estimated from U.S. Department of Energy, *Securing America's Energy Future: The National Energy Policy Plan* (Washington, D.C.: Government Printing Office, July 1981). p. 22.

2 | AFTER THE PEAK: THE THREAT OF HOSTILE OIL

ROBERT STOBAUGH

Oil, the prime mover of industrial life, has become one of its greatest problems. The current patterns of production and consumption, and the political alignments that accompany them, have led the United States—and the world—into a future laden with uncertainty and danger. Although the nation has had a domestic oil industry for about 120 years, the United States has, in just a few short years, become heavily dependent on imported oil. This dependence means ever greater reliance on an unstable part of the world—the Middle East, and especially Saudi Arabia. It would therefore be very much in the nation's interest to reduce permanently oil imports.[1] But contrary to popular impression, increases in domestic oil production is unlikely to be the way to do it. Geology denies that possibility.

THE RISE AND FALL OF AMERICAN OIL POWER |

The oil industry had its origins in the middle of the nineteenth century, when kerosene began to replace expensive whale oil as a source of interior lighting.[2] Whereas most of the kerosene was made from coal, some was extracted from crude oil. But the crude

| 17

oil could be obtained only where it naturally seeped to the surface or from brine water wells. With kerosene priced at $42 a barrel, a considerable opportunity obviously existed for anyone finding a cheap and easily available supply of crude oil. A group of New Haven investors, fortified with a report from a Yale chemist on the economics of refining kerosene from crude oil, formed a company to drill for oil in the vicinity of brine wells in Pennsylvania. The investors hired a railroad conductor, "Colonel" Edwin Drake, to head the venture. The Colonel had neither business nor drilling experience, nor was he a colonel, but he possessed two useful attributes. He was available because he was out of work; and his services came cheaply because he had a railroad pass to get to Pennsylvania. Once there, near Titusville, he struck oil on August 27, 1859. And so the American oil industry was born.

For more than a century thereafter, the production of crude oil in the United States steadily increased. In 1909, the fiftieth year of the industry, U.S. production reached 500,000 barrels a day,* more than the rest of the world combined.[3] And except for several years after World War I, the United States remained one of the world's leading petroleum exporters. As time went on, what became the largest industry in the world—dominated for most of its history by American companies—produced, refined, and distributed oil to an ever wider and more diverse market. Cheap oil gradually shoved aside coal, and so became the basic source of power for an industrial civilization.

A little-noticed but significant change occurred in 1948. Imports—mostly cheap Venezuelan crude—exceeded American oil exports, which meant that the United States had become for the first time a permanent net importer of oil. Nevertheless, the United States continued to produce half of the world's oil in the early 1950's. Furthermore, it had sufficient unused capacity to produce for export markets in an emergency, as happened during the Suez crisis of 1956. But American oil, which was expensive to produce, could not compete with the low-cost crude that had begun to flow in large quantities from the Middle East. Thus, for

---

*For this chapter, *crude oil* includes natural gas liquids, which were 16 percent of the total in 1982.

the stated reason of "national security," but also to protect politically powerful domestic producers, the U.S. government placed
restrictions on imports in the late 1950's.[4] So protected, domestic
oil production continued to climb.

The historic turning point came in 1970, when U.S. spare
capacity vanished and U.S. production reached what proved to be
its peak—an average of 11.3 million barrels a day. From then on,
the level of oil production began to decline. But as demand continued to increase, cheap imported oil took a larger and larger
share of the U.S. market as ever-larger cracks began to appear in
the oil import barrier. In response to sporadic shortages that began
to develop around the country, the Nixon Administration abandoned import quotas in 1973, and imported oil poured in. The
long-term decline in production was interrupted briefly in 1978 by
an on-rush of Alaskan oil, but in 1979 domestic output turned
down once again. As Table 2-1 shows, by 1979 foreign oil accounted for nearly half of American consumption.[5] And in spite
of a substantial drop in consumption—due to the double impact

TABLE 2·1
OIL IN THE U.S.

Year	Consumption (millions of barrels a day)	Production (millions of barrels a day)	Imports (millions of barrels a day)	Imports (as a percentage of consumption)
1960	9.7	8.0	1.8	19%
1962	10.2	8.4	2.1	21
1964	10.8	8.8	2.3	21
1966	11.9	9.6	2.6	22
1968	13.0	10.6	2.8	22
1970	14.4	11.3	3.4	24
1972	16.0	11.2	4.7	29
1974	16.2	10.5	6.1	38
1976	17.0	9.7	7.3	43
1978	18.4	10.3	8.4	46
1979	17.9	10.2	8.4	47
1980	16.6	10.2	6.9	42
1981	15.6	10.2	6.0	38

of increased conservation and severe recession—oil imports still accounted for 42 percent of consumption in 1980 and 38 percent in 1981.

What the table demonstrates is a degree of dependence in recent years that is novel in American history, which in turn means that the United States is vulnerable to a wide range of economic and political threats. The high cost of oil, the resulting effects on the dollar and the international payments system—and supply interruptions—can and have hurt the American economy, as well as those economies of other Western industrial nations and the non-oil developing countries. Beyond this are political dangers that would result from changes in the regimes in the key oil-producing countries. Thus, American imports are not a subject that can be understood in terms of conventional economic analysis alone.

Backed by the American government, U.S. oil companies once dominated the international oil system. But as the American market became more dependent on foreign imports, American influence over the world market has diminished. How did this happen?

The U.S. government itself has never owned foreign oil operations. But at key moments it played a decisive role in making it possible for a handful of the U.S.-based companies to establish foreign operations. These companies, along with two foreign competitors, Royal Dutch/Shell and British Petroleum, dominated the world oil market for about a hundred years.*

Around the turn of the century, the American companies, which had already been exporting oil from the United States, began to search abroad for crude oil. Early on, they found it in Mexico, Rumania, and even Japan. At the end of World War I, the U.S. industry produced two thirds of the world's oil supply from domestic sources and another sixth from Mexico. But because wartime demands had strained world reserves, many in the

---

*The world oil market is defined so as to exclude North America and the communist countries, because these two regions have been insulated from time to time from the general market.[6]

U.S. government were worried about the oil outlook. The major new fields in Texas had not yet been discovered, and so for a few years after World War I the United States was a net importer of oil. "The best technical authorities seem to believe that the peak of petroleum production in the United States will soon be reached," wrote U.S. Secretary of State Robert Lansing in 1919. "The U.S. position can best be characterized as precarious," stated the director of the U.S. Geological Service in 1920. Officials were afraid that the United States would not have adequate foreign supplies. But many in the government, especially in the State Department, felt that foreign oil controlled by U.S. companies was as reliable as if the foreign oil were owned by the U.S. government itself. Thus the U.S. government and the big American oil companies, especially Standard Oil of New Jersey (the largest old Standard Oil descendant, now known as Exxon), pursued a common goal—to place as many foreign sources of oil as possible in American hands.[7]

As the concern over oil supplies became commonplace, the French managed to obtain Germany's share of the oil rights in the Ottoman Empire. But the British controlled most of the oil rights in the Ottoman Empire and, indeed, most of the oil outside North America. Royal Dutch/Shell had aggressively developed production in Latin America and Asia. More importantly, British Petroleum owned the first of the giant oil fields to be discovered in the Middle East, which was found in Iran in 1908.

The interests of the American government and the American oil companies were so intertwined that it was hard to tell who was leading whom. It appears, however, that in the very early days, the government's desire for an American presence in the Eastern Hemisphere, especially in the Middle East, was at least as strong as the companies'. In 1920, Congress passed a law that prohibited foreign-owned corporations from acquiring oil leases on U.S. public lands if their own governments did not allow U.S. firms to explore for oil in territories they controlled. The law, aimed at Royal Dutch/Shell, got the Dutch to open up the Netherlands' East Indies, formerly an exclusive Shell preserve, to exploration by American companies.[8]

The biggest prize of all, or course, was the Middle East. There the U.S. drive succeeded admirably. The United States pushed the British aside, prevented the French from expanding their small interests, and then defended the region (or most of it) from Russian encroachment. In a thirty-year period, from the mid-1920's to the mid-1950's, U.S. companies, starting with no base, gained a dominant position in the area that was to hold the future of the world's oil supply. It was one of the most stunning examples of economic expansion in history. The Middle East nations themselves (at the time, some were scarcely nations) were often little more than spectators to Great Power competition.[9]

The U.S. government first obtained an "open door" for American investment in the British and French zones of influence, including Iraq (part of the Ottoman Empire). The result was that Exxon and Mobil ended up owning about a quarter of the Iraq Petroleum Company. In 1934, Iraq became the second major Middle East exporter, after Iran. A pipeline was completed, and oil began to flow in large quantities.[10]

The U.S. government next persuaded the British government to allow Gulf Oil to enter Kuwait, a British protectorate, in 1934. British Petroleum and Gulf thereupon decided to become partners and so avoid competing against each other in negotiations with the Sheik of Kuwait. The U.S. government also obtained British approval for Standard Oil of California (Socal) to enter Bahrain, a small island off the coast of Saudi Arabia that was a British protectorate.[11] The discovery of oil in Bahrain in 1932 encouraged Socal to begin exploration in that vast desert just a few miles across the water—Saudi Arabia. And there it found an oil field to stagger the imagination.

In 1933, Socal easily outbid the Iraq Petroleum Company (IPC) for oil exploration rights in Saudi Arabia, paying $300,000 in gold, compared with IPC's offer of $60,000 worth of Indian rupees. A few years later, Socal sold half interest in its rights in Saudi Arabia to Texaco, thus forming the Arabian American Oil Company—Aramco.[12]

Aramco sought U.S. government aid on several occasions in order to protect its interests in Saudi Arabia. And the United States, after struggling for so many years to secure a place for its companies in the Middle East, was not about to abandon them.

World War II interfered with opportunities for travel and cut into Saudi Arabia's revenues from the annual pilgrimages to Mecca. An oil company executive in 1941 warned President Roosevelt that King Ibn Saud "is desperate" and needed $6 million quickly. Washington responded with lend-lease assistance. In 1945, the forerunner to the U.S. National Security Council reaffirmed Saudi Arabia's importance, stating, "It is in our national interest to see that this vital resource [Saudi Arabian oil] remains in American hands."[13]

In 1946, the companies again needed help from Washington. When Socal and Texaco decided to sell part of Aramco to Exxon and Mobil, antitrust problems were raised. The U.S. government thereupon provided antitrust clearance, saying that the enlarged consortium was in the national interest, as it would result in faster development of the Arabian oil fields and hence more money for the King. The U.S. government also pressured the British and French governments to overlook clauses in the Iraq Petroleum Company agreement that would have prevented Exxon and Mobil from buying in.[14]

In 1950, the State Department felt that the Middle East was "highly attractive and highly vulnerable" to communism. When Ibn Saud again demanded more money, the companies faced a quandary. They did not want to accede to the State Department's suggestion that they give up rights to territories they had not yet developed and that the Saudi government could auction off. On the other hand, the companies could not raise prices to European customers, because to do so would undercut postwar recovery and the Marshall Plan. Nor did the companies want to raise royalty payments to Saudi Arabia, because this would mean lower profits. The issue was resolved when Aramco began to make payments to the Saudi Arabian government in the form of income taxes, and then deduct equivalent amounts of money from taxes owed the U.S. Treasury—a tax credit. The principle of tax crediting was common practice for other U.S. industries abroad, and oil companies operating in several other countries had already used it. Still, the U.S. State Department expressed some "concern over what in effect could amount to a subsidy of Aramco's position in Saudi Arabia by U.S. taxpayers."[15]

With Saudi Arabia stabilized by the substantially higher revenues from Aramco, the Americans, for the second time in five
years, were forced to turn their attention to Iran, which was then
still the largest Middle Eastern producer. In 1946, in the first crisis
of the Cold War, the United States had put pressure on the
Russians to evacuate northern Iran to keep them from threatening
Middle East oil interests. In 1951, the Iranians, led by Prime
Minister Mohammad Mosaddegh, nationalized British Petroleum's Iranian properties in an attempt to wrest effective control
of their oil industry away from the British. The "seven majors,"*
controlling 98 percent of the world oil market, responded by
instituting a boycott of Iranian oil, and they easily supplied the
world markets by increasing production in the other Middle East
nations—primarily Saudi Arabia, Kuwait, and Iraq. While the
U.S. government made some conciliatory statements toward Iran,
it sided with the majors for two reasons: First, Russian influence
may have otherwise increased in Iran; and second, if Mosaddegh
succeeded, other major oil-producing countries might follow
suit.[16]

With a push from the CIA, Mosaddegh fell and the Shah was
reinstalled. The U.S. government then took the lead in settling
the dispute, encouraging the U.S. majors to join a new consortium
of companies being formed to operate Iran's oil fields and market
its crude. Some majors actually needed prodding because they
were afraid that a requirement to market Iranian crude would
prevent them from increasing production sufficiently in Saudi
Arabia to please the King. But the U.S. government wanted the
majors to participate in Iran because they were the only U.S.
companies considered capable of moving large-enough quantities
of Iranian crude to provide the income deemed necessary for the
new Iranian government. To avoid antitrust problems, the U.S.
majors asked for and received clearance from the Justice Department.[17] The final ownership in the consortium was apportioned

---

*The seven international majors are five U.S. companies—Exxon, Gulf, Mobil,
Socal, and Texaco—and the two British-based companies, British Petroleum and
Royal Dutch/Shell (60-percent-owned by the Dutch).

as follows: American companies, 40 percent; British (BP and Royal/Dutch Shell), 54 percent; and French (Compagnie Française des Pétroles), 6 percent. The Iranians resented the settlement because foreigners still dominated their oil industry, the main difference being that American influence had diluted that of the British. Although this was an improvement, in Iranian eyes, the resentment was to flare openly a quarter century later when the Iranians once again made a major effort to wash away the vestiges of foreign control.

The Iranian settlement of 1954 produced two changes in the ground rules, which also later helped to undermine the American position throughout the oil-producing world. The first was that Iran became the unquestioned proprietor of its own oil fields, then something novel for an oil-exporting country, but within a few years the norm. Second, the U.S. government persuaded the majors to allow some American "independents" to own a small share of the consortium. (Some of the independents, of course, were large companies, such as Standard Oil of Ohio, Getty Oil Company, and Atlantic Refining.) Howard Page, the Exxon executive whose persistence was crucial in forging the agreement, recalled later that the majors agreed because "people were always yacking about it." So, he explained, some independents were allowed in as "window dressing."[18] The independents soon learned that Iranian oil could be very profitable, although their production level was quite limited under the terms of the agreement. Thus their Iranian experience encouraged them to explore elsewhere overseas, and their subsequent growth made certain that the majors would never again be strong enough to organize an effective boycott like the one against Mosaddegh.

The formation of the Iranian consortium represented the zenith of American oil power in the world. In 1955, the five U.S. majors produced two thirds of the oil for the world oil market, the two British majors almost one third. The French had a mere 2 percent.

By the late 1950's, the competition to sell crude to refineries owned by independents caused oil prices to decline in the world oil market. In the meantime, the "posted price"—that is, the official price used to determine host-government revenues—remained constant. This started the chain of events that led to the birth of the Organization of Petroleum Exporting Countries (OPEC). Although the OPEC story started in the marketplace, it moved to the Exxon boardroom. After a 1959 cut in posted prices, Exxon chairman M. J. "Jack" Rathbone persuaded his fellow directors to cut prices again in August 1960, thereby once more reducing the revenues received by the exporting nations. As was the habit in those days, Exxon did not negotiate with the oil-exporting nations; it simply announced the price cuts. The company said that the lower prices were necessary because sales were occurring at sizable discounts. It added, "The pressure on market prices has also been accentuated by new and widespread offers of Russian oil at low prices."[19]

The producing countries were outraged. The Petroleum Affairs director of the Arab League scoffed at Exxon's explanation that Soviet oil was responsible. Venezuelan Oil Minister Perez Alfonzo blamed the cuts on "pressures" from the world's big consuming countries, which he proceeded to identify: "The United Kingdom is the greatest consumer of Western Europe the same as the United States is the biggest consumer of imported oil in the world."[20]

Outside the oil industry, the price cuts scarcely made a ripple. The entire New York Times report was contained in seven sentences on page 41.[21]

The helpless oil-exporting nations had to accept the cuts, and about all they could do was meet among themselves. In September 1960, Iraq invited the five other major oil-exporting nations to a conference in Baghdad. It was at this meeting that OPEC was formed. Years later, eloquent words were to be written about OPEC's beginning: "United in OPEC, they set out to redress the imbalance between cheap oil and imports, and also, in the psychological sense, to redress centuries of colonialism and exploitation."[22] At the time, however, the founding of OPEC was almost a non-event. Although it was formed on September 9, 1960, the story was not reported in the New York Times until September 25. Here is the entire story:

MIDEAST OIL LANDS SEEK PRICE STABILITY |

BAGHDAD, Iraq, Sept. 24—(Reuters)—A five-nation oil conference held here earlier this month voted to demand that oil companies try to restore prices to their former level and keep them steady, it was announced here today.

The meeting, held after the major companies cut Middle Eastern crude oil prices, also voted to form a permanent Organization of Petroleum Exporting Countries to unify their oil policies and promote their individual and collective interests.

Iraq, Iran, Saudi Arabia, Venezuela and the Persian Gulf shiekhdom of Kuwait sent delegates to the conference. The shiekhdom of Aqtar [sic] and the Arab League sent observers.

These states hold 90 per cent of the world's oil reserves, according to the chief Saudi Arabian delegate.

Faud Rouhani, OPEC's first Secretary-General, later said that the oil companies initially pretended that "OPEC did not exist." Of course, OPEC eventually gained considerable recognition. Initially it functioned primarily as a clearinghouse for information and as a forum for representatives of member nations. Perez Alfonzo, one of the founding leaders of OPEC, tried to shape the organization so that it would allocate production; but in fact this was not done until an OPEC meeting in early 1982.[23]

The process set in motion by the Iranian settlement and the establishment of OPEC converged in Libya. In 1956, Libya had granted fifty-one concessions to seventeen companies, including many independents who formed their own groups and whose output was not controlled by the majors. In the early 1960's, the independents began to export large quantities of oil into large European markets, which heretofore the majors had controlled. During the rest of the 1960's, OPEC was still unable to prevent the continuing decline in the price of world oil, which reached a low of from $1.00 to $1.20 a barrel in the Persian Gulf by the end of 1969. The companies and OPEC haggled endlessly over a few pennies per barrel. But by 1970 the situation had changed. Not only had U.S. production reached its limit, but also a number of oil-exporting nations, such as Libya, Algeria, and Kuwait, were approaching production peaks. As a result, Saudi Arabia and Iran were the only nations in OPEC with the ability to expand production substantially.[24]

In May 1970, an accident triggered an historic sequence of events. A bulldozer broke a pipeline carrying oil from the Persian Gulf to a Mediterranean seaport. This pipeline was especially important because the 1967 Arab-Israeli war had closed the tanker route through the Suez Canal. Libya, just across the Mediterranean from Europe, was suddenly in a key position. Colonel Muammer el-Qaddafi, Libya's new dictator, exploited the opportunity by ruthlessly squeezing just the right company—the American-based independent, Occidental—which had no substantial source of crude elsewhere, and thus was almost solely dependent on its Libyan output. Occidental capitulated quickly. At the conclusion of the negotiation, an Occidental executive uttered a few prophetic words: "Everybody who drives a tractor, truck, or car in the Western world will be affected by this." Other companies quickly began to fall.[25]

The overall capitulation of the West occurred in February 1971 at a conference in Tehran. The adroit maneuvering of the OPEC nations, led by the Shah and aided by the vacillation of the American government, gave OPEC their first clear-cut victory over the West. They obtained what was considered at the time to be a large price increase: fifty cents a barrel. America's reign over world oil production was swiftly coming to an end. At that very time began the vast increase in U.S. oil imports.[26]

By the summer of 1973, the stage was set, and center stage was occupied by one country—Saudi Arabia. The demand for petroleum was surging throughout the industrial world. Ordinarily Aramco maintained capacity about 10 percent higher than its actual production requirements, to deal with unforeseen contingencies; another 10 percent was usually available in the summer, at which time demand slackened. These cushions had been adequate in the past. But by the summer of 1973, the only spare capacity in the world belonged to Aramco, and that was equal to just 3 percent of total world production. But world demand was so much greater than expected that even the extra capacity was called into use. The result—no cushion at all. It was just at this time that the United States began to integrate its own voracious

need with that of the world market by lifting oil-import quotas—
so adding a powerful new demand on Eastern Hemisphere oil. The
world oil market was a very tight one indeed by mid-1973.[27]

Simultaneously, the politics of the Middle East were becoming very unstable. In May 1973, President Sadat warned the then
King Faisal of Saudi Arabia that Egypt might soon attempt to
retake the Arab lands occupied by Israel. At a meeting held in
Geneva on May 23, 1973, King Faisal spoke of Sadat's plans to
four American oil executives, each representing one of Aramco's
parents. Faisal, fearful of the appeal of Arab radicals, warned them
that he would not let Saudi Arabia become "more isolated in the
Arab world." Unless the United States gave more support to the
Arab cause, the King said, American interests in the area "will be
lost."[28] The warning, carried to the Nixon Administration by a
convoy of alarmed oil executives, was ignored. The Nixon Administration was more concerned at the time with Watergate.

On October 6, 1973, Egypt attacked the Israeli forces along
the Suez Canal. On October 12, the very epitome of the American
Establishment, attorney John J. McCloy, sent the White House
a personal note from the heads of the four Aramco parents, making two basic points: (1) The Arabs would cut back oil production
if the United States increased its support to Israel, and (2) such
a cutback would have dire consequences on the European and
Japanese economies. On October 17, the Arab oil ministers met
in Kuwait. They agreed to cut exports by 5 percent and recommended an embargo against unfriendly nations. On October 19,
after learning of Nixon's decision to provide $2.5 billion of arms
to Israel, King Faisal ordered a 25 percent reduction in Saudi oil
output and an embargo against the United States and several other
nations. Aramco obeyed immediately. To do otherwise, stated one
American oil executive, "would have resulted in even greater cutbacks, and some oil was better than no oil." Most other Arab
nations quickly followed the Saudi lead.[29]

The cutbacks dictated by the Arabs were less than 10 percent
of the world oil supply, but they caused widespread panic, and
some governments pressed the oil companies to deliver extra oil
to them at the expense of their allies. According to a British civil
servant, Britain's Prime Minister Edward Heath had a "temper

tantrum" when British Petroleum, 48-percent owned by the British government, refused to comply. BP had contractual obligations that prevented them from doing so.[30] And some refiners who lacked an assured supply of crude oil were forced to bid for it at auctions run by the various OPEC countries. In Iran on December 14, a barrel went for $17.34. On December 23 in Nigeria, the price of a barrel reached $22.60. As one refiner explained, "We weren't bidding just for oil; we were bidding for our life." With bids of this magnitude reinforcing the Shah's determination to raise prices substantially, representatives of the OPEC nations met in Tehran on December 22 and 23. They announced a price hike. Effective January 1, 1974, OPEC's take was to be $7.00 a barrel, compared with $1.77 before the October War. As oil production in Arab countries began to creep upward, it became clear that the real crisis was one of price, not supply.[31]

The embargo ended on March 18, 1974, six months after it had begun. But the damage had been done: The oil-producing countries had seized control of the world's basic energy source, and during 1974, Saudi Arabia showed what that control meant. Encouraged by demand from independent refineries for its crude, Saudi Arabia took the lead in raising the OPEC take to about $10 a barrel for the entire year—even though Saudi Arabia was usually considered an advocate of price moderation.

The years between 1974 and 1978 represented a kind of Indian summer for world oil, a period of apparent calm and stability. Demand for OPEC oil dipped because of slow economic growth in the industrial nations, a build-up of production in the North Sea and Alaska, and conservation. Thus, OPEC production in 1978 was slightly lower than in 1974. From time to time, the OPEC producers raised prices, but not enough to keep pace with inflation.

As 1978 began, more and more people in the United States and other Western countries were becoming complacent about the world of imported oil and optimistic about its future prospects. Increasing publicity was given to those analysts predicting that a "glut" of oil would force prices to continue to decline in real terms, perhaps through the 1990's or even to the end of the century.

But the round of self-congratulation about how well the process of adjustment had taken place was not justified. Beneath the apparent calm another profound crisis was developing, for the international energy system that had emerged after 1973 was itself profoundly unstable. Even if the oil-consuming countries had been doing all they should have been doing—which they were not —the stability of the system depended on a set of decisions made by a small group of nations who were the leaders of OPEC. And even before the fall of 1978 these nations had begun to reconsider the policies that had made the temporary equilibrium possible.

Specifically, many OPEC members were asking whether rapid economic development programs would damage their long-term economic and social prospects. Some estimates indicated that up to half of the $400 billion spent by OPEC countries between 1974 and 1978 had been wasted. Moreover, immediate social and political consequences of rapid development were already evident: inflation, unsound urbanization, a wild building boom, a large influx of foreigners, an adverse impact on agriculture and traditional industries, and often a lopsided distribution of wealth. These problems, in turn, led to a weakening of established social and political values, accompanied by disappointment and resentment.

Such experiences pushed OPEC nations to reevaluate their plans for development and hence their need for revenue. The problems created by efforts to establish a self-sustaining non-oil-based economy encouraged members of OPEC to consider stretching out the life of oil reserves by producing less. Of course, there was another alternative—continuing high production levels and then investing the revenues in the West. This option, however, was made less attractive by the difficulty of earning a real return on the investment in the economies of the West, especially in the face of accelerating inflation. Oil in the ground seemed to offer a sounder return than money invested in rapid development or deposited in a Western bank. Especially concerned were the younger members of the ruling cliques, who, looking thirty years ahead, did not want to inherit oil fields pumped dry, bank accounts ravaged by inflation, industrial facilities not competitive in world markets, and societies so churned up that their own political position would be much eroded.

Throughout, developments in the OPEC countries were not accorded much attention in the United States, which had become the largest importer of OPEC oil. Both the Indian summer in the international oil market and price controls at home had shielded Americans from the reality of the situation in energy.

Meanwhile, the United States felt quite comfortable in relying on Iran as a stable ally, as the policeman who would maintain regional order around the Persian Gulf. This close relationship was expressed in the extensive and expensive transfer of highly sophisticated military technology from the United States to Iran. It was also expressed in the toast that President Carter raised to the Shah on New Year's Eve, December 31, 1977. "Iran under the great leadership of the Shah is an island of stability in one of the more troubled areas of the world," said the President. "This is a great tribute to you, Your Majesty, and to your leadership, and to the respect, admiration, and love which your people give to you." But each passing month in 1978 demonstrated more clearly that the people's love was suspect. Domestic unrest and protests increased, eventually encompassing almost every element of society. The Shah's position weakened, although as late as September 1978 few doubted his ability to weather the storm. Within months, of course, the scale of domestic protest forced the Shah into exile. The oil workers played a key role in his downfall when they cut off oil exports late in 1978. This loss of five million barrels per day on the export market turned a small surplus of world production into a shortage.

Thereupon, in December 1978, OPEC announced price hikes higher than generally expected—5 percent, effective January 1, 1979, with further increases scheduled to make the total 1979 price rise equal to 14.5 percent (or 10 percent for the yearly average increase). Other countries—notably Saudi Arabia—increased production to help offset the loss of Iranian production. But unfortunately, the industrialized nations used 7.4 percent more oil in January 1979 than in January 1978. The net result was a shortfall of 1.5 to 2 million barrels a day. The market was suddenly very tight. The price for crude oil not already covered by long-term contracts jumped in early 1979 by as much as $5.00 a barrel above the OPEC price of $13.34 for "marker" crude. The initial spot-market sales were made by oil brokers, but as the price soared OPEC members began to increase their prices for spot-market oil. Sometimes they canceled a long-term contract by invoking the *force majeure* clause, and then immediately offered an identical quantity of identical quality oil to the same customer at the spot-market price.

It was obvious that OPEC members would not allow for long the oil companies to reap easy profits on contracted oil bought at prices substantially lower than those of the spot market. Various OPEC members quickly began adding surcharges on all their oil, even if covered by long-term contract.

After the new government took over in Iran, production sufficient for the needs of the domestic market was resumed. After a few weeks, production rose above two million barrels a day, putting Iran once again into the export market. As Iranian oil began to come back onto the market in early March, other OPEC countries cut back on their production to keep the market tight and the spot price high. Few OPEC countries could resist the temptation—and the internal pressures—to capture some of the advantages of the spot-market price increases in the official OPEC price. On March 26, 1979, the OPEC ministers met in Geneva and announced that the OPEC price scheduled for December 1979 would become effective immediately; but more important, OPEC members were free to add premiums that would raise their prices to whatever level the market would bear. In effect, OPEC had broken down as a price-setting organization. The spot-market prices and the official prices of individual OPEC members continued to climb as Saudi Arabia lost control of the world oil market.

Iran reentered the world oil market in a spirit quite different from that under the Shah. The religious leader, the Ayatollah Khomeini, as well as the new civilian government, made clear that production would never be allowed to return to old levels. Better to sell three million barrels per day at a higher price than five million at a lower price. Also, the consortium—along with westernization—was to be banished from Iran. At last, thought many

Iranians, they had rid the nation of foreign domination of the oil industry for the first time since its beginning over half a century earlier. Indicative of Iran's new policy, the first tanker of oil was sold to a Japanese company, which did not hesitate to turn around and sell at a higher price to an affiliate of Royal Dutch/Shell, a consortium member.

Two subsequent OPEC meetings during 1979—June and December—merely reconfirmed what had occurred in March. OPEC members agreed to disagree. Saudi Arabia attempted to regain some control over the market price by allowing Aramco to produce at 9.5 million barrels daily throughout the last half of 1979 and into 1980. Still, in the face of the high level of Saudi production, reduced world consumption, high inventories, and amidst talk of a forthcoming "oil glut," OPEC members continued to raise their official prices well into 1980. As of July 1, 1980, official OPEC prices, including special premiums of various sorts, ranged from $28 a barrel for Saudi light, to $35 a barrel for Iranian crude of similar quality, and up to $38.21 for the high-quality Algerian crude.

The cut-off of Iranian exports in the winter 1978–79 focused attention on the short-term market impact. But the long-term implications of the Iranian revolution were no less important.

The cut-off revealed that the margin of surplus in the world oil market was more narrow than most experts thought. The "glut"—and talk of the glut—disappeared almost overnight. Moreover, the upheaval in Iran meant a permanent reduction in the availability of world oil. For not only were Iranian exports unlikely to reach prerevolution levels, but other producers, fearing strains of too-rapid economic development, became more cautious about expanding oil output. In addition, it was realized that tensions other than those involving Arab-Israeli relations could result in supply interruptions. The important role that control of the oil fields played in the Shah's downfall meant that the oil fields in other countries would become, even more than before, a prime target of political dissidents. A revival of Islamic fundamentalism, coexisting with radicalism, would ensure a rich supply of political dissidents in Iraq, the Gulf sheikdoms, and even Saudi Arabia, the mother lode of oil on which the Western world depends for political moderation and increased supplies. Large volumes of oil exports were increasingly seen as a sign of political subservience to the West. As the Sheikh of Kuwait said, responding to Queen Elizabeth's compliments on his lavish welfare and development spending: "But, Your Majesty, this kind of spending wins me fewer friends these days."

The Iranian revolution also demonstrated that the major industrial nations were unable to cooperate sufficiently to exercise any control in the upward march of oil prices. An American subsidy of $5 per barrel in May 1979 on imports of middle distillates (home heating oil and diesel fuel) obviously aroused the fears held by the Europeans and Japanese that the United States would preempt the available supply of oil. As oil prices continued to move up, these intra-Western tensions became more acute. Underlying them was a critical difference in perceptions. The official American view was that the heart of the problem was OPEC—essentially a matter of supply. To the Europeans, the essence of the problem was OPEC *and* the United States—a matter of supply and demand. The intensity and logic of the European conviction are hardly yet appreciated in the United States, but it was—and is—a very major factor. The Europeans noted that between 1973 and 1978, U.S. oil consumption had risen by 1.5 million barrels per day, whereas that of the other industrialized nations had fallen by a like amount. In their view, the potential of conservation had barely been touched in the United States; and America's price controls on oil and gas in such circumstances were inexplicable. The scale of U.S. consumption and imports—America's "sheer weight," as Chancellor Schmidt put it—was enough to cancel out whatever any of the other countries might do. This, in turn, made them feel, to varying degrees, helpless or angry or both. The most outspoken critics were the French. President Valery Giscard d'Estaing was quite blunt just before the Tokyo economic summit. When an interviewer remarked that "the Americans have not yet succeeded in reducing consumption," the French President interrupted: "They haven't started."

True, the Western leaders at the Tokyo summit in June 1979 did manage to adopt the principle of limits on oil imports. The United States, for example, specifically agreed to limit imports in

1979, 1980, and 1985 at or below the 1977 level of 8.5 million barrels per day. These commitments were the first of their kind ever taken by the major consuming countries. The commitments may have great importance in the long run, especially as a precedent—provided they are met. But their immediate impact was slight as the Western allies continued their "beggar thy neighbor" policies.

Another important development took place during 1979, which was that high spot prices changed the character of the oil market in basic and lasting ways. Increasingly through the year, the producing countries shifted oil away from contract customers in order to make spot sales. (In one day, for example, the Abu Dhabi National Oil Company cut Gulf Oil from 150,000 barrels per day down to only 20,000.) By late 1979, OPEC nations as a whole were selling about 25 percent of their oil exports at higher than the official contract prices. If Saudi Arabia is excluded, the average rose to 40 percent. The shift to the spot market further eroded the position of the major oil companies, which reduced and even eliminated their sales of crude to independent refiners that had been regular customers, for the majors now needed all the crude they could get for their own systems. The disruption of the established and reliable supply channels that had been represented by contract sales also inherently served to help push prices upward. For it forced more buyers (i.e., independent refiners, major companies, and middlemen) into the spot bidding match. All this meant that the producing nations had successfully become a growing force in the marketing of oil.

At the beginning of 1980, the OPEC countries seemed more and more keen to prove the axiom that reduced production assures higher prices and higher income. At least four OPEC countries reduced output during 1980 to blunt the impact of high inventories, which the oil companies had built up in late 1979.

By September 1980, an uneasy calm had returned to the world oil market—a calm brought about by a reduction in demand, high stocks, and the steady Saudi maintenance of production at a million barrels a day above that nation's normal ceiling of 8.5 mbd. The reduction in demand had resulted from the dampened economic activity and increased conservation brought on in the industrial world by the awesome rise in oil prices. Thus, by September, some spot prices were lower than official prices, and some producing countries were showing a renewed interest in maintaining more traditional marketing relationships. It had taken a year and a half, but the Saudis had, at least temporarily, reasserted their influence over the world market.

But, despite the talk of a "glut" in the press, and the actual slack in the market, bought at painful cost, the basic features of the new world oil market remained highly unstable—in fact, much more unstable than anyone believed. For in September, Iraq invaded Iran, with control of Iran's giant Abadan refinery being a prime target of Iraq.

Oil shipments from both Iran and Iraq were disrupted almost immediately. Subsequent fighting damaged oil facilities of both countries, thereby restricting their oil production levels to a lower level than anyone planned. Thus, in 1981, oil production averaged only 1.3 million barrels daily in Iran and 900,000 barrels daily in Iraq, compared with a theoretical capacity of 4.0 million barrels daily for each country.

The reduction in oil output and the increased uncertainty caused by the Iranian-Iraqi War pushed upward on oil prices once again, even in the face of substantial declines in consumption and a further increase in Saudi output (to 10–10.3 mbd). The increase in Saudi output was an attempt to stabilize the market, whereas most other OPEC countries wanted substantially higher prices. As part of a compromise reached at an OPEC meeting in Bali in December, Saudi Arabia raised its official price for Arab light to $32 a barrel; other Gulf producers were free to charge as much as $36—which most of them did. Spot prices were even higher, reaching $42 for Saudi light, thereby approximating the peak in spot prices reached at the end of 1979 and early 1980.

In early 1981, President Ronald Reagan, newly elected, ordered immediate decontrol of the U.S. domestic oil prices, instead of allowing the gradual decontrol of oil prices instituted by President Carter. This decontrol had a dampening effect on world oil prices in two ways. The higher domestic U.S. prices further reduced U.S. demand. But perhaps more importantly, there were no longer U.S. government controls on price and allocation to moderate competition; hence, anyone buying petroleum—crude oil or products—was encouraged, indeed, in many cases forced, to shop for the lowest cost source. U.S. refiners, in response to sudden and heavy financial losses, began to suspend or cancel high-cost crude oil contracts, an act almost inconceivable in the prior months when security of supply—albeit at times a mirage—was far more important than costs.

In the meantime, Saudi Arabia, by keeping its oil production at the level of 10–10.3 mbd, flooded the market. In April 1981, by which time Saudi Arabian output exceeded 40 percent of OPEC's total, Sheikh Yamani, in a U.S. television interview, announced, "We engineered the glut." His statement sharpened and made more bitter a growing divisiveness within OPEC. Saudi Arabia's price for Arab light remained at $32, while the other OPEC members by and large continued to hold their official prices at $36 per barrel (for Arab light equivalent)—with some attempting to charge special premiums over that. The lower-priced Saudi oil gave the Aramco parents a decided advantage in the marketplace, thereby continuing heavy pressure on the other refiners to shop for low-cost crude. As the months wore on, recession and conservation cut deeper into demand, and the Saudis, instead of cutting back to stabilize prices, continued a high level of production to force the other OPEC members to lower prices. A critical situation for OPEC began to turn into a crisis for OPEC.

In October, 1981, amidst a crisis atmosphere, the OPEC members met in Geneva and agreed to unify prices at $34 (for Arab light equivalent); Saudi Arabia reduced production to 8.5 mbd. The crisis appeared to be over, and the oil refiners were relieved that price stability had returned. But their relief was short-lived. A falling demand, amplified by an inventory draw-down of perhaps 3 mbd, caused spot prices to drop $5 a barrel in just a few months. As Saudi Arabia held its production level at 8.5 mbd, other OPEC countries were forced to cut production.

It was in this crisis atmosphere that OPEC convened a meeting in Vienna in March 1982. It proved to be an historic occasion, because OPEC, for the first time, agreed on production quotas. True, Saudi Arabia refused formally to join the other twelve members in adopting specific quotas, but it did cut output by 500,000 barrels a day to a ceiling of 7 mbd. This level, combined with the quotas adopted by the other countries, resulted in an OPEC ceiling of 17.5 mbd. Saudi Arabia and other OPEC members pledged to cut production further if necessary to defend the $34 price. By late 1982, Saudi Arabia had reduced its production to 5½ mbd, but with some OPEC members producing above their ceilings, market conditions remained unstable and were expected to remain so for some time.

The success of the OPEC members in maintaining the price level in 1982–1983 will depend on their willingness to trim production below the 17.5 mbd level if necessary. The extent to which they will face this problem will depend on when oil companies start to rebuild inventories and the rate of economic recovery.

Over a longer period of time, say 1983–1986, an important determinant of price evolution will be the extent to which oil consumption rises once economic growth in the industrialized countries recommences. The sharpness of this rise will help reveal the extent to which the sharp decline in oil consumption during 1980–1982 was due to recession versus the more efficient use of energy.

Of course, the oil market could become tight overnight—a shot here, a stick of dynamite there. Indeed, the possibility of unrest exists in every single oil-producing country in the Middle East. But by far the most important is Saudi Arabia.[32]

SAUDI ARABIA: A SHAKY FOUNDATION FOR WESTERN CIVILIZATION I

Saudi Arabia is favored by a unique conjunction of huge reserves, extraordinary ease of exploitation, and a population so tiny (5 or 6 million people) that domestic revenue needs at current prices have little practical effect on the level of oil production. Saudi Arabia is the largest producer in OPEC, with 40 percent of total production and 34 percent of total reserves. Estimates of oil reserves have risen dramatically from an estimated 5 billion barrels during World War II to more than 150 billion today. And during the years following the 1973 oil-price explosion, Saudi Arabia's financial holdings have grown from a few billion dollars to well over $150 billion, exceeding those of such rich nations as West Germany and Japan.[33] The pricing system for OPEC oil itself shows the importance of Saudi Arabia, for during normal times all other OPEC oil is priced in relation to Saudi "marker crude."

Producing nations outside OPEC are not likely to undercut Saudi dominance. The Soviet Union, the world's largest producer (12 million barrels daily), exports about 3 million barrels daily, half of which goes to Eastern Europe. Thus, the Soviet Union has relatively little impact on the world market. But the Soviet Union bloc in total almost surely will become net importers—perhaps of several million barrels daily—by the end of the century, thereby placing additional strain on the world oil market. Britain's and Norway's combined North Sea production, which was 2.4 million barrels daily in early 1982, is unlikely to rise above 4 million when it peaks during the 1980's. Venezuelan heavy oil from the Orinoco belt represents a huge supply of oil—perhaps more than 700 billion barrels, or at least four times the proven reserves of Saudi Arabia. And this Venezuelan oil likely will be especially important to the United States, because of the traditional close ties between these two nations. But large investments in both production and processing—to remove large amounts of metals—will result in a carefully paced development. By the year 2000, production is unlikely to exceed 1 million barrels daily.[34]

Over the next decade, Mexico and possibly the People's Republic of China represent the only likely sources of significant new supplies for the world oil market outside of OPEC.

Mexico, of course, has been an oil producer since the early part of this century, and by early 1982 its production had climbed to 2.3 million barrels daily, one third of which was exported. Quite a bit of optimism has been generated in the United States for Mexican oil as estimates of reserves have reached astronomical proportions. Three weeks after taking office at the end of 1976, President Lopez Portillo announced that proven oil reserves were not 6 billion barrels as previously supposed, but 11 billion. By the beginning of 1980 the figure stood at 50 billion barrels (of which about 20 billion represented the oil equivalent of natural gas, although this fact did not appear in some press reports). "Probable" reserves were put at an additional 45 billion, and potential reserves at 200 billion. (Both estimates include about one-third gas.) For comparison, Saudi Arabian proven reserves are some 166 billion barrels of oil.[35]

The euphoria in the United States is not justified. True, the Mexican economy will benefit, but the Mexican oil is quite unlikely to make any important change in the world oil picture. Mexican exports will be constrained by a ballooning domestic oil consumption brought on by a doubling of population by the end of the century—perhaps to over 125 million. Furthermore, developing major new oil fields requires considerable time. Bureaucratic and political problems associated with the Mexican oil industry will further slow the development. Thus, production is likely to be about 4.0 to 4.5 million barrels daily in the early 1990's, with exports not exceeding 2.5 million—less than 4 percent of expected world production. Also, one should remember that even reserves of 100 billion barrels represent less than five years of the world's consumption.[36]

The oil output of the People's Republic of China grew rapidly during the 1970's, reaching a peak of 2.1 mbd in 1979. But so did consumption, so only about a quarter million barrels daily were left for the export market. In the late 1970's, China was looked upon as one of the miracle solutions to the oil crisis. The CIA in 1975 predicted that China's output would be 4.7 mbd by 1980; and, not to be outdone, the U.S. Commerce Department predicted 8.2 mbd by 1988, a level envisaged by the Peking Government by 1990. In fact, Chinese production—principally onshore—had declined to 1.9 mbd by 1982, and any prospects for a major increase in exports rested wholly on offshore areas, which remained largely unexplored as of 1982. The only things certain were high risks, high costs, and long exploration and development times. If China makes any impact ever on the world oil market, it is unlikely to be until well into the 1990's.

Moreover, all these new suppliers are likely to be near their capacity, thus providing no cushion for sudden surges in demand or cutbacks by OPEC producers. Nothing on the horizon suggests that the centrality of Saudi Arabia in the international petroleum market will be challenged in the foreseeable future.[37]

On what kind of country has the world become so dependent? Saudi Arabia is a family business; not an ordinary family business, but one with 10,000 members, for whom the penalty for attempting to marry without family approval can mean death. In 1901, Ibn Saud, penniless and exiled in Kuwait, set out with some forty men on camels to recapture his family's traditional homeland from other Arabs and the Turks. The stuff of high adventure and epic history, his struggle succeeded in 1932, with the unification of his conquests into the Kingdom of Saudi Arabia.[38] King Ibn Saud was succeeded as king by his sons—Saud in 1952, Faisal in 1964, and after Faisal's assassination, Khalid in 1975, and Fahd in 1982.

By 1982, the wealth controlled by the Saud family made the fortunes of legendary Western "oil barons," and even the monetary reserves of the richest industrial nations, look puny by comparison. Indeed, it is reasonable to assume that the Saudi royal family is so wealthy that its primary objective is not maximizing the wealth of the nation it governs, but rather assuring its own survival as the ruling family.[39] Yet there had been so much complacency in the United States about the stability of the present regime of Saudi Arabia that until the Iranian crisis, one was not aware of threats to its existence. But threats certainly exist, and an understanding of them is necessary for an analysis of the energy problem.

Like all families, the Sauds do not always agree amongst themselves. In recent years, the press has reported signs of sharp family disagreement. There was no dispute that Crown Prince Fahd would replace King Khalid (sixty-nine in 1982) when he stepped down or died. But the princes could not agree on Fahd's successor. Fahd himself proposed one of his full brothers, which would have meant passing over the prince next in line—Prince Abdullah, who is Fahd's half brother, head of the National Guard, and thought to be less friendly to the West than is Fahd. Abdullah objected and had enough family support to block a decision at the time.[40] The question was resolved satisfactorily in 1982, when upon King Khalid's death, Prince Fahd did succeed him and in turn was replaced by Prince Abdullah.

Succession crises are not the only internal threat to the family, as the recent histories of neighboring countries suggest. Between 1977 and 1982, political assassinations occurred in Syria, South Yemen, North Yemen, and Iran. And in the last quarter-century, dissidents have overthrown ruling groups in Iran, South Yemen, Iraq, Syria, Egypt, and Libya—albeit some of the rulers were kings put in by colonial powers, and none had the family base of the Sauds. The press has reported some attempted coups in Saudi Arabia, the most publicized being one in 1969 by military officers. Any new regime in Saudi Arabia would quite likely have political and economic goals different from those of the present rulers.[41]

Too little is known about internal relations in Saudi Arabia to make any more solid predictions. But experienced "Saudi watchers," men with years of exposure to different strata of Saudi society, including the highest level of the royal family, are increasingly worried about the corrosive influence of instant wealth. Here are some of their comments:[42] A few years ago, "no one heard words against the government; now one hears, 'This government is intolerable and has to go' "; "I judge the government's chance of survival for a half-dozen years to be quite good, and for a dozen years, fairly good. *But there could be a successful revolution this evening.*"

Indeed, the seizure in November 1979 of the Grand Mosque in Mecca by perhaps 700 militants may well prove, in retrospect, to have been one of the more important developments regarding energy during that fateful year. For it seemed to say—and this, no doubt, was an intention of the perpetrators—that the great stabilizer of the world oil market is itself not stable. That such a conspiracy could go undetected is deeply disturbing. Very little is known about the event; the fact that so much about Saudi internal politics is shrouded in obscurity is hardly a source of comfort to anyone analyzing energy prospects for the 1980's and 1990's.

One of the major external dangers to the Saudi Arabian leaders lies in a possible coalition of radical Arab states supported by Colonel el-Qaddafi, the dictator of Libya. Qaddafi is one of the world's most unusual leaders, to put it mildly. Intensely religious, he has been known to go into the desert alone for a month to meditate. Quite erratic and believed to be behind plots to assassinate some other Arab rulers, he was called a "nut" by Sadat and "crazy" by the Shah of Iran. But he has received substantial military aid from Russia and Cuba.[43]

A neighbor of Saudi Arabia is South Yemen, which with its Marxist government constitutes a major worry to the Saudis. The Soviets and Cubans have been using the country as a staging area for the fighting in the Horn of Africa. South Yemen's artillery battalions, with Soviet officers, helped Ethiopia in its war against Somalia, gaining experience that the Saudis fear could be put to use against the small oil sheikdoms on the Arabian peninsula. Furthermore, South Yemen has been a sanctuary for the Palestinian terrorists believed to be responsible for the 1977–78 assassinations of three North Yemen leaders—two Presidents and a Prime Minister. And the Saudi leaders fear a Palestinian assassination attempt. In early 1979, the rivalry between the Yemens erupted in military conflict, sending shock waves through the entire Arabian Peninsula and drawing direct American involvement.[44]

Iraq, contiguous to Saudi Arabia in the northwest, has flirted with the Soviets on and off for years. To be sure, the Iraqi war with Iran brought the Saudis and the Iraqis closer together. But the radical Iraqi regime historically has been at odds with the Saudis, with basic ideological differences separating radical Arabs from conservative Saudi Arabia. No matter what the outcome of the Arab-Israeli conflict, Arab radicals are fundamentally opposed to rule by a royal family and would want to see the Saudi regime replaced.[45]

Iran's relationship with Saudi Arabia has traditionally been more important to the Saudis than any other except that with the United States. The Iranians have weighed heavily on the minds of the Saud family in two crucial matters: One is oil policy, the other, survival. The nation with a larger population (35 million) and smaller oil reserves than Saudi Arabia might have a good reason to seek to escalate oil prices.

Although fear of the Soviet Union had created a strong bond between Saudi Arabia and Iran, whose territory has been coveted by the Russians since the last century, the two countries have sharply disagreed on oil-pricing policy, and for centuries the Arabs and the Iranians have been traditionally suspicious of one another. Iran's current internal condition, of course, means that it does not pose much of a direct military threat at the moment; it does, however, pose a danger that the turmoil will spread to Saudi Arabia. In December 1981, conspirators—widely believed to be Iranian agents—attempted to assassinate members of the royal family and overthrow the Bahrain government; and by early 1982 Iranian planes had bombed Kuwait. The rulers of the nations around the Gulf were asking themselves: If Iran was engaging in such adventurism while at battle with Iraq, what might it do when the war was over? Saudi Arabian leaders clearly recognized the great danger that existed in the dreams of the Shiite fundamentalists—and in the presence of a large Shiite population in the area of the Saudi oil fields. The Saudi Minister of Interior said that his government would "counter Iranian terrorism and thwart its attempts at hegemony in the Gulf region."[46] In addition to the pressure from leftwing South Yemen and radical Iran, there is concern about the Palestinians, who have important jobs as advisors or oil-field workers in some of the Gulf countries. There have been reports that Palestinian terrorists had been found on tankers.

Control of the Gulf and its narrow mouth, the Straits of Hormuz, is critically important to the noncommunist nations. An almost endless chain of tankers passes through these narrow waters. It is no wonder the United States regards the Arab/Persian Gulf as a security problem second only to that posed by the Soviet Union. In the words of a recent Department of Defense report, "The survival of NATO is as likely to be decided in the Middle East/Persian Gulf as on the plains of Central Europe."[47] The massive dependence of the industrial world on one fragile regime is a frightening reality of modern life.

Still another and larger threat hangs over the entire Middle East, especially the Gulf—of bold Soviet intervention and an increasingly prominent Soviet presence. By supplying arms and advisers and using mercenaries provided by its client states, the U.S.S.R. has gained a strong foothold in the Horn of Africa and in the southern part of the Arabian peninsula. And it has now carried out a massive and brazen invasion of Afghanistan. Meanwhile, the pro-Soviet Tudeh Party holds a strong position among Iranian oil-field workers.

The consequences of continuing Soviet success would be of overwhelming strategic importance—perhaps leading to Russian domination of the world's oil line. Such an eventuality would compound many times over the problem of hostile oil. The U.S.S.R.'s invasion of Afghanistan suggests that it may eventually be prepared to challenge some of the most vital Western interests, which would prove to be very dangerous and unpredictable. This, added to the existing mix of national and regional instabilities, certainly provides still another compelling reason to concern ourselves about the fundamental security of our oil supplies.

Perhaps Egyptian President Anwar Sadat was too quick when he said, on the last day of 1979, that the "battle of energy" had already begun. But the rise in regional instability and the increasingly active Soviet role surely add up to an enormous threat to the continued availability of the oil on which the United States and the West depend for their economic health.

What role does Saudi Arabia play in the analyses of world oil supply during the 1980's and 1990's? As of early 1983, many observers were predicting that substantial excess capacity in OPEC would keep prices relatively steady for some years, following which a slow but steady rise (corrected for inflation) would occur. Indeed, Sheikh Yamani said that he did not expect inflation-adjusted oil prices to increase by much between 1982 and 1990. On the other hand, an April 1981 scenario of the International Energy Agency (IEA) foresaw a shortfall of 3.2 mbd in 1990. In this context, a shortfall does not denote an absolute physical shortage, but rather that, at relatively stable oil prices, the world's demand for petroleum would exceed the supply of oil that producers could or would be willing to produce. The consequence of this demand would be another round of price hikes beyond those of 1973–74 and 1979–80.

There has been much controversy and confusion over projections. What is usually omitted from reports about the projections is the way in which conclusions are affected by assumptions made about a number of very uncertain things. Responsible forecasters can make very different assumptions with very different outcomes. The key uncertainties include:[48]

1. Rate of economic growth in the United States and elsewhere in the world
2. Energy usage per unit of economic output (in other words, amount of conservation)
3. Oil production in Saudi Arabia
4. Oil production in other OPEC nations
5. Oil production in non-OPEC nations
6. Contributions from other "conventional" energy sources— natural gas, coal, and nuclear
7. Contributions by non-traditional sources, such as shale oil, solar, tar sands, geothermal, wave power, and so on

Different assumptions can produce enormously different forecasts. For instance, by making different assumptions on two items —rate of economic growth and energy usage per unit of economic output—specialists have forecast world energy consumption to increase by as little as 60 percent by the year 2000 or by as much as 230 percent.[49]

All forecasts should thus be offered with some modesty. As things stand, it seems reasonable to believe that at current or slightly higher prices, demand for OPEC oil (including consumption within OPEC countries of 5 million barrels daily) could be between 25 and 30 million barrels a day in 1990. But in 1990, the capacity of OPEC nations will probably not exceed 28 million barrels per day, assuming that Saudi capacity is 11 million barrels a day. Thus we come to what is perhaps the controlling uncertainty—Saudi Arabian production.

But how much oil will Saudi Arabia choose to make available? It is an open question. As of 1982, the Saudis had the physical capability to produce 11 million barrels daily, and plans had been announced to increase that capacity to 14 million barrels daily during the 1980's. Some engineers believed that it would be physically possible for Saudi Arabia to increase its output by 1 million barrels daily every year up to a level of 16 to 20 million barrels daily, and then to sustain such a rate until the end of the century.[50]

The royal family favored an increased capacity, knowing it would help keep prices relatively stable. These Saudis were concerned about the condition of the economies of the industrial nations, which were both their chief customers and outlets for their savings. The strongly anticommunist Saudis feared that economic stagnation would increase leftist influence in Europe. Further, the rulers wanted to maintain good political relations with the United States, to which they looked as an ally, an arms supplier, a source of technical advice, and a force to help settle the Arab-Israeli dispute.[51]

Yet even if the Saudis want to keep prices at a moderate level, there is a limit to how much they can increase production in order to do so. Hence a policy of high production and price moderation in the nearer term would still mean higher prices at some later date, when Saudi Arabia would be closer to its production limit.

But the higher prices could come sooner rather than later. There is a growing pressure within the royal family not to allow oil exports to exceed 8.5 mbd.[52] Proponents of this view reason as follows: (1) Saudi Arabia should distance itself from the West and become more friendly with radical Arab elements. (2) Waste and corruption can be better controlled if industrial development is scaled down. (3) The North Yemen labor pool is nearly exhausted, and an increase in migrant labor from other countries could bring about increased political instability. (4) A valuable commodity should not be depleted quickly in order to build up large savings abroad, when the real return on these investments is negative after correcting for inflation. (5) Even after the completion of a massive natural gas project, any oil production in excess of 5 million barrels a day will result in the flaring of natural gas.[53]

The sentiment against high production levels is stronger among some of the younger members of the royal family. They are afraid that the older generation will deplete the oil and gas, spend much of the money, and leave them and their own children with bank accounts shrunk from inflation.[54]

If the present Saudi government were overthrown, the new regime would probably be more radical, less concerned about the effects of its pricing policies on the West, and thus more likely to increase the cost of its oil as rapidly as it could. In any case, the United States would be unwise to base its energy policy on the premise that the Saudis will increase production substantially, thereby moderating any price increases.

We must note, however, that some other observers hold an entirely different view as to how much oil the Saudis will produce. This other interpretation eschews politics in favor of a strictly economic argument. The premise is, "They will produce as much as will maximize their revenues," even if this means producing 20 million barrels daily. This view, of course, is strongly challenged by those who consider other factors, political as well as technical. "I would characterize that as science fiction," said one Department of Energy official. But if the profit-maximizing view is correct, a substantial price rise is a reasonable possibility over the next ten years or so, for the OPEC experience to date has been that more revenues result from higher prices than lower prices (e.g. 17.5 mbd at $30 a barrel is $220 billion annually compared with $140 billion at 30 mbd at $13 a barrel).[55]

Thus, whatever view one holds about the motivations of Saudi decision-makers, the result seems to be the same—eventually higher oil prices, though no one can now accurately predict how much or how fast. If there are no major "accidents" or conflicts, a likely scenario is that oil prices will remain essentially stable in real terms until after 1985. At some point, demand will begin to run up against even Saudi capacity, and with that the Saudis again will lose control of the international petroleum market. Prices will then move up to substantially higher levels—perhaps 50 percent or more above current real prices.[56]

The rate of increase could be gradual. But a number of the past price increases have been triggered by accidents: the 1956 Suez War; the combination of the Suez Canal closure resulting from the 1967 war; the underestimation of European demand by the majors in 1971; and the break of the Trans-Arabian Pipeline by a Syrian bulldozer; the 1973 war; the cutbacks; and the subsequent high prices bid.[57] Who would have thought that an elderly, irate cleric, living in a suburb of Paris, communicating by cassettes with his followers, could have brought Iranian oil production to a standstill? So it is quite possible that some quirk of history will again intervene—an Arab cutback of production in case of another Arab-Israeli war, tankers sunk in the Straits of Hormuz, or a revolution within Saudi Arabia that damages the oil fields, for example. The price rise could then be quite sudden as buyers bid for oil, but it is hoped that the immediate shock could be moderated by the mechanism of the International Energy Agency (IEA), which has developed a plan for allocating oil in case of an emergency. The United States and nineteen other consuming countries are members of the agency, which was established in 1974 to coordinate the energy policies of the noncommunist industrial nations. Along with other IEA members, the United States has embarked on a program to maintain a strategic storage of oil equal to four to six months' supply of U.S. imports.[58] Overall though, the experience of 1979 does not leave one sanguine about the ability of the major importers to work together to offset higher prices.

The experiences of 1973–74 and 1979–80 show us what we might expect from higher real oil prices. Increased prices mean, first, that the United States has to do more work to buy a given quantity of oil. Second, the payments to foreign governments contract domestic demand for goods and services, and in effect become an excise tax, a "drag" on the economies of the importing countries. Industrial nations deflate their economies in the face of oil-induced inflation and balance-of-payments deficits, which further reduces growth and further increases unemployment. Finally, there are massive strains on the international monetary system. In total, the two oil shocks cost the industrial nations $1.2 trillion in lost economic growth from 1974 to 1981.[59]

Higher oil prices in the future would create other conditions that are undesirable.[60] High unemployment, inflation, the efforts by various groups to maintain their relative and absolute economic positions—all create internal political problems. These problems in turn increase the likelihood of political conflict among nations. Since 1973 serious clashes have developed among Western allies over oil and nuclear power, which show that energy questions—involving dependence and vulnerability, employment and growth, the stability of governments—have taken on extraordinary sensitivity. In fact, they have become security issues of paramount importance. Thus, higher oil prices in the next decade—following a decade of tension and suspicion caused by the two oil shocks—could severely strain relations among the Western nations.[61]

About the most optimistic current forecast that can be made is that the world will drift along with a little slower economic growth and a little higher inflation than usual. Indeed, some of the optimists—those saying not to worry about substantially higher prices in the next decade—are basing their outlook on continued low economic growth.[62] Hardly a satisfactory solution, for this would extract a high price in the form of unemployment, diminished opportunity, and the inevitable political conflicts.

U.S. DOMESTIC OIL POLICY I

If oil imports create so many problems, the obvious thing to do is to continue to lower them, or at least to keep them from growing again. Can this be done through a domestic American oil policy? Can the decline in domestic production be reversed and the supply of domestic oil increased? In all the arguments and debates, the charges and counter-charges, of the last decade, three different domestic oil "solutions" can be identified. The oil companies generally propounded two of the solutions. The first was to deregulate oil prices and speedily grant offshore oil licenses. The second was to produce more oil by unconventional means, such as enhanced recovery and shale oil. Opponents of the oil industry offered the third solution—break up the big companies. Yet none of these provides us with a real solution, for none will be able to keep U.S. oil output from falling below its current level of about 10 million barrels daily. This reality has been obscured in the fight over the $1 trillion suddenly created when the 1973–74 and 1979–80. OPEC price hikes dramatically increased the worth of proven U.S. oil reserves.[63] Although the various domestic "solutions" involve interesting and important issues, none is likely to result in as high a level of U.S. oil production as now exists.

The elimination of price controls, indeed, did help in two ways. First, controlled prices had reduced oil exploration to below what it otherwise would have been, although it is impossible to tell by how much. An analysis of oil company budgets, however, shows that exploration and drilling increased substantially, which is not surprising, for the rewards for newly found oil in the United States also increased substantially. But in spite of a 70-percent increase in drilling between 1973 and 1979, U.S. proven reserves declined by one-quarter. From 1979 through 1981, new additions about equaled production, but the outlook from 1982 onward was dimmed by a dramatic reduction in oil drilling in 1982 caused by the so-called "oil glut." Second, the oil industry argued that price controls had been created and administered in a way to generate great uncertainty. This assertion is certainly true. The whole jerry-built structure—"old" oil, "new" oil, "new new" oil, and "strip-per" oil, altogether some seventeen categories in recent legislation—had fostered a chaotic, confusing, and expensive bureaucratic monster. But it is not evident that either price controls or the way they are administered have held back exploration or production to such an extent that they were the dominant cause in the decline in oil reserves.[64]

But it is important that price controls have been eliminated, for higher prices will result in not only more efficient use of oil but also in more oil being found than would otherwise be the case. Yet even with complete decontrol, production of oil from existing fields will likely decline from the existing level of 10 million barrels daily. *In the early 1990's, only 4 to 6 million barrels a day are likely to come from reserves that were known to exist in 1982, including Alaska. It is unlikely that U.S. production will include more than 2 million barrels daily of oil from new fields found between 1982 and the early 1990's. And even this combined total of 6 to 8 million barrels daily could prove to be too high.* Much of the increased drilling and added reserves in 1980 involved very small oil fields that had been known to exist but had just become attractive economically with the higher prices. The amount of new reserves to be added by exploring and developing such small fields is quite limited.

Indeed, the prospects of finding a big field onshore or offshore in the Gulf of Mexico are quite small because these territories have already been intensively searched. Over 2 million wells have been drilled in the United States—four times as many as in all the rest of the noncommunist world combined.

New territories, especially the outer continental shelf and the Alaskan North Slope, are the main hopes for finding a big field.[65] As one oil company executive put it, "Sure, higher prices will help, but a bigger factor is access to new acreage. Even a price of a hundred dollars a barrel won't give you any oil unless you have someplace to drill."[66] Environmental concerns have slowed and will slow the development of the new territories. The drilling off the East Coast that has been done so far has been disappointing, while that off California has been quite encouraging. The big question mark is offshore Alaska. But even if major new fields were found off Alaska and environmental constraints did not exist, finding and developing a major new field in such inhospitable areas could take the better part of a decade.

What about the second proposed domestic solution—new sources from unconventional means? A large quantity of oil—more than half—is left behind in conventional recovery methods. For years, oil companies have been developing increasingly sophisticated methods for extracting a portion of this oil, and not surprisingly, the OPEC price hikes boosted interest in the effort. The newer methods, the so-called enhanced recovery, ordinarily involve the injection of a chemical compound or heat into an oil field. The amount of additional oil that can be obtained depends on the tightness with which the remaining oil sticks to the oil-bearing sands and on the porosity of the sands. Unfortunately, years are needed to determine the effectiveness of any given method for any single field. And as of 1982, enhanced recovery, although moving ahead, was still more promise than reality. It is unlikely that more than one million barrels daily will be made available in the early 1990's through enhanced recovery methods, and this quantity is included in the estimate of 6 to 8 million barrels daily for the early 1990's.[67]

Another potential new source is oil-bearing shale rock. Although considered a new source, oil was actually being distilled from shale in the eastern United States prior to Colonel Drake's oil discovery that started the American oil industry in 1859. Drake's find closed down the shale-oil industry. In Colorado in the early part of the twentieth century, vast shale-oil deposits were discovered. These reserves still dwarf known reserves in conventional oil fields, but the problem has always been to get the oil out. According to a report issued in 1918 by the U.S. Geological Survey, "The production of oil in this country will continue to grow . . . because of the shale resource . . . No one may be bold enough to foretell what tremendous figure of production may be reached within the next ten years."[68]

Subsequently, oil from shale has been said to be within a whisker of economic grasp. Three decades ago, chemical engineering students were taught that if oil prices went up 20 percent, oil from shale would become profitable. Since then, the price of oil has increased by a good deal more than 20 percent in real terms, but it is not certain that shale oil will be profitable. As the price of oil has risen, so has the estimated cost of producing oil from shale. Many engineers and promoters say that the price of oil must go up just another 20 percent for oil from shale to be economic, although others say that it is economic at prices existing in early 1982 *provided environmental issues can be resolved.*

The new government-owned Synthetic Fuels Corporation, which was created in July 1980 with a multi-billion-dollar budget, seemed to be a major step forward for shale oil. Also of apparent importance was a program launched by Exxon, not only the world's largest oil company but also one rich in cash resources and with a long history of excellence in oil and chemical processing. Exxon, deciding to make major investments in synthetic fuels, released a study indicating that 15 million barrels a day of synthetic fuels—eight from shale and seven from coal—could possibly be produced by the year 2010. Such a program, Exxon estimated, would require, in 1980 dollars, about $800 billion in investment.

But by early 1982, the outlook for the shale oil industry was dim once again. The Reagan Administration had little appetite for interfering in the marketplace through subsidies for shale oil facilities and decided to grant government aid to just two projects—one through an agreement to purchase the output and the other a loan guarantee to Tosco for its joint venture with Exxon. But in early 1982, after revising upward an estimate of costs from $3.2 billion to $5.0 billion, Exxon shelved the project.[69]

Existing shale processes are not likely to prove economically attractive unless one expects substantially higher oil prices or unless the government subsidizes the facility. The capital and time requirements would still be huge. A production level equal to about 1 percent of U.S. oil consumption—150,000 barrels a day —would require over ten billion dollars and almost a decade for development. Furthermore, under present technology, water requirements are potentially very large, which would generate opposition from farmers and ranchers. Nor are environmentalists happy about a process that breaks some shale rock into fine particles that float into the sky. Meanwhile, the shale rock that remains expands to a volume greater than it previously occupied, which necessitates filling in some canyons. The so-called *in situ* process, in which the rock is burned underground, involves less environmental damage than conventional means, but shale oil still is likely to make essentially no contribution to the national energy budget by the early 1990's. In fact, it might contribute very little by the year 2000. (Oil from coal is discussed in Chapter 4.)[70]

It seems likely that total U.S. oil output in the early 1990's from all sources (both known and newly found oil fields, enhanced recovery, and oil shale) will approximate 6 or 8 million barrels daily, about 2 or 4 million less than current production.

Indeed, it seems wildly optimistic to believe that the current level of U.S. oil output can be maintained until the early 1990's. To do so would require the finding of 3.7 billion barrels of oil annually; but there has been only five years in the last twenty in which this quantity of reserves has been found.

What about the third proposal, breaking up the companies? Companies in the oil industry have been large, at least since John D. Rockefeller organized the Standard Oil Trust in 1882. And even after the Trust was broken into thirty-four separate companies in 1911, oil companies remained big. In 1981, four out of the top six companies in the Fortune 500 listing of the largest U.S. industrial companies were petroleum firms, with three—Exxon, Mobil, and Standard of California—direct descendants of Rockefeller's Standard Oil Trust. Of the top 50 companies in the Fortune 500 list, over one-third were oil companies.[71]

Divestiture, or "dismemberment," as the companies call it, could take one of two forms. One is a horizontal breakup, in which oil companies would be required to sell off non-oil activities, such as coal, an issue we discuss in Chapter 4. The other is vertical divestiture, which typically would involve breaking up each of the largest dozen or so oil firms into three separate companies—the first restricted to oil exploration and production; the second, to pipelines; and the third, to refining and marketing.

Would vertical divestiture increase the supply of domestically produced oil? This question has traditionally been argued in economic terms: How does one measure the trade-off between increased competition and decreased efficiency? Proponents of divestiture argue that the present pattern of vertical integration makes the firms noncompetitive, and they also say that the great size of firms makes them unwieldy and inefficient. Opponents of divestiture assert more or less the opposite, namely that the industry as it stands is highly competitive, and that the current pattern of vertical integration improves efficiency.

Numerous studies have been conducted on vertical divestiture. A careful review of them leads to a most disappointing conclusion: Economic analyses do not yet enable one to determine whether breaking up the companies would result in any meaningful changes in either competition or efficiency. *What is clear is that there is no evidence that divestiture would have any meaningful impact on the future of domestic supplies of oil.* Moreover, the consequences of a breakup might well be inconsequential to the consumer, on the order of a tank of gasoline a year, but whether a tank richer or a tank poorer cannot be determined.[72] As for the stockholders, any pinch would be hardly felt. Finally, the units remaining after divestiture would have no difficulty in obtaining adequate financing to continue operations. An exploration and production company spun off from Exxon would not, as one book alleges, be a "mom and pop wildcatter." It would remain one of the world's largest firms.[73]

There might well be, however, significant political and psychological effects. Some studies indicate that as many as eight out of ten Americans place some blame on the oil companies for energy problems. Many of them might well assume that breaking up the most visible of those companies would do much to solve the problems, thus increasing complacency and making American consumers even less willing to accept the higher prices needed to dampen demand and stimulate alternatives. Many citizens, however, might derive considerable psychic income from seeing large companies broken up into somewhat smaller ones, and the number of executives earning $500,000 a year substantially reduced. On the other hand, there would be a large multiplication in the number of senior vice-presidents earning over $100,000 a year in the successor companies.[74]

The important point to remember is that there is no domestic oil solution, certainly not in this century, to the problem of U.S. oil imports, no way that production from American oil wells can close the gap of 6 million barrels daily between what the United States produces and what it consumes. Any hopes rest, to varying degrees, on the other energy sources—natural gas, coal, nuclear, solar—and conservation. Our conclusion, therefore, differs fundamentally from the optimistic projections of just a few years ago. In November 1974—one year after the embargo—Administration experts, with the aid of large computer models, argued that domestic production could reach 15 million or even 20 million barrels daily, and that U.S. imports thus could be reduced to zero. They said this would require an eleven-dollar-a-barrel oil price (in 1973 prices), which in fact was not much higher than the 1975–78 prices for newly found oil.[75]

With no possible domestic oil solution, it is obvious that U.S. oil policy must come to terms with the undesirable features of imported oil—the possibilities of supply cutoffs and further higher prices. A supply cutoff, although more dramatic than increasing prices, is actually easier to prepare for, as indeed the United States hopes to do through its strategic storage program. The United States embarked on this program in 1978 with a goal of storing one billion barrels—then about four months' supply of imports. Unfortunately, the program seemed jinxed from the beginning. Shortly after the stockpiling began, the Iranian crisis hit and the resulting tight world oil market precluded additional purchases. Later, as the market loosened, the government began to add oil to the stockpile, which stood at 250 million barrels in mid-1982.

Resumption of the program was certainly important; in fact, the goal should be to store six months of imports. That kind of reserve on hand would help deter any embargo by oil producers, because some producers could not afford to go that long without revenues. Furthermore, it would help provide oil in cases such as the Iranian shutdown of 1978–79 and thereby help prevent runaway markets. The costs associated with the storing of six months' supply—estimated at $5 billion or so a year—sound high, but are small compared with the gains in economic and political security. The United States should also encourage other Western nations to expand their strategic oil reserves as well, which would further diminish the potential effectiveness of a future embargo or disruption.[76]

But strategic storage deals only with a part of the problem. The overall pattern of consumption, which has led to a tight world oil market, is clearly unstable, creating "costs" that are not reflected in prices paid by U.S. consumers. Indeed, U.S. oil policies have encouraged oil consumption to rise. One obvious reason why U.S. oil consumption increased between 1974 and 1978 while that of the other industrial nations decreased is that oil prices in the other nations reflected world levels plus a hefty gasoline tax, while oil prices in the United States were controlled far below world levels. Thus, in 1979 American consumers received a subsidy on oil of $23 billion.[77]

In private interviews some senators expressed serious doubts about the possibility of letting prices rise to the world level.[78] Typical comments: "Everyone is taken in by the conspiracy theory of history. The public doesn't believe that there is an energy problem, and I even hear from well-to-do businessmen, 'The oil companies are capping those wells' "; "Inflation is our number-one problem. We don't want higher prices."

In the face of such doubts, as well as serious congressional and public opposition, President Carter's decision to decontrol oil prices was politically courageous. It proved to be even more courageous as world oil prices continued to rise dramatically during the latter half of 1979. And President Reagan's decision in February 1981 to decontrol prices immediately—although not quite so politically daring—was a further desirable step.

President Carter coupled his decision on decontrol with a request for a "windfall profits" tax on domestic crude oil, that is, a tax on the extra money that would be paid by consumers because of decontrol. Although few oil executives were happy with the tax, many of them recognized that the tax was necessary politically in order to obtain the decontrol of prices. Indeed, without the tax, the President likely would have stopped the decontrol program. Warfare did break out, however, between different segments of the industry as to what portion of the tax would be collected from different segments of the industry. A compromise was finally reached, Congress passed the bill, and President Carter signed it shortly thereafter, almost exactly one year after he had made the request for it.

The law will result in a tax of at least $227 billion over a ten-year period. Although the law has many complex provisions, its essential feature is an excise tax on domestic crude oil on the difference between the free-market price and a defined base price. For example, the tax rate on oil from wells producing prior to 1979 (so-called "old" oil) is 70 percent if owned by a large company and 50 percent if owned by a small company; whereas for newly found oil, the tax rate is 30 percent for all companies. The base price was about $13 for "old" oil and $17 for newly found oil, with the base prices subject to various escalation clauses. Thus, for example, with a market price of $36 a barrel, the tax on "old" oil produced by a large company would be about $16 a barrel; whereas for newly found oil, the tax would be about $6 a barrel. In 1981, some of the taxes were lowered, but unfortunately one very undesirable aspect remained: that the tax also applies to revenues from the sale of oil to be found in the future—a major mistake that will keep U.S. production lower than it would otherwise be. Overall, though, the combination of price decontrol and "windfall profits" tax was a major step forward in the nation's march toward a rational energy policy.

But in spite of this progress, an important fact should not be lost sight of: Even world market prices would still be much too low to reflect the real risks caused by oil imports. These include such things as higher oil prices, slower economic growth, and international political tension. Until President Carter highlighted some

of these issues in his speech on April 4, 1979, virtually *all* participants in the debate had ignored the costs associated with these
risks.[79] Clearly these risks need to be addressed and thought
through.

What do we mean? We are talking about what are called
external costs, or externalities. These are costs induced by oil
imports that are not borne by individual oil consumers, as such
costs are not reflected in the prices involved in the transaction
between producer and consumer—that is, they are external to
those prices. For instance, the cost of cleaning up an oil spill on
a beach on Cape Cod is not included in the price of a gallon of
gasoline in Boston. External costs plus market price equal what is
called the social cost.[80]

Predicting oil prices and their economic effects involves art
as well as science, requiring sensitivity to the political situation as
well as to straight economics. Indeed, by its very nature any
estimate of the total costs associated with U.S. oil imports must
be highly uncertain. But it is so important for policymakers
and the public to have some idea of the possible magnitude
of such costs that we feel compelled to offer an illustration of the
possible, regardless of how tentative and uncertain such an
illustration might be. Our illustration is based on the following
set of relationships, depicted in Figure 2-1, that illustrate how
much it might have been worth to the United States to have
kept its oil imports from rising from the 1975 level of about 6.0
million barrels a day to the actual level of 8.5 million in early
1979.[81]

Arrow	Description of Forces
a	The U.S. policies that caused 2.5 million barrels daily of extra U.S. imports affected policies in the other industrial nations so that their imports were higher than they would otherwise have been (perhaps by 2.5 million barrels daily, although this illustration assumes zero).
b	The additional 2.5 million barrels daily of world oil imports caused world price to be $30 a barrel instead of $20.
c	The $10 difference in world price caused the 6.0 million

FIGURE 2·1
ILLUSTRATION OF POSSIBLE EFFECTS OF INCREASED U.S.
IMPORTS OF 2.5 MILLION BARRELS DAILY (8.5 INSTEAD OF
6 MILLION BARRELS DAILY)

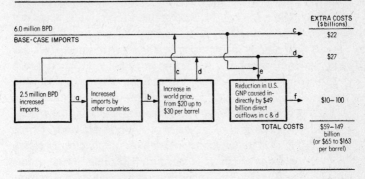

barrels daily of oil imports under the base case to rise in cost by $22 billion yearly ($10 × 365 × 6 million).

d The increased oil imports of 2.5 million barrels daily cost $30 a barrel, or $27 billion yearly.

e, f The outflow of funds from the United States due to the increase in world oil price reduces U.S. national income by contracting demand for U.S. goods and services. The magnitude depends on the amount of funds recycled back to the United States by the oil exporters for investment or purchases, and on the policies (government purchases, transfer payments, changes in taxes, and changes in money supply) undertaken by the U.S. government that offset—or reinforce—the contraction. Government policies will depend on many factors, including the speed of the price rise and fear of inflation, which in itself is exacerbated by higher oil prices, not only by their direct effects but also because of their indirect effects on wage demands.

Note A: Estimates are needed for each of the above forces for each year, with total costs discounted to the present by use of an appropriate discount rate.

Note B: The range of estimates for the va'ues for each force and the probability of each value occurring are dependent on the estimated values of the prior forces. Thus, if one wanted to estimate, say, ten possible outcomes for each of five forces, the total number of possible scenarios would be 10^5. But since each force also depends on conditions in the prior period for that force, the total number of possible scenarios for a ten-year period would run into the billions. For examples of works that have handled complex, multiperiod problems, see Claude L. Pomper, *International Investment Planning: An Integrated Approach* (New York: North-Holland, 1976); Howard Raiffa, *Decision Analysis: Introductory Lectures on Choices Under Uncertainty* (Reading, Mass.: Addison-Wesley, 1967); and Burton Rothberg, "A Decision Theoretic Model of Eastern Hemisphere Oil Exploration," Unpublished D.B.A. thesis, Harvard, 1974.

Although no one can predict with certainty whether the lower level of U.S. imports would have resulted in a lower world capacity to produce crude oil, evidence strongly suggests that it would not have. Those nations that increased capacity during 1976, 1977, and 1978—principally Mexico, the United Kingdom, Iraq, and the Soviet Union—likely would have increased it regardless of whether U.S. imports had stayed at the 6.0 million level or had climbed to the 8.5 million level. Neither can one predict with certainty whether or not Saudi Arabia would have cooperated to keep prices from rising so quickly; but the description above of 1979–82 events indicates the effort that the Saudis made with this goal in mind. If one does assume that world output would have been the same during the Iranian cutoff whether U.S. imports were 6.0 or 8.5 million barrels per day, then the difference of 2.5 million barrels daily of U.S. imports would have turned the 1979 shortage of 1.5 to 2 million barrels daily early in 1979 into a surplus of 0.5 to 1.0 million barrels daily. This swing from a shortage to a surplus almost surely would have had a profound impact on the world oil market. The impact would have been even greater if the United States had had oil in its strategic storage to moderate market forces further.

Admittedly, no one can estimate accurately the total extra costs that occurred because of these additional imports of 2.5 million barrels a day, but a few plausible assumptions allow one to reach an important conclusion: *The costs were huge.* These costs can be classified into several different categories.

1. The first cost was a direct one—the higher level of oil imports caused oil prices to be higher. Not only do U.S. imports impact directly on the world oil market, they also affect the imports of the other industrial nations. If the relationships shown in a recently published study by the Organization for Economic Cooperation and Development (OECD)* are correct, then the additional U.S. imports resulted in additional oil imports by the other industrial nations. Hence, the surplus during 1979 would have been even larger than the 500,000 to 1 million barrels daily mentioned above.[82]

The reason for this tie between U.S. oil imports and the oil imports of other industrial nations is that the United States, with its large market and by its allocation of resources, can make or break various energy options. Without a strong U.S. emphasis on conservation, it is more difficult for other industrial nations to implement additional conservation measures, especially since their consumers pay higher prices than American consumers. A commitment to solar energy in the United States would have made it a much more commercial option for the others. Environmental restraints on nuclear power in the United States had a powerful echo effect on nuclear development in Germany and Japan. In sum, increased American reliance on oil made it more difficult for the other governments to rely on alternatives to oil. But for the purposes of using numbers to illustrate the potential cost of the additional 2.5 million barrels a day of U.S. imports, this impact on the imports of other nations will be taken as zero.

---

*The OECD, of course, is the organization composed of the industrialized, noncommunist countries.

Given the difficulties that we discuss in the Appendix about making accurate forecasts of oil prices, it is clear that any estimate about what might have happened in 1979 is conjectural. But for our illustration, it is assumed that if U.S. imports had been only 6.0 million barrels a day in early 1979 instead of 8.5 million, then the world oil market would have evolved so that the world prices in early 1980 would have been $20 instead of $30 a barrel. In fact, one could make a strong case that the oil price would not even have risen above $16 a barrel, the equivalent of a 10-percent increase in the 1979 year-end price of $14.54 originally planned by OPEC. In such a case, our use of the estimate that the prices would have risen to $20 with imports of 6 million barrels a day will grossly understate the cost of the additional 2.5 million barrels daily of imports.

The assumed increase of the world price of oil by $10 a barrel —to $30 instead of $20—cost the United States an extra $22 billion yearly for the 6 million barrels daily in the base case. The additional 2.5 million barrels daily at their market price of $30 a barrel cost the United States $27 billion yearly. Therefore, the total cost of the 2.5 million barrels daily is about $49 billion yearly —or about $54 for each of the additional 2.5 million barrels daily. In other words, it is possible that the United States might have been spending $44 billion annually to import 6 million barrels of oil per day instead of $93 billion annually to import 8.5 million barrels of oil per day.

To be sure, it is possible to change the assumptions in this illustration and arrive at different numbers for the cost of each additional barrel of oil. But based on almost any reasonable set of assumptions that we tried, the calculated price for the additional oil was substantially higher than the $30 price, and usually it was above $50 a barrel.[83]

2. The second potential cost represents the indirect economic effects of the outflow of the additional $49 billion in direct payments for oil. These indirect costs can vary over an enormously wide range. Whether these indirect costs are low or high depends on a multitude of factors, including the amount of funds recycled from oil exporters back to the United States either for purchases or investments, the speed of any recycle of funds, the gradualness

of any increase in oil imports and prices, the economic policies of the federal government to offset the contraction in demand for U.S. goods and services caused by the outflow of dollars, the degree to which workers demand higher wages because of actual or anticipated inflation related to oil imports, the reaction of the foreign exchange market, the reaction of the stock market, and the effect on investor confidence.

In general, a gradual increase in prices, by allowing adequate time for adjustment, would result in relatively low indirect costs —perhaps only a fraction of the $49 billion annual increase in direct outflows. But a rapid increase in oil prices could create economic costs several times those of the direct outflows and could last for a number of years—as occurred because of the oil price increases in 1973–74 and in 1979. Thus, a relevant range for these indirect costs is probably as wide as $10 to $100 billion. In terms of affecting the cost estimated for the marginal 2.5 million barrels of oil daily, about all we can really say is that these indirect costs might range from about $10 up to $100 a barrel.[84]

3. To these potential costs must be added some social and political risks, difficult to estimate but no less real. Within the United States, increased inflation is socially undesirable; indeed, U.S. leaders have begun to worry seriously about the impact of inflation "on the fabric of American society." Next, U.S. oil imports, even at their present level, are an important contribution to political tensions within the Western community. In the summer of 1978, for example, the United States sought trade concessions from the Europeans and the Japanese, who in turn insisted that the United States restrain its oil imports. The Europeans and Japanese were alarmed by the effects of U.S. demand on the monetary system and on present and future oil prices. A headline in *The Economist* succinctly captured their worry: "Will American oil greed doom the world?"[85] As one foreign leader wrote us, "The energy question gives me more worry than the 20,000 Soviet tanks on the border. The profligacy with which oil continues to be used in the United States is leading us all into disaster." And as the oil-induced recession lingered on, national leaders became more concerned; as West German Chancellor Helmut Schmidt said in early 1982, "Europe is in greater danger than the Ameri-

cans have understood so far. The fabric of the economy and society is endangered by the deepest recession since the middle 1930's. What I fear is economic and social, and therefore political, unrest; political destabilization as a consequence of economic destabilization." Finally, as U.S. oil imports increase, U.S. foreign policy will be more influenced by the desires of the oil exporters, which might involve such things as sales of advanced aircraft to Saudi Arabia and policies toward illegal immigrants from Mexico.

This illustration, admittedly crude, suggests that the total potential costs of the additional 2.5 million barrels daily in early 1979—compared to the 1975 level of 6 million daily—came, in round numbers, to between $65 and $165 a barrel, not counting some potentially quite serious social and political costs. Narrowing this range some suggests that $65–$100 per barrel is a likely result. These costs included a disrupted economy caused by the higher oil prices resulting from a tight oil market. In addition, there are explicit additional costs caused by a disruption in supply.[86] Of course, savings on oil imports by the United States in the future might have a different impact—either smaller or larger—than the conjectures for 1979. But most observers expect a relatively tight world oil market at some future, but unknown, date. Hence, the difference of a few million barrels of oil daily in U.S. imports— even without considering the possible impact of the reduced U.S. imports on the policies of the other industrial nations—could prove to be quite important.

Because we are venturing into heretofore unexplored territory and because any number of refinements in the calculations are possible (such as discounting all future payments to the different times that oil-consuming decisions would be made), we believe that the possible order of magnitudes rather than the exact numbers is important.[87] For convenience, we use the lower boundary of our potential range—say, $65 a barrel or about twice the world market price in 1982—as a reference point in Chapter 9. This is a much lower figure than the $300 a barrel that IEA economists estimate as the cost of oil "saved" through lower economic growth.

It is possible, of course, to construct a much more sophisticated model of the total costs to the nation of incremental oil imports, including an attempt to take into account the lagged responses to high prices. Indeed, since we initially pointed out the potentially high costs of imported oil in the first edition of this book, there has been a proliferation of studies attempting to estimate more closely what the "true" value is. The estimates, of course, vary widely, but one is safe in concluding that investment decisions by individuals and firms, based on today's cost of oil, are dramatically lower than any reasonable estimate of the true cost to the nation as a whole.[88]

One possible solution is to place a tariff of, say, 100 percent on imported oil, thus raising its price to something approaching $65 a barrel. Many economists will recommend a response of this sort when the prices of imports work against achieving some national goal. But it is unrealistic to think that a tariff high enough to reflect the true social cost of imported oil would ever be enacted.[89]

This means that U.S. energy policy should give alternative sources of energy, including conservation, an "equal chance" with the social cost of imported oil. In other words, even with domestic oil prices decontrolled, other energy sources and conservation still deserve U.S. government support.

It also means that the production of domestic oil should be encouraged. New territories for exploration offshore and in Alaska should be opened, under stringent environmental requirements, with mechanisms for the timely resolution of regulatory and environmental issues.[90] Removing the windfall profits tax for new finds of oil and for enhanced recovery oil is desirable as well. Financial payments—perhaps in the form of guaranteed market contracts for the output of the facilities—should be given for new technology, such as coal liquefaction and oil from shale, and greater attempts should be made to reach agreements with environmentalists and farmers.

It may not be politically feasible to add a sufficiently high tariff that would reflect the social costs of imported oil. But, in general, the U.S. should strive to move in a direction in which those social costs would be reflected in the price faced by American oil consumers.[91]

Attention also needs to be given to designing and implementing a system for allocating oil during a supply disruption. The Reagan Administration's desire to use price as an allocator during an emergency may not be politically feasible when the time comes. And a plan designed ahead of the emergency is likely to be better than one designed during the emergency.

We have dwelt on two countries—Saudi Arabia and the United States. Continued reliance on oil means that the future of the world economy will, to a high degree, depend on Saudi Arabia, a nation of perhaps 5 or 6 million people—a highly traditional society, but one going through what may be the most rapid and total social and economic transformation in the history of the world. Dependence here puts the rest of the world in a highly vulnerable position. The very foundation of the international economy will be affected not only by conscious decisions in Riyadh about production levels, but also by other possible contingencies —accidents, a Soviet presence, an unresolved Arab-Israeli conflict, tensions in the Arab/Persian Gulf, shifts in the attitudes of Saudi leaders, or the overthrow of those leaders.

The United States, the world's largest oil importer, is at the center of the world oil problem. It has yet to come to grips with the decline of its influence over the world petroleum market and the true costs of its oil imports. By ignoring the large external costs associated with imported oil, the United States has been encouraging a form of behavior that will drain the world of the commodity. Dependence on imported oil poses a threat to American political and economic interests.

Americans should not delude themselves into thinking that there is some huge hidden reservoir of domestic oil that will free them from the heavy cost of imported oil. Of course, measures should be taken to encourage domestic oil production. But the handwriting is clear. To the extent that any solution at all exists to the problem posed by the peaking of U.S. oil production and the high levels of imports, it will be found in energy sources other than oil.

3 NATURAL GAS: CONFLICTS AND COMPROMISE

I. C. BUPP
FRANK SCHULLER

Natural gas is a premium fuel, the energy prince of hydrocarbons. The 20 trillion cubic feet of the commodity that Americans consumed in 1981 accounted for about one quarter of the country's energy use.* But unlike oil, natural gas has remained for the most part a domestically produced fuel, with only 6 percent imported. Moreover, unlike coal, natural gas burns cleanly, without soot and sulfur emissions; nor does its extraction and transportation cause the environmental damage associated with the black solid. Finally, unlike nuclear power, natural gas poses no waste disposal problem.

Yet, during the 1970's, this energy prince was also one of the fuels for which the words "crisis" and "confusion" seemed particularly appropriate. Twice in the decade—in the winter of 1976–77 and again in the winter of 1977–78—gas supplies were short, resulting in cutoffs that caused the loss of millions of dollars to the economy, much inconvenience, and many hardships for thousands of Americans.

One consequence was a major political battle. As a congressional staff member put it: "When the Carter Administration brought its energy legislation to the Hill, it stumbled into one of the great religious wars in American politics. The war over govern-

---

*Excluding natural gas liquids, which are usually reported with oil production.

ment regulation of natural gas prices goes back a full generation. The Administration's talk about energy waste, its econometric models, and its computer printouts have not been very effective against the deeply entrenched positions of the warring camps."

Following more than a year of deliberation, Congress passed the Natural Gas Policy Act (NGPA) in October 1978, the most comprehensive piece of legislation governing natural gas since 1954 when gas first came under federal price regulation. For a time, NGPA looked like an astonishing success, legislation that almost instantly turned a chronic shortage of natural gas into a surplus—the so-called gas bubble. But by the beginning of the 1980's, it was apparent that this intricate and complex new federal energy law was based on a false assumption. The projection of future oil prices used by NGPA's authors turned out to have been mistaken. Thus, the act represented only a brief pause in a long-fought political war, a temporary armistice and compromise among deeply entrenched and passionate points of view.

Natural gas still poses an overwhelmingly difficult political issue, involving an objective conflict of interest among several groups and several regions, very high financial stakes (perhaps as high as a trillion dollars), and of course correspondingly high passions. "I understand now what hell is," former Energy Secretary James Schlesinger said during the congressional debate over the 1978 bill. "Hell is endless and eternal sessions of the natural gas conference." After the act's passage, one industry executive said that Schlesinger had seen only the beginning.[1]

The basic issue is price. Before the passage of NGPA, the price of approximately two-thirds of the gas produced in the United States was controlled by the federal government. This partial regulation created two very different markets for natural gas: an "interstate" market in which it was regulated; and an "intrastate" market in which it was unregulated.

One objective of the NGPA was to eliminate this dual market. In the process, however, it created yet another dual market —this time between "conventional" gas and so-called unconventional gas from certain types of geologic formations. Under NGPA, the price of the former remains subject to various controls, while that of the latter is unregulated.

As one might expect, controlled prices for natural gas—both before and after passage of NGPA—were considered to be too high by many buyers and too low by many sellers. Indeed, through the smoke of continuing battle over natural gas one sees a single basic issue: Should the price of natural gas be determined by its cost of production and transportation or by its value in the marketplace?

Practically the only thing on which all the warring parties agree is that for the past decade America's proven reserves of gas have been steadily declining. While gas production peaked in 1973 and had fallen approximately 12 percent by 1978, the level of proven reserves peaked in 1967 and by 1981 had fallen some 25 percent, to a volume equal to only ten years at the then-current rate of consumption.

Clearly, new discoveries of natural gas have failed to replace what has been consumed. But the decline of proven gas reserves does not necessarily mean that the United States is running out of gas in any physical sense. Indeed, many, perhaps even most, informed geologists believe that enough gas exists onshore and offshore under the United States' continental shelf to sustain a national consumption rate about equal to the current 20 tcf level for at least twenty-five to thirty years, but at higher prices than Americans are accustomed to paying. Beyond that, there is doubt that even very considerably higher prices would sustain consumption much above the current rate.[2]

The conflict over price is likely to continue. And to make sense of it requires an understanding of how the price of natural gas came to be regulated in the first place.

TOWARD REGULATION

The first gas company in the United States was established in Baltimore, Maryland, in 1816. It sold synthetic gas produced from coal. The organization of similar companies in other cities occurred during the next two decades. The business of all these companies represented the practical application of the discovery by a seventeenth-century Belgian chemist that coal could be burned in a way to yield a flammable gaseous substance. The first large-scale use of manufactured gas in the early nineteenth century in America was for street lighting. Large-scale use of gas for cooking did not take place until late in the nineteenth century.[3]

Toward the end of the last century, high-cost manufactured gas met ever sharper competition from cheap kerosene for household lighting and from electric arc lamps for street lighting. Soon thereafter, central electricity generating stations were developed, and electricity began to compete for the entire lighting market. As the competitive situation stabilized in the early twentieth century, the manufactured gas industry was left with only the market for residential cooking and water heating.

Manufactured gas eventually lost even this limited market to a new competitor: low-cost natural gas, which was found primarily in the South and Southwest, and to a lesser extent in the West and Midwest. For many years natural gas remained an essentially local fuel; the earliest natural gas pipelines, built roughly between 1890 and 1925, were rarely more than 150 miles long. Because they were usually within one state, they could be subjected as public utilities. It was not until after World War II that the technology became available to allow the economical transmission of natural gas by pipeline over long distances. The $50 billion pipeline network that now connects the gas-producing areas of the Southwest, Gulf Coast, and Appalachia to all of the country's metropolitan areas was almost entirely built during the fifteen years after the end of World War II.

While the gas transmission industry was evolving into a nationwide supplier, the markets for its products also were undergoing an evolution. Natural gas came to be widely used for residential and commercial space heating and for a variety of industrial purposes, especially as boiler fuel.

The transcontinental pipelines that carry natural gas from producing areas to urban consumers are, of course, only one part of the natural gas transmission industry. There are also about 1,500 local distribution companies, mostly privately owned, that buy gas from the pipelines and make it available to consumers. To do this, the companies operate a network of smaller pipelines that serve homes and commercial establishments (Figure 3–1). As

FIGURE 3·1
OVERVIEW—U.S. NATURAL GAS SYSTEM, 1975 (NUMBERS IN TCF)

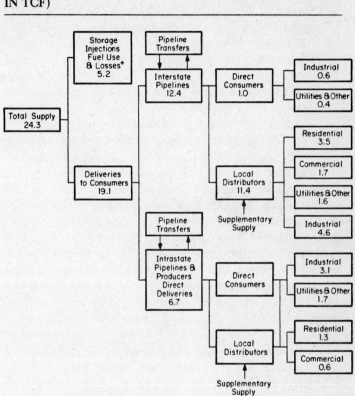

public utilities, the distribution companies come under price regulation as "natural monopolies" from municipal and state agencies.[4]

As soon as pipelines began to cross state borders, regulation by individual states became impossible. Thus, the Natural Gas Act of 1938 created a new government agency, the Federal Power Commission (FPC),* with authority to ensure that the prices charged by the interstate pipeline companies to local gas distributors were "just and reasonable."[5]

But the 1938 Natural Gas Act was ambiguous on a key point: whether the FPC was also to regulate the price of gas in the field that producers charged to the interstate pipelines, the so-called wellhead price. In a historic 1954 decision, *Phillips Petroleum Co. v. Wisconsin,* the Supreme Court ruled that it should, deciding in favor of a suit brought by the attorney general of Wisconsin on behalf of gas consumers in his state. The Wisconsin state attorney general argued that gas consumers needed protection from wellhead price increases that were being "passed through" by the pipeline companies. The court accepted the reasoning that gas producers could exact "excessive" prices at the wellhead, ultimately at the expense of the consumer. But the Supreme Court provided the basis for the current controversy by failing to offer specific criteria for deciding exactly what a "just and reasonable" price should be. The same decision laid the groundwork for a related conflict by creating two distinct markets for the fuel. The FPC interpreted this ruling to apply only to interstate gas, thereby leaving intrastate gas free of wellhead price controls.[6]

Congress immediately set out to overturn the Supreme Court decision. In 1956, both the House and the Senate voted to deregulate the wellhead price of natural gas. Had it not been for a quirk, President Eisenhower, who favored deregulation, would have signed the bill. During the debate on the legislation, Senator Francis Case, who also favored deregulation, indignantly disclosed that a lobbyist favoring the bill's passage had left an envelope containing twenty-five $100 bills to be given to him. Case ordered

---

*The Federal Power Commission (FPC) became the Federal Energy Regulatory Commission (FERC) when the Department of Energy was created.

the money returned and decided to vote against the bill. The lobbyist protested the "inference that it was some kind of a shady deal" and declared that there were "no strings attached." But President Eisenhower, blaming the "arrogant" gas lobby, vetoed the bill, saying that he could not risk creating "doubt among the American people concerning the integrity of governmental processes."[7]

TWO-TIER MARKET: INTERSTATE AND INTRASTATE |

What evolved from the regulation of only part of the natural gas industry were two markets with two different approaches to determining price and, of course, two different prices. The key to understanding the entire U.S. natural gas situation prior to 1978 is to recognize what these differences are. The federal government's regulation of "just and reasonable" prices for the interstate market was cast in terms of the cost of production, or at least on regulators' opinions about the *cost* of production.[8] In contrast, in the intrastate market, supply and demand determined price; thus price was based on *value,* or at least on the buyers' and sellers' opinions about value.

At the time of the *Phillips* v. *Wisconsin* decision in 1954, gas was so abundant and so cheap that producers often flared it as a worthless by-product of their search for oil. In those days, few wells were drilled solely to find gas. The average price of all natural gas sold in the United States in 1953, for example, was nine cents per thousand cubic feet (mcf), or only one-fifth the price of domestic oil with comparable heat content. The regulation of the interstate market initially had little effect on the price of gas, for interstate prices continued to rise moderately after regulation, just as they had before, and the prices in the interstate and intrastate markets remained essentially identical. In fact, gas remained so abundant and cheap that oilmen who found gas instead of oil would curse their luck.

But this situation began to change in the 1960's, when a decline in the gas reserves signaled the end of the era of abundant and cheap gas. In 1967, for example, in the interstate market, the average price of all gas was 17 cents per mcf, whereas the price of newly discovered gas had been allowed to rise to 19 cents, reflecting the FPC's conclusion that the cost of producing gas was rising (Table 3-1). Furthermore, prices in the interstate and intrastate markets had begun to diverge as the price of newly discovered gas sold into the intrastate market had climbed to 22 cents per mcf. The average price of all gas sold into the intrastate market —although not published—began to exceed the average price of interstate gas by a wide margin.[9]

The fact that intrastate prices rose faster than interstate prices suggests that the regulated cost-based price no longer reflected buyers' opinions about the value of gas. And, of course, producers, having a choice between selling gas to one or another of the two markets, preferred to sell where they could get the higher price. The year 1970 marked a turning point in the sales of gas into the two markets. In that year, the new reserves dedicated to the intrastate market jumped from the 1969 level of one third of the total up to two thirds.[10]

True, the FPC permitted the price of newly discovered interstate gas, as well as gas previously committed under long-term contracts, to rise substantially after 1970. In 1976, the price of newly discovered natural gas sold into the interstate market was set at $1.42 per mcf. But the intrastate market had risen even more, to $1.60 per mcf. Accordingly, the intrastate market continued to capture the bulk of the new supplies.[11] During the winter of 1976–77, consumers with gas curtailments along interstate pipelines felt the damaging impact of the two-tiered gas market. The damage would have been much greater if long-term contracts with the pipelines, committing approximately two-thirds of total U.S. gas production to the interstate market, had not been in place.

How does a buyer of natural gas determine its value? In principle, he (or she) does it by assessing the cost of some alternative energy source other than gas. The problem is that when the main alternative to gas is high-priced oil, a *value-based* price for domestic natural gas will be much higher than the *cost-based* price that the government had enforced for interstate gas. In 1977, for

TABLE 3 · 1
PRICES OF U.S. NATURAL GAS, 1966–77
(CENTS PER THOUSAND CUBIC FEET)

	Average Price	Interstate New Contract Price	Intrastate New Contract Price
1966	17¢	17¢	20¢ (est.)
1967	17	19	22 (est.)
1968	17	19	23 (est.)
1969	18	20	26 (est.)
1970	18	n.a.	29 (est.)
1971	19	27	45 (est.)
1972	21	29	63 (est.)
1973	23	37	80 (est.)
1974	27	46	100 (est.)
1975	34	57	140
1976	48	142	160
1977	69	142	190
1978	84	175*	175*

*The base for the natural gas ceiling price that applied for most categories of newly discovered gas. This base price is escalated retroactively from April 20, 1977. The rise is based on an annual inflation adjustment factor plus, for some categories of newly discovered gas, a real growth factor. As of April 1980, for example, the price of natural gas from a new onshore well within 2.5 miles of a "marker well" was $2.48; the price of gas from most other new onshore wells was $2.25. NGPA-78 gives prices in millions of BTUs; we converted this unit to thousands of cubic feet by using 1021 BTU per cubic foot.

Sources: Interstate averages are prices paid to domestic producers by major interstate pipeline companies: 1966–71 from U.S. Senate, Committee on Interior and Insular Affairs. *Natural Gas Policy Issues and Options*, 93 Cong., 1 sess. (Washington, D.C.: Government Printing Office, 1973), p. 220, which also shows that prices paid by interstate pipeline companies are essentially equal to prices paid by major interstate pipeline companies; 1972–76 from Energy Information Administration, Department of Energy, on December 18, 1978; 1977–79 from Energy Information Administration, DOE, *Monthly Energy Review*, December 1979, p. 91. Annual prices represent an arithmetic average of the monthly prices.

Interstate new: 1966–69 from *Natural Gas Policy Issues and Options*, p. 217; 1971–75 from Subcommittee on Energy and Power of the Committee on Interstate and Foreign Commerce, House of Representatives, *Long-Term Natural Gas Legislation*, part I, 94 Cong., 2 sess. (Washington, D.C.: Government Printing Office, January 20–February 2, 1976), p. 470. Prices include area rate ceilings, optional procedures, limited-term contracts, and small producer sales; 1976 and 1977 figures are national ceiling wellhead prices effective on July 27, 1976, for all wells commenced on or after January 1, 1975; Federal Power Commission. *Opinion and Order on Rehearing Modifying in Part Opinion No. 770 and Granting*

Petitions for Intervention, Opinion No. 770A (Washington, D.C.: FPC, November 15, 1976), pp. 12–15. In 1978, prices for newly discovered gas were regulated in interstate and intrastate markets by the Natural Gas Policy Act of 1978.

Intrastate new: 1966–74 from interviews with executives of intrastate pipelines; 1975–77 from arithmetic average of new contracts in Louisiana and Texas, by producers that also sell into the interstate market, rounded to nearest 10 cents; *Monthly Energy Review*, November 1978, p. 78.

example, the average price of all gas sold into the interstate market was 69 cents per mcf, or about one third of the price of oil with comparable heat content; but the price of intrastate gas approximated the price of oil. This meant that a shift to a value-based free-market system—the abandonment of all price regulation—would cause an enormous transfer of real wealth from gas consumers to gas producers.

Who profits from higher prices has been the nub of the dispute over natural gas policy. On one side, for example, the governor of Texas, a gas-producing state, can plausibly assert that "for over twenty-three years, federal regulation of natural gas prices has *undervalued* natural gas in the marketplace, stimulated artificially high demand for natural gas, and provided little incentive for the development and production of additional supplies." On the other side, a public service commissioner from New York, a consuming state, can ask with equal plausibility "whether it is logical as far as the American consumer is concerned to allow the OPEC nations to establish a value of commodity price for our domestic reserves of natural gas."[12]

The controversy goes beyond the basic issue of whether price should be determined by value or by cost. It extends to a question concerning the methods of determining cost.

How much does gas cost to produce? In theory, one can determine a precise production cost for gas. In reality, no one can do much more than guess. Specialists have even disagreed on whether costs of production have really been rising or falling. Jules Joskow of the National Economic Research Association, a respected economic consulting firm, has argued that while drilling costs have been increasing, the unit cost of newly discovered gas has been declining. Professor Henry Steele of the University of Houston, another respected specialist, has maintained the opposite.[13] The prospects for resolving such arguments are very dim, for several difficult issues present themselves.

First, a company that is a going concern will commit a more or less continuous stream of expenditures for exploration and development, much of which it cannot assign to a specific gas reserve. These costs include initial expenditures to determine prospective sites as well as expenditures associated with dry holes.

Second, about one quarter of U.S. gas production comes from wells that also produce oil. In these cases, it is impossible to calculate a meaningful cost of production for gas because of the dominance of joint costs that are related to the production of both oil and gas. Often the two resources are discovered either in the same geological formation or in separate formations penetrated by the same well. Cost analysis for any given producer requires an inherently arbitrary allocation of costs between natural gas and oil. Hence a very wide range of estimates is readily obtainable, depending on the methods and assumptions one chooses to invoke. Different estimates do not necessarily reflect different "real" costs; they reflect instead the differences in the analytic techniques used. As a result, studies placed in evidence before the FPC have shown differences in estimated average unit costs of gas of 500 percent or more for a single company.[14]

Even without the joint costs, attempts to compute cost per unit volume of gas reserves quickly break down. Theoretically, a calculation of discovery costs should be based on the volume of gas discovered by a given expenditure. To do so, two numbers are needed: the total "proven" reserves of gas and the total costs incurred in finding and developing these reserves. But a company encounters a major problem in trying to ascertain the quantity of reserves actually discovered during any given period since reservoir engineers are likely to differ broadly in their initial estimates. Then, during production, unanticipated developments may sharply raise or lower the expected volumes of ultimate recovery as well as sharply raise or lower expected costs.[15]

Of course, after a gas field is depleted and the wells are abandoned, it may be possible, on the basis of some assumptions about the allocation of overhead costs, to reckon the total cost of what was produced. But because few fields are similar enough to support very precise cost comparisons, such information would not be particularly valuable in estimating costs in other fields. In fact, there is no reasonably predictable relationship between money spent on exploration and the amount of gas (and oil) discovered. The disparity reflects differences in producers' business judgment, technical proficiency, and a strong element of luck.

The truth is that calculating the production cost of natural gas, even under the best of circumstances, is highly imprecise and ultimately arbitrary. Most experts would probably agree with Senator Henry Jackson, former chairman of the Senate Energy Committee, who said that it is very difficult to have "a good strong feeling in your stomach that you know exactly what the hell you are doing."[16]

HOW MUCH GAS DO WE HAVE AND AT WHAT PRICE? |

The pricing issue led into the baffling question of supply. During the congressional debate over NGPA, opponents of price regulation maintained that control of wellhead prices had caused the shortages and curtailments of 1976–77. They argued that gas producers would look for new reserves only if the price they were permitted to charge for the gas they found was higher than the costs of finding and producing it. Those who favored price controls did not question this logic. But they did question whether increased reserves would come at too high a price. As one government official put it: "You have to ask yourself, 'What more do you get out of raising the price of natural gas?' . . . Every indication we have is that you get very little."[17]

Experts used two different approaches to answer that supply question. Using historical data, economists typically estimated the supply that would be forthcoming at various price levels. Geologists, on the other hand, typically ignored price. Instead, they related supply to the size of recoverable reserves, based on historic production rates of similar geologic formations. Within both groups of experts, there was deep disagreement.

Some economists contended that supply was not very responsive to price; others stated the opposite. In 1976, for example, the General Accounting Office declared that few additional reserves would likely be discovered at prices above $1.75 per mcf. At the same time that the GAO was painting its pessimistic picture, a task force within the Energy Research and Development Administration estimated that a rise in the price of natural gas from $1.75 to $2.50 per mcf would increase U.S. recoverable reserves by 20 percent.[18]

To add to the confusion, the differences among geologists are at least as large as those among economists. Between 1972 and 1974, the U.S. Geological Survey issued three optimistic reports. At a consumption rate of 20 tcf per year, the different USGS studies projected sufficient gas supply to last anywhere from forty-four to a hundred years. And in 1977, the Central Intelligence Agency estimated that the United States could continue to consume natural gas at a rate of 20 tcf per year for fifty to sixty years.[19] Other equally respectable "stock" estimates contradict all of these relatively optimistic outlooks. For example, in 1974 Shell and Mobil projected total gas reserves sufficient to last only twenty to thirty years at contemporary consumption rates; and in 1976 Exxon estimated an even more meager stock, good for only fifteen to twenty years, although by 1980, Exxon's projections show gas production from domestic sources declining by approximately a third between 1980 and 2000.[20] A range of estimates that varies between fifteen and a hundred years is hardly a sure guide for policy.

THE PARTICIPANTS IN THE NGPA BATTLE I

It is hardly surprising that the battle over NGPA was so bitter and so protracted. Consumers, producers, the people of gas-rich geographic regions and regulatory authorities—all had much to gain or much to lose. No one was neutral.

At the risk of oversimplification, four broadly based factions can be identified: gas producers who wanted deregulation of all wellhead gas prices; interstate pipeline companies whose executives also favored deregulation; the government, whose officials saw huge political obstacles to deregulation; and the majority of the public, which favored price controls.

Each of these groups could point to some evidence that appeared to support its particular combination of beliefs. Each could find "experts" to argue its case in public or before legislative committees, and each, quite naturally, had patrons in either the executive or legislative branches of government, or both. Indeed, much of the debate that the public heard was actually among specialists representing the various factions, drawing upon well-stocked arsenals of competing theories and contradictory data.

Natural gas producers. |

In 1978, there were 6,000 producers, many of whom were selling to the pipelines:[21]

1. Two dozen large companies, mostly integrated petroleum firms, accounting for over one-half of total production.
2. A handful of producing affiliates of certain pipeline companies.
3. Approximately 500 large "independent" producers.
4. Approximately 5,400 small independent producers.

Ben Cubbage, an outspoken member of the Independent Oil Producers Association, summarized the producers' position: "What we are running out of is very cheap natural gas. The vast remaining supplies will not be discovered at current regulated prices. Developing this gas requires immediate deregulation."[22]

Regulated prices, according to producers, often were not high enough to cover either the costs of expanding the potential reserves in existing fields or the cost of finding and developing new reserves.

The intensity of belief among producers was, however, by no means uniform. It varied roughly according to the size of the company. At one end were the small independents, operating in relatively low-quality, small-margin gas fields, and contributing approximately half the U.S. supplies. Jim Daugherty, an independent drilling contractor and gas producer in western Kentucky, captured the independent producers' position: "Hell, yes, there's gas out there, and there's folks right over the state line in Illinois that will pay for it at whatever price it takes to produce it, but that price to produce it ain't the price that those fellas back in Washington say you can sell it for. So we don't plan to drill for gas until it's profitable."[23]

As far as independents were concerned, alternative estimates of price and supply of natural gas were beside the point: The point was that big risks should mean big rewards. So any public policy that tried to moderate such rewards in the interest of other objectives would be unjust. In 1977 and 1978, the independents mounted a well-organized and well-financed lobbying effort to end government price regulation once and for all. Their intransigence helped delay the eventual compromises contained in NGPA.

For the large, fully integrated oil companies at the other end of the producer spectrum, life was not so simple. These companies were struggling to rescue their primary business, oil, from government regulation, and to stave off possible "dismemberment." Taking a low profile on gas, they generally limited themselves to saying that deregulation would benefit the public by stimulating exploration and drilling.

The interstate pipeline companies |

In 1978 the executives of many interstate pipeline companies faced a stark future. Their business seemed mortally threatened because within a few years they would have no gas to transport. One of the few points of general agreement in the NGPA debate was that the two-tier market had greatly reduced the volume of gas transported by the interstate pipelines by effectively excluding them from bidding on gas in the intrastate markets.

Pipeline companies argued that even if higher wellhead prices are necessary to increase gas supplies, the public could still enjoy lower prices because of pipeline economies. If increased gas supplies enabled the interstate pipelines to operate nearer to capacity, their fixed costs would be spread over larger volumes, thereby lowering the cost of transportation. Since the prices that the pipelines charge for transportation, as distinct from the prices they pay at the wellhead, would remain under government control, substantial savings could accrue to consumers who live far from the gas fields.[24]

The government |

During the 1976 campaign, Jimmy Carter pledged to work for deregulation; but once in office, Carter reversed himself and opposed deregulation and value-based pricing, saying that supply, after all, was not very elastic with respect to price. In the summer of 1978, a coalition of very strange bedfellows formed, as both liberal and conservative members of Congress allied to try to defeat a natural gas compromise, but for very different reasons. The legislation seemed to promise prices that would be too high for the liberals' constituencies and too low for the conservatives.' The conservatives also opposed any regulation of intrastate gas.[25]

The public |

If the producers were wrong, if gas supply really were inelastic with respect to price, then the end of wellhead price regulation on newly discovered gas would indeed mean a transfer of wealth from consumers to producers without any compensating economic or social benefit. As Lee White, one of the more eloquent spokesmen for consumer interests, put it, "If there were reason to believe that these excessive drains on the economy and on family income would produce greater volumes of gas than would otherwise be produced, one would be willing at least to consider such an alternative. However, this is not the case. Every econometric model developed to demonstrate this relationship has been picked to pieces by opponents. All we have to go on is the general gut reaction of producers. . . . This is really not good enough."[26]

The public seemed to doubt the reality of gas shortages, to suspect corporate manipulation, and to question the rationale for higher gas prices.[27] The public felt that it was unfair for domestic gas producers to get windfall profits on proven reserves simply because OPEC's price increase for oil had increased the value of gas as well. OPEC's action had abruptly changed the worth of gas, a commodity that was already under great pressure in the energy market. In such circumstances, so dramatic an increase in values would create enormous stakes and correspondingly high passions, and would almost inevitably assure the classic political controversy over who gets what.

Further heightening passions were regional differences. The public in New England and the Middle Atlantic states, areas with essentially no gas production, historically paid a higher price for natural gas than the national average because of greater transportation costs. Furthermore, the 1970's shift of the new gas supplies into the intrastate market raised the fear of chronic shortages in non-producing states.

In contrast, residents of Texas, Louisiana, and other gas-producing states complained that the East Coast residents had blocked offshore drilling, while siphoning off large volumes of gas subsidized at a low price at the expense of the gas producers. Bumper stickers in Texas reflected this sense of frustration: "Turn off the gas and freeze a Yankee."

NGPA AND ITS AFTERMATH |

The major provisions of NGPA are easy to summarize. The basic idea was to permit a carefully managed deregulation of the price of newly discovered natural gas. After a decade of small annual escalations, according to a complicated-looking but actually very simple formula, the price of newly discovered gas will be decontrolled at the wellhead. Meanwhile, the wellhead price of newly discovered gas that is consumed in the producing state is temporarily brought under the control umbrella of interstate gas.

It is easy to see who would lose by the move: first, the producers who were selling gas to the intrastate market. If the newly controlled wellhead price of intrastate gas were less than what the free market price would have been, such producers would stand to lose billions of dollars. Second, the consumers would lose, at least in the short run. "New" gas sold across state boundaries started at $1.75 per mcf and climbed with inflation and an allowed real growth rate. "Old" interstate gas prices would be initially unchanged but as contracts for "old" interstate gas expired the compromise legislation would allow prices to rise to $.54 per mcf, if the original contract price were less. If the original were higher than $.54 per mcf, the government would determine a "fair and reasonable" price.

Since the legislation meant increases in real costs to consumers, it understandably aroused a good deal of public dismay. But the appeal of the compromise was that it offered some real benefits to many producers and distributors as well as consumers. Producers received a higher price for interstate gas than had been legal. The uncontrolled price of unconventional sources of gas allowed producers to explore the high-cost and highly uncertain deep gas as a way of estimating the potential for finding new reserves. Also, the interstate pipeline companies could effectively compete with the intrastate companies for newly discovered gas. And all consumers in non-producing states would have considerably greater assurance of stable gas supplies than in the previous two-tiered market. Finally Washington would gain flexibility to respond to unforeseen events on a truly national basis in the coming years.[28]

Something very important, however, was not changed by the compromise legislation. The residential consumer would still have first claim on the nation's gas supplies, however scarce or abundant they might prove to be. Since the *Phillips* case in 1954, the federal government has assigned priorities among users. The priorities are, beginning with the most important: (1) residential users, (2) industries using gas for feedstocks, (3) industries with gas boilers, and (4) electrical utilities.

But enactment of the legislation quickly provoked controversy and added to the confusion. First, the creation of the gas bubble prompted the DOE to reverse its policy toward natural gas. Former Energy Secretary Schlesinger encouraged industrial users and utilities that had converted from gas to oil to go back to gas. This contrasted sharply with the earlier Administration policy favoring a shift away from natural gas. Second, a vast amount of litigation cropped up as all the players—the Federal Energy Regulation Commission (FERC), gas producers, pipeline companies, the states, and consumer groups—struggled over the interpretation of the NGPA-78.

Producers said that the various price categories of gas were difficult to determine and frustratingly complex to report to the FERC. And they insisted that the confusion and bureaucracy would hamper rapid expansion of production. Interstate pipeline companies complained that they were required to use "incremental pricing" for industrial customers. This meant that industrial users would pay higher wellhead prices than residential customers, who would pay "rolled-in" prices—that is, prices that were a mix of the lower-priced "old" gas and the higher-priced "new" gas. And according to the pipeline companies, the net result would be that high incremental prices would keep industrial users from switching from oil to gas, thereby increasing oil imports. The interstate pipeline companies also were embroiled along with some consuming states in the litigation against producing states, intrastate pipeline companies, and users of intrastate gas.

On the other side, a leading consumerist spokesperson, Ellen Berman of the Consumer Energy Council of America, described the legislation as "extraordinarily complex, impossible to monitor and implement—a total fiasco."[29]

Even a number of persons in the federal government suspected a short-lived truce. In March 1979, several congressmen introduced a bill to extend price controls. Other congressmen proposed legislation to repeal incremental pricing.[30]

But by 1983 many of the early criticisms of NGPA seemed to have been answered. Gas producers and transmission companies had learned how to live with the legislation's complex record-keeping and reporting requirements. The FERC had amended certain pricing rules that producers and pipeline companies had claimed to be obstacles to reserve development.

But many more subtle and more long-term problems with natural gas remained or even became exacerbated by the consequences of NGPA. At the heart of all of them is the continuing price disparity between regulated and unregulated gas. A new "dual market" had emerged. The disparity opened up by NGPA principally had to do with the depth at which gas is found above 15,000 feet. Its price was to remain regulated until January 1, 1985. The price of "unconventional" gas sources—which include gas discovered below 15,000 feet and gas from shale, tight sands, and certain other geologic formations above 15,000 feet—is unregulated.

Gas producers correctly anticipated that unregulated gas would sell at a higher price than regulated gas, which sells at a price significantly below parity with oil on a BTU-equivalent basis. Hence, many producers began drilling wells deeper than 15,000 feet and found substantial reserves. From 1978 through 1980, 695 deep gas wells were drilled. Unlike conventional onshore gas wells, where reserves usually range between .5–6 bcf, these deep wells are estimated to add an average of 7 bcf or more in reserves per well. Gas transmission companies were eager to acquire these reserves, even at prices higher than oil on a BTU-equivalent basis. In early 1981, twenty of the largest interstate pipeline companies reported that although unregulated gas accounted for about 6 percent of their average volume, the price they were paying for it represented about 18 percent of their average wellhead cost of $2.10 per mcf.[31]

In 1982, unregulated gas was selling at prices up to $10 per mcf. This was more than three times the average price of regulated gas and almost double the average price of its strongest competitor, residual fuel oil. Regulated gas, meanwhile, was selling for less than residual fuel oil. Table 3–2 illustrates differences in prices between regulated gas at its highest price and unregulated gas.

These differences produced some novel and sharp disagreements among gas producers about the desirability of further price decontrol. Producers of unregulated gas oppose it on the fear that decontrol will cause the price of their product to decline. Producers of regulated gas naturally support decontrol for the opposite reason.

NGPA has also brought mixed blessings to pipeline companies. While the higher prices permitted by the legislation produced a greater volume of reserve additions than in the years from 1971 to 1978, the higher prices have also created a gas surplus that poses problems for the pipelines and creates confusion for consum-

TABLE 3·2
PRICES OF U.S. NATURAL GAS, 1978–1980
(CENTS PER THOUSAND CUBIC FEET)

	Average Price Paid by Pipelines	Average Price for Highest Priced Category of Regulated*	Average Price for All Deregulated gas**
1978	94	150	150
1979	121	206	229
1980	155	233	414
1981***	174	242	562
1982***	191	253	596

*This is category 102 gas, which is from newly discovered onshore reserves. Gas from tight sands is a regulated source of gas, which is allowed a higher price than category 102 gas. However, gas from tight sands represents less than 1 percent of all gas sold.

**Unregulated gas consists of gas from below 15,000 feet, coal seams, and Devonian shale. Approximately 73 percent of the deregulated gas comes from wells below 15,000 feet. In 1981, gas from deep wells was selling for as much as $10.00/mcf.

***Estimates.

Source: Department of Energy, Energy Information Administration, The Current State of Natural Gas (Washington, D.C.: Government Printing Office, December 1981), pp. 43, 51.

ers. Much of this gas bubble is caused not by new reserves but by increased "deliverability" (the rate at which a gas well can produce gas on a daily basis).

This increased deliverability has resulted from new technologies and production techniques that make it possible to drain gas reserves at a rate faster than in the past. The president of one pipeline explained that in 1978, his company, which had 6.5 tcf of gas reserves, could produce only 1.5 bcf of gas a day, whereas, in 1981, the company's reserves still remained at 6.5 tcf through reserve additions but its production rate had doubled to 3 bcf per day.[32]

Although there is no technical reason why gas wells must produce as much gas as possible, in many cases managers of transmission companies have contractually obligated their firms to purchase all the gas that can be produced. After the higher prices permited by NGPA-78 began to induce more exploration, managers of reserve-short pipeline companies, eager to secure more supplies, began committing themselves to producers with "take or pay" contracts for as much as 90–100 percent of a well's maximum daily production. Thus, as deliverability increased, pipelines found themselves with more gas to sell on a daily basis without a corresponding increase in reserves. Consequently, a surplus developed in which pipelines either had to sell gas or pay producers for undelivered gas.[33]

In 1982 Transco Energy Company was the first pipeline to reduce the price of deregulated gas under contract to $5.00 per mcf under a clause of NGPA that allows pipelines to amend prices if the contract price at the wellhead is higher than the price at the market. Transco decided to do this after paying producers some $65 million under its "take or pay" contract for gas for which it had no market.[34]

Other clauses in gas contracts with producers may continue to haunt pipeline companies after decontrol occurs. During the late 1970's when pipelines were eager to secure gas reserves under liberal terms, their managers granted contracts with variations of "favored nation" clauses. Such clauses stated that if decontrol occurred, pipelines would pay producers of regulated gas either the highest price paid for any gas entering the system or some percentage, such as 110 percent of the price of world oil. If decontrol were to occur, pipelines could be faced with paying wellhead prices for gas that are higher than that of oil at world prices. With wellhead prices higher than that of oil on an equivalent btu basis even before adding on the cost of delivery, managers of transmission companies recognized that they could not compete with fuel oil, particularly for industrial users. Before pipelines will fully endorse decontrol, many will have to find mechanisms by which they can amend their long-term contracts with producers.

Decontrol has different implications for pipeline companies than for gas producers. Producers of regulated gas see decontrol as simply selling gas to the pipeline at higher prices. Pipelines, in turn, see decontrol as only partial deregulation. They see themselves as possibly having to buy gas at higher prices while selling it at existing prices, and thus facing losses for long periods of time. The inability of pipeline companies to raise prices to their customers, whether distribution companies or industrial users, arises from lags in the regulatory process. Interstate pipelines are regulated by the FERC, which sets the rates at which they can sell gas. Obtaining permission for a rate increase takes approximately six months. Thus, these companies face significant periods during which they may incur losses because of an inability to obtain timely rate increases. To a lesser degree, intrastate pipelines face delays from state regulating commissions.[35]

A clear national consensus about natural gas policy has yet to emerge. This uncertainty is epitomized in the waverings of President Reagan on the issue of decontrol. During his election campaign, he proclaimed his endorsement of the decontrol of all natural gas prices. Although he did fully decontrol domestic oil prices once in office, he has not so acted on natural gas. While he continues to advocate deregulation in principle, he has thrashed about for a politically acceptable compromise. The major problem has been the total opposition from gas consumers to further price increases. The political pressures have caused many Republican Senators and members of Congress to take a stand against any new legislation that could cause natural gas prices to increase.

Broad and deep public opposition to gas price increases is readily apparent. So is considerable, and understandable, confusion about what the future is likely to bring. Newspaper and radio advertisements illustrate the conflicting messages that the public receives about natural gas. For example, gas distribution companies in New England attempted to assure the public of the long-term availability of gas in order to encourage consumers to convert from heating their homes with oil to heating with gas. In contrast, fuel oil distributors countered with advertising warning the public to remember the 1976–77 curtailments and the threat that loomed in January 1981 that Boston might run out of gas.

In addition to concern over future gas supplies, the public wonders about future prices. Between the enactment of NGPA-78 and mid-1982, the forty-two million households that use gas saw prices rise from $2.63/mcf to $5.68/mcf. Some observers foresee a sharp jump in natural gas prices when decontrol begins to occur in 1985, since the price of oil has more than doubled over the $15 a barrel that congressmen expected when they passed NGPA-78. The prospect of such a surge in gas prices following decontrol is termed a price "fly-up."

No one can foretell with certainty whether gas prices will indeed "fly up" on decontrol and, if so, by how much. The FERC estimates that average wellhead prices will increase from approximately $2.30 per mcf in 1982 to an average of between $4 and $5 per mcf with decontrol. If wellhead prices had averaged $4/mcf in 1982, then average residential consumer prices would have been about $7/mcf.[36]

Some critics of NGPA have questioned the law's effectiveness in shielding consumers from higher prices. Much of the gas discovered before 1977 is still regulated at prices substantially below the energy-equivalent price for oil. Superficially, one might think that consumers would benefit from the low price of "old" gas. But benefits to consumers are not automatic. Because pipelines can average the price of "old" gas with the price of "new" gas, critics argue that pipeline companies enjoy a "cushion" of "old" low-priced gas that will allow them to pay such a high price for deregulated gas after January 1, 1985, and that the average cost of gas to consumer will fly up. In 1982, the size of the gas cushion created by NGPA pricing rules and the magnitude of the potential fly-up of prices after January 1, 1985, were topics on which the number of different opinions was approximately equal to the number of experts.

Meanwhile, the volume of proved reserves of natural gas has continued to fall in spite of partial decontrol, significantly increased average prices, and the appearance of a temporary bubble following passage of NGPA.

Several factors caused the 1979 bubble. During the winters of 1976–77 and 1977–79, a number of low-priority users were obliged to switch to oil or coal. Many did not switch back. Other industrial users concerned about the continued availability of gas switched out of gas. And users in general began to conserve because of higher prices. The result was that residential and commercial consumption of natural gas grew slightly from 1973 to 1977; meanwhile, industrial consumption plummeted by almost one-third, and electric utility consumption fell by 11 percent. With the passage of the Natural Gas Policy Act some of the natural gas supplies from marginal fields and shut-in gas wells previously held from the intrastate market were offered to the interstate market in response to anticipated price increases in that market. The convergence of decreased supply created the gas bubble.

Most experts expect the bubble, which contains about 3 tcf of gas, to collapse in the mid-1980's. Nor does anyone doubt that it was partly caused by the enhanced incentives for exploration and drilling of the NGPA. Annual drilling footage has increased by almost 20 percent since 1978 and has led to new proven reserves of approximately 15 tcf in 1980 as opposed to 10 tcf in 1977. But a substantial fraction of recent reserve additions have come from wells that developed or extended known fields.

The FERC estimates that 60 to 70 percent of the approximately 65,200 gas wells drilled in 1978–80 were only developments or extensions of reservoirs known before passage of NGPA. By 1982, most industry observers agreed that such fields were near full development. This raises serious questions about long-run supplies of gas from imports, from unconventional sources, and from new conversion or transportation technologies.[37]

True, the United States can supplement its supply by importing natural gas from Canada and Mexico via pipelines. Indeed, since the early 1970's, imports from Canada have been providing about one tcf annually, or some 5 percent of the total natural gas used in the United States. We expect Canadian imports to remain at about that level for an indefinite period, with the price based on world energy values.

As yet, the United States has imported only meager volumes of Mexican gas. Negotiations for much greater volumes of gas broke down in 1978 over price. Although the Mexicans then announced plans to use all their gas internally, many observers expect the United States eventually to import up to one tcf yearly. In the face of recent enthusiasm about Mexican hydrocarbons, it is worth noting that, at most, this would only be 5 percent of total natural gas consumption in the United States.

Whatever volumes of gas the United States imports from Canada and Mexico, the price almost certainly will be linked to the world price of crude oil. After negotiations with Mexico in September 1979, the United States announced an agreement to pay $3.625 per thousand cubic feet for imports of 300 million cubic feet per day, with quarterly adjustments by the same percentage as changes in world crude oil price. At that time within the United States, interstate pipelines were paying domestic producers an average of $1.305 per thousand cubic feet. Just six months later, the Administration announced an "interim" agreement with Mexico, which raised prices 23 percent, to $4.47 per thousand cubic feet. This gave Mexico the same price that was being received by the Canadians, who had been steadily pushing up the price of their natural gas sold to the United States. One executive of a major interstate pipeline referred to the regular negotiations between the United States and Canada over the price of gas as a monologue, with Canada as the master of ceremonies.[38]

Almost all of the gas that has been produced and consumed until now comes from highly porous sedimentary rock, such as sandstone, at depths less than 15,000 feet. But gas is known to occur in other more "unconventional" geologic formations. This makes the question of gas supplies even more bewildering.

Below 15,000 feet, gas is found in two kinds of formation. One is porous sandstone. But the deeper one drills a well, the more it costs per foot. Hence, attempts to develop deep gas wells are very costly. For example, one company told us of spending $5 million to drill and complete a gas well deeper than 15,000 feet, compared with slightly more than $330,000 for a well 3,000 feet deep. Uncertainty is also greater and less is known about the geology of the deep reservoirs because there has been less drilling at these depths. True, some highly productive wells have been drilled in the deep Tuscaloosa trend in Louisiana and Mississippi. The relative success of these deep wells spurred drilling to increase from 414 wells in 1977 to 695 wells in 1980 with expenditures doubling from $1 billion to more than $2 billion in these years. Although these results are promising, it will take some years before the potential is defined. In early 1981, only about 0.4 tcf of the 20 tcf consumed originated from wells deeper than 15,000 feet.[39]

A second unconventional source typically found below 15,000 feet, geopressured brine, faces an additional cost problem because of the need to handle very large volumes of water.

Another unconventional source of gas is in sedimentary rock with low porosity, such as Devonian shale and coal. Because of the low porosity, the rock must be fractured to allow the gas to migrate to the well. Sometimes the fracturing does not work, but even if it does, the output per well is very low relative to that typically found in conventional wells. Although limited experience does not allow projections to be made with confidence, experienced observers believe that gas from these two sources is unlikely to make an important contribution to U.S. energy supply any time in the foreseeable future.

Recent studies have estimated gas volumes from unconventional sources as high as 200 tcf—roughly equivalent to proven reserves from conventional sources. Yet, while unconventional gas sources may represent substantial volumes, numerous impediments hamper their development. Higher prices could help offset some of the uncertainty or possible low productivity of wells. Still, rapid development of unconventional gas sources faces other market obstacles.

First, many unconventional gas sources often are discovered in remote areas far from an existing system of pipelines. Since most pipeline companies first apply for various federal approvals to build the line and then include the costs of the pipeline in the rate base, many executives of such companies are reluctant to proceed in the face of uncertain sources or low volumes when they are presented opportunities for more certain and more prolific conventional sources nearer their main transmission lines. As long as pipelines can secure lower-priced conventional gas, their managers cannot justify paying higher prices and investing in a gathering system for unconventional gas sources for markets, where it competes in price with alternative fuels, especially among industrial users charged incremental prices.

Second, without ready markets, producers refrain from exploring for unconventional gas sources. Higher prices are meaningless without a market. The National Gas Policy Act has deregulated the price of several unconventional sources, and one executive of a major gas-producing company reported a recent contract of nearly $10/mcf for gas from a well deeper than 15,000 feet. Although several companies are drilling in the deep Tuscaloosa trend and other deep gas zones, other unconventional sources from Devonian shale, coal seams, and geopressured brine remain relatively undeveloped in spite of the decontrolled price. In August 1980, the FERC announced an incentive price of 200 percent of the price of new onshore gas to encourage the development of tight sands that have remained untapped even with the increased prices of the 1978 compromise.[40]

In conclusion, there are encouraging signs that considerable quantities of unconventional gas may be found. But it will be years before production of such gas makes a significant contribution to the nation's gas energy supply, and even more years before one can conclude that enough unconventional gas will be available to offset depleting conventional reserves. In early 1981, gas from all unconventional sources comprised only 6 percent of the 10 tcf acquired by the nation's twenty largest interstate pipeline companies. Of this volume of unconventional gas, only about 2 percent or .2 tcf flowed from unconventional sources other than "deep" gas.[41]

Technology heretofore not widely used promises two additional sources of gas. One is synthetic gas (SNG), manufactured from coal. This process was developed in Germany during World War II. In the 1960's, the United States borrowed and improved on the thirty-year-old German technology to produce SNG in several pilot plants established to prove commercial feasibility. But the pilot plants showed the process to be uneconomical at then-current natural gas prices. Later, as gas prices rose and supplies became tighter, several oil companies and gas pipeline firms announced that they would construct commercial SNG plants, mostly in the West, where huge strip mines provided inexpensive coal. As yet, none has been built, and many companies have abandoned their plans in the face of inflation, uncertain operating and construction costs, and environmental concerns. In short, SNG is a long-range possibility at best.[42]

The bright orange flares in overseas oil fields where gas is being burned off as waste have caught the eyes of natural gas companies and policymakers. If this gas could be shipped to the United States, the imports could supplement domestic supplies. Since construction of an undersea pipeline from the Middle East, North Africa, or Indonesia to the United States is an obvious economical and technical impossibility, U.S. firms have turned to the proven technology of liquefying the gas at very low temperatures and pumping it aboard specially designed tankers for delivery to the United States. Here the liquid is regasified and fed into pipelines. As proven reserves of domestic gas declined in the 1970's, imported liquified natural gas (LNG) became the promised salvation for many companies. As Harvey Proctor, executive vice-president of Pacific Lighting Companies, explained in 1977, "The Pacific Lighting Companies, as distributors of gas to southern California, are having to cut back on gas service to low-priority, large-volume customers. These cutbacks will deepen progressively as our supplies decline, until by the early 1980's we will be forced to curtail service to the smaller industries and businesses which have no alternative fuel capabilities. . . . Our two LNG projects, one involving gas from Indonesia, the other from the Cook Inlet in south Alaska, are the only feasible projects which could supply gas to southern California within the critical time period needed to head off the prospect of curtailment of gas service to high-priority industrial customers and the resulting mass unemployment. . . . The impact of delays on these LNG projects is almost too great to be calculated."[43]

The Distrigas Company of Boston became the first importer of LNG, importing LNG from Algeria into Boston in 1974. By 1977 its imports had built up to an annual rate of about .04 tcf, less than one quarter of one percent of total American gas consumption, but locally important. In the spring of 1978 two other much larger LNG projects began operating. The El Paso Natural Gas Company began to import Algerian LNG to two terminals on the East Coast, one in the Chesapeake Bay, the other near Savannah, Georgia, at an annual combined rate of about one-third tcf per year.

An additional ten projects for large-quantity LNG importation were being planned in 1978. But in December, the administrator of the Energy Regulatory Agency of the Department of Energy denied applications by Tenneco and El Paso Natural Gas for two large LNG import projects from Algeria. These decisions signaled the Carter Administration's deep reluctance to see LNG imports increase beyond their current modest levels for long-haul shipments. DOE, however, sets a higher priority for LNG projects nearer the United States, such as the proposed project in Trinidad.

Even if federal government policy should change, new LNG projects face at least three additional obstacles.

The first is a dispute over safety. Some scientific experts have claimed that the handling and transportation of LNG poses great hazards to the public. Accidents to LNG tankers entering port or while unloading, accidents at LNG storage facilities, and motor vehicle accidents involving trucks that transport LNG—all threaten the public with the risk of potentially catastrophic explosions and fires. Equally reputable scientists support the gas industry's view that such risks are under control. They cite the special design features and operating requirements of LNG ships and storage facilities as protection against catastrophe, and argue that highway transport of LNG is no more hazardous than the transportation of gasoline.

As with the nuclear safety controversy, there seem to be serious gaps in government-sponsored research and development programs to answer the issues that are in dispute. There is, for example, no good experimental basis for predicting the consequences of a collision between an LNG ship and another vessel. Gaps in scientific knowledge such as these create so much uncertainty that a wide range of risk assessments is possible.

Cost is a second obstacle to the wide-scale use of LNG. To build facilities for a typical project requires over $2 billion, most of which is needed for the liquefaction plant and the specialized ocean-going ships. If absolutely nothing were paid to the exporting country for the value of the gas, a price of at least $2.50 per mcf would be required to cover operating expenses and amortization of this capital investment. Because of such high handling and delivery costs, the Algerian government, in its initial contracts with U.S. firms, accepted prices for the value of the gas (exclusive of handling and delivery) that were equivalent to only a small fraction of the OPEC price for oil.

But virtually all gas specialists expect that gap to narrow in the future, a view reinforced by indications that OPEC members are considering ways to control the world market prices for LNG. Indeed, in spring 1980, Algeria demanded a wellhead price for gas from El Paso comparable with the world price of oil. Negotiations in which the federal government intervened on behalf of importing companies went unresolved with the U.S. refusing to pay the higher price, Algeria shutting the valve on exports, and El Paso scrapping its billion-dollar LNG project.

A third obstacle is that importation of LNG puts the United States in virtually the same position of foreign dependence that characterizes the importation of oil. The difference is that radical Algeria rather than conservative Saudi Arabia would dominate the market. No doubt, in the stalemate with Algeria in 1980, policymakers recognized that price concessions for LGN importers would prompt Canada and Mexico to seek equivalent or better terms for exports from across the U.S. borders through existing pipelines.[44]

In general, the Natural Gas Policy Act and any subsequent legislation could have three possible outcomes on the vexing question of future gas supplies in the long run. First, higher prices might stimulate exploration to such an extent that the discovery of new reservoirs would support consumption in excess of the current 20 tcf per year, say, 25 tcf per year or more. In that case, new electric generating plants might even be permitted to use natural gas. This seems, on the available evidence, to be the least likely outcome, but it is possible.

Second, and only slightly more likely, is that higher prices could fail to stimulate more than the current 10 tcf of new discoveries per year.

The third and most likely outcome is that annual discoveries will range between 10 tcf and 25 tcf per year. Within that range, a figure closer to 10 tcf means further restrictions on the industrial use of gas as boiler fuel and as feedstock, plus stern enforcement of mandates to convert existing gas-fired industrial and electric utility boilers to coal. A figure closer to the upper end of the range means little change in present use patterns.

It is tempting to say that the most likely outcome is in the middle. But, of course, no one really can say for sure. The essential point is that the nation should not plan on greater quantities of natural gas. Indeed, it will be a challenge to find enough new gas reserves to maintain production at current levels.

4 COAL: CONSTRAINED ABUNDANCE

MEL HORWITCH*

During the 1970's coal was rediscovered, and coal's resurgence continued throughout the decade. America's most abundant fossil fuel had powered the country's shift from an agrarian to an industrialized society in the late nineteenth and early twentieth centuries. But with the appearance of cheap and convenient oil and natural gas shortly after World War II, coal experienced a dramatic decline in key markets, and soon the local coal delivery truck, the coal-fired boiler used in the factory, and the steam locomotive practically vanished from the American landscape. When President Truman battled United Mine Workers' president John L. Lewis in 1946 during a debilitating coal strike, coal supplied about half of America's total energy needs. When the White House threatened to use the Taft-Hartley injunction in 1978 during a much longer coal strike, coal accounted for less than 20 percent of total U.S. energy consumption.

The Arab oil embargo of 1973 and the shocking realization of America's growing dependence on foreign oil triggered the public's rediscovery of coal, and for a few years coal acquired unaccustomed glamour. Suddenly the United States began to be called "the Persian Gulf of coal," and the resource itself was

---

*with the assistance of Frank Schuller

termed the "great black hope." The coal industry was characterized as "a somewhat frumpy middle-aged ballerina rushed out of
semiretirement to fill an unanticipated gap in a show that must
go on. Suddenly the old girl is back in demand." And so a "new
age of coal" was proclaimed. During the 1970's, the airline flights
that linked the coal areas of Appalachia and the Midwest with the
financial centers of the East Coast were soon booked with bull-
market deal makers eagerly attempting to acquire coal mines or
reserves. At the very least, coal was thought to be the "transition"
fuel until effectively inexhaustible energy sources, such as fusion
or solar power, became available.[1]

President Carter also made coal's rebirth official in April 1977
when he unveiled his National Energy Plan, which gave coal a key
role. Carter specifically mentioned the seemingly huge disparity
between America's coal resources and coal's current use. Although
coal comprised about 90 percent of total U.S. energy reserves, he
said, it provided only 18 percent of total energy production. Accordingly, the President called for over an 80-percent increase in
coal production by 1985—from about 680 million tons in 1976 to
over 1.2 billion tons.* He further proposed an expanded program
of research and development in such areas as mining, burning,
liquefying, and gasifying coal, and also pushed for the conversion
from scarcer fuels to coal "whenever possible."[2]

Indeed, the United States is a Persian Gulf of coal; according
to one estimate, it possesses about 27 percent of the earth's coal
reserves. But projections of U.S. coal reserves vary widely. The
U.S. Geological Survey estimated total identified U.S. coal resources at about 1.7 trillion tons, and postulated hypothetical U.S.
coal resources in unmapped or unexplored areas at another 1.8
trillion tons. Projections of recoverable reserves range considerably
—from about 150 billion tons to 475 billion tons. But it is safe to
assume that the United States has enough coal—if one looks only
at the physical resource itself—at any reasonably expected level of
production for at least the next hundred years.[3]

---

*This is the energy equivalent of an increase from about 7.9 million barrels of oil
per day to about 14.5 million barrels per day, according to the 1977 National
Energy Plan.

In 1980, after the shock produced by the turmoil in Iran, a new surge of interest developed for coal as well as for liquid and gaseous synthetic fuels derived from coal. In March 1980 the President's Commission on Coal, established as a result of the 1977–78 strike in the industry, made a series of recommendations to encourage conversion to coal-fired boilers by electric utilities and industry in general. The commission claimed that its recommendations, if implemented, would replace the equivalent of more than 2 million barrels per day of imported oil with "readily available" coal by 1990. At about the same time, the government similarly launched a massive $12-billion plan to accelerate the conversion of utilities to coal, with funding to come from the windfall tax on oil.

U.S. coal exports also took off, increasing from about 66 million tons in 1979 to about 93 million tons in 1980 with steam coal's share rising from about 22 percent to 28 percent of the total. Signalling this development, in mid-1980, the World Coal Study —an international study project with over 80 participants from 16 coal-producing and coal-consuming countries—described coal as a "bridge to the future." It predicted that world coal production would need to rise 2.5 to 3 times between 1977 and 2000 to meet world energy requirements. Attention and activity shifted toward the growing international trade in steam coal. The group also forecasted as much as a 15-fold increase in the world steam coal trade between 1977 and 2000. As if to make such optimistic assessments official, the leaders of seven industrialized nations, including the United States, at an economic summit meeting in Venice in June, 1980 declared, "Together we intend to double coal production and use by 1990."

But in the years since, the bullish rhetoric and expectations have run into a rather more bearish reality. Part of this change resulted from sluggish economic growth; part from surprisingly effective energy conservation. In addition, the Reagan's Administration's radical shift in energy policy reduced near-term hopes for coal, and expectations for the growth of coal production have diminished. The so-called transition to coal is proving a difficult and over-inflated concept. Given the policies of the Reagan Administration, coal's future, more than ever before, will depend on coal's intrinsic market attractiveness and its basic attributes. True, the United States has an abundance of coal, but coal in turn has an abundance of problems. Its greatest positive attribute, as the General Accounting Office observed, may be simply that "there is a lot of it."[4]

This is not to say that the coal industry will not experience future growth in the short term. Moreover, the longer-term prospects for coal—fifteen to twenty years—are brighter, with coal's share of its current markets increasing. Even now, coal companies are having some success in managing a difficult operating situation. New participants with strong managerial, technological, and financial resources are entering the industry, and new technologies, particularly in the area of coal utilization, may ultimately provide more convenient and less environmentally hazardous ways to take advantage of coal's plentitude. Moreover, the continuing growth of the international steam-coal trade is one of the most significant new developments in the energy field.

THE SHORT TERM |

A ubiquitous and diverse set of obstacles still stands in the way of accelerated coal development. These constraints are not all of equal importance, but all have a common major characteristic: Each will require considerable time to be overcome, if it can be satisfactorily resolved at all. These obstacles are partially systemic, partially environmental, and partially cultural and sociological. Although they are interrelated, for purposes of clear discussion each barrier will be examined separately.

The System |

The coal industry can be conceived as a system that produces, transports, and consumes coal. Consumption is the place to begin, because it triggers activity in the rest of the system and because consumption constitutes the major short-term bottleneck in the system.

Although coal production climbed during both world wars, it

suffered serious declines during the postwar periods. Coal could not compete with petroleum and natural gas in key sectors, and after the Second World War, it totally lost its hold on the transportation, residential, and commercial markets, and, to a somewhat lesser extent, on the industrial market. On the other hand, electric utility consumption grew substantially, particularly after 1960, and caused coal demand to achieve record levels in the 1970's.

But even within the electric utility industry, coal's share of the total electric generation market declined between 1955 and 1972. Import controls for oil, which were initially established in 1957, were subsequently relaxed for heavy fuel oil used by boilers, and were finally abandoned completely in early 1973. Stricter clean-air standards were passed in the sixties, which also had the effect of favoring oil over coal. Therefore, oil—not coal—was the attractive fuel for utilities in most areas in the late sixties. In addition, by the end of the sixties coal confronted still another challenge to its utility market: large nuclear power plants. In short, by the early seventies coal's last bastion—its relative position in the utility industry—was threatened by oil and gas, increasing environmental regulation, and nuclear power.

But the prospects for greater consumption of coal appeared to brighten considerably after 1973. Although not directly caused by the oil embargo, coal prices rose after 1973. But the subsequent oil price rise increased coal's relative cost advantage. Moreover, there was a growing realization of significant delays in bringing nuclear power plants on line.

Federal policy after 1973 also enhanced coal's position in the utility sector, beginning with the Energy Supply and Environmental Coordination Act in 1974. ESECA authorized the Federal Energy Administration to order power plants and other "major fuel-burning installations" to substitute coal for oil or gas as their boiler fuel, a policy termed "coal conversion." But this initial attempt to substitute coal for petroleum was not particularly effective, primarily because of environmental regulations. By mid-1977, of the seventy-four conversion orders issued by the FEA, only fifteen had received approval from the Environmental Protection Agency.[5]

On the other hand, the deregulation of natural gas prices and the decontrol of oil are effectively discouraging the installation of oil and gas boilers for new generating plants. This policy, along with management considerations of fuel price and security of supply, has increased the market for coal.[6]

The competition from nuclear power has weakened, the cost of oil and gas has increased, and government policy has encouraged conversion to coal. Nevertheless, the utilities' overall ability to change their fuel mix in the short term is limited, and they are also postponing certain coal-fired facilities. Coal's share of the total mix of fuels used to generate electricity will increase gradually. The National Electric Reliability Council, which compiles utility data and forecasts, estimated in 1980 that coal's share of the total fuel used by utilities as measured in kilowatt hours would only increase by about 2.5 percent between 1980 and 1989—from 50 percent in 1980 to about 52.5 percent in 1989.

The utilities' cautious behavior results from the radically different environment that the electric utilities faced after 1973. Rarely does such a stable and prosperous industry confront the kind of upheaval and uncertainty that the electric utilities have experienced since 1973. Until then, the historic annual growth rate for the industry hovered between 7 and 7.5 percent. The growth rate has since plummeted, and the electric utility industry has grown at far below recent historic rates. Recent projections of annual growth rates range between approximately 1 and 3.5 percent for the next decade, and some respected analysts think it could be even lower.

The general causes for the decline in the growth rate seem clear. One reason is the overall slowdown in the U.S. economy, which, of course, affected the industrial sector, which consumed about 37 percent of the output of electric utilities in 1980. Another obvious reason is that the price of electricity rose considerably after the 1973 oil embargo as utility costs increased. Between 1972 and 1975, the average residential electric price increased by over 13 percent per year, and has continued to rise since then; industrial prices increased even faster.

These price increases, along with government legislation and regulation, have encouraged energy conservation in manufacturing processes, appliances, and buildings—all of which work to reduce growth in the demand for electricity. Other factors tending to constrain the growth rate of utilities include government air-pollution regulations and licensing procedures (which increase costs) and related difficulties in raising capital for new plants. The environmental challenge to utilities has produced a need for utility managers to be innovative in terms of strategy and decision-making. Some have succeeded; some have not.[7] The possible difficulty in obtaining financing for coal-fired plants (as well as nuclear) could prove especially significant, with a severe impact on the growth of demand for coal. According to a recent study, one result of tight capital markets would be for the United States to continue using about as much natural gas and oil in the utility sector in 1995 as the nation did in 1980. The Reagan Administration hopes that new tax incentives will encourage utility investment.[8]

The problem for utility managers—and consequently for forecasting future utility coal consumption—is that this radically different and difficult environment might very well continue to change in unpredictable ways. The National Electric Reliability Council has warned that the future electric power supply would be in "jeopardy" if planned generating units were significantly delayed and if demand picked up. In fact, this group saw possible power "deficits" in the near future in certain regions.

In any event, long-term planning for the electric utility industry, a task which was once relatively simple, is now a difficult and uncertain responsiblity occupying, as it frequently did not in the past, senior management. As *Electrical World* observed, "The [electric] load-growth pattern—or lack of it—since late 1973 has no precedent in utility history. The excursions we have experienced clearly show that traditional trending methods no longer apply, especially for the years in the immediate future." The days of regular, steady growth, comparatively short construction lead times, guaranteed fuel supply, and easily obtainable financing are over. In short, utility electric-load forecasting, as one utility planner noted, is "not easy" anymore.[9]

Even if capacity forecasts could be more certain, there would still be great difficulties in deciding what kind of plant to build. Many estimates indicate that the total electricity-generating costs of nuclear and coal (with desulfurization systems) are nearly the same. Thus, the decision to build one or the other is not a straight-forward task of selecting the lower cost option. The coal strikes of 1977–78 and 1981 demonstrated the importance of maintaining a strong interconnected electric transmission system and of relying on a diversity of fuels. The regions that were struck imported large amounts of electricity that were generated by oil and nuclear plants. After the 1977–78 strike, two analysts for the Common-wealth Edison Company observed that "the advantage of having a mix of fuels is obvious: the eggs are not all in one basket. This offers some protection against monopoly pricing, strikes, em-bargoes, and weather effects."

These uncertainties explain why utilities have remained cau-tious about adding generating capacity and about committing themselves to a fuel source, and why, therefore, forecasts for coal use at the end of the 1980's can vary so much. It is, above all, demand that will determine the coal industry's growth. As even a rather bullish report by the National Coal Association observed, "Without a market, a coal mine will not be opened or ex-panded."[10]

The growing use of long-term coal delivery contracts gives even greater importance to utility demand uncertainties in deter-mining overall coal production, because such contracts explicitly link the opening of new mines and the expanding of old ones to utility decisions. In 1982, about 80 percent of U.S. coal produc-tion was sold through long-term contracts. The practice coincided with the rise of the utility market, the associated increase in power plant size, the growing desire by some utilities to use low sulfur coal from large Western surface mines, and the increasing capital expenses encountered by coal companies and utilities. Without such contracts, coal companies are increasingly reluctant to open major new mines, which further hinders expanded production.[11]

To comprehend other barriers, one must know something about the geographic distribution of coal reserves and its relation-ship to mining methods. Coal mined in the United States is usually categorized as either Eastern or Western. About 55 per-cent of coal by weight—but only 30 percent by heat content—is estimated to lie west of the Mississippi, far from the traditional

Eastern markets that use it to generate electricity (steam coal) or to make steel (metallurgical coal). Western coals are also generally lower in sulfur content by weight; and sulfur dioxide, of course, is a prime atmospheric pollutant when coal is burned. Consequently, Western coals are generally less polluting, although they also provide less energy per pound. So, on a comparable basis of heat value, the difference in the emission polluting potential between Eastern and Western coals lessens, although it is still significant.

Most Eastern coal—about 80 percent of its demonstrated reserve base—must be extracted by underground mining methods. Much Western coal—about 45 percent of its demonstrated reserve base—can be surface-mined (strip-mined), since the seams often lie less than two hundred feet below the surface. The overburden—the earth above the seam—is blasted and removed by giant draglines or by huge shovels, and the exposed coal is loaded onto trucks, which move it to railroad sidings. According to the 1977 Surface Mining Control and Reclamation Act, the mining companies must then reclaim the land. Moreover, laws in many states already required reclamation.

Surface mining is more efficient than underground mining, which recovers only 50 to 60 percent of a seam's coal. Up to 90 percent may be recovered through surface mining, and the average productivity of surface mines in 1980, measured in tons per worker-day, was slightly less than three times that of underground mines. And by 1980, surface mines produced about 60 percent of total U.S. output.[12]

This geographic distribution of coal profoundly affects another systemic barrier, the transportation network that links the production and consumption of coal. Coal is shipped by various modes of transportation and at times is even transshipped—for example, from trucks to barges. In 1981 about 59 percent of all domestically distributed coal was shipped by rail, 14.5 percent by river barge, 14.5 percent by truck, 9 percent used at mine-mouth generating plants, and 3 percent transported by other methods. It is important to remember that the transportation of coal can be a difficult and complex operation, especially when compared to the ease with which oil and gas can be moved through pipelines and in tankers. Although barge can be the least costly method of transporting coal where available, the coal industry will have to rely on the railroad to carry a major share of planned new tonnage because that mode is the only realistic option in most cases.[13]

The increasing dependence on the railroad will be especially great in the West, which is estimated to be the major growth area in coal production, because its low sulfur coal can be surface-mined as well as because of the expected growth in the use of coal by Western utilities. This makes the railroad the key means of transport, because it is already in place—although not necessarily with sufficient capacity—where there are no navigable waterways. The Federal Energy Regulatory Commission estimated that the railways would carry 62 percent of the coal for new electric generating units between 1977 and 1986.[14]

Can the railroads deliver? In the East, there is already a well-established coal rail network, and many consumers, producers, and railroaders believe that the lines—despite some short-term delays—can handle the additional business. More uncertain is the ability of the railrods to carry the expected growth of coal traffic in the West. The principal carriers of Western coal are the Burlington Northern, Chicago and Northwestern, Union Pacific, and the Denver and Rio Grande. To service the large surface mines of the West, these railroads are increasingly using "unit trains," which consist of a chain of about a hundred hopper cars with each carrying a hundred tons of coal. But thus far the railroads in the West have generally been able to deliver the coal on schedule.

Railroads also face other problems. For one thing, Western railroads create their own set of environmental and social hazards. Frequent unit trains can rumble through towns, disrupting whole communities and, in effect, cutting a town in half. Auto traffic is delayed, and general inconvenience engendered. Various studies also project an increased number of train-related accidents. Meanwhile, the cost of bypassing such communities altogether—or of building numerous bridges, overpasses, or underpasses—presents a significant and still largely unknown factor in the economics of coal rail transport.

The dependence on the railroad for coal transport also presents the government with a very complex set of economic, bureaucratic, and political problems. Involved is the cost of coal and, with coming deregulation, whether or not the railroads can increase freight rates. In the late 1970's, the city of San Antonio claimed that the rates charged by the Burlington Northern for shipping in coal from Wyoming made it more economic for the city to buy Australian coal. Two national goals were pitted against one another: creating an expanding market for coal on the one hand, and revitalizing the American railroad industry on the other. The Department of Energy backed the first objective by trying to hold the line on coal freight rates and the Department of Transportation supported the railroads and the second objective. Naturally, a number of rival bills, which support either controlling coal freight rates or the right of the railroads to raise prices, have been introduced in Congress. And disagreements between coal interests and the railroads over freight rates continued into the early 1980's.[15]

There is some chance that the railroads might not carry all the increased output of the West, for they face potential competition from slurry pipeline systems in which mined coal is successively cleaned, pulverized, mixed with water, pumped through a pipeline, and dewatered for use. In 1982 only one slurry pipeline operated in the United States, a 273-mile line transporting 4.8 million tons annually from Peabody Coal Company mines at Black Mesa, Arizona, to a Nevada utility. But at least five new pipelines have been proposed, including one that would transport 25 million tons of coal annually more than one thousand miles from Wyoming to Arkansas. Slurry pipelines seem to have a cost advantage for long-distance high-tonnage runs of coal, though not all studies agree with this conclusion. In any case, their potential development could keep railroad freight rates lower than they would otherwise be.[16]

But the decision to build slurry pipelines is not likely to be decided solely on the basis of cost. Political and environmental considerations are also important. The railroads, determined to maintain a dominant position, have fought legislation at both the federal and the state level that would give slurry pipelines the right to eminent domain across land owned by the railroads. But pipeline sponsors, through successful court suits and state legislation, are gradually obtaining eminent domain power, without which most proposed pipelines are stymied. It does appear that sufficient water exists for slurry pipeline operations (slurry pipelines, in fact, use less water than mine-mouth generating plants or coal gasification plants), but the water is not yet legally available. And in the West, water rights are a volatile issue. In mid-1978 a coalition of railroad interests, environmentalists, and Western congressmen decisively defeated a coal slurry pipeline bill. Moreover, the Reagan Administration backed off from support of federal slurry pipeline legislation on grounds of states' rights. But by 1982, a new slurry bill was under consideration on Capitol Hill that would grant slurries eminent domain if they had Interstate Commerce Commission certification and obtained water rights from the states.[17]

Further, a cloud of uncertainty hangs over any decision having to do with Western coal transportation. There is still some question whether the projected high growth in demand for Western coal will actually develop, at least before the mid-eighties. It must be remembered that both President Carter's energy plan and the 1977 Clean Air Act Amendments call for the "best available control technology" pollution-control equipment for desulfurization—or so-called scrubbers—on all new utility plants. If implemented, this policy would tend to reduce the market for low-sulfur Western coal, and to increase the demand for higher sulfur Eastern coal, because the key economic reason for preferring low-sulfur Western coal—scrubbers not being required—is removed. But the actual impact of the regulation is not clear. Because it is so much less costly to produce surface-mined Western coal, and because smaller scrubbers can be used, less limestone is needed in the scrubbing process, and the amount of solid waste disposal—sludge—is reduced. Therefore, Western coal may still be able to compete for the large Midwestern coal market. Moreover, the Clean Air Act appears to be a permanent feature of coal policy-making. After initially threatening to severely modify it, the Reagan Administration took a surprisingly hands-off stance toward a review of the act in the early 1980's. A strong Clean Air Act is likely to remain in force, though perhaps modified, for the rest of the decade.

Meanwhile, until the early 1980's, other factors, such as environmental regulation, court litigation, and environmental impact statements, have also slowed the rush to mine Western coal. But in 1981 the Reagan Administration, as part of its deregulation energy orientation, lifted the Department of Interior's de facto moratorium on leasing coal reserves on federal lands—which represent at least 60 percent of all Western coal reserves. In 1982 the Interior Department initiated the largest coal lease sale in U.S. history—offering seventeen tracts totaling about 2.24 billion tons.[18]

So the development of an efficient coal transportation system finds itself in a Catch-22 situation. On the one hand, if demand substantially increases, the railroads face a severe challenge in transporting the additional coal. On the other hand, there are enough uncertainties about the actual demand for coal to inhibit the railroad's ability to raise the capital required to prepare for the explosive growth, if indeed it does come about.

In short, a critical obstacle to massive coal production is the short-term systemic barriers. Coal demand, particularly from utilities, triggers the rest of the system, and that demand is the crucial factor. Utilities are hedging because of their own set of doubts; meanwhile, the railroads, which in the short term provide the key link between increased production and increased consumption, also hesitate and therefore may not possess the capacity to meet the system's needs. Finally, the producers wait for long-term contracts, especially in the West, before opening new mines. Consequently, all parts of the system are hindered from assembling the required capital, which in turn reinforces the delays in increased coal production and improved coal transportation.

Environmental Barriers

A second major hurdle to massive increases of coal utilization in the near term lies in the resource's physical properties and setting. Coal possesses the troublesome attribute of generating a seemingly endless string of environmental hazards that are ubiquitous and pervasive. As soon as one hazard, such as sulfur dioxide emissions, is identified and solved, it seems that another possible environmental danger associated with coal, such as carbon dioxide emissions, becomes a source of controversy.

As it is, serious environmental problems exist at practically every part of the coal system. During production, underground mining can result in acid drainage, subsidence, and coal workers' pneumoconiosis (black lung disease). Surface mining requires careful reclamation, or the unrestored land will usually remain scarred and unproductive. As already discussed, the transportation of coal creates its own set of environmental effects, including disruptions of communities by unit trains and possible depletion of water by slurry pipelines. Finally, coal consumption generates still another set of serious environmental hazards, including emissions of sulfur dioxide, nitrogen oxide, acid rain,* trace elements (including arsenic, cadmium, mercury, lead, fluorine, and beryllium), and carbon dioxide into the atmosphere, thermal and chemical discharges into water, and the solid-waste-disposal problems of coal ash. In fact, the very process of reducing sulfur dioxide emissions with scrubbers creates a new pollutant, sludge.[19] This entire array of environmental problems creates such a complex—and politically and socially charged—set of issues that it is difficult to envision an easy technological fix to deal with all of coal's environmental effects.

These diverse environmental hazards work in diverse ways to harass large-scale coal utilization in the short term. The need for better data in some areas, such as the extent and precise causes of acid rain—whether it comes from burning coal or automobile exhaust—will take time. Similarly, environmental hazards have obviously led to greater government regulation, which extends the time needed to open mines and power plants. Such regulations lead to battles between pro-industry and environmental forces in courts, government agencies, and legislatures, which further increases lead times.[20]

The potential environmental impacts of coal also substantially alter the market for key segments of the coal industry. For example, as mentioned earlier, the 1977 Amendments to the Clean Air Act, which limit sulfur dioxide emissions and require desulfuriza-

---

*Acid rain refers to rainfall of relatively high acidity due to sulfur and nitrogen emissions from power plants and automobiles.

tion treatment on all new coal-fired power plants, may substantially reduce the attractiveness of low-sulfur Western coal for Eastern markets.

At least one potential hazard of burning coal (and other fossil fuels as well)—the emission of carbon dioxide into the atmosphere —could have worldwide implications. This ultimately may well be the most difficult environmental problem. A report from the National Academy of Sciences has warned that a warming of the earth's temperature due to the "greenhouse effect" from increased carbon dioxide emissions might pose a severe, long-term global threat. The Academy went on to say, "The climatic effects of carbon dioxide release may be the primary limiting factor on energy production from fossil fuels over the next few centuries." The warning was soon echoed by other experts. Massive, long-term climate changes, including the melting of the polar icecaps and the shift of prime agriculture zones, have been suggested as major consequences.

There is disagreement as to how much of the increasing carbon dioxide is due to coal burning and other fossil-fuel combustion and to the cutting down of forests. It is certainly true that fossil fuels other than coal produce carbon dioxide. Still, the implication is clear: Coal and other fossil fuels may produce over time a global environmental hazard. Indeed, many critics (including, it should be noted, some advocates of nuclear power) have portrayed coal as the same kind of major danger that nuclear power is alleged to be by its critics. At a recent conference, a pro-nuclear speaker devoted his first twenty minutes to the potential carbon dioxide problems of coal. So, for the first time, it is possible to envision an absolute environmentally imposed limit to the use of coal in many parts of the world. In contrast, other researchers downplay this environmental hazard.[21]

The carbon dioxide issue aside, there were those, like the members of the Rall Committee on Health and Environmental Effects of Increased Coal Utilization, who suggested that it was environmentally safe to proceed toward the original Carter goal of 1.2 billion tons by 1985. (This committee's report was submitted to the Secretary of Health, Education, and Welfare at the end of 1977, who in turn transmitted it to the President.) But the Rall

Committee also said that strong environmental and safety measures must be followed, and stressed the uncertainties in information and data collection. The committee recommended rigorous compliance with all air, water, and solid-waste environmental regulations, universal adoption of the best available pollution-control technology on new coal-burning plants, rigorous compliance with reclamation standards and mine health and safety standards, and "judicious" siting of coal-fired facilities.

It may very well be that under such strict standards, environmental degradation may not be significant. But in the "real world," strict adherence to the recommendations of the Rall Committee may not be possible for a variety of economic, political, bureaucratic, and technological reasons. In mid-1978, for example, a Massachusetts utility agreed to convert an oil-fired plant to coal only after the federal and state governments exempted the utility from laws that would require scrubbers; it now uses low-sulfur coal instead. In addition, the state had to guarantee that it would not impose tougher environmental laws on the plant for ten years.[22] Moreover, the battle in 1982 to modify the Clean Air Act and the 1977 Surface Mining Control and Reclamation Act shows how environmental standards can be attacked and changed.

People Barriers |

Another significant problem with coal is people. Unlike other widely used energy sources—oil, nuclear and natural gas—coal is more "people-intensive," and because it is, a number of short-term barriers to large-scale coal utilization are raised. Steady increases in coal production, particularly in underground mines, depend on at least three key factors: the coal labor force and its productivity, managerial effectiveness and commitment, and the history and culture of the Eastern coal fields.

Labor force and productivity are usually the only human factors that receive attention. To understand the coal work force, one must remember the decades of mutual distrust between labor and management, the historic stark poverty of the Eastern coal fields, the dangerous and humanly exhausting nature of the work itself, and the miners' feelings of long-term exploitation. No won-

der that there have been several severe labor-management wars
since the beginning of the twentieth century. Not surprisingly, the
coal work force and the union that represented it, the United
Mine Workers of America, were often violent in asserting their
demands. Before World War II, the UMW's president, John L.
Lewis, proudly called his union "the shock troops of American
labor."[23]

When Lewis made that claim, the UMW possessed about
half a million working members. The postwar decline in production, the rapid mechanization of underground mining (which
Lewis encouraged), the move from more labor-intensive underground mining to less labor-intensive surface mining, corrupt and
ineffective union leadership after Lewis' reign, the shift of production to the West (which was outside the UMW's Eastern strong-
hold), and new competing unions—all these took their toll. By
1965, the UMW had approximately only 90,000 working members, which represented about two thirds of the total coal work
force. With the rise in coal production in the early seventies, the
UMW experienced rapid growth. By 1976, the UMW had well
over 160,000 working members, or about 75 percent of the total
work force, but the UMW's control over coal production was still
declining. Between 1972 and 1980 the share of coal produced by
UMW mines fell from 75 to 44 percent.

Still, even if the UMW's control of coal production is reced-
ing—temporarily or permanently—its legacy of conflict, defi-
nance, and distrust of management remains. Moreover, in the coal
fields there is a "new breed" of miner, who is young, militant, and
frequently well educated. A thirty-year-old vice-president of a
UMW district in southern West Virginia said of his members,
"Now, they're very intelligent. They don't think the company is
doing them a favor by hiring them. They think they're doin' the
company a favor by workin'." Indeed, coal mining is attracting
skilled workers from other occupations. The average age of the
UMW miner was 43 in 1971 and 37 in 1975 and 1980.

Coping successfully with the enduring posture of confrontation of the coal work force is critical for stable, growing coal
production. Accomplishing as much will not be easy. In 1977, for
example, there was an epidemic of wildcat strikes, and in 1982

there were threats of new wildcat strikes to protest Federal proposals to limit fines for mine safety violations.[24]

In any case, productivity in underground mines fell drastically after 1969. The decline in the 1970's has been variously attributed to the provisions of the Mine Health and Safety Act of 1969, changes in mining conditions (such as the quality of seams), higher coal prices (which may encourage extracting the substance from less productive seams or mines), the introduction of a number of inexperienced miners, the requirements of additional personnel due to union agreements, unscheduled interruptions due to wildcat strikes, and absenteeism. However, in what is a significant bright spot for coal, productivity began to increase at the end of the decade. Between 1980 and 1981, it rose about 7 percent for underground mining and about 9.9 percent for surface mining—for a total industry-wide increase of 8.4 percent.[25] But it is too early to know if this is a long-term trend.

One thing the operators did not see, or at least did not publicly acknowledge, was inadequacy in their own managerial ranks. Although an increasing number of mining engineers are now being trained, coal companies across the country still suffer from a shortage of qualified mining foremen, mine superintendents, and professional general management talent. And firms vary greatly in their interest or commitment to upgrade management staffs, with most coal companies only now beginning to hire professional labor-relations experts and administrators, and to recruit at schools of management. The traditional reluctance to recruit managers from outside the industry stems from the sound belief that mine experience is necessary for managing coal production. But the same perceived requirement tends to spill over into nonproduction areas, which significantly limits the talent pool for new managers and also constrains managerial creativity and innovation in such areas as labor relations.[26]

This does not have to be the case. There are a few underground mines, union and nonunion, which are highly productive, and management policy and behavior are important factors in their success. For example, the productivity of one coal company that operates underground mines in western Kentucky is 50 percent greater than most neighboring mines with similar seams. The firm is nonunion, but it pays basic union-scale wages and provides substantial production incentives, profit sharing, private medical insurance, and a retirement plan; it also pursues a policy of no layoffs and places great emphasis on recruitment. The firm's vice-president explained, "Our money and fringe benefits are better than anybody else's coal mine. Our miners are, perhaps, the richest working people in Kentucky. They have fancy homes. Some of them have boats which they take to nearby lakes. Quite a few are golf fans. They have expensive vacations. And why not? A few of these miners make—in salary, overtime, bonuses and profit sharing—as much as $25,000 a year."

Up to 1977 the firm never experienced a wildcat strike. When striking union members from other mines occasionally picketed the firm's mines, the company made a tacit agreement with its employees—the miners would try to get to work, but they would also avoid any confrontation with the pickets. If they were unable to get to the mine, they would return home. "We appreciated," said the vice-president, "that the decision of a miner to come to work can sometimes create tensions within his family, especially if there is a close relative who is out of work because of his union's strike." Although there are other factors that contribute to the firm's success, its consistent and innovative labor-relations policies and its commitment to implement them are key.[27]

The effects of endemic poverty are also powerful impediments to labor peace and stable production. Coal has been so closely associated with massive social deprivation for so long that a few boom years cannot be expected to erase basic social scars. Several close observers of Appalachia have seen coal and its after-effects as destroyers of both the human and natural landscape. In addition, certain Eastern coal-mining regions still suffer from poor public services.

But the Eastern coal regions generally have never been entirely isolated from mainstream industrial America. Moreover, prosperity has come to the coal fields. In 1978, the average wage of a union coal miner was between $17,000 and $18,000. The comparable nonunion figure was about $23,000.[28]

In spite of this increasing affluence, however, old and deep-seated social problems remain. Fundamental issues of labor productivity and motivation, managerial thinness, distrust of coal operators, and social insecurity generally still exist. Such human problems present the coal industry with difficult, though not impossible, operating barriers. These problems require dedication, patience, and time, and therefore will impede the increased production of Eastern coal in the short term.

Taken together, the three major types of barriers to the massive short-term utilization of coal—which are systemic, environmental, and human—stand in the way of our relying heavily on coal as an alternative to imported oil.

THE LONG TERM |

Although coal may not be a panacea for our immediate energy problems, it will continue to experience steady growth. Moreover, its prospects by the turn of the century are much brighter because of three trends: the growing participation of a diverse and strong set of established companies that are newcomers to the industry, the associated emergence of new technologies that permit cleaner and more convenient ways to utilize coal, and the growth of a significant world steam coal trade.

The New Participants |

To understand the long-term importance of the newcomers, it is necessary to review briefly the dramatic changes that have taken place in the coal industry since 1960. Until then, the coal industry consisted primarily of coal-mining companies and a few steel firms and utilities. It was also regional and isolated, and was confined almost entirely to east of the Mississippi. Management was basically home-grown and the labor force was aging. And finally, the industry was experiencing a rapid decline in the railroad, industrial, and residential markets. In short, coal in 1960 was the prototypical "sick" industry.

But during the decade that followed, especially the latter half of it, the earlier decline of coal production and employment within the industry halted and then slowly began to rise, thanks to increased demand from utilities. Also in the late sixties, petroleum firms became major forces in the coal industry as they began to buy operating coal companies, acquired coal reserves, and established totally new coal subsidiaries.

In 1966 Continental Oil Company acquired the mammoth Consolidation Coal Company. At the time Consolidation was the second largest coal producer in the United States, with an annual production of about 49 million tons, or about 9.5 percent of all U.S. production. Two years later Standard Oil of Ohio and Occidental Petroleum Corporation also acquired major coal companies, while Ashland Oil created an affiliate to mine Western coal. Exxon, the largest petroleum firm in the world, also entered the coal industry during the latter half of the sixties, acquiring large federal coal leases in Wyoming and several hundred thousand additional acres in Colorado, Montana, North Dakota, and Illinois. Exxon subsequently established the Monterey Coal Company to operate underground mines in Illinois, and the Carter Mining Company to conduct its Western mining operations. By 1974 at least seventeen of the twenty-five largest petroleum companies had entered the coal business in some fashion, and it was clear that a new group of firms with strong managements and massive financial and technological resources had a large stake in coal.[29]

But this large-scale entry by petroleum firms has become a source of controversy and may place another obstacle in the way of further development of the industry. Some people are afraid that the oil companies will come to dominate the coal industry, with the result that competition within the coal industry or between oil and coal will be limited. Fear of such concentration of market power or of reserve control in the energy field by a few huge oil-based, but increasingly diversified, energy companies has resulted in demands for horizontal divestiture of the petroleum firms. In its typical form, horizontal divestiture would force major oil producers to get out of all but one major energy resource (coal, uranium, or oil/natural gas). Its practical effect would be to force the oil companies out of coal.

Proponents of horizontal divestiture argue that each major energy source can be substituted for another, especially in the production of electricity. Therefore, a firm with interests in more than one energy source might delay the development of a competing fuel. Moreover, the proponents say, there is a great deal of regional variation in the control of coal production or of reserves, and in some areas, especially the West, control is already highly concentrated.[30]

But the opponents of horizontal divestiture cite a number of studies or opinions from such diverse sources as the Federal Trade Commission, the American Petroleum Institute, the U.S. Department of the Treasury, the National Coal Association, the U.S. General Accounting Office, and the U.S. Department of Justice. These studies show that the coal industry, even with the entry of oil firms, is still quite competitive. Using the most common measure of competition within an industry, concentration of production, we find that the top four firms, after increasing their control of production during the sixties—from about 21 percent in 1960 to about 31 percent in 1970—slipped some during the seventies, to about 21 percent in 1980. As for coal reserves, the top four holders controlled only about 16 percent in 1980. Meanwhile, the American Petroleum Institute reported that in 1980 oil firms controlled about 19 percent of all U.S. coal production and about 22 percent of U.S. reserves. Such concentrations do not appear alarming. According to economic theory, collusion is usually prevented and competition is usually protected when the top four firms control less than 50 percent of production. There is also evidence to support the notion that oil firms spend a disproportionately large amount of money on coal research and development. In 1975, their research investments accounted for about 60 percent of total private funds spent on coal research, at a time when their share of production was 20 percent. In sum, the industry remains quite competitive, and if anything, the entry of oil firms has made the industry stronger.[31]

Nevertheless, the mere threat of horizontal divestiture may restrain coal activity by some oil firms.[32] At one point, it was also thought that competition could be protected by methods short of horizontal divestiture, such as existing antitrust laws, setting limits on the share of reserves any single firm can control, and innovative federal leasing policies. The last could have been especially effective. About 40 percent of all U.S. coal reserves (by weight) and at least 60 percent of all Western coal (by weight) lie in government land. Through its huge ownership of the coal reserves in public lands, the government could do a great deal to control regional concentration. But the massive leasing sale begun by the Interior Department of the Reagan Administration has signaled an abandonment of such an approach.[33]

By the mid-seventies, additional participants and new patterns had emerged which will help shape U.S. coal production for the next twenty-five years. Other types of large companies have joined oil firms in starting or significantly increasing steam-coal production, a pattern which brings in a still larger base of corporate, managerial, and technical resources. Some of the new participants are those whose main business is the extraction of natural resources, principally Amax and Utah International. These two firms are now respectively the seventh and twenty-first largest private holders of coal reserves in the United States.* Also by the mid-seventies, the production of coal from utility-owned captive mines—mines that produce coal primarily for the parent company's own use—increased significantly; as recently as 1970, no utility ranked as one of the top fifteen coal producers in the United States. But in 1980 no less than three utilities—American Electric Power, Pacific Power and Light, and Texas Utilities—were among the top fifteen. This kind of production represented a significant attempt by certain utilities to cut into the fragmented coal demand-supply network and to integrate vertically. In 1982, the Federal Energy Regulatory Commission forecasted that the share of coal mined by utilities would grow from 14 percent in 1978 to 20 percent by 1985.

Although the coal production of steel-company-owned captive mines did not increase substantially, U.S. Steel, one of the two steel companies among the top fifteen coal producers, had decided to diversify and sell steam coal, used to produce electricity, as well as to continue mining metallurgical coal for making its own steel. This meant that still another kind of large firm with huge coal reserves now produces steam coal.[34]

---

*In 1976, Utah International merged with General Electric, at the time the largest merger in U.S. history.

In many ways, the most intriguing new participants are the engineering firms and other high-technology companies that have recently moved to enter the coal industry. State-of-the-art technological expertise is now coupled with control of coal. A dramatic example of the pattern is the formation of the Peabody Holding Company, which in 1977 acquired Peabody Coal and instantly became the largest coal producer in the United States and fourth largest holder of reserves. The holding company was comprised of Newmont Mining Corporation (a diversified international mining company), Williams Company (a diversified fertilizer and chemical manufacturer), Bechtel Corporation, the Boeing Company, Fluor Corporation, and Equitable Life Assurance Society of the United States. Bechtel and Fluor are engineering firms, and both have designed and built gasification and liquefaction plants of various sizes. Bechtel is also trying to develop and promote slurry pipeline systems. An even more startling new entrant is the huge chemical firm, Du Pont, which in 1981 took over Continental Oil and its coal subsidiary Consolidation.[35]

Plans for multiorganization and multisector coal activities also appeared with greater frequency in the middle seventies. These are joint ventures comprised of two or more firms and frequently involving some form of government participation through direct funding or some other type of subsidy. Such enterprises bring together significant managerial, financial, and technological resources, while limiting the risk of each participant, and therefore make possible very large, risky projects in coal. Such projects came into being for large-scale surface mining, particularly in the West, and have been proposed for developing coal gasification or liquefaction plants.[36]

The Wesco and ConPaso projects exemplified such new patterns of organizational relationships. Essentially, both were efforts to mine massive amounts of coal from the Navajo Indian Reservation in the northwest corner of New Mexico, to gasify the coal into high BTU gas,* and then to feed it into nearby gas pipelines. Both

---

*BTU stands for British Thermal Unit—the heat required to raise the temperature of one pound of water by 1° F at or near 39.2° F. Gas with an energy value exceeding 900 BTUs per cubic foot (cf) is generally labeled high-BTU gas. Low-

projects involved the participation of a gas company, and both were to use the proven Lurgi gasification process. The projects, however, were delayed indefinitely, due to regulatory decisions, inflation, lack of water access, difficult negotiations with the Navajo Indian tribe, and the general demise of synfuels in the early 1980's. Elsewhere similar efforts have been proposed and abandoned.[37]

New Technologies |

Until the 1960's, technological innovation in the coal industry focused on mining operations. Although fragmented, it was reasonably successful, involving as it did the participation of mining equipment companies, the U.S. Bureau of Mines, and operating firms. The system permitted a rapid diffusion of several innovations, including the shuttle car in the thirties and forties and the continuous mining machine in the fifties. The traditional pattern of innovation has persisted, although the government, the larger coal companies, and foreign firms are now playing greater roles.

Meanwhile, a new kind of innovative activity has emerged that could greatly improve coal's long-run prospects. On the one hand, increasing attention is being given to making the direct combustion of coal more efficient and cleaner. Such an approach makes sense, because direct combustion of coal accounts for about 85 percent of total coal usage. One of the most promising areas for continued research is fluidized-bed combustion, in which a fossil fuel is burned in a bed of granular particles held in suspension in an air stream. The government has sponsored work in this area for a number of years. This process offers significant potential for increased efficiencies and reduced emissions of sulfur oxides. Studies have estimated that the cost of energy using fluidized-bed combustion is potentially lower than that of energy from burning coal with scrubbers. Still, a number of technical probems remain, although there is hope that this technology will become available in the eighties.[38]

BTU gas has a heating value of 100–200 BTU/cf and medium-BTU gas, 300–650 BTU/cf.

The other significant, long-term direction of coal research and development is in gasification and liquefaction. Such work is less fragmented than the pattern exhibited in traditional technological innovation in the coal industry. In one sense synfuels are attractive because a convenient infrastructure already exists to transport oil or gas. Moreover, energy in either of these two forms is cleaner than can be had by the direct combustion of coal, because the technology to curb pollution from burning oil and gas is more developed and less expensive.

Liquefaction in particular is one weapon against increasing dependence on foreign oil. It is being used for precisely that purpose by another country with plentiful coal reserves, the Republic of South Africa. Although oil-trading ties with its previous major source of foreign oil, Iran, were severed with the overthrow of the Shah, South Africa seemed prepared in early 1979 to survive this shock. It had planned well. It had stored large stockpiles of crude in abandoned coal mines; in any event, coal supplied about 80 percent of the country's total energy needs. Moreover, South Africa has an extensive liquefaction capability. One facility is already operating, and another much larger liquefaction plant will be on line in the early 1980's. At that point, oil-from-coal will account for about 35 to 50 percent of South Africa's total petroleum consumption.

Historically, by contrast, the American synthetic fuel effort has been less intense and less focused, never given the priority it possessed in South Africa. Although some work on coal gasification and liquefaction took place in the United States before 1960, the Department of Interior's Office of Coal Research ignited the beginning of current interest by sponsoring a relatively small research effort during the 1960's. In 1963, OCR signed a contract with Consolidation Coal Company to support Consolidation's ongoing Project Gasoline effort. The company's president G. Albert Shoemaker happily told a Wall Street audience in November 1964: "Thus far we have demonstrated that our method is technologically feasible and in an area of such economic attractiveness as to encourage moving into the pilot-plant stage in the near future." After building a small pilot plant in the mid-1960's, Shoemaker was still quite optimistic: "While our projections must be confirmed in the . . . pilot plant, we believe this development offers the potential of creating a major new market for coal."

OCR also sponsored other synthetic fuels (oil and gas made from coal) projects during the 1960's, including efforts by the Institute of Gas Technology and FMC Corporation. Optimistic comments on the prospects for a "flourishing" synthetic fuels industry continued to be heard during the middle and late 1960's.[39]

Oil and gas companies considered coal a potential feedstock for their refineries, pipelines, and petrochemical plants. The lure of synthetic fuels led them to acquire coal, particularly in the West, where at the time no large market existed for steam coal. In fact, a Texaco official openly said in 1977 that his firm had acquired coal reserves during the sixties because of the optimistic forecasts made for synthetic fuels. Meanwhile, Exxon, in addition to acquiring reserves in the late 1960's, began to build up a coal and synthetic fuels research department.

By the early seventies, however, more discouraging estimates for the cost of getting oil and gas from coal emerged. The "economic attractiveness" mentioned by Shoemaker was a mirage, and the flush of optimism vanished when all participants discovered that liquefied or gasified coal was much more expensive than petroleum or natural gas. A respected engineering study of six gasification processes in 1976 found synthetic gas costs ranging from $3.88 to $6.72 per million BTUs compared to a regulated interstate natural gas price for newly found gas of about $1.40, and an unregulated intrastate gas price that hovered around two dollars per million BTUs. And in 1979, estimates for synthetic crude were over $30 per barrel. Moreover, the government's first attempt to build a liquefaction demonstration plant, the clean-boiler-fuel Coalcon project, was stopped in the mid-1970's on grounds that still more pilot-plant work was needed, and that other technologies appeared more promising.

The government then shifted away from backing large-scale demonstration facilities and primarily toward funding several promising technologies, mostly at the pilot-plant level. By early 1979 the Department of Energy had authorized only two gasification demonstration plant designs, and continued to fund at least three joint pilot or demonstration liquefaction facilities.[40]

The panic created by the Iranian crisis in the spring of 1979 dramatically changed the United States' policy toward synthetic fuels, which had always suffered from a lack of commitment or from general ineffectiveness. But during the spring of 1979 a wave of enthusiasm for synthetic fuels engulfed the House as it considered and passed an amendment to the Defense Production Act of 1950, which directed the President to achieve a production goal for synfuels of the equivalent of 500,000 barrels of oil per day. At the same time, a pro-synfuels campaign was also mounted by private citizens and the media.

Then on July 15, 1979, President Carter unveiled a new energy policy that had as its core an $88 billion proposal for a crash, massive synfuel program—to be financed mostly out of the windfall tax proceeds. The President's proposal called for the equivalent of 2.5 million barrels of oil per day by 1990, largely from coal liquids and gases and oil shale but also from biomass, peat, and unconventional gas. To promote synthetic fuels development, the President also proposed establishing an Energy Security Corporation that would have the authority to provide price guarantees, federal purchase agreements, direct loans, loan guarantees, and energy bonds.

With the President's proposal, the status of synfuels as an energy option momentarily was totally transformed. On the one hand, enthusiasm for synfuels erupted on an unprecedented scale. In November 1979 the Federal Energy Regulatory Commission approved the "rolled in" sale of natural gas from the forthcoming world's first commercial-scale high-BTU coal-gasification plant in North Dakota. By March 1980 commercial-scale units, costing about $2 billion, were being planned for Massachusetts, Kentucky, and Louisiana (as well as Poland and West Germany), and demonstration projects were being scheduled for Tennessee and California.

On the other hand, a number of diverse groups cautioned against a crash, massive synfuels effort for a number of reasons: uncertain, but increasing, cost estimates; various adverse environmental effects; technological risk; and poor strategy (becoming locked-in to an enormously expensive option too early). Instead, most skeptics recommended a more modest effort with the emphasis on learning more about a range of synfuels technologies during the 1980's basically through laboratory work and pilot plants, and then allowing the free market a greater role in deciding what contribution synfuels will make.

In any case, for better or worse, a synfuels industry seemed on the verge of being created. Congressional conferees in March 1980 approved the general framework for an independent twelve-year Synthetic Fuels Corporation. Splitting synthetic fuels development into two phases, the SFC was authorized to spend $20 billion during its first four years (although some administration officials thought that the high oil prices would mean that relatively little of this money would have to be spent). During the second phase, to last eight years, the SFC would focus on developing commercial facilities based on technologies proven during the first phase. The proposed spending ceiling for this stage was $68 billion. The SFC would have an interim goal of at least 500,000 barrels per day by 1987 and not less than 2 million barrels per day by 1992. Moreover, Congress obviously wanted to keep the SFC lean and to avoid bureaucratizing it by limiting it to 300 full-time professional employees and to $35 million per year, adjusted for inflation, for administrative expenses. The bill that established the SFC was signed into law on June 30, 1980.

But with the assumption of the presidency by Ronald Reagan in 1981, plus falling oil prices and high interest rates, enthusiasm for synfuels quickly diminished. As of mid-1982, only two major synfuels projects, both backed by forms of government subsidies, were under construction: the Great Plains coal gasification project in North Dakota and the Union Oil shale oil venture in Colorado. Three huge projects had been cancelled: the Exxon-Tosco shale oil project in Colorado, the Gulf Oil SRC-II coal liquefaction project in West Virginia, and the American Natural Resources–led WyCoal coal gasification project in Wyoming. In May 1982, eighteen months after its first meeting, the SFC had yet to sign a project-support agreement. Perhaps three of the original sixty-three entries would eventually be sponsored by the SFC. Certainly, there was very little chance of even coming close to the ambitious goal of a synfuel production equivalent to 500,000 barrels per day by 1987 and 2 million barrels per day by 1992.

The call in 1979 and 1980 for an enormous, crash synfuels effort represents both a technocratic and supply-oriented solution to the energy crisis. Its attraction was obvious: the convenient utilization of the nation's great resources of coal and oil shale. Its risks were both obvious and hidden: high development costs, high end-product costs, inflationary impacts, environmental hazards, premature technological selection, and the creation of a highly visible political effort, which means that, after grandiose promises and vast expenditures, a possible backlash might destroy whatever long-term benefit synfuels could have otherwise provided, if the crash program fails. As has happened before with synfuels, the various economic and technological risks overwhelmed possible long-term political gains, and the greatest opportunity in U.S. history to develop a significant synfuels industry vanished in the early 1980's.[41]

The synfuel program demonstrates how the dominant force in coal industry R&D and the promotion of innovative activity has become the federal government, which has shifted its energy research priorities. In 1963, out of a total federal energy R&D budget of about $330 million, only $11 million was spent on coal, while over $210 million was spent on nuclear fission. But by fiscal 1980 the Department of Energy research budget allocated about $663 million (or about 19 percent of the total) for coal and about $954 million (or 28 percent) to nuclear fission, with almost half of coal's money going to gasification and liquefaction. However, under the Reagan Administration's policy to encourage private sector development and marketing of new energy technologies, the pattern of continued growth of federal R&D funding in coal has been radically reversed. For fiscal 1982, $366.8 million was appropriated for Department of Energy coal R&D and only $90.8 million was requested for fiscal 1983, though much of funding responsibility for synfuels was placed in the SFC.

In the private sector, coal-related R&D spending by oil firms rose from about $5.5 million in 1971 to an estimated $42.4 million in 1976, which meant that coal's share of all oil firms' total R&D budgets had increased from 2 percent to 10 percent. Furthermore, coal-related R&D by oil firms is generally less fragmented than the traditional technological innovation process in the coal industry. Oil company research directs itself toward developing whole systems (not just specific components of a process), and the approach usually involves coordinating various technologies and different organizations. And because oil and natural gas companies are intersted in gasification and liquefaction, they are playing key roles in the new, integrated kind of R&D now emerging in coal. As a result, of the thirty-six proposed synthetic fuels projects identified by the Bureau of Mines in mid-1976, oil and gas companies sponsored twenty-two.[42]

THE INTERNATIONAL STEAM COAL TRADE |

A significant source of optimism for coal's long-term future is the rise of steam coal exports in the early 1980's. The world coal trade has been growing since 1960. Between 1960 and 1979, the amount of coal traded on the world market more than doubled, from 113.3 million tons to 252.4 million short tons. Most of this coal—about 70 percent of the international coal traded in 1977 —has been metallurgical coal used for steel production. But in the past few years the amount and percentage of steam coal—used for the production of energy—traded on the world market has increased enormously.

While the World Coal Study's optimistic numbers can be debated, its message was clear and correct: World steam coal trade in the next twenty years will increase rapidly, and this growth is one of the major new elements on the energy scene.

Total U.S. coal exports rose from about 66 million short tons in 1979, to about 91 million short tons in 1980, and to about 112 million tons in 1981. The burgeoning steam coal export market was a major contributor to this dramatic increase in U.S. coal exports. In 1980, about 27 million tons—or 29 percent of total U.S. coal exports—were steam coal; in 1981, about 45 million short tons, or 40 percent of total U.S. coal exports, were steam coal. Between 1980 and 1981, U.S. metallurgical coal exports increased by 3 percent, while U.S. steam coal exports increased by over 68 percent. In the future, metallurgical coal trade should experience relatively little growth. On the other hand, growth in the steam coal trade over the long term should remain vigorous.

This expansion in steam coal trade offers tremendous opportunities for coal producers throughout the world. Most forecasts expect the United States to assume a larger share of the growing steam coal market. For example, one typical midpoint estimate shows the U.S. share of a rapidly growing world steam coal market increasing from 18 percent in 1985 to 25 percent in 1990 and to 38 percent in 2000.

It should also be noted that other countries are vigorously improving their steam coal export capabilities or have the potential to increase coal exports significantly. In 1981, the major competitors were Australia and the Republic of South Africa. In fact, South Africa surpassed Poland as the leading exporter of steam coal to Europe, partly due to the wave of strikes in Poland during the first half of 1981. However, an equally important success factor is the effective strategy at both the national and corporate levels in South Africa to vigorously encourage coal exports. Especially impressive was the construction of one of the most efficient coal logistical infrastructures anywhere in the world. But in the United States, there is considerable argument over whether the U.S. should spend several billions of dollars to equip its ports for large coal-carrying ships.

There is little doubt that the United States will continue to remain the world's largest exporter of coal and will increase its export volume and market share. What is in question are the timing, rate of growth, and the absolute magnitude of potential U.S. exports. But the actual results will depend as much on corporate strategic decisions and other managerial factors as on national policy.[43]

THE DISAPPOINTMENT AND THE HOPE |

Despite its much-touted abundance, coal will not become our major near-term solution to the energy problem. Its use, however, will grow, and it will play an increasingly important role in certain sectors. But coal's potential long-run strengths—new, strong participants, new kinds of technological innovation, and growing steam coal exports—are emerging. The industry is more vigorous than it has been for decades; it is no longer isolated, and a large, rich, and diverse set of firms now participate. Finally, until the Reagan Administration, the government had pumped massive amounts of money into the coal industry to encourage the development of new technologies.

The strategy for coal is clear: to concentrate on long-term answers and strategies, such as through technological and managerial innovation and steam coal exports, while seeking acceptable ways to utilize coal's steady short-term growth. Nevertheless, U.S. energy policy must cope with the inevitable disappointment that is even now beginning to develop as it becomes clear that coal cannot be *the* transitional energy source. It also must cope with disappointments that might arise, such as from difficulties caused by slacking demand or by overambitious synfuels or coal-export programs.

These disappointments could engender a pathology that in turn could further cripple coal's prospects in the short term. The industry is still conflict-ridden, with, at times, the environmentalists pitted against industry, industry against government, and labor against management. Such pathology was exhibited during the coal strikes of 1977–78 and 1981. Fundamental problems in labor-management relations—more mining foremen, skilled labor managers and specialists, and generally better qualified middle-level managers—and in environmental questions remain and are still hotly debated. Heroic efforts to reach some sort of accommodation between the various conflicting interests in the coal industry have had only a limited impact. One such attempt was an undertaking called the National Coal Policy Project, which sought to achieve some consensus and cooperation between two long-term antagonists: industry and environmentalists.

This group even claimed to have achieved an "80 percent agreement" between industry and the environmentalists in 1978, when the draft report was issued.[44] But since then, the slackening demand and the softening on environmental regulation by the Reagan Administration have once again pushed coal back into its historic position of a boom-and-bust and conflict-torn industry.

Because of its obvious abundance, too much too soon has

been expected from coal. Less attention has been placed on coal's intrinsic and enduring characteristics—on its market appeal, its diverse environmental problems, and on the key features of the industry. Coal usage will grow, but so will disappointment as demand cycles up and down, environmental battles continue, and labor strife remains. Methods to deal calmly and reasonably with coal's short-term problems have not been successful. We should recognize that coal is not a panacea and miracle transition for America's energy needs. Our overall long-term focus should include serious programs to utilize coal more cleanly either in direct combustion or possibly as a liquid or gas, and to export steam coal more efficiently and effectively. Such a posture will permit more freedom in meeting U.S. energy needs, including choices involving coal.

5 NUCLEAR POWER: THE PROMISE MELTS AWAY

I. C. BUPP

By the end of 1974, the political and economic establishments of the Western industrial countries had agreed on a common response to OPEC and dependence on imported oil: As the 1960's had been a decade of oil, the 1980's would become a decade of nuclear power. President Nixon unveiled Project Independence, which called for atomic energy to provide 30 to 40 percent of America's electricity by the end of the 1980's and even more—up to half—by the beginning of the twenty-first century. French Premier Jacques Chirac expressed the view of most Western leaders when he declared, "For the immediate future, I mean for the coming ten years, nuclear energy is one of the main answers to our energy needs."[1]

For the government and business leaders committed to atomic energy, the years since for the most part have brought frustration. The nuclear promise has turned into the nuclear disappointment.

Critics have argued that nuclear power plants are unsafe or uneconomical or both. The critics have also attacked the industry for failing to develop feasible, safe, and acceptable methods to dispose of radioactive waste materials, and they have charged that worldwide growth of the nuclear power industry will result in the spread of the materials and know-how required to produce atomic bombs. Moreover, since 1979, issues concerning the basic safety and costs of nuclear power have emerged that have drained the industry of its optimism. During the past ten years internal concern has done as much to halt the growth of nuclear power as external dissent.

Some of the critic's apprehensions about the safety of nuclear power were confirmed by events that began in the predawn hours of March 28, 1979, at the "Three Mile Island" nuclear power plant located near Harrisburg, Pennsylvania. In the days following these events, millions of people around the world came to believe that something that was supposed to be impossible had almost happened: an accident that might have killed thousands of people.

The accident at Three Mile Island began with a simple pump failure. As the operators tried to cope with this rather routine problem, an important valve failed to work the way it was designed, effectively causing a huge leak in the reactor's cooling system. More than two hours passed before the faulty valve was discovered and shut. During this time, hundreds of thousands of gallons of radioactive water poured into the building housing the reactor. Some of this water was pumped to storage tanks in an auxiliary building, but these tanks quickly spilled over.

Meanwhile, the plant's operators were being misled by poorly designed instrumentation. The operators believed that there was too much water in the cooling system, when in fact there was far too little. Because of this misinterpretation, the operators took actions that essentially eliminated the system's ability to remove heat from the reactor core.[2] As a result, the fuel in the core sustained an amount of damage that is still unknown three years after the accident.

After three years, most of the radioactive water that had been spilled into the reactor buildings is still sitting there. This is because the experts have had a lot of trouble agreeing how to remove it, and what to do once it is removed. They have had even more trouble deciding what to do about the reactor core that partially melted down during the accident. Final agreement is still months away. The clean-up process is dragging into years, rather than the months first estimated. Before the process is finished, presumably in the mid-1980's, the costs are almost certain to exceed one billion dollars.

The accident now stands as a crucial watershed for the entire nuclear industry. It caused regulatory delays and changes which, in turn, led to even higher costs for new plants. More importantly, it focused attention upon the uncertainties that were already cropping up over reactors in operation as well as those under construction. Well before March 1979, new orders by American electric utilities for nuclear generating equipment had all but stopped.

Less than half a dozen reactors were purchased between 1975 and 1982. Moreover, in the same period there were about sixty cancellations of plans for reactors previously ordered and more than twice as many deferrals for periods ranging from five to ten years. During 1980 and 1981 alone, work or planning on about twenty-five more plants was either halted or indefinitely postponed, even after, in several cases, expenditures of between $200 million and $400 million.

It's not attitudes that have changed. Nuclear advocates among the government and business leaders and their allies from the scientific and engineering communities will still say that there is no realistic alternative to increased reliance on nuclear power. For them, it is not so much the technology of choice as the technology of necessity. Neither have the opponents of nuclear power changed their views. Some nuclear critics, motivated by images and associations of Hiroshima and nuclear war, go beyond such pragmatic questions and want to put "the atomic genie" back in the bottle as soon as possible and at any cost. No technical or economic facts will easily erase for them the image of the mushroom cloud. Others attack atomic energy as a product of an entire social and political order to which they are opposed.[3] This has been a prominent theme among some opponents in Western Europe and Japan. But in the U.S., the most influential critics have been those who have challenged the nuclear industry with pragmatic, not ideological, questions.

Nuclear advocates still readily admit the existence of some technical and economic uncertainties, particularly with respect to nuclear waste disposal. But they steadfastly maintain that these problems are tractable. This assumption is what separates the nuclear advocates from many of their critics. The advocates implicity accept the motto: For every problem, there is at least one feasible solution.

Pragmatic questions do suggest the possibility of pragmatic answers. But in this case there are wide differences of opinion about how to interpret even basic scientific facts. There are equally wide differences about who should assume the burden of proof when varying interpretations imply a choice of conclusions about the safety and economy of nuclear power. The fundamental disagreement is over how to deal with uncertainty. The resolution of differing opinions over how to deal with uncertainty, over how much risk is acceptable or how safe is safe enough—all this requires judgment in which values play as large a role as scientific facts.

The most directly related to Three Mile Island of these issues is the inflammatory one of reactor safety. The unresolved problem of the used-up, or "spent," fuel from reactors also stands in the way of new orders and threatens the operation of both plants in the pipeline and those already on line. For it is not even clear that all of the plants that are today producing electricity can continue to do so throughout the 1980's. If some currently operating nuclear plants were forced to shut down because there was no place to put their spent fuel, or because of safety considerations, it would be anyone's guess whether new ones would be permitted to start up. Moreover, plant shutdowns would mean that the absolute output from nuclear power a decade from now could actually decline from where it is today.

In the absence of broad consensus on how to interpret issues such as waste disposal, another basis for interpretation has emerged. In the U.S., the new questions are: Do we need it? Can we afford it?

It is important to remember that the only application of atomic energy is to produce electricity. In early 1982, the American electric utility industry had the capacity to produce about 550 "gigawatts" (GW) of electricity.* The entire electric utility industry contributed the equivalent of about 11 million barrels of oil per

---

*One gigawatt is equal to 1 million kilowatts (1,000 megawatts), or the equivalent of 42,000 barrels of oil per day in an oil plant operating full time, or the equivalent of 20,000 barrels of oil per day at the typical operating rate of the U.S. electric utility industry.[4]

day of energy in 1982. About 55 GW, or 10 percent of this capacity, was nuclear. However, these nuclear plants were generating about 12 percent of the electricity actually produced. The discrepancy between capacity and actual generation exists because electric utilities try to operate nuclear power plants full time. In industry jargon, these plants are "base-loaded," which means that they normally account for a higher percentage of electricity actually generated than of generating capacity.

In early 1982, there were about seventy-five operational nuclear power plants in the United States, accounting for the 55 GW of generating capacity. Construction work was proceeding on about sixty plants, representing about 65 GW of new capacity. About 20 other plants—representing about 25 GW of capacity—remained on the drawing boards of various companies. In fact, work was actually started but had subsequently been stopped on a half-dozen or so of these. Hence, about 90 GW of nuclear generating capacity remained "in the pipeline" in the United States.

However, it would be extremely surprising if all of this capacity actually entered service in the 1980's and early 1990's. More cancellations and delays appear very probable during the 1980's. The fate of many of the plants depends upon the continuing commitment of a relative handful of people. Two companies in the southeastern United States together own fourteen of the twenty deferred, but still not formally canceled, plants (T.V.A. with eight and Duke Power Company with six); and five of the other six deferred plants are only in the preliminary planning stage, with four of them concentrated in the Pacific Northwest.

All in all, a good guess is that about 50 of the 60 plants still under construction in mid-1982 will enter service in the 1980's. The approximate 55 GW of capacity that they represent would double the entire contribution of nuclear power to a total of about 110 GW. The fate of the other 35 GW of capacity in the pipeline is indeterminate. But, even if it is all eventually completed, the resulting total of 145 GW (55 GW operational plus 90 GW in the pipeline) is the extreme upper limit of any realistic projection for nuclear power in the United States for the rest of the twentieth century.

This is only a little more than a third of what had been officially projected as recently as 1975.

It is important to know that, concurrently, most forecasts of probable electricity demand growth in the 1980's have been also revised downward by half, as well. For about twenty-five years, from the late 1940's to the early 1970's, there was rapid and steady growth in demand for electricity in all of the industrialized countries. This growth averaged about 7 percent per year. Since 1974 the situation has changed dramatically. Highly erratic but generally slow growth and even periods of decline have replaced the rapid and steady pattern of the 1950's and 1960's. Between 1975 and 1980, projections of future growth rates were successively scaled back. By 1982, few experts were predicting a return to steady 7 percent growth before the end of the century. Nearly all foresaw half that or less.[5]

Between 1973 and 1979 the reserve margin of the nation's electrical generating system rose from about 20 percent to about 30 percent, compared to a desired level of 20 to 25 percent. If the capacity additions scheduled at the time of the Three Mile Island accident had actually materialized as planned, the nation's electricity reserve margin would have been greater than 40 percent by mid-1982 because of lower than anticipated demand growth in most regions of the country. As the sixty-odd nuclear plants still being built are completed and enter service during the 1980's, the industry-wide reserve margin will climb to 30 to 35 percent and remain in that range—with a few regional exceptions—throughout the decade, depending on decisions about how oil and gas-fired plants are operated.

Even if demand for electricity were to suddenly increase, new nuclear plant orders would have no significant impact on the country's energy supplies until the 1990's, since it takes twelve to fourteen years to plan, build, and license an atomic power plant. And it is far from clear that the issues that have halted new orders and left plants half-built can be resolved in the next few years.

The prospects for nuclear power through the 1980's are a shadow of the confident appraisals of the early 1970's. To understand why, it is necessary to go back some years and review the evolution of the business and the federal government's role in it.

THE EARLY COMMERCIAL TRIUMPH |

A group of scientists led by Enrico Fermi operated the first man-made atomic reactor in 1942—in a converted squash court at the University of Chicago.[6] The first power-prototype atomic reactor to be connected to an electricity distribution network in the United States began operation in late 1957, at Shippingport, Pennsylvania. It was a very different machine from the first reactor in Chicago. The first device and others built during World War II as part of the government's Manhattan Project were called piles, for they were little more than piles of graphite blocks into which uranium fuel rods were inserted. The Chicago pile was not designed to produce anything; its purpose was merely to demonstrate the feasibility of starting and controlling a nuclear chain reaction. The graphite slowed down, or "moderated," the neutrons produced by the splitting uranium in order to sustain and to control the process. The later piles of the Manhattan Project also used graphite as a neutron moderator, but were designed to produce plutonium, a new element for use in atomic bombs.

The reactor in Shippingport had a different purpose: to turn the heat of fission into electricity. Its uranium fuel sat in a steel chamber through which ordinary water was circulated at high pressure. An intricate system of pipes, valves, and pumps allowed this circulating water to slow down—to moderate—the neutrons, and to carry heat from the fuel chamber, the reactor core, to an electricity-producing steam turbine. The second large American reactor to produce electricity was based on a similar design. It also used ordinary water as a neutron moderator and as a coolant, but instead of maintaining the water in the reactor core under high pressure, it permitted it to boil off into steam.

Naturally enough, these designs were dubbed pressurized water and boiling water reactors, and together were known as light water reactors. The term *light water* distinguished them from yet another design that used a rare compound of oxygen and a form of hydrogen called deuterium to transfer heat from its core. The descriptive name of this compound was heavy water, and the devices using it were known as heavy water reactors—the design favored by the Canadians.

Pressurized water reactors, boiling water reactors, and heavy water reactors by no means exhaust the technical possiblities for generating electricity from nuclear fission. Since World War II dozens of other systems have been tried around the world. The first reactor to be connected to an electricity network—in England in 1953—used graphite piles as its moderator and carbon dioxide gas to remove heat from its core. During the 1950's, such gas-graphite reactors were the basis of British and French efforts to produce nuclear electricity. The fifteen-year attempt by Britain and France to make the gas-graphite design the basis of the world's nuclear electricity program effectively ended in 1967. A decade later, no manufacturer offered gas-graphite plants for sale. By the early 1970's, the world market for nuclear power plants was dominated by the light water systems that had been developed in the United States as a direct outgrowth of the American Navy's nuclear submarine propulsion program. Only the Canadian heavy water system—nicknamed CANDU—survived as potential competition.

In December 1963, the Jersey Central Power and Light Company announced its purchase of a 515-megawatt light water reactor from General Electric to be built at a site called Oyster Creek. To explain its decision, Jersey Central offered a novel reason: The Oyster Creek nuclear power plant would produce electricity more cheaply than any other generating system. Also unique was that the federal government did not participate. For the first time a reactor would be built to produce electricity in the United States without a direct subsidy from the Atomic Energy Commission. General Electric had offered to build the entire facility for a price that, over the several years of the project, could change only to correct for inflation.

Jersey Central's decision was widely regarded as a milestone in the development of nuclear power technology. It was accepted as proof that the day when reactors would be sold in direct competition with conventional generating plants was very close at hand, if indeed it had not already arrived.

Spokesmen for General Electric maintained that the low cost

of the Oyster Creek plant was not unique.[7] At about the same time, GE was also furnishing another utility in upstate New York, Niagara Mohawk, with the major components for its Nine-Mile Point nuclear plant at prices "in line" with those for Oyster Creek. In addition, the company published a price list for nuclear power plants of many sizes. The Westinghouse Electric Company was quick to match GE's price quotations with its own for the pressurized water system. Few informed persons in either industry or government publicly questioned the rosy picture for the future of nuclear power that these events seemed to foretell.

In the months following the purchase of the Oyster Creek plant, four American reactor manufacturers—G.E. and Westinghouse, joined by Babcock and Wilcox and by Combustion Engineering—committed themselves to deliver complete nuclear power generating stations at firm prices, subject to change only for inflation. The reactor manufacturers would assume responsiblity for the cost of materials and equipment manufactured by other companies as well as for managing the entire construction project. The manufacturer would turn over the completed plant to the owner, who merely had to start the generating equipment. Such facilities were called turnkey plants, and the Oyster Creek turnkey contract was followed by eight others. These sales were regarded as proof of the reality of commercial electricity generation from light water nuclear reactors.

In 1965, American utilities placed their first orders for nuclear plants for which the manufacturers no longer provided firm price guarantees. The next two years produced a "great bandwagon market" for nuclear plants as utilities ordered nearly fifty systems totaling about 40 gigawatts of electrical generating capacity. The intense competition among the four reactor manufacturers was waged in terms of plant prices and confidential ancillary guarantees on fuel and other factors affecting plant operating costs. In most cases, a utility considering the purchase of a reactor could solicit secret bids from each of the four manufacturers and then bargain among the lowest bidders for the most attractive supplemental guarantees. This remarkable buyer's market was characterized by continuous downward revision of the *estimated* cost of electricity from nuclear plants.

Advocates of nuclear power were ecstatic, many speaking of a "revolution" that had been accomplished. "Nuclear reactors now appear to be the cheapest of all sources of energy," Alvin Weinberg, director of the Oak Ridge National Laboratory, told the National Academy of Sciences in 1966. By 1968 authoritative forecasts for continued rapid growth of nuclear generating capacity were being made by government and industry. These forecasts, with their astonishingly low cost projections, would have seemed incredible to even the most bullish proponents of nuclear power only five years earlier.[8]

A CHANGE IN GOVERNMENT REACTOR POLICY

In the mid-1960's, just as the great bandwagon market for the light water system was getting going, the federal government's power reactor research-and-development program underwent a major transformation.[9] A close look at the circumstances surrounding the drastic change in government policy and internal organization suggests that it was only indirectly related to the rapidly unfolding commercial prospects for nuclear power; instead, it was the culmination of a ten-year-long squabble between the Atomic Energy Commission and the congressional Joint Committee on Atomic Energy about the proper scope of the federal government's role in developing and bringing advanced reactor systems to the marketplace.

Lewis Strauss headed the Atomic Energy Commission during much of the Eisenhower Administration. He was a conservative Republican who believed that the chief responsiblity for developing the technology to produce electricity from nuclear fission lay with private industry, not the federal government. Several powerful New Deal Democrats on the Joint Committee thought otherwise.[10] Years of increasingly bitter disagreement between Strauss and the Joint Committee Democrats left a residue of antagonism and distrust that affected the government's nuclear power program long after Strauss's departure. In fact, federal power reactor development policy during the mid-1960's was more heavily influenced by the issues of the 1950's than by contemporary events and their implications for the 1970's.

In November 1964, Milton Shaw, a protégé of Admiral Hyman Rickover, was named Director of Reactor Development for the AEC. His main objective was to turn the commission's nuclear power research-and-development activities into the kind of aggressive government-controlled program that Democrats on the Joint Committee had wanted. Shaw was only secondarily concerned with the surprising commercial success of light water systems. The key problem of reactor development, as seen by Shaw and the AEC, was that light water technology wasted uranium. This perceived technical deficiency called for an accelerated government-controlled effort to develop systems that would use uranium more efficiently. A large number of new reactor technologies held this promise. The most sophisticated, and the best according to this criterion, was the "breeder" reactor. But between light water systems and breeder reactors were a number of "second generation" concepts, such as high-temperature gas reactors.

For some time, several different concepts had seemed to the AEC's technical staff to offer roughly equal promise for second-generation nuclear power plants. Prior to Shaw's appointment, the AEC had already taken the position that electric utilities would have to make their buying decisions from the menu of these various second-generation designs. In early 1964, the AEC had solicited proposals for joint government-industry projects to build prototypes of one or more of these new designs. For the rest of the year—the crucial period preceding the great bandwagon market for light water—the staff of the AEC was preoccupied with sorting out the technical pros and cons of the next reactor technology.

Shaw turned the government program even further away from the remaining development problems of light water systems. He wanted to skip the second-generation technologies and move directly to establish the liquid-metal fast breeder reactor as the highest-priority government research-and-development effort. During 1965, Shaw successfully reoriented the AEC program. His liquid-metal breeder reactor program would attempt to do for this new technology what Admiral Rickover's naval propulsion program had done for light water systems: provide a solid technical base for a prototype construction project. For the first time, the AEC's power reactor research-and-development program would meet the demands articulated for years by the Democratic majority on the Joint Committee on Atomic Energy. It would assume full, not partial, responsibility for shepherding a new reactor technology from engineering concept to full-scale prototype demonstration.[11]

But Shaw's success had an unforeseen and unfortunate consequence of great importance for today's problems. The time devoted by AEC officials to bringing about this policy change and their willingness to sacrifice other goals to meet the new commitment to the breeder reactor diverted the government's managerial attention and fiscal resources away from other huge unsolved problems that remained in the development of light water systems.

LIGHT WATER: AN INCOMPLETE SYSTEM

Many business executives are familiar with looking at manufacturing or service operations in terms of systems that require certain inputs to produce some product. Descriptions of nuclear power technology that appeared to fit this approach were common during the mid-1960's, and indeed still are. That technology is often described as a way to produce electricity from steam turbines, in which uranium fission is substituted for the burning of oil, gas, or coal to make steam. According to this beguiling description, nuclear energy is little more than a novel way to boil water. The board of directors of General Electric reportedly viewed the company's decision to enter the nuclear power field as a decision merely to integrate the company's business "backward" into steam-boiler manufacturing. Their customers were subsequently persuaded to buy "nuclear steam supply systems," not "atomic reactors."[12]

The phrase *nuclear steam supply system*, though perhaps technically correct, obscures a crucial point. In nuclear power technology, the pertinent system is much larger and far more complex than simply a new way to make steam to turn a turbine. In fact, the nuclear power system is an interconnected set of subsystems that extend far beyond the atomic generating station itself. The reliable production of electricity from nuclear fission requires the operation of a fuel supply system to provide uranium; a fuel preparation system to "enrich" the uranium and package it in appropriate form; a power-plant operating system to build and maintain the reactor and associated generating equipment; and a spent-fuel treatment and disposal system. Moreover, these several systems are not connected in a simple one-way fashion. There are complex technical and economic linkages among them, and each depends on the other in complicated and often subtle ways. Cheap and reliable electricity from nuclear power requires one of the most demanding creations of modern society: a highly interactive set of extremely sophisticated industrial processes and services spread across many separate plants and requiring many specialized management skills. To believe that nuclear power is merely a new way to boil water is to believe that open-heart surgery is merely a new way to relieve minor chest pains.

In the mid-1960's, the light water reactor development job was far from complete, for only pieces of the massive interdependent enterprise were actually in place. Yet the government's policies, combined with assumptions about the willingness and ability of private industry to complete whatever supposedly minor tasks remained, created the unfortunate illusion that the research-and-development task for light water systems was all but complete. It was as though a fleet of modern jet aircraft, such as Boeing 747s, had been sold to some less-developed country, with the aircraft and engines working perfectly. But to become operational, the fleet obviously would require the support of a sophisticated group of ancillary operations and services, such as airports, air traffic control, and a skilled crew. In short, the aircraft and its engines would be useless without a complex and highly interdependent infrastructure. Of course, such a comparison is only an analogy. Yet it captures an essential reality about the great bandwagon market of the 1960's: Nearly everyone involved in the initial commercial success of nuclear power helped to create and to sustain the illusion that a difficult task that had barely been started was, instead, almost finished.

In order to sell a nuclear power plant to an electric utility, its manufacturer had to demonstrate that it would produce electricity cheaper than coal or oil. The trouble was that there was no real evidence to sustain the reactor manufacturers' claims. The nuclear power plants that were being sold in the mid-1960's on the *promise* of cheap electricity would not actually begin to operate until the early 1970's. But from the mid-1960's until the mid-1970's, there was little or no effort by reactor manufacturers, by the purchasers, or by the government itself to distinguish fact from expectation on a systematic basis.

In the last half of the 1960's, the buyers were obliged to accept on faith the sellers' claims that nuclear power could produce electricity more cheaply than coal. Each new buyer was, understandably, cited by the successful vendor as proof of the soundness of the vendor's economic claims, and such proof was accepted by other utilities in the United States and abroad, as well as by those companies already committed to light water plants. In this way the rush to nuclear power became a self-sustaining process.

The reactor manufacturers had earlier absorbed large losses from the original nine turnkey projects, but they had expected these losses, which in any event seemed to be more than offset by the marketing and advertising victory that followed. Nevertheless, it soon became apparent that things were not as bright as they might have appeared in the fever of the great bandwagon market. By the end of the 1960's there was already considerable evidence that the 1964–65 cost estimates by government and industry for electricity from light water nuclear power plants had been low.[13] But since the illusion of a completed research-and-development job served so many interests, a consensus quickly developed that the causes of the initial cost overruns were fully understood and were being dealt with.

The nuclear power community had ready explanations and ready solutions. First, economies of scale were seen as a powerful tool for lowering the cost of electricity from nuclear plants. By the late 1960's, light water manufacturers were offering ever larger plants for sale. In 1968, manufacturers were taking orders for plants *six* times larger than the largest then in operation.[14] Second, there was widespread confidence that "learning" effects and design improvements in such key areas as fuel life would help to compensate for the unexpectedly high costs of the plants themselves.

In 1971, M. J. Whitman, an Atomic Energy Commission official, told the Fourth Geneva Conference on the Peaceful Uses of Atomic Energy that "the evolution in the costs of nuclear power . . . would under normal circumstances, be classified as a traumatic, rather than a successful experience." However, "many of the trends which have affected the rise in the investment costs of nuclear plants have had similar effects on alternative methods of generating power."[15] Whitman also asserted that the atomic energy's cost difficulties were a "prelearning" experience and that future costs would inevitably decline because of learning effects. He concluded that the cost of a nuclear plant delivered a decade after the first commercial sale in the United States would be more than 200 percent higher in real terms, but labeling this a period of "intense learning," he predicted that learning effects would begin to lower costs for plants coming into operation in the late 1970's.

During the first half of the 1970's, these sorts of explanations and remedies constituted an unchallenged conventional wisdom about the economic status and prospects for nuclear power. That wisdom provided the basis for a new surge of nuclear plant orders, and one would not have known from the apparent evidence of the bandwagon market and the claims that went with it that the economic problems of light water systems had barely begun. Nor would one have known that they were directly related to criticism of atomic power plant safety. At the time, most business and government references to such criticism dismissed it as a transient phenomenon related only to local power plant siting decisions. Yet by the early 1970's, the still less than fully developed battle over reactor safety was already having a major effect on the cost of nuclear power and on the ability of industry to complete the job of putting the entire nuclear energy supply system in place.[16]

THE COSTS OF THE BARGAIN |

Since the end of World War II, suspicions and fears had, of course, often been expressed about atomic energy. Many of the same scientists who first saw the great promise of the discovery also stressed its terrible dangers. For most of those who later worked to turn the promise into reality, these dangers, though real enough, were completely manageable. Convinced of this by their own knowledge and experience, they were impatient with outsiders who raised questions. But the outside doubts would not go away; in fact, they grew in both number and intensity as the years passed.

Nevertheless, the nuclear community, and especially its most prominent scientists and engineers, had the credibility to persuade government and business leaders that its view was the technically correct one. By the early 1970's the general tendency among the Western world's business and government establishments was to accept the judgment of the nuclear advocates that doubts about nuclear safety were confined to a comparative handful of noisy and misguided people.

This assessment of the situation was unfortunate. Policymakers overlooked an important political reality: The judgment of the nuclear power community about the acceptability of its technology was being effectively questioned in the United States and in almost all of the Western countries. Moreover, the issue was becoming more, not less, troublesome at the very time of OPEC's price increases.

As opposition to nuclear power developed in the Western democracies, government officials and the affected business executives and nuclear scientists responded in remarkably similar ways. They initially defined the problem as a distortion of certain well-established scientific facts. Given the correct information, the public at large would quickly realize that there was no merit to the questions raised by nuclear critics who were merely exploiting public ignorance. All questions about nuclear safety would vanish as soon as the facts were known. This, of course, has not happened.

Most advocates believed in 1983, as in 1970, that, as one

electric utility executive told us in an interview, "Atomic energy's promise to rescue the world from energy starvation is being killed by the critics, the courts, the bureaucracy, the press, and the politicians." Thus, most persons in the nuclear business insist that the persistence of the critics and their political and legal victories have little or nothing to do with the scientific merit of the allegations made.

Most nuclear critics naturally disagree. The basic problem, in their opinion, is technical. The nuclear critics steadfastly maintain that neither the government nor the nuclear advocates have satisfactorily answered the questions they have asked about reactor safety and reliability. Indeed, the first thing that impresses an observer of the dispute between the two sides is the breadth and depth of the apparent disagreement among their respective experts. For each of the scientific or technical questions that the nuclear critics have asked about the risks of nuclear power, it was easier in 1983 than in 1970 to find seemingly qualified technicians and scientists prepared to give contradictory answers. In fact, since the early 1970's it has been virtually impossible to make any substantive statement about reactor safety that would not be challenged by either nuclear advocates or nuclear critics as inaccurate or misleading. It does seem, however, that some critics, notably the Union of Concerned Scientists, have shifted the burden of proof to the nuclear advocates on certain key technical issues. But at the same time one must be sympathetic to the frustrations of responsible, technically competent nuclear advocates. One Harvard physicist, Professor Harvey Brooks, speaks for them: "What drives me up a wall is that conservative expressions of scientific caution are seized on by nuclear critics as admissions that nuclear power is unsafe. Unfortunately, extremism on the part of some critics stimulates equal extremism on the part of a small minority of the proponents, which then tends to alienate more scientifically cautious persons and put them, in the eyes of the public, into the critics' camp."[17]

Brooks's comment captures a good deal of what has been going on in the nuclear safety controversy. What it misses is the poisonous legacy of the early years of nuclear power promotion by the industry, the Joint Committee on Atomic Energy, and the Atomic Energy Commission.

A major reason for the persistence of reactor safety criticism is the way the introduction of light water technology was managed by American industry and government.[18] First, the developers of nuclear power had too narrow a view of their task. In many instances they did indeed behave as though they were building and selling a Boeing 747, and leaving the development and construction of airports, radar, and pilot skills to some later date.

A cavalier attitude toward the "outside world" was a second crucial error. During the years of early public visibility—the great bandwagon market—the government agencies and the business interests with the most to gain from successful innovation largely monopolized the technical information about it. Their impatience with questions from outside the club surely contributed to their critics' sense that they were hiding something. By impugning the competence or even the rights of outsiders to question their judgments, government and industry advocates of nuclear power helped to create the impression that much of the "truth" about atomic energy's dangers was being distorted. Government documents support the contention that much concealment and distortion did in fact occur.[19]

The nuclear advocates' case has also been damaged by the heavily negative connotations attached to nuclear technology. Talk of "unprecedentedly deadly materials," "invisible radiation killers," and lone psychotics or terrorists fashioning atomic bombs may all seem melodramatic and irrelevant to a nuclear engineer. But it is powerful stuff, and the fears it arouses resist the rational calculus of economic costs and benefits more strongly than most officials have supposed.

The nuclear critics have also been helped by the growing demands of many in Western society for more participation in matters that affect them. In the past, it was usually easy for proponents of technological change to establish the desirability of their proposals and implement them. That those who directly benefited were generally different from those who paid the price could usually be overlooked. Those who challenged "progress" could be dismissed as irrational. Much of this has changed during the past generation. An increasingly representative society guarantees the nuclear critics a base of political power, which means that resolution of the nuclear safety controversy will require more than a consensus of established scientific and engineering judgment.

By the 1980's disagreement among apparent experts had spread into yet another technical area: the economics of nuclear power. A tangle of contradictory expert opinions similar to that which for years had characterized the nuclear safety imbroglio had by 1977 overtaken the question of whether nuclear power was, or could ever be expected to be, a relatively cheap source of electricity. It was virtually impossible to make any substantive statement about the economic performance of nuclear power without touching off a rancorous dispute.

The controversy touched every important factor on which the economic performance of a nuclear power plant depended: the respective investment costs of coal and nuclear generating stations; the proper way to deal with inflation in allocating this investment cost to each kilowatt hour of electricity produced by the plants during their assumed lifetimes; respective fuel and fuel-related costs; and the appropriate way to discount future cash flows in allocating the fixed and variable costs of nuclear and coal-fired power plants.[20]

After hearing weeks of expert testimony on the subject, the Public Service Commission of Wisconsin concluded that "there is a wide range of views in this record concerning the relative economics of nuclear and coal-fired generation. These views range from nuclear power's being much less costly than coal to coal's being much less costly than nuclear, *and include the view that it is impossible to tell* [emphasis added]." The staff of another state public service commission—New York's—summarized yet another lengthy review with a terse conclusion: "There is no credible bottom line comparison of the total generating costs of nuclear and fossil facilities which can be extracted from this record."[21]

In my opinion, no credible bottom line comparison can be extracted from any existing data. In short, a decade after OPEC quadrupled the price of fossil fuels—and two decades after nuclear power supposedly first gained a competitive edge over coal—it is still plausible to assert that atomic energy is or is not competitive, depending upon the choice of assumptions that suits one's interest.

Whether an analyst supports or opposes nuclear power, he or

she adopts assumptions and cites evidence about relative capital and fuel costs, power plant capacity, and other factors that maintain one or the other position. Consciously or unconsciously, those arguing whether nuclear power is cheaper than coal are simultaneously arguing the larger issue. This means that we should expect no early resolution of the traditional question about the economics of nuclear power. In the coming years there is little chance of an unbiased scientific consensus on whether nuclear power is cheaper than coal.

This is scant comfort to executives of companies already committed to continued growth of nuclear power, or to others who hoped for an end to the stalemate that had developed in the 1970's. For by 1982 the traditional dispute about relative economics of nuclear and coal plants had been superseded by a new and more troubling question about the relative economics of nuclear and oil-fired plants. At the end of the 1970's, most data suggested that the marginal cost of electricity from the nuclear plants that would enter service in the mid-1980's would be in the approximate range of four to five cents per kilowatt hour, expressed in constant late-1970's dollars. This would guarantee that nuclear power would be a bargain compared to oil: Since $30 per barrel oil translates into a *fuel-only* cost of electricity from oil of about five cents per kilowatt hour, any reasonable capital charge plus variable operating and maintenance expenses would increase this to a minimum of about seven cents per kilowatt hour.[22]

But this was before the Three Mile Island accident, and before the astronomical interest rates of the early 1980's turned all predictions on their heads. By 1982, it was apparent that the marginal cost of electricity from the nuclear plants that remained under construction would, in real terms, be at least twice that which had been anticipated less than three years earlier. This means that electricity from nuclear power plants will become prohibitively expensive unless oil prices (in 1982 dollars) climb into the $50-per-barrel range by the end of the decade, and into the $75-per-barrel range by the early 1990's.

In absolute terms, the astonishing increase in projected nuclear capital costs between 1978 and 1982—from about $1 billion per plant to an average of $2 billion—represents a staggering, indeed backbreaking, financial burden to companies either contemplating or trying to build a reactor. It all but guarantees that during the decade of construction the equity of these companies would be severely diluted. Under these conditions, the common stock dividends required to retain access to capital markets for construction financing would be a return of the power company's capital to its shareholders. In other words, building a nuclear power plant means partial liquidation of corporate assets throughout the decade-long construction process.

Already by mid-1977 there was a national de facto moratorium on the purchase of nuclear generating equipment in the United States. By 1983 there was no realistic prospect that the moratorium would end until at least the early 1990's when plans will probably have to be made either to replace worn-out machinery or to accept a deterioration in the reliability of the nation's electricity generating system.

The strongest advocates of nuclear power persist in their optimism that the moratorium on orders could be ended sooner. But even these nuclear proponents generally concede that U.S. electric utilities would not order additional reactors until drastic changes occur in the environment affecting utility planning and investment decisions: The ability to clean up Three Mile Island, both technically and financially, has to be proved; the capital costs of building a nuclear power plant have to stabilize, an accomplishment possible only if construction and regulation achieve impressively higher efficiencies; and a federal program to guarantee effective management and disposal of radioactive waste has to be established.[23]

WASTE: A BOTTLENECK IN THE SYSTEM |

Periodically nuclear power plants must be refueled, the spent fuel assemblies removed and replaced with fresh ones. In the 1960's and early 1970's, government and industry planners assumed that the spent fuel would be reprocessed to recover still-useful fissionable material from useless and dangerous waste materials as soon as enough reactors were in operation to support the large-scale facilities required for economical reprocessing. Both the government and the nuclear industry postponed important technical decisions about the treatment and disposal of the waste materials pending the start of large-scale reprocessing.[24]

Meanwhile, people both in and out of government have worried about the proliferation of nuclear weapons. International treaties and government secrecy notwithstanding, for thirty years the major impediment to such proliferation had been the scarcity of nuclear explosive material. Even in the 1970's its manufacture remained so difficult and so expensive that it was beyond the reach of all but a few governments. But arms-control specialists argued that widespread reprocessing of light water reactor fuel would produce a great deal of material that could be used to make atomic bombs. The plutonium that would be recovered during reprocessing for use as a supplemental reactor fuel could also, though with some difficulty, be used to make nuclear explosives. Moreover, the 20 kilograms or so of plutonium that is theoretically necessary to manufacture an atomic bomb is a mere accounting error compared to the tens of thousands of kilograms that will be routinely handled by an economically viable reprocessing facility.[25]

Consequently, in October 1976, the Ford Administration warned the American nuclear industry that fuel reprocessing might become unacceptable. Six months later, the Carter Administration transformed the warning into an outright prohibition of indefinite duration.[26] For the American nuclear industry, the new government policy also transformed what had been regarded as a relatively minor technical problem, the choice of specific methods to dispose of radioactive waste materials, into an acute operational problem—what to do with spent fuel.

Because the industry was forbidden to reprocess the spent fuel, it has been piling up in storage areas, those specially designed pools of water at nuclear power plant sites. The reactor storage pools are generally large enough to contain the entire reactor core if it must be removed for any reason, as well as one to three years' discharge of spent fuel. One year's normal discharge usually corresponds to about one third of the total fuel in the reactor. By 1983 most operators of nuclear power plants had expanded the capacity of their fuel storage areas by installing redesigned holding racks.

But "re-racking" is only a temporary help. The fuel storage pools at most operating American nuclear power plants could be filled by 1986, and a few even earlier. As these plants exhaust storage capacity, their owners will be forced to transfer spent fuel to other locations or to build and license additional storage capacity—or to shut the plants down altogether.

One expedient would be to transport spent fuel to one or more centrally located common storage pools. Such "away from reactor" pools (AFRs) would be comparatively cheap to build and could safely store fuel for many years. A dozen or so such facilities, each about the size of an average industrial warehouse, would accommodate all the spent fuel that is likely to be produced for the rest of the century.

Technology is not an issue here, with the technical aspects of spent fuel storage being eminently straightforward. Instead, what is at issue are considerations such as whether commitment to a new type of nuclear facility is wise; who is best suited to manage storage and where; whether further growth of nuclear power should be encouraged or allowed before "final" repositories are available; how the risks of storage, transportation, and disposal should be distributed within society; and, of course, the ubiquitous question of how large a risk is acceptable.

The situation is further complicated by the fact that public perceptions of how serious the waste disposal problem is do not closely match those of many government officials, industry executives, academic experts, or even technically informed anti-nuclear activists. Most experts on both sides of the fight over nuclear power are much less worried about solving the waste disposal problem than the public at large appears to be. Yet, the federal government has also lost the confidence of many elected officials in state and local governments, who do not trust the federal government to resolve competently and without bias what they and their constituents perceive to be "the problem," nor to make the inevitable value tradeoffs in an acceptable way.

Because of public perceptions, AFRs pose a considerable not-in-my-back-yard political problem. In September 1977, Illinois Attorney General William Scott told a congressional committee that General Electric's announced plan to increase spent fuel storage capacity at a company-owned facility near Morris, Illinois, was unacceptable. "Illinois will not passively allow itself to become the nation's dumping group for high-level nuclear waste—when a proper review is complete, General Electric will not be permitted to expand its facility," he said.[27]

By 1978 objections to warehousing spent fuel in AFRs had become concrete. At least seven state legislatures had imposed various prohibitions on the construction or expansion of local nuclear waste storage facilities, or on the transport of radioactive waste into the state. One of the strongest was a California statute which actually prohibited future construction of nuclear power plants until the state "finds that there has been developed, and that the United States through its authorized agency has approved, and there exists a demonstrated technology or means for the disposal of high-level nuclear waste."

In this political environment, large-scale reliance on AFRs could easily be dismissed as a stall that allows the industry to avoid solving the real radioactive waste disposal problem. Of most concern to those opposed to AFRs is that such facilities might become de facto substitutes for a permanent solution to the waste disposal problem. Nuclear critics want to avoid a situation in which large-scale, supposedly interim spent fuel storage facilities allow the continued operation of nuclear power plants in the absence of real progress toward safe, ultimate disposal of radioactive waste.[28]

The Reagan Administration, like Carter Administration before it, believes that the technology and know-how necessary to proceed with a safe waste disposal demonstration program are now in hand. Both Administrations also have shared the notion that proceeding with a safe waste disposal demonstration program is a better solution, both technically and politically, than merely shuffling assemblies of spent fuel from one storage tank to another. In 1981, the Reagan Administration sought legislation to authorize such a demonstration program. Neither the Senate nor the House, however, were able to settle upon the details of the legislation, although they generally agreed upon the wisdom of building a demonstration facility. The obstacle is bitter disagreement over whether or not the federal government should have the authority to build AFRs. In the House of Representatives, the prospects for compromise are particularly dim.

Even where existing federal jurisdiction is more clear-cut, in the area of military waste disposal facilities, similar controversy has arisen. The Carter Administration had proposed a Waste Isolation Pilot Plant (WIPP), in which suitably packaged wastes from atomic weapons manufacture would be deposited in a salt cavern several hundred meters below ground in southeastern New Mexico. WIPP had initially become the focal point of a scientific debate about the adequacy of salt formations as a radioactive waste disposal and again in 1981 when real technical difficulties developed at the WIPP site. The WIPP project has also stirred a debate over relative state and federal responsibilities for certifying the acceptability of specific disposal sites.

Since the late-1970's it has been clear that there are indeed large gaps in scientific knowledge about long-term radioactive waste disposal.[29] But it was also clear that there were sharp differences of opinion about the meaning of these gaps. For example, while few informed persons believed that there simply was no radioactive waste disposal problem, many did believe that the outstanding technical issues were relatively minor and could be easily overcome. Similarly though, while few informed persons believed there was no solution whatever to the radioactive waste disposal problem, many did believe that very serious technical uncertainties abounded and that efforts to resolve them would turn out to be expensive and time-consuming.[30]

The basic disagreement between the two views is over the question: "How safe is safe enough?" The building and licensing of nuclear power plants, before a community-wide consensus existed on this fundamental question, proved very costly for everyone involved. It was especially damaging for the federal government's nuclear research-and-development and regulatory agencies whose credibility and even legitimacy were demolished in the eyes of many citizens. Repeatedly during the 1960's and early 1970's, government officials had acted less like umpires than partisans, defending the nuclear advocates against the nuclear critics. Many persons still fear that the government will manage radioactive waste disposal in the same way it managed the light water system, pressing forward prematurely and thus generating serious health and safety problems.

Some scientists and industry spokesmen argue that introduction of breeder reactors would considerably simplify the problem of isolating radioactive wastes from the environment. The reason is that breeder reactors would "burn" the plutonium that is a by-product of light water reactor operation, and hence, theoretically, eliminate the need to isolate this particularly long-lasting radioactive element from the environment. Like most technical questions having to do with the safety of nuclear power, the degree to which consumption of plutonium in breeders would lower the long-term hazards of radioactive waste management is hotly disputed by apparently qualified experts.[31]

Moreover, many nuclear critics claim that even if breeders did simplify the radioactive waste isolation problem, their introduction would create a new hazard: enhanced possibilities for the illicit manufacture of nuclear explosives from plutonium.

The debate on these issues rages in the absence of much relevant evidence. Contrary to a widespread impression, even the world's most technically advanced breeder-reactor development program (in France) is decades from making any significant addition to that country's nuclear power supply. One small pilot plant, called Phoenix, is in operation. Construction is well underway on a second, much larger plant, Super Phoenix, that is scheduled to begin operation in 1985. But even Super Phoenix is not a prototype for commercial breeder reactors. Yet another, still larger plant will be needed to demonstrate commercial (that is, economical) power production. The French government will not proceed with a third breeder reactor until the mid-1980's. In the United States, Congress has authorized, and the Reagan Administration strongly supports, construction of the Clinch River Breeder Reactor. This plant is intermediate in size between Phoenix and Super Phoenix. But the project is already years behind schedule and hundreds of millions of dollars over original cost estimates. Its future is extremely uncertain.

Events beyond the early 1990's are, of course, anyone's guess, but the history of the light-water-reactor development effort cautions against expecting too much too soon from a new and highly complex technology. Certainly for the indefinite future there is no realistic possibility that breeder reactors can have any practical effect on the waste disposal problem.

Meanwhile, because distrust of the government is so high on nuclear issues, it will be enormously difficult to find a program for waste disposal whose acceptance extends beyond the nuclear industry's own scientists, engineers, and executives. As a practical matter, the nuclear advocates who urge haste in developing and implementing a spent-fuel management and waste disposal program have little means of producing that outcome. The nuclear critics who prefer less haste, however, have numerous mechanisms by which they can express their discontent and slow down the program's progress. These include outright veto in the case of state legislatures and time-consuming court challenges in the case of environmental groups.

Decisions on radioactive waste disposal will have to be supported by a body of scientific evidence and a range of informed technical judgment that will withstand the most searching independent scrutiny. It seems clear that a condition for any relief of the spent-fuel bottleneck is massive and rapid improvement in the vigor and technical quality of the federal government's radioactive waste disposal program. By 1980, the Department of Energy had put in place a program of geological research to locate and characterize potential repository sites in a variety of different geological environments. This was an all important first step toward resolving the radioactive waste disposal problem.[32]

The government under President Carter was, for a change, candid. It admitted that gaps do exist in the scientific understanding of the long-term environmental effects of radioactive waste disposal. A program of investigating several different geologic media before proceeding with full-scale repository construction— if it is carried out—will build on the already existing agreement among a wide range of scientists that safe and secure radioactive waste disposal in conventionally mined repositories is *probably feasible*—a proposition with which even many prominent nuclear critics agree. The scientific problem is to carry out the experiments in the field and to analyze the data to identify specific sites.

But the Carter program—though it represented real progress

—was *only* a first step. Great conflict over how safe is safe enough seems certain to persist. It is unlikely to be eliminated or even very significantly reduced by clarification of the outstanding technical questions.

Meanwhile, the Nuclear Regulatory Commission is trying to decide whether the granting of new licenses for reactors should be tied to progress on radioactive waste disposal. The Commission is also reviewing its siting standards for nuclear power plants.

It is a good bet that the NRC will link progress on waste disposal to new reactor licenses. It is a better bet that the NRC will issue more stringent criteria to regulate the location of new reactors close to large population centers. Some members of the Commission have admitted that any significant modification of reactor siting standards would oblige the agency then to consider the very difficult question of whether to allow older plants that do not meet the new standards to continue operation. It is, of course, virtually inevitable that any or all NRC decisions on these matters will provoke legal challenges by the aggrieved parties.

In the months following the accident at Three Mile Island, chaos developed in nuclear power plant licensing and regulation. In effect, during 1979 the nuclear licensing machinery of the federal government was brought to the same kind of halt that followed a 1969 Federal Court decision on the Atomic Energy Commission's non-radiation related regulatory responsibilities.[33] At that time some eighteen months were needed for the AEC to adjust its rules and procedures to comply with the Court's mandate.

Although the post–Three Mile Island licensing moratorium did end in 1980, considerable uncertainty and even outright confusion remained about many key aspects of NRC reactor licensing policy. In 1981 and 1982 the Reagan Administration was not very effective in improving matters, despite numerous pronouncements about the importance that the President attached to streamlining NRC procedures.

An especially important reason why the circumstances in the 1980's is more complicated than those a decade earlier is that the NRC does not retain the old AEC's effective monopoly over nuclear regulatory policy. Instead, at least a dozen independent agencies and bureaus in the Executive Branch alone claim jurisdiction over various aspects of nuclear power plant licensing and operation. Differences on both strategy and objectives exist among these organizations. In certain cases many are proceeding at direct cross-purposes.

In Congress, the 1960's monopoly legislative authority of the Joint Committee on Atomic Energy has been replaced by competition among as many as two dozen separate committees and subcommittees; again, often moving at cross-purposes or in direct conflict. No locus of potential central power or authority is readily apparent.

Because the organizational confusion is based on real policy —even value—differences, confusion over basic reactor licensing policy will persist for the foreseeable future. Working out some of these differences, building some effective coalitions, and putting together some workable compromises will take considerable political imagination, skill, and luck.

What nuclear power experienced in 1979 was not a reactor core meltdown at Three Mile Island. It was a regulatory meltdown in Washington.

The central fact about the environment in which the political meltdown occurred is that the nuclear advocates and the nuclear critics—both in and outside the federal government—can in large measure block each other's goals, frustrate each other's policies, and hence prevent the development of any coherent strategy in reactor licensing. The 1979 nuclear regulatory meltdown was, in short, a breakdown of the American democratic political process.

Nuclear Power Outside the United States |

At the beginning of the 1980's the reactor manufacturing industry in the noncommunist world had the capacity to build about fifty nuclear power plants per year.[34] For the rest of the century, however, the combined markets of the developed and developing countries will probably provide this industry with only 10 to 20 percent of the work for which it is equipped. The coming years will bring intense competition as reactor manufacturers defend their manufacturing capability in a "buyer's market" that contains hardly a handful of customers. None of the major manufacturers except France's Framatome will enjoy a significant domestic market for their product for at least ten years.

Among the industrialized nations, France's nuclear program will see the most progress. Until the election of the socialist government of François Mitterrand in 1980, France was the only country, other than the Soviet Union, where reactors were still being ordered and built, essentially in accordance with plans developed in the mid-1970's. Mitterrand's victory was followed by several months of uncertainty about the future of his predecessor's ambitious reactor construction program. Within a year, however, it was apparent that because of lowered projections for growth in electricity demand, the socialists would slow the rate of orders for new reactors during the mid-1980's perhaps by fifty percent. However, the ultimate objectives of the French nuclear program would not be changed. Nuclear power will provide as much as two-thirds of France's electricity by the 1990's. Moreover, France will continue with a strong breeder reactor development program. The Mitterrand government is said to have decided that an aggressive nuclear program at home, and a nuclear industry capable of playing a strong role in the international nuclear power market, if it returns, is an important component of French industrial policy.

In contrast, the nuclear program is stalled in the Federal Republic of Germany, much as it is in the United States, and for many of the same reasons: violent disagreement over "how safe is safe enough" in a political, administrative, and judicial structure that gives nuclear critics significant advantages over nuclear proponents. A major difference between the United States and Germany is that in Germany nuclear critics have been motivated more by ideological than pragmatic concerns.

Japan probably has the greatest "need" for nuclear power. So several Japanese companies, evidently confident of a domestic market for at least three to six reactor orders per year, have entered into discussions with KWU in Germany and Westinghouse in the United States. Their view is toward licensing arrangements that could provide the foundation for a Japanese reactor export capability by the end of the 1980's. Nonetheless, between 1980 and 1982 the future of nuclear power in Japan became more, not less, uncertain. Growing concern over the reliability and costs of American pressurized water reactor technology, technical problems involving the first Japanese fuel reprocessing plant, and the continued lack of a politically acceptable radioactive waste disposal plan all combine to raise huge doubts about the future of nuclear power in Japan.

By mid-1982 only seven countries seemed to be significant nuclear power growth markets for the rest of the decade: Italy, Spain, Argentina, Brazil, South Korea, Taiwan and Mexico. Of these, nuclear plant manufacturers have considered Mexico to be the "plum"—with potential sales of as many as twenty plants before the end of the century. Then, in the spring of 1982 the Mexican government announced an indefinite deferral of its plan for a major nuclear construction program because of falling oil prices and reduced worldwide demand for oil.

Elsewhere, even among the other six potentially large-scale importers, nuclear power probably will not grow by very much in the 1980's. The Brazilian nuclear program has been a story of frustration and deep disappointment involving a series of construction fiascos, and consequently huge cost overruns. South Korea and Taiwan, with fourteen plants under construction, plus one operating in South Korea, are probably saturated, unless the world economy turns sharply upward in the near future.

Italy, Spain, and Argentina may each purchase one or two nuclear power plants. So, for that matter, might a host of other countries: South Africa, Finland, Belgium, Greece, Portugal, Turkey, Rumania, Yugoslavia, China, Egypt, and Canada. But in the case of each of these countries, as indeed everywhere in the world, such purchases will be highly vulnerable to economic and political circumstances that are today simply unpredictable.[35]

In both the developed and the developing countries, adverse economic conditions—some directly attributable to oil price increases—and bearish forecasts of electricity growth have combined to inhibit the growth of nuclear power. It is also evident that political opposition has everywhere played an important part; in fact, in no country can politics and economics be easily separated.

It has now become popular for nuclear critics to maintain that "nuclear power has failed the test of the marketplace."[36] This seems disingenuous. The worldwide controversy that the nuclear critics have themselves produced has been at least partly responsible for rising nuclear power costs. Capital costs increased in real terms chiefly because of major design changes to contain nuclear accident hazards. The Three Mile Island accident caused further real cost increases by demonstrating the need for additional design changes and by throwing into chaos an already unstable regulatory environment.[37]

The opposition to nuclear power is by no means a homogeneous political movement either across countries or within a given country. In Europe and Asia, as in the United States, some nuclear critics oppose the technology in absolute terms and want existing facilities dismantled as soon as possible. Others appear prepared to accept plants that are either operating or under construction, but oppose new commitments. Still others are worried about specific issues—reactor safety, nuclear weapons proliferation, waste disposal—but claim a willingness to accept nuclear power in principle. In addition, some persons, who seem to be more numerous, or at least more visible, outside the United States, oppose nuclear power as a symbol of an entire social structure that they reject.

Although there are wide variations across countries in the forms that opposition to nuclear power has taken, it is evident that there are certain conditions under which this opposition can influence nuclear growth and others that, at least in the short term, effectively preclude it from doing so.

For example, reactor siting decisions are subject to local or provincial government approval in the United States, the Federal Republic of Germany, Canada, Japan, and Sweden; but not in the United Kingdom or France. In general, local or provincial government involvement works to the advantage of the nuclear critics. Licensing decisions can be challenged in the courts in the United States and the Federal Republic of Germany; but not in Canada, France, Japan, Sweden, or the United Kingdom.

In Sweden, the United Kingdom, and France, authority to certify the "need" for a new reactor rests unambiguously with the national government. In the Federal Republic of Germany and Canada, it rests with regional governments, as to a growing degree

it also does in the United States. In this area, too, regional governmental control is an asset for nuclear critics.

On the whole, the evidence of the 1970's strongly suggests
that in the developed countries nuclear power is vulnerable to
criticism where political authority is fragmented by federalism
and/or where judicial authorities exercise broad mandates to challenge administrative agencies. Conversely, nuclear development
benefits from centralization of government and narrow limits on
rights of judicial review. Only in the two quite different countries
of France and the U.S.S.R. have nuclear advocates been able, for
the time being at least, to keep nuclear decision-making free from
a tangle of procedural knots that will take time and political power
to undo.

Many American nuclear advocates, however, often speak and
act as if they do not understand that the explanation for the
striking success of the French nuclear program is not their
"greater rationality," but rather is deeply imbedded in the bureaucratic structures of this European country itself. Licensing reform
is not merely administrative rationalization. It is modification of
basic *rights* of political participation.

During the 1960's and early 1970's the major political parties
in Western Europe were generally favorable, or at least indifferent, to nuclear power. Although conservative parties remain
largely pro-nuclear, some new patterns began to emerge in the late
1970's. Minority "center" parties in Scandinavia became decid-
edly anti-nuclear, while liberal parties in the Federal Republic of
Germany and the United Kingdom split on the issue. This was an
important development since many of these parties held the balance of power in coalition governments in several countries.

The large social democratic parties of Central and Northern
Europe—in Austria, Switzerland, Denmark, the Federal Republic
of Germany, Norway, Sweden—were all deeply divided over the
nuclear issue and, as a consequence, often lost significant political
power. The powerful communist parties of Southern Europe—in
France, Italy, and Spain—remained strong nuclear advocates, although they typically demanded nationalization of various sectors
of the industry. Across Western Europe, an anti-nuclear alliance
of farmers and urban intellectuals faced an equally odd pro-nuclear

coalition of urban workers and members of the industrial establishment.

In 1982, there were about 255 operational nuclear power plants in the world. These plants represented an aggregate electrical generating capacity of about 160 GW. About one-third of this capacity was in the United States. The rest was widely dispersed among 21 other countries of which only three, France, Japan, and the U.S.S.R., accounted for more than 10 percent each.[38]

The world's 1982 total of about 160 GW of operational nuclear capacity represented about 35 percent of the approximately 460 GW that had been ordered since the first power producing reactors were purchased in England in the early 1950's. At the current rate of construction, approximately two-thirds of the reactors that had been ordered—representing about 200 GW —will enter operation during the 1980's, more than doubling the world's aggregate nuclear generating capacity. Only the United States, the U.S.S.R., France, and Japan will, respectively account for more than 10 percent of worldwide generating capacity.

The future of the other approximate 100 GW that remained "on order," or, in some cases actually under construction in 1982 was extremely uncertain. For only in France and the U.S.S.R. was it reasonably sure that all of the reactors that in 1982 were either on the order books or under construction would be completed on schedule or even completed at all.

Elsewhere, this question is only one of the many questions about the future of nuclear power. For the United States, which still has both the world's largest nuclear program and the most real alternatives to nuclear power for the 1990's, the uncertainties are particularly vexing.

Consider first the seventy-five reactors that were operating in 1982. Without expansion of spent fuel storage capacity in the early 1980's many of these plants will be forced to shut down in the late 1980's. The time left to develop such capacity is short. It will require at least three to four years to design, license, and build new, at-reactor storage facilities. "Away-from-reactor" (AFR) facilities are available in principle, but the means to move spent fuel in significant amounts from power plants to AFR's is not. Several years of design, construction, and licensing lead-time are involved here also. Yet in 1982 this increasingly acute operational problem remained far down the list of nuclear programs receiving sustained and competent attention either in or outside the federal government.

Should the government try to prevent the non-safety-related shutdown of operating reactors in the 1980's? The answer is pretty clearly yes.

There is no significant safety problem associated with indefinite interim spent-fuel storage. Moreover, while the operating nuclear power plants supply little more than 10 percent of the country's total electricity demand, their regional importance is far greater. New England, the upper Midwest (especially around Chicago), and the southern Atlantic states all receive more than one-third of their electricity from nuclear power, even if no more nuclear plants go into operation. Although we cannot predict the precise effects of a widespread shutdown of operating reactors in the 1980's, it is a good bet that it would cause a major regional, if not national, economic catastrophe.

A vigorous government effort to find a scientifically acceptable solution to the disposal problem is the key to eliminating the spent-fuel bottleneck that threatens reactor shutdowns in the 1980's. Maintaining the momentum of the government's waste disposal program will require a compromise on the AFR issue. It seems sensible for Congress to give the federal government authority to build and operate some minimum level of emergency temporary fuel storage capacity. This is necessary to guarantee that no reactors will have to be shut down merely because there is no place to put spent fuel.

But, what about shutting down reactors for safety reasons—poor design, poor location, or poor management? Making such a decision obviously requires excellent and delicate judgment, for the stakes, whatever their exact magnitude, are plainly large. The key point, however, is that the burden of proof shifted decisively during 1979. The Three Mile Island accident vindicated the pragmatic nuclear critics, notably the Union of Concerned Scientists, in one of their main contentions about the industry—poor management.

In the words of the President's Commission that investigated

Three Mile Island, "To prevent nuclear accidents as serious as Three Mile Island, fundamental changes will be necessary in the organization, procedures, and practices—and above all—in the attitudes of the Nuclear Regulatory Commission and, to the extent that the institutions we investigated are typical, of the nuclear industry."[39]

In the 1980's the burden lies squarely on nuclear advocates and regulators to satisfy skeptical people that nuclear plants are being designed, built, and operated with the competence and skill that the country was so long, so monotonously, and, it turns out, so incorrectly assured were already commonplace. The nuclear industry and its regulators will also have to stabilize nuclear capital costs. With cost estimates for new plants ranging as high as $3 billion, the traditional argument over the relative costs of electricity from nuclear and coal has become moot. The blunt truth is that the investor-owned electric utility industry is simply not able to bear the financial burden of decade-long, multibillion-dollar construction projects. Unless real nuclear capital costs are, at long last, stabilized during the 1980's, the nuclear promise will have melted away forever.

The nuclear critics also face an important challenge. They must be sufficiently objective to recognize that proofs of design and management competence can never be absolute; some unknowns and imponderables will always remain. The best that we can ever expect is to be able to exercise judgment on incomplete data and partially tested theory.

But three years after the Three Mile Island accident evidence of any progress, especially on the government side, remains sparse. In January 1980 a Washington law firm that had been hired by the Nuclear Regulatory Commission to analyze the accident in Pennsylvania found the agency still "incapable" of supervising safety at nuclear power plants: "In our opinion, the Commission is incapable in its present configuration of managing a comprehensive national safety program for existing nuclear power plants adequate to ensure public health and safety."[40] Nearly three years later no one had made much progress in rectifying the situation. Can it be so obscure to the friends of nuclear power in the executive branch of the federal government and in the United

States Congress that if the Nuclear Regulatory Commission cannot unambiguously establish its competence and its legitimacy in the very early 1980's, the nuclear dream will, indeed, be forever shattered? Cleaning up the debris from the 1979 regulatory meltdown in Washington is at least as important to the future of nuclear power as cleaning up the debris from the near reactor meltdown at Harrisburg.

On the order of $40 billion has been invested in the sixty reactors still under construction in 1982. If their owners are unable to complete and bring them into operation, the consequences would be disastrous, not only for the stockholders but perhaps for the entire financial community.

Then, too, the approximate 65 GW of generating capacity that the nuclear plants under construction represent are the equivalent of about 1.5 million barrels of oil a day in new energy supplies. While it is true that not all of the nuclear capacity would actually displace or forestall oil consumption in the 1980's and beyond, as much as one-third of it might.[41] Because of the foreign oil issue and because of the large amounts of money involved, the question of what to do with partially built nuclear power plants will be one of the most acrimonious energy policy questions of the 1980's. For any one person, the answer will require a complex judgment about reactor safety, the prospects for waste disposal, and expectations about future growth in electricity demand.

It has to be stressed that this judgment involves a very real dilemma. First, it is obvious that both federal and state governments should proceed with a great deal of caution in licensing new nuclear power plants for operation. Here, even more so than in the case of operating reactors, the burden is on those who seek or want to approve such licenses to have answers to specific technical criticisms of the standards and practices that have governed their design, siting, and construction and that will govern their operation and inspection. Still, failure to allow a completed nuclear plant to begin operation would mean financial disaster for its owners. In many cases, the cost of the plant will substantially exceed the net worth of the company or companies that have built it. The unadorned truth is that there is no easy way to write off the tens of billions of dollars invested in partially built nuclear plants. The investment is an enormous outstanding bill that comes due for someone—investor, lender, ratepayer, or taxpayer—during the 1980's and 1990's.

The waste disposal problem had made extension of the plant order moratorium into the middle or late 1980's highly probable before Three Mile Island. That accident, the regulatory meltdown that followed, and the growing financial problems of the electric utility industry have combined to make such an extension a virtual certainty for the 1980's.

As recently as early 1978, Sir Brian Flowers, one of the European pioneers of atomic energy, declared: "Nuclear power is the only energy source we can rely upon at present for massive contributions to our energy needs up to the end of the century, and if necessary beyond."[42]

In the United States there is simply no reasonable possibility for "massive contributions" from nuclear power for at least the rest of the twentieth century. Nuclear power offers no short-term solution to the problem of America's growing dependence on imported oil.

What about the longer-term, the early twenty-first century? One basic fact seems reasonably clear as far in the future as the early decades of the next century: for the United States nuclear power—even then—will probably be the chief alternative to coal for base-load electricity production.

Is such an alternative needed? This is a very difficult question to answer, in part because we can do little more than guess about how much new base-load generating capacity will then be required. There are major uncertainties about the health, safety, and environmental impacts of coal. Energy policymakers in the early twenty-first century may well want a non-oil or a non-gas alternative to coal for base-load electric power production. If the nuclear dream is allowed to vanish in the 1980's and 1990's, the only presently feasible alternative may not be available.

Hence, we believe that serious efforts should be made in the early and mid-1980's to sustain the nuclear option by keeping existing plants in operation and licensing those under construction to begin operation, subject to the tests and conditions that we have described. It is worth repeating that these are not easy tests.

A widely respected and generally sympathetic observer of nuclear power wrote in early 1980: ". . . without a fundamental reform of our society's institutions for dealing with nuclear power, . . . we can expect it to wither away."[43]

We agree, and we also worry that "fundamental reform" simply may not be possible.

6 | CONSERVATION: THE KEY ENERGY SOURCE

DANIEL YERGIN

There is a source of energy that produces no radioactive waste, nothing in the way of petrodollars, and very little pollution. Moreover, the source can provide the energy that conventional sources may not be able to furnish.

The source might be called energy efficiency, for Americans like to think of themselves as an efficient people. But the energy source is generally known by the more prosaic term *conservation*. To be semantically accurate, the source should be called conservation energy, to remind us of the reality—that conservation is no less an energy alternative than oil, gas, coal, or nuclear. Indeed, in the near term, conservation could do more than any of the conventional sources to help the country deal with the energy problem it has.

If the United States were to make a serious commitment to conservation, it might well consume perhaps 30 percent less energy than it now does, and still enjoy the same or an even higher standard of living. That saving would not hinge on a major technological breakthrough, and it would require only modest adjustments in the way people live. Moreover, the cost of conservation energy is very competitive with other energy sources. The possible energy savings would be the equivalent of the elimination of all imported oil—and then some.

How could this come about? One must understand that there is very great flexibility in how much energy is required, and how much is actually used, for this or that purpose. To give a simple example, toast can be made on a barbecue, in a broiler—or in a toaster. The end product is the same—toast—but the methods employed to make it vary greatly in energy consumed and waste produced. The making of toast illustrates the central point of this chapter—that much less energy than is now consumed can be used to achieve the same end.[1]

The barriers to the potential savings through conservation are very great, but they are rarely technological. Although some of the barriers are economic, they are in most cases institutional, political, and social. Overcoming them requires a government policy that gives this "energy source" a chance equal in the marketplace to that enjoyed by conventional sources of energy.

But why should the country place greater emphasis on conservation?

We have already discussed the substantial difficulties and very considerable social costs that attend excessive dependence on foreign oil, the limited productive capacity of domestic oil and gas, the high uncertainties of increased reliance on nuclear power, and the moderate growth that might be expected in coal. Conservation may well be the cheapest, safest, most productive energy alternative readily available in large amounts. And conservation is a quality energy source. It does not threaten to undermine the international monetary system, nor does it emit carbon dioxide into the atmosphere, nor does it generate problems comparable to nuclear waste. And contrary to the conventional wisdom, conservation can stimulate innovation, employment, and economic growth.[2] Since the United States uses almost a third of all the oil used in the world every day, major reduction in U.S. demand would have a major impact on the international energy markets.

A firm commitment to conservation is also required for American foreign policy to become credible on energy and nuclear proliferation issues. How can the United States ask the Europeans and the Japanese to give up the fast breeder reactor and reprocessing if it does not hold out some alternative—that is, less pressure on the international oil market? How can the United States ask its allies to join in significant foreign policy initiatives that might affect oil supplies from one or another producer without helping to compensate them by reducing demand—a political problem dramatized by the seizure of the American Embassy in Tehran in November 1979? In fact, foreigners often seem to pay much greater attention than do Americans to the relation between U.S. energy demand and these kinds of issues. For, in their eyes, the oil problem is not merely an OPEC problem, a supply problem. It is a problem of supply and demand—a problem of OPEC, on one side, and of the U.S. and other consumers on the other.

THREE TYPES OF CONSERVATION |

One can pick up a piece of coal, hold it in one's hand, and say, "This is coal." Conservation is far harder to grasp and comprehend. While it involves a host of different things—heat pumps, insulation, new engines—it also involves changes in methods, and even more important, an ongoing commitment to promote and implement conservation. To clarify matters, we can identify three categories of energy conservation, although the boundaries among them are fuzzy. The first two are not desirable. The third is.

The first category of conservation is out-and-out *curtailment*. When supplies are suddenly interrupted, energy saving is forced as factories are closed and working days lost, and people cut down on driving because they cannot obtain gasoline. This is what happened when interstate natural gas ran short in 1976 and 1977, during the coal strike of 1977 and 1978, and during the gas lines of 1979. The country can expect more curtailment in the future if sensible actions are not taken now.

A second category is *overhaul*, dramatically changing the way Americans live and work. An extreme example would be the outlawing of further suburbanization, forcing people to move into the urban center and live in tall buildings not equipped with places to park a car. Very few people would willingly accept that kind of energy conservation program.

To many people, energy conservation has suggested only curtailment or overhaul—something repressive and most un-American, involving cutting back, rationing, and unemployment. They have seen it as the product of an anti-growth crusade led by the granola-chomping children of the affluent. Unhappily, some of the language of the Carter Administration—such as President Carter's insistence on "sacrifice"—strengthened this unpleasant and misleading imagery in the mind of the public, although Carter generally supported conservation. President Reagan, who generally did not, went further in emphasizing the negative imagery when he declared that conservation means "we'll be too hot in the summer and too cold in the winter."

But there is a third way to think about conservation: as a form of *adjustment,* entailing such things as insulating the house, making automobiles, industrial processes, and home appliances more efficient, and capturing waste heat. This can be called *productive conservation,* which encourages changes in capital stock and daily behavior that promote energy savings in a manner that is economically and socially nondisruptive. Its aim is to use less energy than has been the habit to accomplish some task—whether it be to heat a home or to make a widget—in order to prevent disruption later. Conservation, therefore, is not a theological or ideological issue. It should be pursued not as an end in itself, but as a means toward greater social and economic welfare, as a way to promote the well-being of the citizenry. As two prominent analysts, Lee Schipper and Joel Darmstadter, have expressed it, "The most impelling factor in encouraging conservation action is the cost of not conserving."[3]

The Obstacles |

One major roadblock to productive conservation is its very character—it is a highly fragmented area of inquiry that certainly lacks glamour. There is in this country a natural-enough desire for a technological fix, preferably one big one, that will solve all energy problems—another Manhattan Project, another man-in-space program. Indeed, some survey data indicate that many Americans simply assume that high technology will step in to "save" them just in time.[4] It is certainly easier for the Federal government to organize itself to do one big thing, but, alas, that is not what productive conservation is about. It involves 50,000 or 50 million things, big, medium, and little, and not in the one centralized place where the energy is produced, but in the decentralized milieu where it is consumed. Conservation is prosaic, even boring.

At an energy conference in Los Angeles, the oil people told the heroic story of tapping Alaska's North Slope; the nuclear people talked about advanced nuclear technology; the coal people discussed synthetic fuels and slurry pipelines. The engineer from Los Angeles' Department of Water and Power then stood up to explain how it got the residents of Los Angeles to go along with an effort that substantially reduced consumption of electricity: "We advised citizens to do such things as shut their curtains at night." Here was a conference devoted to the great energy crisis, the moral equivalent of war, and here was a man who was saying that the solution is for people to do such bold things as close their curtains at night.

This is why, when an aide to one of the most powerful senators on energy issues was asked why the distinguished legislator has never given a speech on conservation, the aide replied, "It would either be filled with platitudes or so specific that everybody's nose would fall into his Rice Krispies."[5]

The lack of drama has restricted not only policy and public attention, but also scientific interest in conservation-oriented research. As one physicist has observed, "Little glamour has adhered to research in heat transfer at modest temperatures, relative to heat transfer at the temperature of a nose cone at reentry into the atmosphere; or the hysteresis losses of rubber tires, relative to the neutron losses in nuclear reactors."

A second obstacle to conservation is the way the energy debate has been shaped in this country. When the crisis broke in 1973, the country turned to the experts, the people who had spent their working lives trying to increase energy supplies through oil, gas, coal, and nuclear. Not surprisingly, these people forcefully advocated a rapid further build-up of conventional sources, and their voices were powerful. After all, they belonged to organizations set up to accomplish such tasks, and the organizations had often been admirably effective at doing this, and in the process contributed much to the general welfare. Even if economic self-interest had not been involved, points of view, convictions, and experience acquired over many decades of working to provide more energy would naturally have caused these people to emphasize energy production rather than conservation.

Their voices were all the more powerful because the other side was so weak. What serious "expert" would advocate dampening demand? What economic entity had an interest—economic or otherwise—in promoting such a view, lobbying Congress, spending millions to advertise the case? As Roger Sant, formerly assistant administrator for conservation in the Federal Energy Administration, observed: "Outside of perhaps the insulation manufacturers, there is no organized conservation industry in this country. So we have nothing to compare to the energy producers in terms of marketing, distribution, and lobbying. The oil companies and utilities are busy talking up how much they need to produce. But no one's out there wholesaling conservation by the ton and barrel." The conservation industry has grown considerably since 1975, but it is still a fledgling. Thus, the energy suppliers pretty much shaped the terms of the debate, and established what was important and what was not.[6]

The discussion has become much less one-sided. The Carter Administration, in its first year, gave an imprimatur of seriousness to the case for conservation. Introducing his first energy program in April 1977, President Carter declared that conservation "is the cornerstone of our policy." Encountering a good deal of political resistance as well as apathy, the Administration subsequently retreated, eventually focusing its efforts on synthetic fuels. In sum, the effort to reshape the national energy debate to the point where conservation would be regarded as a serious energy source was slow, halting, and wholly inadequate during the 1970's. Today, however, conservation—aided by a lengthening record and a shift in public attitudes—is at last being taken seriously across a broad spectrum of American society.[7]

A third obstacle to productive conservation may be summarized by the maxim, Let the market do its work. As should be clear, we are convinced that American energy prices should reflect the realities of the world market and should not be artificially restrained. But decontrol of rising real prices is not enough. Even if prices did begin to rise substantially tomorrow, conservation would still be seriously hampered by political and social barriers. Excessive faith in the market tends to obscure the difficulties and requirements of the needed transition away from the world of imported oil. Just because prices go up does not mean that people will take certain steps—or will have easy access to capital even if they do want to take those steps. Time has been telescoped for the energy problem. Thus, the process of adaptation needs to be speeded up.[8]

The question of price is one of the main reasons why the entire energy debate has been so bitter. Any significant change in energy prices raises real distributional issues—some people will be hurt and others stand to gain. To say that these issues are secondary is to ignore the way interest groups and regions assert their claims in the American political process. Therefore, an effective conservation strategy has to look for methods to mediate the distributional claims and has to provide incentives and cushions to reduce the hardship of higher prices on lower-income consumers.

The fourth barrier is a fundamental misconception about the relation of energy use and economic growth. Many believe in what might be called the iron law of the energy—GNP link. Some economists, as well as a number of decision-makers in business, labor, and government, have believed that there is a direct, even inevitable, one-to-one correlation between economic growth and consumption of energy, and accordingly, that encouraging conservation could easily plunge the nation into serious economic straits. The *Energy Report* from the Chase Manhattan Bank went so far as to say that "there is no documented evidence that indicates the long-lasting, consistent relationship between energy use and GNP will change in the future. There is no sound, proven basis for believing a billion dollars of GNP can be generated with less energy in the future." And an internal communication of one of the seven major oil companies said, "There is no empirical evidence to indicate that the coupling of energy to economic growth can be uncoupled." The basic idea behind the iron link was pungently expressed by the head of the Texas Railroad Commission:

TABLE 6·1
RATIO OF ENERGY GROWTH TO ECONOMIC GROWTH
IN THE UNITED STATES

	Unit of Energy for Every Unit of GNP	Economic Growth Rates (percent)
1950–55	0.63	4.3
1955–60	1.10	2.2
1960–65	0.81	4.8
1965–70	1.45	3.2
1970–75	0.65	2.1
1975–79	0.57	4.4

Source: Herman Franssen, Energy—An Uncertain Future: An Analysis of U.S. and World Energy Projections Through 1990 (Washington, D.C.: Government Printing Office, 1978), p. 17, updated.

"This country did not conserve its way to greatness. It produced itself to greatness."[9]

But the iron link has, in fact, yet to be convincingly demonstrated. It remains unproved, as can be seen by looking at the historical record and by comparing the United States with other advanced industrial countries.

There has been wide and erratic variation in the relationship between energy and GNP in the United States. Table 6-1 expresses the ratio of energy to gross national product—that is, the amount of energy growth for every unit of GNP growth. As can be seen in the table, the ratio varies from .57 to 1.45.

Going back to the late nineteeth century, the variations in the relationship between energy and GNP are even greater. As a study by the Conference Board has summarized, "Energy use and economic growth are certainly not independent of one another, but the link between them is more elastic than is commonly assumed."[10]

A similar insight is obtained by comparing the American experience with that of other advanced industrial countries (Table 6-2), which suggests that the realm of possibility for energy savings in the United States is rather broad.[11] Thus, West Germany

TABLE 6·2
COMPARATIVE ENERGY/OUTPUT RELATIONSHIPS,
1980

Country	Gross National Product per Capita (dollars)	Energy Consumption per Capita (tons of coal equivalent)	Energy/GNP Ratio Tons of Coal Equivalent per $ Million GNP	Index (U.S. = 100)
United States	11,500	10.4	9.1	100
Britain	9,100	4.9	5.4	59
Canada	10,300	10.1	9.8	108
France	12,300	4.8	3.9	43
Japan	9,400	3.9	4.2	46
Mexico	2,400	1.8	7.8	86
Spain	5,500	3.0	5.4	59
Sweden	14,300	6.3	4.4	48
Venezuela	4,000	3.1	7.7	85
U.S.S.R.	5,200	6.0	10.7	118
West Germany	13,400	6.4	4.8	53

Sources: Energy Decade; World Energy Industries; United Nations; Handbook of Economic Statistics

Note: GNP expressed in dollars per capita vary widely from year to year because of changes in exchange rates.

consumed about half as much energy for each dollar of gross product as the United States, and France even less. Of course, such comparisons cannot be taken as perfectly equivalent, because of obvious differences involving such factors as exchange rates, political culture, government policies, geography, import dependence, and industrial structure. The broad comparisons do indeed mask a great deal of variation among sectors within countries.[12] Even so, the comparative data seem to make clear that substantial but non-disruptive energy savings are possible in the United States; for while the differences among these societies are important, they are not as important as the fundamental similarities— a common set of problems, a common technology for heavy industry, a common architecture, and common modes of transport.[13]

More people are coming to recognize that the iron link is not ferrous at all, but on the contrary, elastic. A far-ranging and innovative study of energy prospects in Western Europe by "Nine Wise Men" of the European Community has argued that decoupling (or "disassociation") is essential as a policy goal in order to maintain economic growth in western societies. In releasing a report projecting that energy consumption would increase more slowly than economic growth in the years ahead, the manager for energy economics at Shell U.S.A. simply announced, "We have found that we could decouple the two."[14]

When the Lights Go Out |

The case of Los Angeles after the embargo provides a dramatic example of how flexible energy use can be. The Department of Water and Power (DWP) provides the city with electricity, half of which is generated from oil. Air-quality control restrictions require the DWP to use low sulphur oil, thus limiting possible sources. Like most utilities, the DWP had enjoyed very rapid growth—a yearly average of 7 percent between 1950 and 1969, and 5 percent in the early 1970's.[15]

In November 1973, shortly after the Arab oil embargo went into effect, the DWP realized that 11 million barrels of already contracted North African low-sulphur oil (more than half its annual consumption of oil) would not be delivered. Early in December, newspapers ran stories with panic headlines like "What to Do When the Lights Go Out."

Facing a substantial shortfall in electricity production, anxious city officials discussed ways to reduce consumption. They talked about limiting the work week, instituting rolling blackouts in various neighborhoods, and hiking prices massively. But they feared that major loss of jobs would result from reducing the work week, that the rolling blackouts would be a nightmare to administer, and that massive price hikes would arouse a storm of protest.

In the middle of December, an ad hoc committee, representing a broad coalition of civic, business, and labor leaders, came up with an alternative—to set mandatory targets for reductions for all customers—but to leave it to the customers themselves to implement the specific cuts. And so, in mid-December, the city council adopted a two-phased Emergency Energy Curtailment Plan, the purpose of which was to "significantly reduce the consumption of electricity over an extended period of time, thereby extending the available fuel required for the production of electricity, while reducing the hardships on the city and the general public to the greatest possible extent."

Under Phase I, to go into effect immediately, customers were to cut back on their use, compared to the same billing period of the previous year. There was a stiff penalty for noncompliance: a 50 percent surcharge on the entire bill. The aim was to reduce the city's total electricity consumption by 12 percent. Phase II, to go into effect at a later date, set higher targets. The penalty for noncompliance with Phase II was to be even more severe—a cutoff of service. But the city never needed to institute Phase II, because Phase I was so successful; moreover, penalties for Phase I were never even applied (although, of course, neither officials nor consumers knew at the beginning that this would be the case).

The response to the targets of Phase I, to everyone's surprise, went far beyond the targets themselves.

	Target	Actual Reduction
Residential	10%	18%
Industrial	10	11
Commercial	20	28

The total drop was 17 percent, against the target of 12 percent. Much of the adjustment in commercial establishments, which accounted for 50 percent of electricity usage prior to the cutback, was done mostly through better control of lighting and air-conditioning. The Los Angeles Dodgers met their target by the simple expedient of starting baseball games at 7:30 instead of 8 P.M.

Philip Hawley, head of the ad hoc mayor's committee and chief author of the Los Angeles Plan, has observed, "It was important to tell people what the specific job was, to have them understand what was expected of them, to give them specific energy reduction targets. . . . Our job was to reduce the usage of energy, not to mandate life-styles, not to reduce hours that businesses were open, and not to indulge in costly methods and select certain segments of the economy, but to protect employment to the maximum degree possible, and to try to do this in a way that would result in a minimum of job loss or preferably no job loss."

In May 1974, two months after the Arab embargo was lifted, the program was suspended, but its impact could still be felt a year later; in May of 1975, total electricity sales were 8 percent lower than the 1973 level. In addition, there had been a far greater reduction in DWP consumption than in that of the three other largest electric utilities in California, none of which had adopted such a program.

Los Angeles, in the course of a crisis, had stumbled onto a very effective program—a combination of price and regulation that might be called a semi-market approach. The program brought dramatic savings with a minimum of sacrifice and disruption, and required virtually no investment. Two factors made for the program's success. The first was a broadly based consensus emerged among civic leaders that this plan was the fairest and most effective response to a pending crisis. Second, while the program set targets, it still possessed a great deal of flexibility and left it to consumers to figure out how and where to make their own cuts, to make their own decisions about "essential" and "nonessential" uses. What this Los Angeles experience tells us, fundamentally, is that in many circumstances, great flexibility exists for energy use.

Of all the evidence, the most compelling is what has happened on a national scale. Considerable flexibility has been demonstrated between energy and economic activity. By 1981, the United States was almost 18 percent more energy efficient than it had been in 1973. That is, it took 18 percent less energy to generate each unit of gross national product—a dramatic demonstration of the flexibility between energy use and economic activity.*

Let us now look at the possibilities for conservation in the United States. The discussion is organized by consuming sectors, each of which poses different problems. (See Table 6-3 for a breakdown as to sectors.)

---

*Although, as we note later, part of this greater efficiency reflected a shift in economic activity away from energy intensive production and activities.

TABLE 6·3
U.S. ENERGY CONSUMPTION BY SECTOR, 1981

Sector	Consumption (oil equivalent, mbd)	Percent of Total Consumption
Residential/ Commercial	12.2	35
Industrial	13.8	39
Transportation	9.2	26
TOTAL	35.2	100%

Source: Monthly Energy Review

Transportation focuses on the automobile, where the existence of only a few manufacturers makes regulation an effective way to communicate the need for energy saving. Industry is characterized by a larger number of decision-makers, generally informed about costs and alternatives and likely to respond to clear economic signals. Buildings, on the other hand, involve millions of poorly informed decision-makers within a highly decentralized milieu where market imperfections loom large and where the capital stock has a very long life.

TRANSPORTATION |

The abrupt transition into the era of expensive and insecure oil has focused attention on the transportation sector of our economy. For the most part, conservation involves a multitude of decision-makers. One exception does stand out—the automobile, which is the largest single component in the transportation sector. Of course, millions of individuals make decisions about buying and using automobiles every year. But only a few producers are engaged in automobile manufacture, and they are its key decision-makers. Moreover, the automobile is the one and only consumer product that exerts a disproportionate and indeed massive effect on energy consumption. Insofar as oil is the most important part of the series of problems that comprise the "energy problem," the automobile is at the heart of it. While the transportation sector uses a quarter of the energy consumed in the United States, it uses half the oil. The car in turn uses the bulk of the transport sector's energy. To put the matter into world scale: almost one out of nine barrels of oil used in the world every day is burned as gasoline on the American highway. The American automobile owner consumes an amount of petroleum products almost equivalent to American oil imports. Interrupt oil, and the American automobile is interdicted. The car, then, is a very big piece of the energy puzzle.[16]

The Auto Way of Life |

American society, as it has evolved since World War II, has become enormously dependent on the automobile, both as a means of transportation and as a source of economic activity. Most suburbs, whose development has depended on the private auto, would be stranded without it. In addition, one out of every five workers in the United States is involved in the manufacture, distribution, servicing, or commercial use of vehicles. In other words, the future of the American economy is intimately involved with the future of the car. Finally, of course, the automobile is a wonderful invention, providing easy mobility, offering people the opportunity to go—by themselves or in groups—where they want and when they want—traffic conditions permitting.

Until the 1970's, energy was not much of a consideration either for those designing and marketing cars or for those buying them. The easy availability of gasoline was simply assumed.[17] That has changed. The old relationship between Americans and their cars, at least with their old-style cars, is a thing of the past.

The automobile is certainly amenable to becoming more efficient through technological fixes—and rather swift ones, since the auto stock turns over more rapidly than most other forms of capital. Because about half of the American automobile population is replaced within five years, an improvement in mileage efficiency, which is a form of conservation, can make itself felt quickly on the international energy market.[17]

Stretching a Gallon |

Increasing the miles obtained from each gallon of gasoline (mpg) is a form of conservation that has very little effect on life-style.[18] Autos for the 1974 model year, which went on sale just before the embargo, averaged 14 miles per gallon. The average for domestically produced models was even lower—12.8 mpg. In the same year, it was quite possible to purchase comfortable European or Japanese imports that got 20 to 30 miles to the gallon. Not only was mpg low in American-made vehicles, but it had been declining since the middle 1960's. The auto industry blamed the decline on government safety and air-pollution regulations instituted in the late 1960's. The pollution-control devices did impose a penalty— about 5 percent in 1975—but far more important was weight, the single most important factor in determining fuel economy, which had been increasing rapidly. For example, between 1968 and 1973, Chevrolet's full-sized V-8 four-door sedan gained 500 pounds, an increase typical for all the auto makers. The main reason for this was the development of larger and heavier engines for higher performance, the growing array of accessories and options, and other design changes that responded to marketing imperatives. Some accessories, like airconditioning, imposed double penalties, adding to weight and consuming energy directly.[19]

Bigger cars meant more value added, higher prices, and a larger profit margin for manufacturers. As a prominent auto executive pointed out in an interview with the author, "One of our top people in the 1950's was known for having said, 'Small cars mean small engines, small windows, small doors, and small profits.' " Also, competition from imports kept profit margins low on small cars.

Thus, before 1973, fuel efficiency was given a very low priority, and it was difficult for anyone inside Detroit management circles to argue convincingly that gas economy would find any response in the marketplace. Moreover, the manufacturers themselves tended to discount the dangers of any energy squeeze: World oil reserves were increasing and the real price of gasoline, declining. Detroit was also suspicious of what it thought might be oil-company special pleading.[20] "The industry was unprepared for the magnitude and the suddenness of the crisis," an executive observed. "In a way, the embargo was a boon because it raised the question of vehicle efficiency from an issue for debate within management to one of the highest priority for action."

As things turned out, the embargo helped those in management who wanted to give mileage greater attention, but who had consistently lost out when intracompany decisions were made. Once the oil crisis broke, auto-engine efficiency became a public policy issue. This was a reversal, for in the past, government policy had fostered increased auto use at the expense of mass transit.[21]

Four policy alternatives for reducing gasoline consumption were apparent. One was a substantial increase in gasoline prices through some mix of price deregulation and higher taxes. Intense political opposition ruled out this option in the middle 1970's. Thus, prices did not go up to encourage people to buy a more efficient car the next time, and prices certainly did not signal manufacturers that fuel economy should remain a matter of high priority. Indeed, prices deceived both auto buyers and auto makers. At the end of 1978, the real price of gasoline—that is, the price corrected for inflation—was no higher than in the halcyon days of 1960, the year that OPEC was founded. Prices began to rise again at the gasoline pump in real terms only with the second oil shock of 1979 and then with President Carter's courageous decision to move toward decontrol of domestic oil prices. In fact, inflation had actually cut the value of the federal gas tax 60 percent between 1959 and January 1980.[22]

A second method to promote efficiency that is common in Western Europe is a graduated tax on horsepower or weight.[23] But a tax of this kind can inhibit engineering innovations that could make even large cars much more efficient. A third approach was a flat minimum mileage standard for every car, but this would have placed American-manufactured cars at a disadvantage compared to imports.

Standards and Regulations |

In any case, the issue of increased fuel economy was considered too important to be left to the industry and the marketplace. The federal policy finally adopted was the establishment of fleet-average mileage standards.* It is attractive because it sets a target and allows the manufacturer the flexibility to experiment with ways to meet it. It assures them that their competitors will also have to meet the goal. For all cars manufactured after 1977, the Energy Policy and Conservation Act of 1975 established the following fuel economy standards:

Year	MPG
1978	18
1979	19
1980	20
1985	27.5

Thus, between 1973 and 1985, the efficiency is supposed to double. The Act also provided that standards be set subsequently for trucks and vans, and imposed substantial penalties for failure to meet the targets.

Much of the auto industry vigorously opposed the standards, which puzzled many people, including the then-president of the United Auto Workers, Leonard Woodcock, who told a Congressional committee in 1975, "Unfortunately, the industry comes down here and always in their public postures takes a very hard line, which, frankly, they do not pursue when we have conversations with them. I do not know what it gets them, because it puts them in a position where their word is, very frankly, doubted." In fact, as GM was publicly protesting the standards, the company was already taking weight out of its models (downsizing) as the quickest way to improve efficiency. Ford did not oppose the standards, already having concluded that they would constitute the least disruptive form of regulation, which was inevitable.[24]

The issue of regulation, in fact, was at stake for the manufacturers. The automobile industry is currently in the process of becoming a regulated industry, which it does not like. The move began in the middle 1960's with the passing of auto pollution and safety regulations. But the fuel efficiency standards, which could affect profits and market share, were considered more threatening. The manufacturers' bind is understandable, for they are asked to

---

*Fleet average means that the target applies to the average mileage of a manufacturer's entire production. Thus, individual models might fall below the target.

deal at one and the same time with pollution and safety, which can add weight and so reduce miles per gallon, and with the demand to increase efficiency. All this, plus the consumer who wants high performance and an agreeable sticker price—and who sometimes cares about fuel efficiency and sometimes does not.[25]

So it is no wonder GM's president was exasperated when he said during the 1975 hearings on fuel economy, "We do not want any handouts, we do not want any taxes, and we do not want any regulations . . . we do not like that sort of thing." In 1978 Henry Ford II also attacked the move to regulations, saying, "It is no secret that the automobile industry has been the prime target of those who have presumed to tell the American people, through single-minded and hastily drawn regulations, what is best for them." Yet in the same statement Ford approved of the three main forms of regulation: "I am not at all reluctant to say that some automotive regulations have been needed . . . Some obviously desirable goals such as reduced emissions of pollutants and increased passenger protection in the event of accidents could not have been achieved as readily without uniform, across-the-board government mandates. In retrospect, I think it is fair to say also that the law requiring greater fuel economy in motor vehicle usage has moved us faster toward energy conservation goals than competitive, free-market forces would have done."[26]

Despite their complaints, the auto makers hastened to meet the fuel economy standards, and have succeeded. The cumulative fuel savings that will result from the targets set up to 1985 could be as high as 20 billion barrels over the years 1975–2000—twice the reserves on the North Slope of Alaska.

But these potential savings need to be qualified. Actual driving results are lower than the Environmental Protection Agency tests indicate; by as much, in some circumstances, as 20 percent. Moreover, an unexpected boom in light truck sales in the late 1970's may have skewed the fleet composition and thus projections, although the recent trend toward small cars may have compensated for that surprising growth.[27]

Nevertheless, the march to the 27.5 mpg fleet average is well along toward completion and is unlikely to be interrupted. Attention now focuses on the issue of possible standards for the period beyond 1985.

Should the mandate be 40 to 50 miles per gallon for 1995?

There are technical barriers to further improvements. The major gains so far have been effected by weight reduction—the average U.S. car will have probably lost about 700 pounds between 1974 and 1981—and by the importation and commercialization of Japanese and European technology (some of it from foreign subsidiaries of American auto makers). These relatively easy options will soon have been fully exploited—at a cost of perhaps $10 to $20 billion out of a total industry investment of $80 billion by 1985. Thereafter, substantial technological innovation is needed in materials, engines, and design; and this kind of innovation, as opposed to styling, was not until recent years a major priority for the industry and its suppliers.[28]

Yet the technical problems are generally thought to be manageable. A car that meets fuel-efficiency goals—as well as safety, environmental, and comfort goals—appears within reach in current technological horizons. The existence of such cars as the Volkswagen diesel Rabbit, at 40 mpg, points to the technical plausibility. Indeed, there is reasonable discussion today about the possibility in the mid-1990's of an 80 to 90 mpg car, otherwise known as the "cucumber on wheels."[29]

The question for Detroit is what kind of market will exist for such a car, and at what cost it can be achieved. Will Detroit be capable of making such an adaptation? For the American manufacturers are in a considerably weaker position today than when they were first faced with standards in the middle 1970's. A substantial part of the American auto market has been lost to imports, especially to the Japanese companies. In 1960, Japan produced just 715,000 cars and trucks, compared to 7.9 million in the United States. Two decades later, Japanese production—now about 11 million vehicles—had overtaken that of the United States. In 1981, 1.68 million Japanese cars were sold in the United States.[30] Japan Inc. had overtaken Ford as number two.

The sudden swing to fuel efficiency as a major criterion by a much wider segment of the market caught Detroit unprepared. The sales of the American manufacturers plummeted, and, to varying degrees, they have been thrown into financial difficulties. In fact, the American companies might well be grateful for the initial fuel-efficiency standards against which some argued so strenuously, for without the push from mandated standards they might have found themselves even less well prepared, and in an even worse financial position than they currently are. Or there might have been a serious trade war between Japan and the United States because of even greater imports from Japan. As it is, in response to growing domestic pressures in the United States, Japan agreed in 1981 to set "voluntary restraints" on its auto exports to the United States. The American auto industry today is the single most compelling and disturbing case of an industry whose products and processes have been rendered obsolete by the sudden change in factor cost and availability engendered by the oil shocks.

In early 1979, Henry Ford II expressed a hope that the federal government "would give up" on efforts to push for tighter post-1985 fuel-economy standards. He expected that plenty of oil could be available from a variety of conventional and unconventional sources. That would hardly be the guiding premise in the auto industry today, as it struggles to adapt. Moreover, Detroit can be much more confident that consumer demand will support their efforts to manufacture more efficient vehicles, although the possible volatility in such demand—combined with declining real costs per mile driven as fuel efficiency increases—suggest that additional higher standards are needed to help shape the market in the post-1985 period and to protect the auto industry.[31]

The biggest constraint is financing—how to find the funds necessary to make the necessary capital investment, especially with reduced sales. True, some Detroit executives expect that substantially higher gasoline prices will cause a speedup in the turnover of the American automobile stock, and they hope to capture a large share of the expanding market. Indeed, one executive spoke privately of a "golden era" for auto manufacturers during the 1980's. But unless something of this sort occurs, then American manufacturers will have a very difficult time financing the move from the 27.5-miles-per-gallon standard in 1985 to a 50-mile-per-gallon standard by 1995.

Whereas in the middle 1970's the auto industry regarded the government as a nuisance and threat to be kept out of its business, circumstances now force it to look to Washington as a potential partner. The nation in turn finds itself asking how difficult it will be to sustain an auto industry turning out cars with a fuel efficiency adapted to the requirements of the time. A 50-mile-per-gallon fleet average might well save 2 to 3 million barrels a day by 1995 over what would be consumed if fleet averages remained at 27.5 miles per gallon.[32] But the cost is not yet clear.

A number of minor modifications in car care and motorist behavior could promote significant savings. One is the enforcement of the 55-mile-per-hour speed limit, which also reduces highway fatalities. Planning and consolidation of daily driving trips and better knowledge about the most efficient travel routes could save upward of a million barrels of oil per day. Flextime— to relieve congestion on mass transit facilities and roads—could also reduce gasoline demand. Significant savings can also come from proper maintenance. Poorly tuned engines and improperly inflated tires can impose a penalty of 6 to 10 percent on fuel usage. Keeping the national auto fleet properly maintained could bring considerable savings, perhaps equivalent to half the oil flowing through the Alaska pipeline. But the trend toward self-service is leading to worse maintenance. Just the simple requirement that all such stations have functioning, easy-to-use tire-checking equipment could in itself save significant gasoline.[33]

Ride Sharing |

Another way to increase the efficiency of the vehicle population is by increasing the number of riders per vehicle. Ride sharing— van and car pooling—could have a large impact on consumption with relatively little disruption. Table 6-4 indicates, in particular, the efficiency of van pooling. The focus here is on the trip to work, for about 35 percent of all vehicle miles are to and from work. Occupancy is at or below 1.4 persons per vehicle, compared to 2 or above on recreational and social trips. Moreover, over half of all work trips go to sites with 100 or more employees; 75 percent to sites with 50 or more employees. There

TABLE 6·4
ESTIMATES OF ENERGY REQUIRED BY VARIOUS
URBAN TRANSPORTATION MODES, 1977
(BTUs PER PASSENGER MILE)

Mode	Total Energy*	Operating Energy†
Van pool	2,400	1,600
Bus	3,100	2,600
Heavy rail transit (Old)	4,000	2,500
Commuter rail	5,000	2,600
Light rail transit	5,100	3,800
Car pool	5,500	3,700
Heavy rail transit (New)	6,600	3,600
Average automobile	10,200	7,900
Single-occupant automobile	14,200	11,000
Dial-a-Ride	17,200	9,700

*All forms of energy, computed on a door-to-door basis, adjusted for roundabout journeys. Includes energy to build and maintain road, track, and equipment.

†Propulsion only.

Source: Congressional Budget Office, Urban Transportation and Energy: The Potential Savings of Different Modes. Study Prepared for the Senate Committee on Environment and Public Works (Washington, D.C.: GPO, 1977), p. xvi.

have been many efforts to encourage ride sharing since 1973, many of them unsuccessful because they were promoted by highway departments that did not care. Where there has been committed leadership—for instance at 3M in Minneapolis, TVA in Nashville, and ARCO in Los Angeles—the results have been very good. This points to what might be a growing trend. Employers will take more responsibility for helping their employees get to work. In effect, travel, like subsidized meals in the company cafeteria, will become a fringe benefit. Positive incentives—from priority parking spaces to perhaps free transit on the company van—are required to make such systems work. Ride sharing is clearly one of the best short-term improvements on our current transportation system.[34]

Mass Transit |

The greatest uncertainty in the transportation sector can be found in the potential contribution of mass transit—fixed rail and bus systems—to energy conservation. The nub of the problem is to find a system flexible enough to connect the low-density suburb where the commuter lives with his workplace, which might be either in the high-density core or in dispersed sites around the city. During the many years of low and declining real price of gasoline, mass transit came to carry a lower and lower proportion of commuters. Systems were run down, neglected, and, as in the case of the Los Angeles trolley, actually disbanded. The challenge facing mass transit is to offer a service that is flexible, convenient, and comfortable, that does not entail a status drop for the rider, and that does not leave the rider feeling exposed to crime.

Much of the literature on mass transit today raises serious questions about the energy efficiency of such new rail systems as BART in San Francisco and the Washington, D.C., Metro. These systems, it is said, not only involve very high capital costs, but may actually use more energy than they save because of the energy required first for construction and then to get the passengers to the stations along the line. Moreover, critics point out that the construction of new systems can produce quite a disruption of an urban area.

Buses, on the other hand, can be a very energy-efficient way to move people about, especially if special lanes and other incentives are used to encourage bus riding. Of course, if a trip takes twenty minutes by car and fifty minutes by bus, most people who have the option will take the car. That would be an argument for more frequent service in smaller buses, rather than less frequent service in stretched buses.

In present circumstances, it seems quite premature to write off mass transit as unable to make a much larger contribution. For one thing, capital allocation since World War II has favored the car. Street and highway construction has produced a subsidy to the automobile, much of it paid by the federal government in years of low inflation, when mass transit was considered a local responsibility. Mass transit systems were allowed to deteriorate; capital budgets were constrained; operating budgets are still inadequately supported (a similar imbalance favored the truck over the railroad for transporting freight). Living patterns and behavior patterns that were the norm may change in an era of rising real costs of gasoline, and help provide the density that supports a mass transit system and encourages its use. Indeed, there could be a demand for mass transit considerably beyond the capacity of present systems. In addition, one can see, as with the Washington Metro, how a mass transit system can change the character of a city, knit a metropolitan area together, and maintain a vitality in an urban core.

Finally, to have observed the difference in two major urban areas during the gas lines of 1979—in Los Angeles and Boston—is to perceive how vulnerable in the era of expensive and insecure oil is a city without a viable mass transit alternative. Sometimes, of course, the idea that mass transit might function well in the urban United States seems beyond the realm of human comprehension. Yet, such systems do work reasonably well in other modern industrial societies, which is one of the many reasons why the mass transit option should not be written off, but rather experimented with and invigorated.[35]

"No Gas" |

Attention to the "cucumber on wheels" for 1995 should not divert attention from an immediate problem affecting the transportation sector—the likelihood of supply interruptions and OPEC price leaps in the context of constrained world supplies. The gas lines of 1979 should serve us as a reminder. Thus, there is a strong case for seeking to restrain and reshape gasoline demand in the very near term through a gas tax. Such an effort could be highly desirable for two reasons. First, it could take pressure off the world market and world prices for oil, and thus help to prevent—or at least blunt—future price and supply shocks arising in the chronically unstable international supply system. So much is obvious from the overwhelmingly large place U.S. gasoline consumption holds in world demand, and the relative flexibility that exists in how we use our cars. Second, such an effort could be necessitated in the context of an emergency, to restrain U.S. demand should an interruption occur. So it would be desirable to have it in place prior to the occurrence of an emergency.

These measures would encourage—and depend upon—the developments discussed so far: more efficient cars, convenient mass transit, ride sharing and van pooling, and better planning of all trips by auto.

The Energy Policy and Conservation Act of 1975 mandated that the United States establish a standby rationing plan for an emergency. Five years later, in 1980, a plan finally went on the books. This standby plan provided for a white market—that is, citizens could buy and sell their rationing coupons. This built needed flexibility into the plan.

A rationing system does offer more control over gasoline consumption. But it also brings a complex bureaucratic structure, and creates a second currency in the form of coupons. Rationing initially does look equitable, and psychologically it may be. In practice, this well may not be the case.

Exceptions and appeals would be numerous, and cumbersome to deal with. What seems equitable to a resident of New York does not necessarily seem equitable to a resident of Wyoming. A gas tax with rebates is functionally quite similar to rationing with a white market. It involves much less bureaucracy; the rebate can be constructed so that it actually favors lower income groups should this be necessary to overcome any inequitable effects of the tax. Some have suggested that a gasoline tax also involve a tax shift —that is, leading to a corresponding reduction in some other tax, such as Social Security.

In September 1981, President Reagan allowed Presidential authority to implement the emergency standby plan to expire. The Administration subsequently rescinded the plan itself. Reagan then vetoed a congressional effort to reconstitute the Presidential authority. So at this writing, the United States has no plan and the President no authority to respond to a disruption of oil supplies and panic among motorists. Congress, however—all too aware of the intense political pressure during a crisis—will probably try to devise a new plan.

The arguments for a tax over rationing are quite strong, at least in terms of taking steps to reshape demand and so help avert future supply crunches with their attendant gas lines and other disruptions. Some have even argued that a tax mechanism could be used as a preferred substitute for rationing in a supply interruption. Our politicians and policymakers have been excessively timid on the subject of a gas tax. Compare U.S. gasoline taxes to those of other Western countries:

TAX ON REGULAR GASOLINE, JANUARY 1982 (U.S. DOLLARS PER U.S. GALLON)

United States	$0.15
United Kingdom	1.12
West Germany	1.06
France	1.35
Italy	1.70

Source: International Energy Statistical Review.

It would certainly seem sensible to make greater use of tax in order to promote energy efficiency in the transportation sector—not as a punitive measure, but in order to help ensure that people do have some security in their ability to get about from one place to another.[36]

Some observers argue that a tax is not needed if efficient cars result from mandatory regulations. In fact, though, a gasoline tax still is needed to bring the price up to the real cost of gasoline to society; otherwise, an inefficiently high level of driving will occur and gas guzzlers will not be retired at an appropriate and early time. Others argue that a high tax would make it unnecessary to regulate mpg's and fleet averages. We wonder, in any case, whether a tax of such magnitude would ever be levied. Thus, a definite rationale exists for a combination of a gasoline tax and mpg regulation.

MANUFACTURING INDUSTRY

Industry is characterized by constant self-awareness. Ever greater effort goes into computing and comparing, in order to better allocate resources, balance processes, and improve product. In other words, industry has a bottom line, and profits are its final test.

Consequently, because energy in the 1950's and 1960's was very cheap, an effort to save it was hardly a priority concern for most U.S. firms. "When I first came to the company," recalled a textiles executive, "we didn't pay any attention to gas costs because we couldn't find them." But the 1973–74 dramatic increase in energy prices provided an incentive—though not always a powerful one—for American business to seek energy-saving innovations as part of a broader effort to reduce energy costs.

The process of industrial energy conservation can be classified in three major broad and somewhat overlapping categories: (1) *Improved housekeeping*, which means such things as furnace maintenance, adjustment of lighting, fixing of leaky steam traps. Often, surprisingly large savings can be realized here with little or no investment. (2) *Recovery of waste*, which frequently involves familiar technology. One of the most important aspects is the recovery of waste heat, a major task for industrial retrofit. Another is the cogeneration of electricity and steam. Still another is the reclamation of waste products. To recycle aluminum, for example, requires only 7 percent as much energy as does getting aluminum from ore.[37] (3) *Technological innovation*, which requires major redesign of processes and products and considerable investment in capital stock that embodies the more efficient technologies.

Since the early 1970's, industry has been struggling to integrate energy saving into its bottom line. That there has been progress can hardly be doubted, and the pages of a publication like *Energy User News* contain claims of substantial energy savings in many firms, as seen in Table 6-5.

When explored in terms of pay back on investment, the savings can be dramatic. American Can at a big New Jersey facility reduced energy consumption by 55 percent with an investment of

TABLE 6·5
ENERGY SAVINGS IN VARIOUS U.S. FIRMS

Firm	Reduction	Time Frame	Comment
Burger King	17%	1974–77	50% by housekeeping
Lockheed (Los Angeles area factory complex)	59%	1972–77	Almost no investment
Tenneco	17%	1972–77	(1) 50% by housekeeping (2) Recycling waste heat
Colgate-Palmolive	18%	1973–76	Mostly housekeeping
Exxon (U.S. refineries)	21%	1972–77	80% with little or no capital investment (11.3 million barrels a year)
Western Electric (Kansas City plant)	38%	1972–77	Almost no investment
Frito-Lay	20%	1972–82	Per pound of snack chips

Source: Energy User News, April 11, 1977; April 18, 1977; June 13, 1977; October 31, 1977; February 20, 1978; and April 12, 1982.

$73,000, and the annual savings amounted to $700,000. The Parker Company, a large manufacturer of automotive parts, put $50,000 into saving energy and ended up saving $1.2 million a year on energy costs. The comment of that firm's senior industrial engineer is well worth noting: "Everyone is looking for the innovative approach to energy conservation. That's not where it is. There's nothing sensational about how we saved energy. It's been a whole new ethic for conservation."[38]

A surprising amount can indeed be accomplished by simple, good housekeeping. But there are limits to even the best housekeeping, and over the longer term, especially in energy-intensive industries, greater efficiencies will require investment in new equipment and plants. The evidence on industrial energy conservation is contradictory, and the time span since the embargo relatively short. Still, it has become quite common recently to claim that energy saving in the industrial sector is proceeding rapidly and sufficiently, which is to suggest that conservation energy is being widely tapped.

At this point, it would seem fair to say the following: Energy conservation is proceeding more rapidly in the industrial sector than in any other part of the economy, and the process has been accelerating since 1973, helped along by one of the most positive developments in the American energy picture—the growing status and importance of the corporate energy manager.

Between 1973 and 1981, industrial production rose 20 percent, while industrial energy use declined by 9 percent—indicating a decrease in energy usage per unit of industrial output of 24 percent. But important qualifications are needed. The usefulness of recent data has been sharply constrained by the recessions in the mid-1970's and in the early 1980's.[39] For instance, a substantial decline in demand for aluminum led to the temporary shutting down of older, less efficient aluminum smelters, thus leading to an apparent, but not real, improvement. Moreover, the mix of U.S. industrial output has been changing, so that the share produced by energy-intensive industries is declining. An analysis of the decline in energy intensity in U.S. industry between 1973 and 1980 attributed half the gains to shifts in production mix and half to greater efficiency in energy use. (The latter included both a continuation of the pre-1973 trend and the additional effort stimulated since).[40] On the basis of what is known today, therefore, it would seem sensible to conclude that, although industry has posted the best record so far of any sector, it remains far below its potential. Despite the relative flexibility of American industry when compared to that of other countries, conservation has been much slower and more uncertain than it need be. Why?

The Barriers |

A number of important barriers retard conservation in industry. To begin with, effective conservation is not something that happens automatically. It requires an organizational response, usually at three levels. There must be a strong and persistent interest and commitment by senior management. There must be an effective energy unit in the company—that is, engineers and managers with the authority of the senior levels behind them, who can implement change at the plant and in the office. And finally, conservation must be built into the fabric of operations, so that energy use is constantly monitored and so that conservation becomes part of the employee's work habits and an element in the manager's annual bonus. "One of our biggest problems is getting people at the plant level to take energy conservation seriously," Goodyear's corporate energy planner has observed. "Yes, even after all this time." The importance of commitment and persistence at all three levels cannot be exaggerated. Indeed, backsliding is often easier than maintenance. "Like all housekeeping, the benefits soon slip away without constant attention," noted an executive of Armco Steel, the nation's seventeenth largest industrial energy user. That point was underscored by the energy manager of a major airline: "We lost our two full-time energy managers in early 1981, and for the first time since we started keeping records our energy use began to rise."[41]

How to get and maintain that commitment—and implement it? In many firms, energy is not a significant cost, and so energy saving, whether by housekeeping or by investment, remains a low-priority concern. In such circumstances, the benefit to society of energy saving exceeds the benefit to the individual firm. And current energy policies widen the cost gap between society and the firm by posting prices that do not take into account replacement costs or the externalities that result from dependence on imported oil. But, of course, there are firms for which energy is a large part of costs—for Allied Chemical, 10 percent of sales; for Armco Steel, 15 percent of sales. Even if they want to save energy, some of these firms may not have the capital available to do so.

Another most important barrier is the very high rate of return demanded by many firms for the type of investment in which energy savings is usually categorized. The high "hurdle rates" frequently seem to cluster around 30 percent after taxes. With accelerated depreciation and an investment tax credit of 10 percent, this corresponds to a two-year payback.[42] Companies base the high "hurdle rates" on the judgment that conservation measures do not have the strategic impact of a new product or additional capacity, and that they are easily postponed—this, despite the very low risk involved in energy-saving investment. This remains the case despite the second round of sharp energy price rises that began in 1979. Other uses within companies may win higher priorities for the use of scarce capital. Inflation, high interest rates, recession, and uncertainty about future markets all inhibit the allocation of funds even for conservation investments that do meet hurdle rates. Then, too, incomplete data and inadequate information about the appropriate technology can engender doubts about making an investment in conservation.

It can also be very difficult to read and adjust to the environment. The president of Inland Steel complained, with some justification, about the lack of "consistent economic, energy, and other regulatory signals which can be used as a basis for orderly decision-making."[43]

The confusions are multiple. The first, obviously, concerns price. Managers are told that the value of energy is increasing; yet the real price of No. 6 industrial fuel oil decreased between August 1975 and August 1978—not exactly a signal for increased effort to save energy. There is even more uncertainty about the future: Will the real price increase or decrease? In 1979–80, oil prices shot up, but in 1982 some experts were predicting substantial falls in the price of oil. Every time there is some slack in the oil market, there is considerable discussion and publicity about an oil glut.

The uncertainty extends to other aspects of the future energy environment. What will be the preferred sources of energy? What will happen to natural gas regulation, and where will decontrolled natural gas prices equilibrate relative to oil? Changing expectations of price will profoundly affect investment decisions. The president of Pan American World Airways explained why that company would not order any more energy-efficient aircraft: "These two airplanes were ordered at a time when airlines could justify the purchase price because everyone was projecting a $2-a-gallon fuel price by the end of 1982 and a price of $3 by 1985 . . . At the end of 1982, fuel will probably cost less than it did at the end of 1980." Corporate managers continue to hear predictions about an abundance of new, conventional domestic energy sources. How secure will domestic and foreign supplies be? And great confusion exists about the thrust and impact of government policies, especially those involving incentives, regulations, and allocations. Many smaller firms doubt whether conservation will pay off financially. Many firms, large and small, are afraid that if they trim energy use now, they could end up being penalized (compared to companies with more energy "fat" on them) by a rationing system imposed in some future crisis.

For larger companies, the simultaneous push to conservation and coal conversion has created a real quandary. The two compete for investment dollars, and a shift from oil and natural gas to coal can actually increase the number of BTUs required per unit of output.[44] A leading energy consultant explains why management postpones making investments in conservation, even when the payback time is only two or three years: "They're waiting because of a fuzzy picture on fuel costs and they're waiting for signals from the government."[45]

Cogeneration: Industry's North Slope |

One aspect of industrial conservation stands out, for American industry has within its grasp an Alaskan oil strike, a major new source of energy waiting to be developed. This type of conservation energy deserves special attention because of its potential scale and because its availability largely depends upon requisite decisions being made in the political process. The source is sometimes called *combined heat and power*, a term awkward enough to be designated CHP, and perhaps for that reason better known in the United States as cogeneration. But the meaning is simple enough —the combined production of electricity and heat (the latter for either process or space-heating purposes).

Today there are two independent energy delivery systems. One is composed of utilities in which electricity is centrally produced, be it by coal, nuclear fission, oil, gas, or hydropower. As the electricity is produced, the heat from the power plant steam goes up (indirectly) a stack and into the air—or into lakes and rivers

—as waste. In the second system, companies generate their own steam for use in the industrial process; in fact, almost half of all energy used by industry is consumed just to produce steam.[46] What cogeneration means is the integration of the two systems.

Cogeneration can take two forms. In the first form, steam (or hot water) from a power station is delivered by pipes to homes and offices to provide heat and hot water. Such systems, called district heating, are quite common in both Eastern and Western Europe, with about a thousand in nine of the countries of the European Community. District heating schemes, however, are economical only when urban density is high and subscription to the system general. Up to now it has been thought that, for most American cities, the cost of putting in the pipes and other parts of the system would be prohibitive, although recent studies for St. Paul and Minneapolis have suggested a more promising potential. Steam can also be transmitted from power plants to specific consumers nearby. An Exxon refinery in New Jersey, for example, buys its steam from a power station a mile away, just as Harvard buys steam from a generating plant on the Charles River. Consolidated Edison pipes steam to over 2000 office buildings and apartments in Manhattan. Other firms and power plants are exploring such symbiotic relationships.

The second type of cogeneration, with by far the most significant potential, comes from the combined production of electricity and steam at industrial sites. Here the firm produces not just steam but also electricity as a by-product of generating the steam. The process, called topping cycle, can be explained simply. Energy is used to produce combustion at temperatures up to 3600° F in order to get steam that need not be any hotter than 400° F. Obviously, a great deal of energy is wasted in the process. In cogeneration, the high temperature is used to make gas vapor or very high pressure steam, which drives a turbine or a rotating shaft, which in turn generates electricity. As in a power plant, the waste from this process is steam, except that in this case the steam is not waste, for it then goes on to be used for industrial processes. The energy is thus *cascaded* from uses that require high temperatures to those that require lower temperatures. This is called high-quality and low-quality energy uses.[47]

The advantages of cogeneration are substantial—about half as much fuel is used to produce electricity and steam as would be needed to produce the two separately.* And it appears that the return on investment for many industrial firms (and for other establishments, such as hospitals and shopping centers) is quite good. Furthermore, cogeneration gives companies an important hedge against almost inevitable increases in energy prices and against brownouts and other interruptions of supplies, whether caused by oil producers, coal strikes, or bad weather. For utilities, cogeneration can reduce the need to build new nuclear or coal-fired power stations, at a time when marginal costs are higher than average costs—and at a time when the political obstacles to such new capacity are difficult to surmount in any event.

As with so much else in conservation, cogeneration does not require a major technological breakthrough, but rather regaining a path that was abandoned. Around the turn of the century, many industrial establishments in the United States produced their own electricity as well as steam, but they eventually gave it up.[48] For one thing, the utility regulatory system scared them away from cogeneration. For another, the declining real price of electricity (which for industrial consumers was cut in half between 1940 and 1950), combined with lower unit prices for larger consumers, made cogeneration even more unappealing.[49] Companies, therefore, chose to stay in the businesses they were in and to leave electricity to the utilities. In 1950, 15 percent of the nation's entire electricity supply was generated by industry; by 1973, only 5 percent, a figure that differed markedly from other countries. Twenty-seven percent of all West Germany's electric power is produced by industrial firms, half by cogeneration. British industry produces 20 percent of its own electrical needs.[50]

A number of analyses suggest substantial energy—over twenty percent of total industrial energy use—could be saved in the United States through cogeneration investments that are economically sound.[51]

---

*At a typical electric utility generating plant, up to two thirds of the fuel's potential energy is lost as discharged waste heat.

In other words, industry is sitting upon an easily recoverable, relatively cheap new source of energy. Is it quickly being exploited? Not especially. Why? Because we have here a near-perfect example of obstacles being not technical, but almost entirely institutional and organizational.

There are two key obstacles to industrial cogeneration. The first is represented in the point where industrial cogenerator, utility, and utility regulator meet. The cogenerator cannot unplug himself from the utility, because he will sometimes have to buy extra electricity to meet his needs. At other times, he will have extra electricity which he will want to export, that is, send into the utility grid. So his questions are three. What will the stand-by electricity cost? Will he be able to feed his electricity to the utility? And if so, at what price?

As things now stand, the whole system discourages cogeneration. The cheap rates for bigger users and the absence of marginal pricing still reduce the incentive for industrial firms to cogenerate, while utilities do not want electricity produced by cogenerators. As a regulated monopoly, the utility industry has an allowable profit based upon a return on capital, and an industrial firm's generating capacity cannot figure in the utility's capital base against which the utility rates are calculated. Meanwhile, the industrial cogenerator, even if he does get the utility to accept his electricity, may find himself in a regulatory thicket; for as soon as he sends electricity across the street, he may be deemed a public utility, subject to a number of federal and state regulating bodies, all of which only complicate his life with more forms, more hearings, more lawyers, and more uncertainty.

Fortunately, the environment is changing. The 1978 National Energy Act has eased the danger of industrial firms' being categorized as utilities, and also presses utilities to become more receptive. Moreover, while some utilities remain hostile, others already short of capital and afraid of having insufficient generating capacity in the 1980's, are showing a willingness to accept electricity into their systems from wherever they can get it.* Slowly, the regulatory system is adapting to the needs of conservation in

---

*Perhaps ownership of the cogenerating facilities could be vested in the utilities.

general, and electricity rates are in the process of being revised so that they encourage, rather than discourage, cogeneration. This is a very difficult, complicated, and time-consuming problem. It is at one and the same time highly technical, highly political, and highly important.[52]

The second key obstacle is that many companies fail to see the great advantages that cogeneration might bring them—they want to be in the business they are in, not in the electricity business. They also demand a much higher rate of return (sometimes twice as high as normal investment, as high as 30 percent after taxes) for such an ancillary investment as cogeneration, whereas utilities are satisfied with a much lower rate.[53]

Cogeneration is only one of the major ways to save energy in the industrial sector. Altogether, it may be economically possible to cut industrial energy use by more than a third through cogeneration and conservation efforts, and to do so at a cost a good deal less than that required for investment in conventional energy sources. Before the 1979–80 price hikes, the total capital investment required was estimated as some forty or so billion dollars less than that required for investment in conventional energy sources.[54] Such as assessment is admittedly rough. After all, energy is used in so many different ways in industry that a quantification of potential savings is very difficult to achieve.

Indeed, a number of major firms have been surprised to find out how great is the flexibility between energy use and economic activity. Union Carbide, one of the largest industrial energy users, had projected in 1974 a 3.8-percent compounded growth in energy use through 1990. So far, it has experienced an absolute decline in energy use year-by-year since 1974. Gillette set a 10-percent energy reduction goal in 1973 in its U.S. operations. By 1981, it had reached a 30 percent reduction in absolute consumption, while its sales were up 83 percent. "Our energy savings have required very little investment," Cameron Beers, the firm's corporate energy manager, has noted. "Rather, they are a sum total of a variety of little things. We keep thinking we've just about done everything, but new ideas keep springing up." Emphasis on the flexibility is gaining attention. American Telephone and Telegraph has established a dramatic goal for its own operations: that its business double between 1973 and 1984, while its energy consumption decreases in absolute terms. In other words, negative energy growth is AT&T's target.[55]

Of course, potential savings cannot be predicted with any great precision—either for a single firm or for an industrial sector as a whole—because of the diversity of energy use, incomplete knowledge, and uncertainty about means and timing of implementation. But one can certainly be highly optimistic about the possibilities.

Price signals have become somewhat clearer, but still are in need of clarification. Prices should reflect the real value that energy has today. Hence, those supporting, for instance, a system of continued price regulation of natural gas face the fact that such a system strongly retards energy conservation in industry—and increases the prospect of much higher prices later. It is obvious that senior management will not take energy-saving investments more seriously until they are convinced that their firms will be paying more for energy in real dollars in the future than today. On the other hand, higher prices are not enough, since the world oil price does not reflect the total social cost.

Thus some increase in price must be matched with other policy-induced mechanisms that will accelerate conservation and give it an equitable chance to compete with conventional sources of supply. In particular, these mechanisms need to reduce the high hurdle rate, and thereby increase the rate of energy-saving investment and so speed up the turnover of machinery and other capital stock. Between 1947 and 1973, the ratio of energy to output actually did decline in all U.S. manufacturing. The major reason? More efficient technologies embodied in new plants and equipment. As Myers and Nakamura point out, "Turnover of capital stock and expansion of the size of stock have been the principal means by which reductions in energy-output ratios have been achieved." But this can be a very slow process. "An obvious implication for government policy is that tax or other policies that promote investment will speed energy conservation." A most important point follows from this observation: While low economic growth reduces absolute energy consumption in the short term, it most certainly will slow energy conservation over the longer term by retarding investment in more efficient plants.[56]

Any general stimulus to investment will encourage energy efficiency. The 1978 National Energy Act provides a 10-percent tax credit for conservation investment. But given the subsidies and external costs of other energy sources, as well as the high hurdle rates, 10 percent seems much too low. Consideration should be given to larger tax credits, plus accelerated depreciation and energy-conservation loans. These are especially important in a period of lagging economic confidence, high inflation, high interest rates, and high uncertainty—and recession and consequent low investment.

There is a widespread unexamined assumption that rising energy prices will generate the "right" amount of cost-effective energy conservation investments. This assumption does not work out very well in the real world where energy is not the only consideration. Indeed, a survey of 2500 companies in energy-intensive industries found that most reported energy savings are attributed to housekeeping, *not* to significant capital-investment programs. Just because energy prices are high does not mean investments will be made. For, at any given time, there are many more claims on corporate funds than there are funds. There may not be sufficient cash flow to cover the high capital costs associated with major new capital investments, and borrowing may be difficult because of credit restrictions and high interest rates. Moreover, there may be a pronounced gap between the firm's interest and the nation's interest—both in terms of time horizon and in return on investment. The measure of cost-effectiveness to a company, which pays the same for a marginal barrel as for an average barrel, is quite different for the United States, which is interested in the least costly energy investment, and for which the marginal barrel may be far more expensive. These constraints and this gap make a strong argument for larger incentives to accelerate industrial energy conservation and facilitate industry's adaptation to the new energy era.

The widespread belief that high energy prices will generate just the "right" amount of investment is so widespread that it is important to elucidate how the problem appears to managers who must grapple with it. "From the standpoint of what is technically feasible, most chemical companies—and I imagine companies in other industries as well—would concede that a good deal more can be done," the chairman of Union Carbide pointed out. "Yet, under current conditions, not everything that can be done will be done. And you may well ask why is it that, in light of rapidly rising energy costs and the national need to reduce energy consumption, we do not provide unlimited budgets for energy conservation projects. The short answer is that we do not have unlimited budgets to run our business. And as energy costs go even higher, the amount of capital available for energy conservation will shrink even further. . . . What must be understood is that as the price of energy goes up, a massive transfer of income is also taking place —between the companies that sell petroleum and the second-tier companies like my own that use it in the process of manufacturing other products. . . . The problem for companies in a highly competitive industry like ours is that our increased energy costs are not easily passed along to our customers. We are faced with the very difficult choice of advancing the projects we must have to sustain our business, or allocating the money to conservation projects. And, quite frankly, we are sometimes compelled to defer the conservation."

Other measures should also be implemented. Currently, the government has a weak voluntary program in which companies report on energy saving. The data, however, is, as already suggested, obscure, difficult to analyze, and often misleading. The reporting system should be made more meaningful, and the voluntary targets for savings strengthened.[57] Finally, information and education efforts should be intensified, especially for smaller firms, which find that their organizational resources are strained by the additional task of energy management.

Dow's War on BTUs |

There is nothing automatic about the integration of energy consciousness and energy efficiency into the bottom line. But once the considerable barriers to energy conservation are surmounted, the savings can be very considerable. So the story of Dow Chemical indicates.

The case is worth serious attention, for Dow is one of the largest industrial energy consumers in the United States, ranking with U.S. Steel and Alcoa. Thus Dow had good reason to be very sensitive to the sudden price changes in one of its key inputs, natural gas. It was also able to translate sensitivity into action. In the late 1960's and early 1970's, Dow correctly interpreted market signals and long-term trends ahead of most other major American corporations, and it managed over ten years to reduce its energy consumption (per pound of product) by 40 percent—putting it at the forefront of major chemical companies.[58]

Two features of Dow's situation made it special. First, the firm has traditionally been oriented to energy saving. The hobby of H. H. Dow, the company's founder, was power—in the literal, not political, sense. "He loved to generate power in ingenious ways," said J. E. Mitchell, Dow's director of corporate planning. "Right from the beginning, H. H. Dow spent money for efficiency in power generation that was not justified." Dow's interests were shared by the plant manager in Midland, Michigan, Merle Newkirk, who is still known around Dow's headquarters for having been "a nut on power efficiency." He, too, paid little attention to the economics of investment in power, but rather drove for more and more energy saving. Thus, Dow introduced cogeneration into its plants in the 1920's. A continuing tradition of intense interest in power efficiency was established as well.

The second feature had to do with the development of the company. In the 1940's and 1950's, the Texas Division, operating in the Gulf States, underwent an enormous growth on the basis of cheap natural gas—which at first was available simply for the cost of gathering it. The original Midland Division, based in Michigan, continued to use coal, which meant its costs were higher than those of the Texas Division. "We were under the gun to lower costs," recalled Mitchell. "It was a noose around our necks."

The cost crunch became critical during the 1954 recession, when there was a marked downturn in Midland's contribution to corporate profits. The general manager of the Midland Division launched a program to try to compensate for the division's reliance on coal. He instituted an increasingly elaborate system to keep track of the amount of steam and electricity used in the various manufacturing steps, so providing, on a monthly basis, data on cost of energy per pound of product. "From day one," Mitchell recalled, "Midland knew it was fighting an uphill battle on energy costs." The situation improved, but the division recognized that it could never be competitive with the Texas Division, which was expanding in an almost explosive way in the 1950's and early 1960's.

In 1967, reports began coming to headquarters about developing shortages of natural gas, and a study was done in Midland, which forecast pressure on natural gas supplies as prices of interstate and intrastate natural gas began to diverge. In 1968, the director of U.S. operations was persuaded that all energy prices would increase. He coined the phrase "the war on BTUs"—and ordered it waged throughout the company.

But the Texas Division was reluctant to accept such projections. "People had gone down there in the 1940's and 1950's when gas was cheap," Mitchell said. "The people in Texas said, 'It can't happen here.' "

It was not until 1970 that the senior management of the Texas Division finally came around. What helped convince them was that the price of natural gas went up 10 to 15 percent in 1970 and 1971. But even corporate management in Midland was not fully convinced of how serious the problem was until one intrastate natural gas contract increased $5 million in one year.

In 1972, Mitchell presented to the firm's executive committee a prescient forecast of the energy future and what it could mean for Dow. He predicted increasing dependence on imports, tightening supply, and significantly rising prices. The years 1973–80 he called "the Arab era," the result of which would be "a wild, scrambling worldwide fight for hydrocarbons." He added, "There can be no real security of supply during a scrambling readjustment." As for Dow's course, "The only short-term solution is intensive conservation effort." The executive committee agreed, ensuring that there would be full support at the top for an intensified war on BTUs.

The company thus had its institutional traditions, the experience of the Midland Division in how to save energy, and now it also had top management support behind conservation. Throughout the company, targets were set for the amount of energy that each pound of product should require, and daily corporate reporting of theoretical and actual balances of energy was instituted for all operations. The outcome was taken into account in annual job-performance reviews and in the annual merit-raise procedures. Key personnel are now kept constantly informed of energy prices and trends. This procedure, in the words of a conservation specialist in the Texas Division, has "sensitized all levels of supervision to the need for conservation." Thus, Dow's efforts went from the simplest kind of housekeeping (turning off motors when not needed) to retrofitting (putting in heat exchangers) to designing entirely new plants that yield more product with less energy.

Several lessons emerge from the Dow experience. There is a strong need for accurate measurements of energy consumption in order to establish targets, evaluate results, and assess managerial repsonsibility. Commitment must come from the top to make clear that conservation is a bottom-line concern and not a public-relations ploy. "Because top management gave it such strong support," said Gerald Decker, corporate energy manager from 1967 to 1978, "everybody gave it top priority. That was the secret." Moreover, as another Dow executive expressed it, "Most things in energy conservation are not based on new knowledge, but rather the applying of knowledge we already have in a different environment." The simpler and cheaper things are done first, and then progressively more capital investment is required. "There are no gimmicks left for us," said Mitchell. "From here on, the only way to save BTU's is by reengineering, by building new plants, by spending more capital. The easy part is over."

But Dow's "easy part" in itself makes a very dramatic point: With relatively little capital investment, Dow was able to increase the productivity of its energy inputs by 40 percent, and make a substantial contribution to company profits in the process. Dow had stronger incentives than most other firms prior to 1973, but still the lesson is clear.

BUILDINGS |

Between 36 and 40 percent of U.S. energy consumption is used to heat, air-condition, light, and provide hot water for homes, commercial structures, and factories. The residential sector alone uses 20 percent of all the energy used in the United States. The use in the individual home breaks down like this:

Space heating	53%
Hot water	14%
Cooling	5%
Air-conditioning	7%
Other	21%

During the 1950's and 1960's, efficient energy usage was increasingly neglected in the construction of new buildings and homes. In New York City, office buildings put up between 1945 and 1950 used half as much energy per square foot as those built between 1960 to 1965. The difference? The older buildings use natural light and have windows that open, whereas the newer buildings are sealed and depend on mechanical systems for lighting, heat, and air-conditioning. The same trend is evident in private housing, where convenience and fashion also promoted an increase in the use of energy-intensive household appliances.[59]

Cleverer Buildings |

Since 1973, energy has ceased to be neglected. "Architects are now in a period of major reassessment in which the entire selection of materials and assemblies is being examined to determine whether they can perform to satisfy the new energy conservation demands," Richard G. Stein, one of the nation's most energy-conscious architects, has observed. "Many of the materials that would normally be slowly phased out will now be abruptly rejected. ... The hope for the future lies in the fundamental reversal in our present commitment to the sealed building, with its massive plant for manufacturing the air and delivering it at predetermined temperatures and velocities and its large lighting apparatus that substitutes a universal switch for selectivity."[60]

This same reassessment is being made by builders and buyers. How extensively? It is not yet clear.

But there are certainly some significant examples of change. The modern, tall, glass-faced, sealed office building of the 1960's and 1970's is an energy-intensive creature, annually using between 150,000 and 250,000 BTUs per square foot—even up to 400,000 BTUs per square foot. But a new IBM facility at Southfield, Michigan, without computer operations, uses only 51,000 BTUs per square foot, a third to a fifth of what the building might have used had it been built in the early 1970's. While the drop in consumption is dramatic, there is nothing dramatic about the methods—double glazing for the windows, more insulation, and lower lighting levels.[61]

The General Services Administration has established an energy target of 55,000 BTUs per square foot per year for its new office buildings. "It is important to realize," said Fred Dubin, the consulting engineer who helped the GSA (and a number of companies) establish that target, "that the order of magnitude of these savings in the new and existing buildings can be done with readily available off-the-shelf hardware, equipment, and systems—with thoughtful, discriminating, innovative design."

Buildings, as some architects express it, are becoming even more "clever" in their use of energy. Requiring no conventional heating plant at all, the twenty-story headquarters of Ontario Hydro in Toronto (a city that is definitely cold) uses only 65,000 BTUs per square foot. The warmth is provided entirely by capturing the waste heat given off by lighting, office equipment—and employees.[62]

Similar changes are likely to follow through design changes in new residential construction. The National Association of Home Builders constructed and monitored two similar homes in the Washington, D.C., area. One was the bestselling model of a merchant builder; the other, a house based on that model, but redesigned to conserve energy through using "off-the-shelf products and techniques." Between February 1978 and January 1979, the energy-efficient residence used 49 percent less energy than the conventional home—for a savings of $545 for the year. A test house constructed by the Oak Ridge National Laboratory will require only 20 percent as much electricity for heating, cooling, and water heating as would a conventional house. Between 1977 and 1979, some fifty low-energy houses were constructed in Saskatchewan province in Canada. Strong conservation measures were combined with passive design in these homes. Their space-heating requirements proved to be only a fifth to a third of that of conventional housing in the area. The added costs, including ventilation systems, ranged between $2500 and $4000. Since then, more of these houses have been built, with energy savings up to 90 percent relative to conventional houses—and adding only about 5 percent to the building cost.[63]

The continuing development of what has been described as "energy-conscious design" will promote increasing energy efficiency in new construction. For some, such design comes as a reaction to obvious waste, over-engineering and over-lighting, to what is seen as an excessive artificiality in modern building and an insensitivity to the natural environment.[64] For more people, however, emphasis on energy-conscious design is much more the result of a perception of rising costs and the uncertain supply of energy.

The trend is being reinforced slowly by changing building codes and loan requirements, which increasingly stress energy efficiency. Local governments are developing their own standards. Seattle, for instance, is investigating different approaches to make conservation in buildings an "equal option *with* generation."[65]

Another important factor is movement away from a "first-cost mentality" to life-cycle costing. Traditionally, the purchase price of a house, rather than that price plus operating cost, has been the chief concern of builder, buyer, and financing institution. Two thirds of all the new single-family homes in 1971, for instance, were built for speculative sale. The builder was therefore interested in keeping the selling price down, and worried much less about longer term energy costs.[66] Obviously, a shift is occurring to looking at life-cycle costs in some form, which has been encouraged not only by the interest of the buyer, but also by lenders concerned about rising utility bills' affecting mortgage payments and underinsulated homes losing value.[67]

Retrofit |

The trend toward energy-conscious design is promising, but there is a catch, a large one. Unlike the auto stock, the building population turns over very slowly. In 1972, a record year for new housing starts, new homes accounted for less than 3.5 percent of the total stock; in the depressed housing market of the early 1980's the number was much lower.[68] Moreover, major constraints will slow down the diffusion of new designs. These constraints range from building and health codes to availability of materials, to trade-union practices, to the education received by future architects and engineers. So new building designs can have a substantial impact only in the long term.

In order for energy saving to be promoted in existing buildings, an aggressive retrofit campaign must be mounted. *Retrofit* is a space-age term, describing the upgrading of a complex system through the insertion of improved components. In the case of Dow, it has meant the addition of new equipment to existing manufacturing processes. In buildings, it generally means changes in equipment and structure to improve thermal and lighting efficiency.

The evidence so far indicates that a program of retrofit brings savings that astonish those who embark on the strategy. IBM, for instance, was already aware of rising energy prices before the embargo, and so launched a conservation campaign in early 1973. The initial goal was to reduce energy use by 10 percent in thirty-four major locations in the United States. The savings have far exceeded the goal: by the end of 1977, consumption was 39 percent lower than the 1973 preconservation levels. If the company had not embarked on this campaign, its energy costs for the period 1974–77 would have been $90 million higher. That realization, observed a senior IBM executive, "provides a powerful incentive to save." What really impressed the executive was that two thirds of the savings was achieved with little or no capital investment. "In the past," he said, "abundant and low-cost energy supplies did not make conservation a key management concern, and so initial energy conservation measures yielded large savings without capital investment . . . The methods of achieving these initial savings are not very technical or profound. They amount to turning off lights, changing temperatures, shutting down equipment when not needed, fine tuning building systems, and other similar techniques." By 1980, IBM had been able to reduce its energy use (per square foot) by about 48 percent—for a dollar savings of $225 million. How far can IBM go in energy efficiency? "I keep getting asked that question," commented John Honeycomb, director of energy programs for IBM. "Sure, there's a ceiling. We just don't know what it is. As energy costs go up, so does the ceiling. We certainly haven't struck the bottom of the barrel."[69]

Its electricity supplies threatened by the coal strike of 1977 and 1978, Ashland Chemical, a division of Ashland Oil, found that in a matter of weeks it could cut back on electricity use by 25 percent in the buildings that comprise its headquarters complex with little investment and "little inconvenience." The lessons cited by the official in charge of the program provide an insight into the barriers to conservation: "Our management group was generally surprised at the extent of our success, and the amount of discretionary items that use electricity. Unfortunately, it might well take an imminent crisis like the coal shortage to motivate the type of action that we initiated. The key elements here are to develop a sense of participation on the part of all the employees because all the employees can contribute in some manner to energy savings . . . A crisis situation gives one the opportunity to effect change of this nature. Once the change has been developed, it is considerably easier to maintain the change. . . . In addition to the strong emphasis on communication and participation on the part of the employees, another lesson that developed from this experience is that a little additional planning during the design and construction of a physical facility would give the management of that facility considerable more flexibility and opportunity for savings on electrical use."[70]

Sixty-Seven Percent Less |

The possibilities in the residential sector parallel those in the commercial-industrial sector. The American housing stock is characterized by extreme diversity. Of the 80 million or so all-year residences in the United States, 50 million are detached single-family houses. More than a third of all residences were built before 1940, when there were few or no standards for insulation. In the late 1950's, the spread of air-conditioning and electric heating provided an impetus for thermal insulation. Only then did insulation manufacture become a major industry, and double glazing and storm windows gained consideration in new housing. Even so, the economics at the time did not exactly create a clamor for significant thermal protection. By some estimates, 30 percent of the residences in the country may be completely uninsulated. Altogether, two thirds probably need additional thermal insulation.[71]

What savings are possible? The Federal Energy Administration found, with a test house in the Washington, D.C., area, that adding standard insulation devices decreased the total annual energy requirement of the house by 25 percent. Additional insulation increased the energy savings to 35 percent. Standard Oil of California conducted a three-year demonstration study of homes in Portland, Spokane, and Seattle. With an investment of $981, the fuel consumption of the Portland house was reduced by 50 percent, with a rate of return on the investment of about 25 percent. The study concluded that 50 percent energy savings are possible as economically attractive investments in a substantial part of the nation's housing stock. These results are consistent with a number of other tests around the country.[72]

The Washington Natural Gas Company, serving the Puget Sound area, went into the energy conservation business after the embargo, selling "conservation kits" for attic insulation. By "kit," the company meant that it not only provided but also installed the insulation, guaranteed it, and financed it. The cost was about $200. The reduction in heating energy, 22 percent. The company advertised the kit with the message that it would cost consumers more not to buy it than to buy it. By November 1977, the utility had sold 14,000 such kits, and it estimated that its advertising and promotion created a demand that led to an additional 42,000 jobs for other contractors. The utility is now selling a more elaborate kit, which includes attic insulation, pilotless natural gas furnace, and automatic day-night thermostat. This, the company estimates, has reduced energy used for heating by an average of 36 percent.

Such programs also help the utilities cope with sometimes urgent problems of supply. Washington Natural Gas estimates that the savings in the 56,000 homes insulated as a direct or indirect result of its program has freed gas for 16,500 new houses without requiring any new supply. "What all of that meant," said the utility's president, "was that we had been sitting atop a new gas field for years, and didn't recognize it."[73] This was a most valuable discovery at a time of rising prices and supply uncertainty for natural gas. Similarly, some electric utilities hope that retrofit can reduce the need to invest in new generating capacity, and help avoid some of the difficult choices between coal and nuclear.[74]

Important evidence for the value of retrofit comes from Twin Rivers, New Jersey, a community of 3,000 well-constructed residences a few miles from Princeton. For five years, a group from the Center for Environmental Studies at Princeton University intensively studied actual energy consumption in this community. The results are extraordinarily rich for understanding energy use in the real world. The researchers found that a 67-percent reduction in annual energy consumption for space heating was possible with a relatively simple package—interior window insulations, basement and attic insulation, and plugging of air leaks. The costs were not high. The conclusions point to the great potential of systematic conservation: "Among the ways of conserving household energy, there are no spectacular technical fixes. There is only a catalog of small fixes, many of them drab and unimpressive in isolation. It is therefore easy to dismiss conservation of household energy as an incremental business and to seek bigger solutions elsewhere. But the catalog is fat, and many of its entries are cheap. With patience, groups of small and even tiny fixes can be put together into large assemblies that overall can produce impressive results. . . . It does not appear to be impossible, in fact, that under present technology and economic conditions, space heat in houses could be a minor rather than a major consumer of fuel."[75]

What would be good for the homeowner and for the utility would also be good for the nation. If simple retrofit packages—

ceiling insulation, storm windows and doors, caulking, weather stripping, furnace adjustments, plugging of air-bypass flows—were aggressively pushed by a strong national program, it could be possible by the end of the decade to cut in half the energy currently used for residential heating—and do so at costs considerably lower than those of any other energy source.[76]

Where Is Policy? |

Yet, only grudgingly encouraged by government, progress toward a meaningful retrofit program has been disappointingly slow. This failure of public policy has been one of the biggest lapses in the nation's lapse-ridden effort to cope with the world of imported oil.

For the first three years after the crisis, senior government policymakers in the energy area suffered from an excessive faith in the efficiency of the market. Prices, they thought, would stimulate just the right amount of retrofitting and just the right changes in construction practices for new buildings. A small example: In March 1975, an official in the Department of Housing and Urban Development requested permission to change minimum property standards to increase energy efficiency by promoting "maximum reduction in cost with a minimum, if any, increase in construction cost." HUD higher-ups rejected the request, saying, "Although most of the items submitted are energy saving, it is more effective to have the market dictate the additional thermal requirements."[77]

Those who advocate exclusive reliance on price forget about the considerable imperfections in the very decentralized housing market with its millions of decision-makers. The homeowner is typically ill-informed about conservation, how to analyze energy use and calculate savings, whom to go to for advice and installation, how to finance, what to put in. Another problem is mobility. By 1970, only 54 percent of all household heads were living in the same houses as 1965. If you think you are going to move in a couple of years, why invest?[78] Moreover, many whose houses most need retrofit are the people least able to afford it. What those who argue for exclusive reliance on the free market forget is that there are real people with real problems, for whom high energy costs create genuine hardships. One such real person is Florence Leyland, an elderly woman who owns a three-bedroom house in Waltham, Massachusetts. In one twelve-month period, Mrs. Layland had to spend $550 of her $3,223.20 total income, all of which comes from Social Security, on heating.[79]

Some encouragements for retrofitting were included in the Energy Policy and Conservation Act of 1975 and the Energy Conservation and Production Act of 1976: A modest program of weatherization assistance for the elderly and the handicapped; targets for improved efficiencies of appliances; and demonstration projects and energy audit procedures.

The 1978 National Energy Act provides for a 15-percent tax credit on investments in residential conservation, but not to exceed $300. Although better than what has happened so far, the proposals are still rather modest, and still do not do enough to give conservation the chance it needs and deserves.

One must ask how effective even the various efforts to date will be in overcoming the obstacles described by the Governor's Energy Advisory Council in Texas: "In the absence of government leadership, typical consumers will experience a long period of high expenditure for energy until they come to demand energy efficiency as a priority. The period can be shortened and its impacts lessened by the adoption of appropriate government policies." Recent survey data point to the inadequacy of the current levels of tax credits. Seventy-one percent of respondents supported government programs that help homeowners to improve the energy efficiency of their homes. Current programs apparently play a negligible role in motivating people to act. Although 79 percent of homeowners were aware of the federal tax credit program, only 3 percent who had made an energy-efficiency improvement said the tax credit was important to their decision. But, some will say, the price system will eventually take care of everything. In this survey, 54 percent admitted that "more can be done to make (my) home energy efficient."* Of those, 76 percent said that the main reason they have not done more to make their homes energy

---

*No doubt, quite understated.

efficient is that they "can't afford it." High interest rates have further impeded retrofit investments.

It is nothing short of ridiculous that now, a decade after the embargo, the United States does not yet have an adequate national program of incentives to encourage sufficient investments in retrofit. The speed with which retrofit can deliver substantial savings argues for a much more stimulative public policy that includes the development of innovative financing mechanisms. Such a policy would signal the importance of retrofit and would encourage homeowners, entrepreneurs, and manufacturers. It would make retrofit economically attractive for some homeowners, and not only attractive but possible for others. Standards and regulations also need to be pushed. So do demonstration projects. Residential homes comprise the most decentralized sector of energy consumption, and therefore public education and information is particularly important. The market cannot function efficiently if people lack relevant information. Since 1981, however, the efforts at the federal level to make up for market imperfections have actually been rolled back, and information programs have been killed.[80]

But how to encourage the development of an efficient system that will actually deliver conservation to the individual homeowner? The National Association of Home Builders Research Foundation has projected that the retrofitting of 40 million single-family homes might require the establishment of 6,000 retrofit businesses, each generating at least $400,000 of business a year (at least 500 homes a year) and many thousands of jobs. Some system of licensing, training, and control will be required. But it must also be recognized that as independent operators, retrofit contractors will encounter the considerable skepticism that homeowners feel toward the home-improvement industry and the "aluminum siding boys."[81]

One way to speed up retrofit is to ensure that such entities as utilities and independent heating-oil marketers have a stake in it, so that they deliver conservation along with energy.[82] How would they do this? They would do energy audits for the house, recommend retrofit measures, subcontract to independent businesses to do the work, but guarantee the work themselves, thus maintaining quality control and reassuring homeowners. In this way, automatic day-night thermostats and furnace adjustments can be combined with structural changes. To help finance the work, the utility would "loan" the money to the customer, who would pay it back as part of the monthly bill or when he sells the house. Many utilities are moving in this direction. For some, it is a strategy to manage load growth and so avoid having to make commitments to expensive new central generating capacity. Others have responded more reluctantly to the prodding of legislation and public utility commissions.

Certainly, the effectiveness of utility involvement has been demonstrated by a number of utilities that have launched retrofit programs. The Tennessee Valley Authority, for instance, launched a home-insulation program in August 1977 that includes free home-energy audits, zero-interest loans, and post-installation reinspection. As of June 30, 1981, some 491,000 homes had been surveyed, and 210,000 consumers had received loans for 404,000 weatherization installations.

Many other utilities are either launching or considering similar programs. In some instances, they have been prodded by innovative state bodies, such as California's Public Utilities Commission. In other instances, as with New England Electric System, they have acted on the basis of internal re-evaluations of their long-term strategy.

Whatever the sources, and they are usually mixed, the consequence has been summed by Charles F. Luce, chairman of New York's Consolidated Edison: "It is said that when Thomas Edison invented the incandescent light, his idea of an electric utility was a company that would supply not only electricity but also a complete lighting service. Instead of selling only kilowatt hours of electricity delivered to the customer's property, the utility would sell an illumination service installed on the customer's premises. . . . But as our industry evolved, it supplied only electricity, and its facilities stopped at the customer's meter. How efficiently that customer used the electricity delivered to his property by the utility was not regarded as the utility's concern. Today the utility industry is moving back to Edison's idea; not thus far as the supplier of illumination but rather as an industry vitally concerned with how efficiently its customers use energy on their premises."

For a national retrofit strategy to have maximum effect, there is also a need to raise the level of skills of those diagnosing and doing retrofits—the creation of what Robert Socolow has called a new profession of "house doctors"—specialists who understand the thermal dynamics of housing and have a high degree of competence in retrofits.[83]

Retrofit, of course, can mean things beyond insulation and storm windows. The heat pump is a device that became commercially available in the 1950's, but is still far from being widely used. Its working principle is simple: In the summer, the pump removes heat from the interior of a building and discharges it outside. In the winter it does the opposite—extracting heat from the outside and pumping it into the building. It can deliver the desired interior comfort much more efficiently than conventional electric heating, for the heat pump can produce up to three times as much output in thermal energy as it receives in electrical energy input. The heat exchange is also important for assuring adequate ventilation in tight houses—related to the whole question of indoor air pollution.[84]

Standard setting and efficiency labeling have now begun to be applied to home appliances. If accelerated, the effort could also lead to substantial savings without affecting people's standard of living. Because energy use by appliances has been increasing much faster than energy use by heating systems, the savings could be very important. Almost a third of residential energy use—6 percent of the national total—is now consumed by major home appliances.[85]

One respected group of researchers at the Oak Ridge National Laboratory has concluded: "A judicious combination of government regulations (appliance efficiency standards, thermal standards for construction of new residences), incentives for weatherization of existing houses, and research and development to produce new technologies can yield a future in which residential energy use in the year 2000 is at roughly the present level. Such a combined program can also provide large economic benefits to households."[86]

Behavior |

Increased efficiency in existing and new buildings will result not just from one set of decisions or from one overall fix, but from an interplay of factors—prices, incentives, regulations, research and development, changing techniques and methods of operation, and changing human attitudes. That last should not be underestimated. The consequences of behavior are crucial. Reducing the thermostat from a twenty-four-hour setting of 74 degrees to 68 degrees during the day and 60 degrees at night can reduce heating loads by as much as 20 percent. Setting air-conditioners at 78 degrees instead of 72 degrees can reduce energy requirements by 15 percent. As the Princeton Twin Rivers project found, some residents use twice as much energy to heat and cool their townhouses as do other residents in identical structures. Retrofit must therefore be combined with an ongoing, consistent, clear, and non-threatening public education campaign. Homeowners otherwise may assume that their one-time decision to weatherize allows them thereafter to forget about energy—which it certainly does not.[87]

It is of great importance to close the energy information gap. Vast amounts of bad and contradictory information have confused the American response to the energy issue, at the individual as well as the national level. Those who want to do something do not know what to do, or whom to believe. This gap costs the United States many, many barrels of oil.

One of the most successful Department of Energy programs has been a sophisticated information out-reach program called "Low-Cost/No Cost." A clear, carefully prepared booklet was mailed to all homeowners in New England. Also included was a small device to restrict the flow in the shower to save hot water. Surveys afterward indicated that this information enabled the average homeowner to reduce consumption to the extent that about every eight dollars invested in the program saved about one barrel. To have imported that barrel at the time would have cost $26 to $30; to have produced it as synthetic fuels, were such fuels available in 1980, might have cost $50 to $60 a barrel. In this case, there is no question which is the low-cost energy source.

It is striking that it took almost six and a half years after the embargo for such a publication to be distributed in such a sensible manner. This omission underlines what a surprisingly inadequate effort has been put into the communications effort (which should be distinguished from pure exhortation). A major reason is that many of those in leadership positions in the executive branch and Congress, as well as state governments, have conceptualized the energy issue primarily as a "high-tech" problem, and have not realized that the reality in the 1970's was and in the 1980's continues to be just as much, if not more, a "people problem," a communications problem. These leaders prefer a "Manhattan Project" to "Madison Avenue," failing to note that neither analogy is particularly relevant. Others have assumed that prices are the be-all and the end-all, that price signals, like chromosomes bearing the genetic code, carry well-defined information about what to do. But prices only convey information about relative scarcities; they do not tell a homeowner whether a flow restrictor in the shower will save hot water. (And, it might be added, they do not provide people with capital.)

Fortunately, an underlying shift in public thinking suggests that the American people are becoming more interested in and responsive to energy efficiency than in the past. A poll taken in 1979 for the Alliance to Save Energy found that, for the first time, a majority of Americans (65 percent) believe that U.S. energy consumption, if not curtailed, will lead to "severe cutbacks in our lifestyle." In earlier years, people would have replied that conservation—rather than *not* conserving—was the threat. A subsequent survey found that 58 percent of the respondents believed that major energy savings should or would come from improved efficiency, while only 30 percent thought the savings "would come from cutbacks in living standards." There was a tendency to comprehend the viability of conservation as a major energy source, in the near term, as indicated in Table 6-6.

CONCLUSION I

Conservation is a blanket term that covers several sectors, many activities, and many different kinds of decision-making. It is there-

TABLE 6·6
"THE ONE OR TWO THINGS
THAT WOULD HELP IMPROVE
THIS COUNTRY'S ENERGY SITUATION FASTEST"

Saving energy	36%
Coal	23%
Oil and natural gas	21%
Solar energy	20%
Nuclear energy	14%
Synthetic energy	10%

Source: Roger Seasonwein Associates, Union Carbide.

fore difficult for public policy to cope with. But let us try to analyze the overall potential in three ways—by projection, by inventory, and by observation.

Many projections about future energy demand have been bound by conventional wisdom, folklore, the inability to incorporate political forces, and the habit of looking at things from the supply side.[88] One of the most significant efforts to break habit's shackles is the recent report of a panel on energy futures assembled by the National Academy of Science. The panel looked at four different plausible scenarios for energy demand in the United States. The scenarios were constructed out of careful engineering analyses of trends in various sectors, combined with econometric and input-output analyses. The results were extraordinary—that in the year 2010 "very similar conditions of habitat, transportation, and other amenities could be provided" in the United States using twice the energy consumed today, *or almost 20 percent less than used today.* And this is with continuing economic and population growth. The fundamental conclusion is "that there is much more flexibility toward reducing energy demand than has been assumed in the past."[89]

Another way to assess the overall potential is through inventory, which can be done by physical modeling. Here, analysts take accessible, often off-the-shelf technologies and compute the cumulative effect on energy consumption of their substitution for conventional technologies. Two scientists followed this procedure in a study for the American Physical Society based on the year 1973.[90] They calculated the savings that would arise from such steps as

- Installing heat pumps
- Increasing refrigerator efficiency by 30 percent
- Reducing heat losses from buildings by 50 percent through better insulation, improved windows, and reduced infiltration
- Implementing cogeneration for half of direct heat applications in industry
- Using organic waste in urban refuse for fuel
- Improving automobile efficiency by 150 percent over 1973 levels

The results are very impressive:

(in millions of barrels per day)

Total U.S. energy consumption (1973)	36
Potential savings	−15
Hypothetical consumption	21

This hypothetical consumption is 40 percent less than the actual consumption in 1973. *In other words, in 1973, the same U.S. living standard could theoretically have been delivered with 40 percent less energy.* These savings, in BTUs, are almost as much as all the oil—not just imported oil—used that year.[91]

The results fly in the face of conventional wisdom. Yet the changes required are considerably less daunting than developing the breeder reactor or making a wholesale conversion back to coal.[92] Sometimes one concludes that the real challenge of energy conservation is not to do it, but rather to believe that it can be done.*

---

*The physical-modeling approach has been carried much farther in a major new study, *A Low Energy Strategy for the United Kingdom*, by Gerald Leach, Christopher Lewis, Ariane Van Buren, Frederic Romig, and Gerald Foley (London: Science Reviews, 1979). Rather than starting with elasticities and some large model of demand, it takes as its starting point the investigation of energy use, and the multiplicity of changes and adaptations that might reduce the amount of

There is yet a third way to conceptualize the real potential for energy conservation, and that is by observation, using such information and understanding as is gained in this chapter. One notes the difference between cars that get 13.5 miles to a gallon and cars that get 33.5 miles to the gallon; between industrial plants that do organize themselves to reduce energy per unit of output by 30 percent and those that do not; between homes that are retrofitted that use 40 percent less energy than homes that are not. Here is evidence for a wide band of flexibility in energy use with current technology.

Public Policy |

But the reader should not be deceived. Nothing will happen automatically, and the obstacles to conservation are manifold. To overcome them in a politically acceptable and nondisruptive way requires adroitness. The movement toward greater energy efficiency, toward greater tapping of conservation energy, will be governed by a complex interaction between government and society. A public policy is required that shapes strong coherent signals, all of which point in the same direction.

It is disheartening to compare the role of public policy in the

---

delivered energy required to provide a service. Energy demand is broken down into some 400 separate categories determined by end-use, fuels, and appliances. Projections of demand are then laboriously built up, "brick by brick." The conclusion? That gross national product could triple in the United Kingdom in the fifty years 1975–2025, but that a series of simple, known technical fixes could keep energy demand pretty much where it was in 1975. The work shares the same spirit of energy pragmatism that, we hope, is central to our own volume, for *A Low Energy Strategy* makes the following points that apply to all Western societies: that there is "immense scope for energy conservation"; that "a low energy future" need *not* be "bleak and repressive"; and that major social change is not required. "Britain —and by implication other countries—can move into a prosperous low-energy future with no more than moderate change. All that is necessary is to apply with a commitment little more vigorous than is being shown today by government, industry, and other agencies some of the technical advances in energy use which have been made, and are still being made, in response to the oil price increase of 1973–74." But, as this chapter has argued, the barriers can be considerable to that somewhat more vigorous commitment. The computer time for the *Low Energy Strategy* study, it might be noted, was provided by British Petroleum, and is to that oil company's credit.

United States with that of other Western countries, especially when one remembers that the United States is the dominant energy consumer on the world scene. The Reagan Administration sought to cut conservation expenditures to just $22 *million* for 1983—compared to an oil import bill (in 1981) of $77 *billion.* Canada, for instance, has established an extensive program to facilitate conservation. The program was instituted after comparing the costs of developing new Canadian hydrocarbon resources with the costs of retrofit. The Canadian expenditure level is twenty times as *large* as the conservation budget requested by the Reagan Administration, although Canada has only one-tenth the population of the United States.

The French government, convinced that an "energy transformation" was at hand, embarked on a major energy conservation program, perhaps the most ambitious in any major industrial country. While some of its elements would not be suitable to American society, the program does indicate how a democratic society can make conservation a high priority without being high-handed. One of the most significant lessons to emerge from the program is the absolute need for coherent signals. As Jean Syrota, the director for energy in the French Ministry of Industry, expressed matters: "You have to put things together. You have to do regulations, financial incentives—not only price—and publicity all at the same time. These three means of action must be coordinated. . . . It is indispensable to be helped strongly by politics, by the government, especially by the government. . . . If the government's actions are not positive, then they are negative, harmful. If government does not show interest, then all sectors of society imagine that it is not important."[93]

Yet there is something ironic about the French program, for France's energy consumption per capita is only 40 percent of America's. Also, what it does has far less impact on the international energy system, since it uses only about 10 percent of the oil that the United States does.

It would be a serious mistake, however, to focus exclusively on the potential roles of the federal government. Energy use, in contrast to energy production, is highly decentralized—in every home, every vehicle, every office. In the last few years, there has been a growing recognition that those levels of government—states and localities—that have the most direct contact with people in their daily lives have a major role to play. The federal government can set the overall signals; it can make sure that the traffic lights are all synchronized on green for energy efficiency. It can, for instance, help provide that incentives, particularly capital, are available to end-users and to the intermediate vendors, such as local governments. But the states and cities are the implementers. States have a great deal of say over transportation. Cities have considerable influence over such matters as housing construction codes, zoning, master planning for land use, property tax assessment, and the operation of hospitals, schools, and other municipal buildings. However, as Henry Lee, former Director of the Massachusetts State Energy Office, has observed: "Having the capability to act does not necessarily signify that this capability will be utilized." Many communities have hung back, on the assumption that energy is something over which they have no control.

Some communities do stand out for their innovative experimentations in this area—Seattle, Washington; Portland, Oregon; Davis, California; St. Paul, Minnesota; Hartford, Connecticut; Franklin County, Massachusetts. In several cases, the locality was galvanized into action by constraints on conventional energy sources (the exhaustion of cheap electricity and natural gas options for Seattle and Portland), and turned to conservation energy as an alternative to expensive new generating capacity. The localities have looked to energy efficiency not only as a way to keep energy costs down, but also to rejuvenate the housing stock and promote general economic development. There is a belief, Lee notes, that "these programs will result in an increase in economic activity and an improvement in the quality of life in that city. This attitude contrasts with the pervasive notion that such programs would cause a deterioration in life-style and unnecessary hardships." But cities, under considerable financial pressure, are unlikely to move forward without assistance from the federal government.[94]

What conclusions emerge from this investigation into three very different energy-consuming sectors of American society?

First, there is a great deal of flexibility in how and how much energy is used for various activities and to deliver various services and amenities. In the past, it did not matter greatly how much energy was consumed for this or that purpose. There was little economic rationale in attending to these questions. It was cheaper to leave windows broken in a factory than to repair them. But the world has changed. It is no longer economically, politically, or environmentally sound to ignore possibilities for much greater efficiency in energy use.

Second, the best way to conceptualize conservation is as an alternative energy source. As such, we can compare it to other sources in terms of payback, ease of recovery, disruption, and environmental effects. Which is cheaper—a barrel of new production in some distant and hostile terrain, with the risk of a dramatic increase in price, or a barrel saved by insulation? How many BTUs are produced by a dollar invested in synthetic fuels—and how many BTUs produced by a dollar invested in retrofit? Which is safer—continued reliance on imported oil, or the heat pump? Real choices about direction do exist. In general, conservation appears to be the energy source that calls for the greatest emphasis in the short and middle term, since it is often the cheapest, most accessible, and least disruptive.

The United States can, in effect, quickly produce millions of barrels per day of conservation energy—at least more quickly than other energy sources. In 1973, such a view would have been regarded in most quarters as heresy—or nonsense. But comprehension has grown. Recently an oil company executive observed that the oil-refining industry is saving 135,000 barrels a day of oil equivalent against 1972 in its refinery operations. This, he pointed out, is almost three times as much as the projected output of the largest shale oil plant expected to be operating in 1990, a multibillion-dollar undertaking. "Although it does cost the oil industry money to realize energy savings, it is much less than the capital costs of an alternative energy scheme, whatever it might be," he stated. "In addition, the lead time to produce the savings involved is a matter of months rather than years." In other words, energy efficiency is one of the choices in deciding on the energy use required to run a refinery. The larger significance of the statement is that it illustrates the developing consensus that conservation is in fact an alternate source of energy. Obviously, conservation is no final answer in itself, as some are quick to remind us. The energy newsletter of Citibank said, "It cannot be stressed too strongly that this country cannot conserve its way out of the energy problem," and instead argued that increased domestic production could provide an alternative to imported oil. But those who so argue are more and more hard pressed to demonstrate that domestic oil, gas, coal, or fission provides any final, or indeed even any better, answers than does conservation. Conservation certainly buys the United States time, and given the difficulties that attend the other sources, provides more immediate relief than do high-capital, high-technology alternatives.[95]

Third, conservation energy is not so simple to recover as it might seem. Unfortunately, it is a diffuse source, and it has no clear constituency in the way that oil, gas, coal, and nuclear do. Public policy must be its champion. With such a commitment, many different strategies will be needed. Public policy must create a hospitable environment for the expeditious exploitation of this source. If we had decades, then the market alone, working through gradual rise in prices, would be sufficient. But the decades are not there. For conservation to make the kind of contribution it should in the relevant time span, there must be found that adroit mixture of measures—of price, regulation, incentives, information, and research and development. Only in that way can conservation actions become as economically attractive to individual decision-makers as they are to the society at large.

The American system is particularly responsive to incentives. Up to now, the failure of public policy has been its inability to assess the true prices and true risks of conventional alternatives, and its consequent inability to measure against them the costs of incentives that will promote conservation.

Certainly $34 a barrel of oil is stimulating conservation that would not have occurred at $13 a barrel. Pointing to the recent record, a leading energy industry spokesman declared, "See, price works." But the blessings have been mixed. For with the price shocks have come high inflation and the deepest recession since the Great Depression. Public policy has an important role in correcting market imperfections and taking into account the social cost of oil in order to facilitate a smooth transition and so avoid costly price shocks in the future.

What are the "principles" of a meaningful energy conservation policy?

1. The pricing system should give clear and consistent signals about energy. This means decontrolled energy prices that eventually reflect replacement costs. But these prices should be accompanied by measures that reduce the hardships for lower-income persons.

2. Incentives should give conservation a fair chance against imported oil, including a premium on oil prices to reflect the social costs.

3. A permanent information and education campaign should be maintained. The market will not operate efficiently if information is not available.[96]

4. A broad-ranging conservation research-and-development program should be instituted.

Each of the three energy-consuming sectors need somewhat different strategies. All should build on existing programs.

1. Automobile manufacturing involves very few decision-makers. Regulatory policies applied with flexibility are most effective. Higher gasoline efficiency should be pursued in post-1985 standards, but in a way that takes into account the capital investment problems facing the auto industry. Buses and car-pools should be stimulated, and perhaps free public transportation should be experimented with in a few cities. The unthinkable—a moderate increase in the gasoline tax, either rebated or used to reduce other taxes—should be thought about.

2. For industry, while subsidies are useful for demonstration projects, the preferred method to encourage conservation should be substantial investment tax credits, accelerated depreciation, and loans (the last is especially important for smaller businesses). To such signals businessmen habitually respond. Firmer conservation targets should be set for major energy-consuming industries, but familiar and flexible methods should be used to encourage them.

3. Buildings involve the greatest number of decisionmakers. Regulations perhaps geared to performance, not specifications, are

extremely important for encouraging energy-conscious design in new construction. They can be encouraged through federal loan agencies and savings and loan associations, which can also encourage retrofit through their lending policies. This suggestion is an example of the principle that existing and familiar institutions should be used to deliver conservation to the public. Another example would be the giving to utilities of a major stake in retrofit, that is, for generating conservation energy. For the homeowner, direct subsidies, extensive tax credits, and perhaps exemption from property taxes for conservation improvements—these are required to speed and spread retrofit. Certainly the marginal costs of imported oil justify such assistance, thus making conservation as valuable to the individual homeowner as it is to the society, and also making the signal visible, not merely a haze on the horizon.[97]

The United States might use 30 percent less energy than it does, with virtually no penalty for the way Americans live—save that billions of dollars will be spared, save that the environment will be less strained, the air less polluted, save that the dependence on OPEC oil and an unstable region will be reduced, and Western society will be less likely to suffer internal and international tension. These are benefits Americans should be only too happy to accept.

7 SOLAR AMERICA

MODESTO A. MAIDIQUE*

During most of this century, solar energy seemed to interest only dreamers, tinkers, and political radicals of one sort or another.** But because of the oil embargo, and subsequent price increases, renewables have become a serious alternative source of energy. The issue has now become *how much, what kind*— and *when.* According to Denis Hayes the organizer of International Sun Day, "Forty percent of our energy could come from solar energy by the year 2000 if we make some dramatic moves *now.*" The editor of *World Oil* disagrees, saying that the source will have the impact over the next quarter-century of "a mosquito bite on an elephant's fanny."[1]

The two estimates lay out the range of the debate on the near- and middle-term potential contribution of renewables to America's energy needs. It is possible that renewables will end up little more than that mosquito bite—that is, not provide any significant addition to America's energy mix. It also is possible for renewables

---

*with the assistance of John Ince
**We use the terms "renewables" and "solar energy" interchangeably. Some people mistakenly assume that solar just applies to active hot water systems, when in fact it encompasses—as we shortly point out—a wide variety of renewable energy sources.

to meet as much as a fifth of the country's equivalent of the current amount of imported oil.

Just a few years ago, one could have only speculated about the possibilities for solar. Today, however, we have several years of experience behind us in the "modern" renewables era. Just how have renewables measured up so far? The growth rates of renewables in the last five years have been impressive: From 1975 to 1980, dollar sales of solar equipment, including active passive and photovoltaics, increased 777 percent; wind increased 352 percent; biomass equipment, 257 percent; and geothermal 128 percent.[2] Solar America, however, is not a certainty. In order to achieve a 23 percent penetration, high growth rates must be maintained for at least another decade in the solar sectors.

To achieve this level, solar energy must have a fair chance in the marketplace against conventional energy sources, some of which are heavily subsidized. This means continued governmental incentives, sustained research and development programs, expanded information efforts, creative financing techniques, careful attention to legal and institutional impediments, as well as sensitivity and flexibility in the face of unanticipated environmental consequences. A commitment to solar energy must also be sufficiently strong to weather the effect of vacillating political policies and shifting short-term economic conditions. If these conditions are met, it is not unrealistic to envision a twenty-first-century Solar America, a society that relies more on renewable sources of energy than on exhaustible hydrocarbons.

Certainly, in terms of dollar outlays, government support during the Carter Administration increased dramatically. From fiscal years 1975 until 1980, the federal government's appropriation for solar increased steadily from $42 million to $623 million. Fiscal year 1981 was the first year that President Reagan exerted influence over the solar budget, primarily through recisions and deferrals. In that year, the research budget declined to $471. For fiscal year 1982, Carter had recommended $576 million, Reagan recommended $170 million—and Congress passed $275 million. In fiscal year 1983, Reagan had again recommended figures around the $73-million mark.

The sharp reversal of attitude toward renewables under the Reagan Administration was evident from the following statement of Reagan's first Energy Secretary James Edwards: "It will take fifty to one hundred years before solar can make a significant contribution to our energy program."[3]

In order to comprehend the potential for renewable energy, its diversity must be understood. Renewable energy is not a single new energy technology, but a broad term that covers a diverse set of technologies, some new and some quite old. It includes proposals for colossal microwave satellites and huge ocean platforms, as well as for wood, Colonial America's principal fuel. But all of the renewable technologies have an important common denominator: unlike coal, gas, and oil, they are inexhaustible for the humanly foreseeable future. The unifying concept is that renewable energy is the energy which arrived on the earth from the sun "recently" (i.e., during the last hundred years or so).[4]

The Department of Energy has divided renewable into eight different individual categories which can be organized into three major groups:[5]

1. *Thermal (heating and cooling) applications*
   Heating and cooling of buildings—including hot water heating
   Agricultural and industrial process heating
2. *Fuels from biomass*
   Plant matter, including wood and waste
3. *Solar electric*
   Solar thermal electric—such as the "power tower"
   Photovoltaics—solar cells
   Wind—windmills
   Ocean thermal electric
   Hydropower—hydroelectric dams

Each of the individual categories can be further elaborated. For instance, biomass includes not only wood, but also sea algae, gasohol, vegetable oils, and gasified manure.

Renewable requires new ways of thinking about energy. Procuring energy has conventionally meant buying fuel—oil, gas, and coal. Most forms of biomass also require buying fuel, but other types of renewable energy will mean buying equipment. The fuel —sunshine, wind, water, or temperature gradients—is free. Thus, frequent purchases of fuel must be measured against a one-time investment in equipment.

Would the coming of renewable energy bring, as some have suggested, fundamental changes to American society? Technological change generally implies some degree of social change, and that will surely be the case with renewable energy. But the "revolutionary" impact of solar has been exaggerated. Certain industries and firms would be affected much more than society as a whole.

The spread of solar heating and the other on-site technologies, such as agricultural and industrial process heating, small windmills, small dams, and local usage of plant matter, could have significant impact on the traditional distributors of energy—the utilities. They could find themselves partially bypassed, leading to a leveling off or actual decline in demand for their services.[6] The managerial responsibility for generating energy would then, at least in part, move out of the hands of the utility executive into those of the energy consumer himself. Still, a shift of this sort hardly means the disappearance of the utilities or a revolutionary transformation of American society, as some "small is beautiful" advocates have argued. In short, on-site renewable energy technologies are unlikely to trigger a fundamental decentralization of American society.[7]

A reasonable assessment of solar prospects requires analyses of very diverse forms of energy, and we have, therefore, chosen to concentrate on four of the most important options. The first, solar heating, is what most people think of when they think of solar energy. The second, biomass, especially wood and waste, is already making an impact.[8] The third, solar electric, has been a leading recipient of research funds.[9] The fourth technology, photovoltaics, converts light to electricity using semiconductor technology, the basis of the transistor and integrated circuit industry. Each of the four renewable options differs in its level of technological advancement, its market potential, and the economic and institutional barriers it faces.

SOLAR HEATING |

Solar heating is one of the most technically developed on-site renewable technologies.[10] It is hardly a new technology, but rather represents a return to a path abandoned only during the last hundred years or so. Up until that time, most human cultures sought to incorporate the sun itself into the design of its architecture. The surviving baths at Pompeii, for example, demonstrate the use Romans made of solar water heating. Channels carrying water to the baths were built open to the sun and lined with grooved black slate, so that the water became heated as it ran through the grooves on its way to the bathers. The Mesa Verde cliff dwellings in Colorado were constructed with massive rock overlays, which provided shade from the high and hot summer sun, but allowed the rays of the lower winter sun to penetrate. Over the centuries, many very different cultures have designed and built structures that embody the basic principle of solar architecture found at Mesa Verde.[11]

Today, a design that manages to take advantage of the sun with few or no moving parts is called passive solar heating. The structure itself is sited, constructed, and landscaped so that it becomes in effect a large solar collector. South-facing window space is maximized; walls are situated so as to facilitate air convections and provide storage for heat at night; and windows have two panes so as to retain a maximum percentage of heat during winter months and at night. Passive design also includes such features as roof overhangs, skylights, rock beds to store heat, and solar greenhouses.[12]

Such architecture, ignored for several decades in the United States, has received increasing attention since the embargo. Energy-conscious design, where conservation and solar energy overlap, can be very effective. In Nacogdoches, Texas, for example, a retired Air Force colonel built a U-shaped passive house. In his previous home, which was nearby, he paid $850 a year for winter heating and summer air-conditioning; in the new house, the annual bill fell to $260. The passive approach also works in the colder climates; in Maine, an 8,000-square-foot, energy-conscious commercial building saved its owners about $400 a month in heating bills. In Davis, California, an entire development of over 250 homes has been built along these principles.[13]

There is a fundamental proposition underlying the effective solar design employed in these structures. First, the heating needs of the building are minimized by improved insulation, weather-stripping, and similar conservation practices. Only then is an investment made in active solar heating. In sum, the maxim is: conserve first, then heat. In this manner the total investment required—in conservation and solar design—can be minimized, for conservation substantially reduces the cost of the solar design required. This improves the return on the overall investment, for, in general, investment in conservation yields the highest economic return, followed closely by passive solar design, and then by active solar hot water heating and space heating.

Much experimentation and learning—and relearning—is now occurring with passive solar heating. Passive design, however, has a drawback. Its major impact will be on new structures, and as noted in the preceding chapter, the building stock turns over slowly. Also, the rate of penetration of passive architecture is highly sensitive to local building markets. In Denver, a dozen developers demonstrated that with careful planning passive solar can be effectively marketed. They staged a sixteen-day tour in 1981 that attracted over 95,000 persons and generated $2.5 million in immediate sales and an additional $6.3 million in deferred sales.[14] In many other regions of the country, however, passive solar technology encounters the cold stares that most innovative architectural features face.

The amount of energy captured by passive solar designs is difficult to document. But it appears that at the national level the pace of dissemination of passive technology remains slow. The National Association of Homebuilders Research Foundation (NAHRF) estimates that less than one percent of new homes incorporate a comprehensive package of passive solar design features. Why?

Although a number of individual design features are incorporated in a growing number of homes, "It's the old problem of technology transfer," said Ralph Johnson, executive director of the NAHRF. "The existing data on potential savings are very poor and the information provided by the government cannot be understood by anyone other than a mathematician or physicist. When a builder puts up a house he is risking his own capital. He'll stop awhile before spending an additional $10,000 to put up a house that looks different, operates differently, and may overheat in summer. He has to be pretty sure of the data and know that he can recoup his $10,000."[15]

The full impact of passive design will not be felt until the next decade. The pace will be affected by the rate at which knowledge and experience are disseminated and by the overall health of the housing industry.

While passive solar systems will make their principal impact on new buildings, active solar systems can be retrofitted onto existing structures as well as incorporated into new ones. Active systems are so called because they involve mechanical moving parts. Panels about three feet by seven feet are bolted on the roof. Generally made of aluminum, glass, plastic, and copper, the panels catch and concentrate the sun's rays, which in turn heat water, air, or some other medium that flows in pipes through them. Fans or pumps then circulate the medium through a heat exchanger in a water-filled storage tank. The hot water in the storage tank can be used either directly or to heat the house by pumping it through a conventional radiator network. (See Figure 7-1.)

Active solar heating and solar hot-water heating are variations on the same system, differing principally in cost and scale. Three solar panels may satisfy the hot-water needs of a house, whereas a hot-water and space heating system in the same house may require ten or more such panels. The larger system will cost several times more, but will also save several times as much fuel. A solar heating system does not, however, completely eliminate the need for conventional sources. The most cost-effective design typically meets one half to two thirds of heating needs, which means that a backup conventional heating system is required for periods of sustained cloudiness. And, of course, conventional electric power is needed for lighting and appliances.

As of January 1983, there were about 400,000 residential solar heating installations, mostly just for hot water, in the

FIGURE 7·1
PASSIVE SOLAR HOME

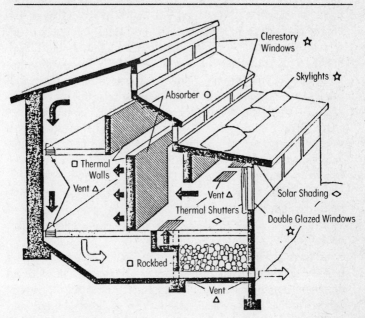

Clerestory Windows ☆

Skylights ☆

Absorber ○

Thermal Walls □

Vent △

Vent △

Thermal Shutters ◇

Solar Shading ◇

Double Glazed Windows ☆

Rockbed □

Vent △

Recognition Factors

□ Storage Mass
☆ Solar Collection Areas
○ Absorber
△ Heat Distribution
◇ Heat Regulation Method

Source: U.S. Department of Energy, "Passive and Hybrid Solar Energy," January, 1980.

United States. Still, the American solar industry is well behind its counterparts in other nations, such as Japan, Israel, and Australia. Israel, with a population less than 2 percent that of the United States, has 400,000 domestic hot water systems.[16] Israel, of course, has more sunshine than much of the United States, but the explanation for the wide disparities in penetration rates lies deeper in the personal habits of other peoples of the world. For instance, Japan now has over 2 million solar hot water installations. True, Japanese homeowners use considerably less hot water than Americans and, therefore, can be satisfied with smaller systems with fewer collector plates. And instead of electric pumps, smaller systems can incorporate the use of pressure from the heated water to move the water around—what is known as a thermosyphon system. This approach can be much more cost effective than more elaborate and larger systems; in 1980 alone, 250,000 thermosyphon systems were sold in Japan versus 10,000 in the United States.[17]

The solar heating industry has the classic characteristics of a new industry with small entry barriers—fragmentation, with no dominant design or leading manufacturer. A great deal of entrepreneurial energy is evident, as hundreds of firms—hungry and hoping for their share of a potentially huge market—compete under such names as Sun Works, Sun Power, Sunsave, Sunspot, Sunburst, and Sunco.

In this environment, some affiliates of major corporations have found the revenues too small and the margins too tight to support their heavy overheads and, as a result, have withdrawn. For example, Exxon, Libby-Owens Ford, PPG Industries, and Olin Brass have all exited from the flat plate collector business.[18]

One can expect more major changes in industry structure with marginal competitors dropping out and leading firms emerging. But what comes out of this will not constitute a high-technology industry. Rather, a given company's strengths will come from its ability to refine its product lines and to work out an effective system of promotion and distribution. As one solar heating executive observed in an interview, "Solar is a hard sell. The key to success in this business is marketing and logistics." This will require effective selection and training of distributors, plus innovative advertising and the development of quality controls. The solar industry might well follow the industry-structure model provided by the central air-conditioning business, where a handful of firms dominate the manufacturing, but where installation and service are local businesses.

Although solar heating is a growing industry, it is far from clear that solar heating will fulfill its potential as a real alternative to imported oil. There are two barriers, economic and institutional, that must be overcome for solar heating to make a significant contribution. First, possible customers for solar heating want a fast return on their investment—that is, to recoup in a few years the dollars spent on installing a system through dollars saved on fuel costs. The fuel savings need to be substantial, for a hot-water heating system typically costs $2000–$3500 for a single family home, from a few hundred dollars to $5,000 for a passive space heating system, and for an active space and hot-water heating system, $5,000 to $13,000. The Energy Project at the Harvard Business School distributed 4,000 questionnaires to a randomly selected population across the country. Three key points emerged: (1) The idea of solar heating is very attractive. (2) People are poorly informed about how such systems work and how to get one installed. (3) On average, a five-year payback—that is, the investment recovered in fuel savings in five years—is necessary to attract serious consideration. And in order to get 80 percent of the respondents to think about installing a system, a two-year or better payback was required.[19]

Yet tens of thousands of people are buying solar systems today. The marketing manager of a leading solar firm described the solar consumer as "a man in his late forties or fifties, typically an engineer or an architect earning forty to fifty thousand dollars a year. He buys equipment for status or philosophical reasons. Economics are not a factor." This profile, however, is changing. Solar energy is also being adopted by some middle-income people in their thirties. A California solar-user profile indicated that over half of those that applied for the state tax credit for solar equipment were in the middle-income range ($20,000–40,000). Moreover, the size and character of the solar market will be expanded by a provision in the Military Construction Act of 1979, which stipulates that if "cost effective," that is, if they can pay for themselves over the next fifteen to twenty-five years, solar heating systems must be incorporated into all new military housing and 25 percent of remaining new military construction.[20] But it is clear that in order to make an important contribution, solar heating must become accepted by a much broader range of people than is currently the case, and basic household economics will be an important factor.

Our surveys of business executives, as well as homeowners, support the contention that the rate of return, perceived as too low, constitutes the critical economic obstacle. The problem is accentuated because the difficulties of analyzing solar by conventional methods are considerable, and they bias the comparisons against solar. To begin with, analysis must take into account weather, technology, and the cost of the fuel assumed on the comparison. An eight-year payback for a new house with electric hot-water heating in Albuquerque, New Mexico, may become a forty-year payback for an existing gas-heated house in Augusta, Maine. Beyond this, several considerations very much in solar's favor are often overlooked.

First, energy saved with a solar system can be considered tax-free income. For a homeowner in a high-tax bracket, this can be important. Secondly, as energy costs rise in excess of the inflation rate, the value of the solar investment increases. That is, one purchases a system at today's prices and realizes savings at tomorrow's energy prices. Thirdly, any capital appreciation of the solar system will be taxed at capital gain rates upon resale of the home. Fourth, federal and state tax credits, formulated in recognition of the fact that solar does not carry many of the social and external costs of conventional fuel, can cover more than half of the capital costs of a solar system for the homeowner, in effect doubling the return on investment.[21]

There are two other important economic barriers. One is the cost of borrowing money.[22] The other is the possible increase in property tax that might result from the installation of solar heating.

Powerful institutional barriers also impede the acceptance of solar heating. One of the most formidable is building codes. Each

American locality has its own code—the result of geography, climate, building materials, and local political forces. Frequently the codes do not provide for solar energy and where they do, the sheer complexity of the procedures can discourage a prospective solar user. A New Hampshire man, for example, wanted to install solar hot-water heating. He applied for a building permit to make the necessary modifications in the structure of his house, but an official in the town planner's office told him that solar energy was not in the building code's lexicon. So, after going through all the documents, hearings, and other procedures required to obtain variances from building codes, he decided he did not want solar after all.[23]

Another institutional barrier is the level of skills required to install and maintain solar systems. The construction industry, like other fragmented low-technology industries, does very little research and development, and is slow to adapt to technological changes. Indeed, recent experience suggests that poor installation is a far greater problem than the reliability of the solar equipment itself, and can cast a shadow over the future of the industry.[24] Since most installations are site specific, the degree of care, patience, imagination, and experience required is great. There is, however, some reason for optimism; many firms now have experienced workers and maintain high standards. But worker turnover and inadequate training remain serious problems for other firms.[25]

Another obstacle is legal uncertainty. Access to the sun is not a transferable property right in most of the United States. Yet such a guarantee is essential to eliminate one of the main risks associated with installing solar energy—loss of access to the sun. The sun's rays strike solar collectors in the United States at an average angle of 35 degrees (plus or minus 20 degrees, depending on location). Obviously, light must pass through the air space above a neighbor's property before it can be collected. Without legal protection, a rational potential solar buyer will think twice before committing capital to an energy source that depends on a neighbor's whims—or on the growth of his trees, or on the construction of a high-rise apartment house.[26] In November 1980, a Wisconsin Circuit Court judge ruled against a solar homeowner who wanted to prevent his neighbor from constructing a home that would have obstructed the sun's access to his solar collectors. Presently under appeal to the State Supreme Court, the case was considered to be a possible landmark case and it underlines the thorny legal questions that confront a potential solar homeowner.

The attitude and role of utilities has been in many cases a major stumbling block. Most solar-heated homes will still need to be connected to electric utilities for a source of backup supply. Thus, the rate structure and attitudes of utilities are very important to the successful implementation of solar heating on any scale. As things now stand, utility rate structures can discourage conversion to solar, affecting institutions as well as individual homeowners. A Massachusetts bank, for example, decided to make a major investment in an advanced design solar space and hot-water system for one of its new branch offices. All went well until the bank found that its application for the low all-electric rate had been turned down by the local utility. The power company claimed that by using solar space and hot-water heating, the bank had forfeited its right to the all-electric rate, even though it employed no conventional fuels—that is, no oil, gas, or coal. Because loss of the right would have nullified any savings that might have been achieved with the solar system, the bank reversed its decision, abandoned plans for an overall solar space heating system, and installed only a smaller system for hot-water heating. With the smaller system, the bank managed to qualify for a lower electric rate, but was still denied all-electric status.[27]

Initially, many utilities, seeing solar heating as a new competition, were indifferent or even hostile to it.[28] But the high cost and uncertainty that surrounds the addition of new central generating capacity is changing the minds of many executives. They increasingly view solar heating as a potentially useful way to manage their demand growth. Some utilities now offer technical or financial assistance. Pacific Gas and Electric, the nation's largest private utility, now offers rebates roughly equal to the value of the interest paid on a loan needed to purchase a solar hot water system.[29]

The Tennessee Valley Authority has assumed a leadership role in promoting solar heating in the seven-state region it serves. Since initiating a solar domestic hot water program in 1978, the TVA can claim 25,000 installations at an average cost of $3,200. That saves homeowners an average of $150–200 annually. TVA offers homeowners a free energy survey, low-interest, long-term loans, referral services for solar installers, as well as follow-up inspection to assure quality control. Pat Harris, TVA's director of public relations, indicated the reasoning behind their ambitious program in solar: "As an integral part of our planning process for load management over the next twenty years, we compared solar and conservation alternatives to central station alternatives. We have verified that these programs are cost justified not only compared to the costs of building new capacity, but also when compared to the operating costs of existing capacity."[30]

Without utility support, or at least cooperation, the spread of solar heating will be greatly retarded. A survey in Pennsylvania concluded that "if solar energy is ever to achieve substantial adoption rates, utilities will have to play a pivotal marketing role."

A key question still remains: How to assure solar heating a fair chance in the marketplace against conventional sources?[31] First, economic incentives are necessary in order to offset subsidies given to conventional energy sources and help the diffusion of innovation. Such incentives should be framed with the traditional innovation pattern in mind—that is, the problem is to get over the sluggish first phase, and then allow the industry to proceed on its own momentum.[32] The 1980 Windfall Profits Act allows credits of 40 percent of the cost of qualified active solar heating on principal residential buildings up to $10,000 through 1985. In addition, many states offer generous tax credits.

California offers a 55 percent credit, which, combined with facilitating legislation, has helped speed up the pace of solar installation. At the beginning of 1983, there were an estimated 150,000 active solar heating installations in California, almost half of the total in the nation. Solar heating is now a $250-million industry in the state with a current employment of over 4,000 persons. Thus far, well over 100 manufacturers and 200 installers with solar experience are doing business in the state.

Extrapolation of California's projections to the remainder of the country, however, is complicated by the mix of fuels employed, climate, architectural characteristics of the housing and commercial building stock, the rate of new building construction, and—most important—incentives. Solar hot water and space heating, however, is technically feasible across the entire country, but the rest of the country lags behind California. Indeed, one of the main arguments of this chapter is that vigorous action by the federal executive branch and Congress—and their state counter-parts—will be required to minimize this lag.

Several other states have followed California's lead. Arizona, Massachusetts, Vermont, and Oregon have instituted state tax credits of 25 to 35 percent for renewable energy installations. In Arizona, where the state tax credit can be taken by the builder while the homeowner takes the federal tax credit, the installation rate tripled from 1978 to 1979. But it is too early to tell how much of the rapid advances made in Arizona and California are a result of the tax credits by themselves, and how much is the result of the overall legislative climate and the activist role of the state energy commissions. An early conjecture is that it is the overall program rather than any one single factor that has led to an accelerated solar adoption rate in both states.[33]

Since solar heating equipment is a capital good, the value of tax credits is limited unless accompanied by appropriate financing. The "solar bank" passed by Congress in early 1980 would have helped meet that need, although the initial level of funding was much too low and subsequent budget reductions by the Reagan Administration have effectively killed the program. Therefore, a great challenge remains in educating financial institutions in the evaluation of solar heating.

Building codes must also be reformed to facilitate action by state legislatures and city councils.[34] Therefore, a model solar heating code is required. The code would need to take into account regional differences, and would also need to include provisions on sun rights and recommendations for property-tax exclusion.

WOOD AND WASTE: OLDER THAN ROMAN POOLS I

The ideal solar collector has already been designed. Requiring virtually no maintenance, it is economical and nonpolluting; it uses an established technology and stores energy. It is called a plant.[35]

Indeed, organic matter from plants and animals, or biomass, constitutes a major near-term and accessible form of solar energy. According to a 1980 study by the Office of Technology Assessment, biomass under "business-as-usual" conditions could contribute up to the equivalent of 3 million barrels of oil by the year 2000, most of it from commercial forests. With vigorous government support, the report argues, up to 8 mbd may be achieveable. The potential is also large on a worldwide basis. Photosynthesis stores more than ten times as much energy annually in plant form than is consumed by all mankind. But very little of this energy is tapped, particularly in the developed countries.[36]

This has not always been the case. Less than a century ago, wood was the United States' principal fuel. As recently as 1900, wood accounted for 25 percent of the country's total energy,[37] but by 1976 it provided less than 1.5 percent, or about .5 million barrels per day. And most of the 1.5 percent—.4 mbd—came from the forest products industry, which burns tree wastes. The resurgence of biomass as residential heating fuel as well as in the forest products industry and in selected industrial uses is indicated by growth to .8 mbd by 1979.[38] And by the end of 1981, wood use approximated one mbd. This, however, still lags far behind wood heating in other countries like Sweden and Finland where 8 and 15 percent of their energy needs are met by wood.[39]

The theoretical potential of biomass is very large, but within the continental United States, most of the land suitable for biomass production is legally withdrawn from timber harvesting or is already used to produce food feed, fiber, or timber. Thus, only about 20 percent—480 million acres—is commercial forest land that could under optimal conditions be considered available for fuel. Even 20 percent would make for the equivalent of 3 million barrels a day. But the achievement of this level faces three serious obstacles. First, there is opposition from environmentalists. Second is the limited infrastructure for wood harvest and distribution, and third, insufficient knowledge of proper forest management techniques. Another 5 mbd is potentially economically recoverable from municipal solid and liquid wastes and from animal manure. This recovery could also help to solve the problem of what to do with the waste generated in America.[40]

There are several different methods for *bioconversion*, which is the term for the transformation of biomass into usable energy. One is the simple direct burning of solid wood or other plants. The second is the conversion of biomass into a liquid. Brazil, for instance, had a goal of replacing 20 percent of its gasoline with alcohol derived from plant matter, primarily sugar cane, by the end of 1980.[41] A third method is a biological process in which bacteria break down organic waste into methane gas. Considerable research is now going on to develop new sources of biomass, such as quick-growing plants, that would provide greater energy intensities.[42]

Brazil's ambitious goal to convert its entire fleet of motorcars to alcohol by the end of the 1980's, combined with the corn and wheat surplus produced by President Carter's grain embargo to the Soviet Union, resulted in overly optimistic expectations regarding the potential of gasohol in the United States. Gasohol is a blend of 90 percent gasoline and 10 percent ethanol ("grain alcohol") that can be used directly in U.S. automobiles without any modification to existing engines and is close to being economically competitive. First, one can say that extrapolations from the Brazil expectations on alcohol may not be justified. Indeed, Brazil has scaled down its original targets.[43] Furthermore, Brazil has considerably different land costs and availability than the United States, and agricultural labor rates and other factor costs are also considerably lower. Second, beyond a sustained level of 2 billion gallons of ethanol per year (.12 mbd of oil equivalent, about 2 percent of present imports), competition for grain and sugar feedstocks may increase food prices significantly. This is not to say that ethanol from grain and sugar feedstocks does not present an attractive and also presently economic alternative to reduce dependence on imported oil, but simply that the large contributions from biomass will come from other sources.

For the remainder of this century, wood and related waste products will continue to be the United States' principal source of domestic biomass. There are three major markets where the potential 3 mbd of additional wood and wood waste could be consumed: the forest products industry, residential wood heating, and industrial firms and utilities that employ coal-fired boilers that can be converted to wood.

Today the main consumer of wood for energy generation is the forest products industry, which derives over half of its total energy needs from burning primarily bark and mill waste. But the industry could become almost self-sufficient in about a decade without great difficulty by burning additional quantities of wood and wood waste, thus saving an additional million barrels of oil a day equivalent.[44]

Another major market for wood is residential wood heating. Sales of wood stoves have been booming since the oil embargo. One survey estimates that the number of installed wood stoves has increased from one million in 1974 to well over five million in 1980. If the new stoves' wood-burning capacity were used at the same rate as the old capacity, a fivefold increase in home wood consumption—from .1 mbd to .5 mbd—would be realized.[45]

A third category of potential use is in industrial firms and utilities that presently employ coal-fired boilers. Wood and dry crop wastes have an energy content of about 16 million BTU per ton. By comparison, coal—wood's old rival and still, for many purposes, its principal competitor—ranges from 16 million BTU per ton for Western coals to 25 million BTU per ton for the good Eastern coals.[46] In other words, wood is roughly comparable in heat content per ton with Western coal. However, the economics of any further comparison are influenced by two offsetting factors: Coal is easier to transport and to use than wood and dry crop waste; coal, however, is a notoriously bad pollutant, whereas wood contains, on the average, less than one tenth of the sulfur content of the black mineral.[47]

Yet the constraining effects of both factors can be dealt with. Coal pollution can be greatly reduced by adding scrubbers. And the difficulty in transporting wood can be reduced by chipping it or possibly by compressing it into half-inch-diameter wood pellets that are more convenient to handle. Such being the case, the cost of these processes must be included in any fair economic comparison. But wood can be obtained at economic prices only if the consumption point and the source are within approximately a hundred miles of each other. At longer distances the economics generally favor coal. But when the costs of sulfur scrubbing are included, shipping the wood becomes economical over an additional several hundred miles. A full comparison can be extremely complicated, but the important point is that, under many circumstances, wood and dry crop wastes can compete with coal.

Burning wood can be very economical. One firm in Tennessee installed a $2.3 million boiler capable of firing 500 tons of pellets or wood chips per day, and has found that the savings in conventional fuel costs provided a payback of less than five years.[48] A utility in Vermont, Burlington Electric, generates one third of its electricity production with wood.

A large increase in wood burning would necessitate either the management of present forests for fuel source or the establishment of large "energy plantations" devoted to the growing of energy crops. The latter constitutes one of the best hopes for long-term renewable energy, and it is beginning to attract considerable interest.

However, three barriers stand in the way. The first is cost. For energy plantations, biomass would represent the main income, not a supplementary one, as for timberlands. When forest economics are analyzed on the basis of cutting down the entire tree for energy alone, the cost of the wood increases dramatically. But research in improved tree cultivation and tree species could reduce this cost by half during the next decade.[49]

The second obstacle is land—a great deal of which would be required for large energy plantations. But improved techniques could reduce the amount of land required.[50]

The third is pollution. In some areas where residential wood use has grown rapidly, the build-up of particulate emissions has caused great concern. When wood is burned at low temperatures, which is the common practice in wood stoves, the emission level increases dramatically. In residential use, improper burning methods and the resulting pollution definitely constitutes a near-term constraint, which warrants the concern of appropriate regulatory bodies. By comparison, industrial fuel-wood burning, which takes place at a high temperature, produces virtually no emissions.[51]

There is much to recommend wood and forest waste as a

source of energy. The process of growing trees is familiar, the economics are attractive in many situations, pollution is low, and storage capability is inherent. In the short term, the oil equivalent of 2 mbd of energy may be achieved by the increased use of wood and wood waste in residential heating and in the forest products industry.[52]

The other major near-term biomass source is municipal and animal wastes, which a biological process can turn into perhaps an additional mbd of useful energy.[53] Organic waste can be transformed into a low-BTU gas, containing methane. In less sophisticated forms, the technology has been used in sewage-treatment plants since the turn of the century.

There are several varieties of longer-term potential biomass sources. They extend from sugar-producing trees that can be harvested on an annual basis to microorganisms that can live on simple nutrients and may produce a hydrocarbon harvest in a matter of hours, not weeks or seasons. Further out in the horizon is the use of genetically engineered enzymes or microorganisms to optimize the fermentation of crops into hydrocarbons.[54]

Federal energy policy should encourage bioconversion research, especially for small and medium-scale products. A major effort is needed to familiarize foresters, farmers, and businessmen with the benefits and potential of biomass.[55] Bioconversion incentives should also be incorporated into utility regulations.

Meanwhile, large biomass projects, such as energy plantations, may not have an impact in this century. But well-developed, locally based technologies could provide 6 percent of U.S. energy needs by the end of the century, as opposed to roughly 2 percent today.

SOLAR ELECTRIC |

High in the French Pyrenees sits a sparkling ten-story parabolic mirror that looks from a distance like an oversized diamond nestled in a sloping green valley. It is a 1 megawatt solar furnace—a power tower.

In 1977 this solar furnace, which lies near the town of Font-

Romeu, was the only solar thermal electric system in the world that was pumping power into a conventional electric grid. Although the structure was designed primarily for achieving high temperatures for research purposes, the French tapped off some of the heat to prove a point: that solar energy could be used to generate conventional electric power.[56]

The system works by reflecting the sun's rays onto a large parabolic mirror via an array of smaller mirrors perched on an adjoining hillside. The parabolic mirror focuses the incident light onto a small area where a boiler is placed. The steam produced by the boiler is piped down to a small building that contains a 100 kilowatt steam turbine-generator combination.

Under the Carter Administration, the solar thermal electric program, better known as the power tower, commanded nearly a fifth of the entire federal budget for solar energy.[57] Although the widely publicized Barstow power tower in the Southern California desert was completed and operating in 1982, the Reagan Administration's cutting of the solar budget has put further development of the power tower into limbo.[58] The power tower is only one of several renewable sources of electricity. Some are familiar, such as windmills and hydroelectric dams. Others are in the early stages of development, such as solar salt ponds and photovoltaics, while still others are quite speculative, such as ocean thermal conversion and microwave space power satellites.

Wind |

Wind energy offers the hope of near-term, cost-effective power generation. This source includes small wind machines—of 1 to 15 kw, and now numbering more than one million worldwide—all the way up to large machines of greater than 100 kw.

Most wind machines involve a multiblade rotor, resembling an airplane propeller, facing into the wind, and spinning about a horizontal axis. This fixture is mounted on a tower and connected to an electric generator. Another increasingly popular concept is a vertical axis system which resembles a gigantic egg beater.

In one important respect, wind energy is especially attractive: Wind can be available continuously throughout a twenty-four-hour day as opposed to the diurnal pattern of direct sunlight. But the wind speed is intermittent and unpredictable, which means that the typical unit operates only at 25 to 35 percent of capacity. To greatly oversimplify, small wind energy systems can be economic at sites with wind speeds that average 12 mph or greater. Large wind systems will be economic with a steady wind averaging 15 mph. At some of the most attractive sites, the projected cost of electricity generated from large windmills is 8 to 14 cents per kilowatt hour, but none has been built yet that demonstrates this cost level. Several wind experts further project that at sufficient production levels (50–100 machines annually) third generation– wind machines can produce electricity at 3 to 4 cents per kilowatt hour.[59] Still, many observers expect that wind machines will be cost competitive in a number of locations with conventional fuel in the mid- to late-1980's.

More than twenty companies, including corporate giants like Alcoa, Bendix, Boeing, General Electric, Grumman, Hamilton Standard, and Westinghouse, as well as various entrepreneurs, are today actively competing to develop large-scale central power wind generation. The favored concept is the "wind farm," a cluster of wind generators at a site of steady strong wind that are connected to a grid system. U.S. Windpower, Inc., developed one of the first U.S. wind farms, consisting of twenty machines, each of 30 kilowatts, at Crotched Mountain, New Hampshire. This Massachusetts firm has recently begun a farm with 100 wind machines at 50 kilowatts each (a total of 5 megawatts) at the Altamont Pass in Northern California.[60] The most ambitious project in the United States has been proposed by Windfarms, Ltd., at Kahuku Point in Hawaii. This $350 million facility would ultimately provide 80 megawatts of power to Hawaii Electric Company which would amount to 10 percent of Hawaii's electricity needs. However, as of March 1982, Wayne Van Dyke, president of Windfarms, expressed concern over the combined effect of high interest rates and cutbacks of federal funding on wind energy systems research, and on the financial viability of that project.

Projections of wind power for the United States are impressive. The California Energy Commission estimated the century-end potential of California alone at 1300 megawatts—the equivalent of one large nuclear power plant. A Domestic Policy Review Panel for Solar projected that wind would provide 8 percent of total U.S. electricity by 2000. And the Worldwatch Institute projects that wind energy could provide 20–30 percent of total electricity in some countries by the year 2000.[61] Equipment reliability on large-scale windmills is far from established, as evidenced by a sequence of mishaps, one in Washington state and the other in Southern California, where shortly after the facilities were dedicated, strong winds ripped machines from the ground.[62] Before one can place much confidence in these projections, a good deal more experience has to be accumulated.

Other potential barriers to wide use of wind power involve safety, television interference, land use competition, aesthetics, and noise.

Hydro |

The solar electric technology currently making the largest contribution is hydroelectric power. In 1980, rivers provided the source for 23 percent of the world's electricity—5 percent of total world energy consumption. Yet these levels appear to be far below the hydro potential. The World Energy Conference estimated that the world has utilized only 17 percent of potential generating capacity. Europe and the United States have, respectively, exploited 60 and 40 percent of their total hydro potential. Developing countries, which are feeling most acutely the strains of high oil import bills, have the largest untapped resources. Asia, Africa, and South America have utilized barely 8 percent of their potential capacity.

The turbine technology invented in France in 1820 and the development of electric power transmission in the early twentieth century made possible large-scale hydroelectric development, which has included some of mankind's most heroic engineering achievements. The world's most powerful dam, the Itiapu, between Brazil and Paraguay, will soon provide as much electric power as 13 nuclear power plants.[63]

In developed countries, most sites for large-scale hydro power are already in use. Further development primarily depends on "low-head" hydropower, produced as small or medium-sized dams. The U.S. Army Corps of Engineers estimates that of the 50,000 existing dam sites in the U.S. only 3 percent are now used for hydroelectric power. Many of these dams—used for flood control, irrigation, water storage, or recreation—could be retrofitted, upgraded, and expanded without interfering with the existing purpose of the dam. The Corps of Engineers estimates that 120,-000 megawatts of potential power exists at these sites.

Other sources are, however, less sanguine about the potential of hydropower. The New England River Basins Commission emphasized the danger to fish runs, sports, and lakeshore ecology and estimated that only 300 of the 10,000 existing dams in New England could be developed both economically and with adequate respect for the environment. The passage of the Public Utilities Regulatory Policy Act of 1978 (PURPA) has given a great boost to low-head hydro development. There has been a rush for permits and licenses for small and medium-sized hydro sites throughout the United States. In many cases, what is involved is the refurbishing of existing dams. The economics of hydro development is such that once the high initial development and construction costs have been covered, the facility generates returns that escalate with competitive energy prices, with virtually no cost escalation, into perpetuity. Moreover, the development of small hydro is built upon existing technology.

The Public Utilities Regulatory Policies Act is especially useful to producers of electricity from renewable sources in dealing with utilities. PURPA includes three provisions that are advantageous to power producers that generate less than 80 megawatts from solar, wind, or biomass, and hydroelectric sources. (Small power producers of this kind are exempt from Public Utilities Commission regulation.) First, the utility must purchase power generated by the small power producer at the utility's "avoided cost." (In other words, the utility must pay at a rate comparable to its most expensive fuel displaced.) Second, the utility must provide standby power at approximately its average rate. Third, it must provide interconnection with the grid. Cogenerators are similarly benefited. "The importance of PURPA is that it allows for competition in the production of electricity, and creates the potential for 12,000 megawatts of electricity from renewables and cogeneration," says Richard Menson, director of the Solar Lobby.[64]

The future of PURPA is far from secure, however. A district court judge in Biloxi, Mississippi, ruled in 1981 that several provisions of that act violated the states' rights guaranteed under the Constitution. The Supreme Court of the United States subsequently ruled against the Mississippi judge. But the Court has agreed to hear an appeal on another PURPA case.

Solar Salt Ponds |

One of the most intriguing renewable electric technologies is the solar salt pond. A solar salt pond is a shallow body of water—10 to 20 feet in depth—covered on the bottom with a layer of highly saline water. On the top of the pond sits another layer of less saline water. The difference in density between these layers prevents mixing of the water. The pond then acts as a huge solar collector, with temperatures on the bottom reaching 200°F. The pond then provides sufficient heat to drive a turbine. Feasibility research has been jointly conducted by DOE and Southern California Edison at a proposed 1 Mw, 64-acre facility at Salton Sea, California, but the future of that program is now uncertain in the face of budgetary reductions. In Israel, experimental ponds have been successfully demonstrated, most notably the 150 kw Ormot two-acre test pond at the Dead Sea.[65]

Photovoltaics: Room for Breakthroughs |

The logic of photovoltaic conversion is very persuasive. Silicon, the principal raw material used in the manufacture of photovoltaic cells, is the most abundant solid element on earth. And photovoltaic cells alone convert sunlight into one of the most highly prized energy forms—electricity.[66]

Presently, photovoltaic cells are generally made through similar processes to those used by the semiconductor industry to manufacture transistors and integrated circuits, though several radically new processes have been proposed. Pure silicon is selectively "contaminated" with different gaseous impurities at high temperatures. These impurities define electrical boundaries between the elements of cells that are connected by depositing a thin layer of aluminum on the circuit. The resulting cells are photovoltaic—that is, they will generate an electric voltage when light falls on them. The theory behind the phenomenon was first developed by Albert Einstein in his classic 1905 paper.[67]

The early photovoltaic cells were used to provide electricity for orbiting space satellites, with clusters of them covering the butterflylike wings that opened when the satellite achieved orbit. Cost was not then a problem; reliability, technical performance, and sophistication were the key considerations.

These early cells were manufactured under the same tightly controlled and costly processes used for making transistors for aircraft electronic systems. They were indeed very expensive. Early systems cost as much as $1,000 per peak watt, more than a thousand times the cost of producing electricity by conventional means.[68]

But what happened to the transistor industry is now starting to happen to photovoltaics. The space program's need for lightweight, reliable electronic amplifiers created a constant, strong stream of federal purchases for what were then often $200 transistors.[69] The rapid fall of semiconductor prices is now legend. A commercial version of the same transistor can today be purchased for a few cents. The cost of photovoltaic cells has also been dropping dramatically. The average commercial price for photovoltaic systems in 1977 was about $16 per peak watt and $9 in 1981.[70]

Even though present price levels reflect a decrease in cost to less than a hundredth of the original satellite cells, they still restrict the current market for photovoltaics to special applications, such as irrigation pumps, unmanned railroad crossings, remote microwave repeaters, marine battery recharging, and pipeline leak warning systems. But the market for these photovoltaic applications grew at 60 percent annually, from $8.6 million in 1977 to $56 million in 1981.[71]

At the heart of the cost reduction problem is the high cost of purified single crystal silicon. As one experienced semiconductor executive explained, "Eighty percent of the cost of a photovoltaic system is in the materials, and eighty percent of the material cost is in the silicon."[72]

A number of approaches are being pursued to reduce costs. Some companies are seeking to streamline the purification, crystalization, and fabrication processes. Two expensive steps involve "growing" the single crystal silicon into a cylindrical ingot and then slicing that ingot into solar cells. Those two steps are circumvented through one streamlining process in which a continuous ribbon of silicon is slowly drawn up from a vat of molten silicon and wound onto a drum. The ribbon is then cut into rectangular-shaped wafers that allow the surface area on the solar array to be better utilized.

Several other companies have placed their bets on manufacturing techniques that can use substantially less pure silicon. Still other firms have been experimenting with alternative materials that can be formed into wafers up to 100 times thinner than the crystal silicon cell. Perhaps the most exciting thin film and overall photovoltaic solution is the amorphous or uncrystallized cell. The amorphous technology avoids the crystallization steps and uses much less semiconductor-type material; moreover, the cells are considerably more durable than other thin films or materials. The biggest drawback for amorphous cells is their low efficiency level, a prime target of current photovoltaics research.[73]

Sanyo, the Japanese electronics company, recently announced plans to build a $50-million manufacturing facility that will produce amorphous cells for electric watches, calculators, and toys. It is unclear whether the experience it gains with these cells, which operates at very low efficiencies, will be applicable to large-scale energy production, where higher efficiencies are more important than portability. But it is clear that Sanyo is making a major commitment, in the context of Japan's Project Sunshine, to the amorphous technique and to solar in general.

The continued reduction of costs could open up vast markets for on-site residential and commercial uses, particularly in the Third World, where utility grids are not usually highly developed, especially in outlying rural areas.

One industry executive estimated that at least 85 percent of the potential market for photovoltaics in the near term will be in the Third World. Taking a larger view, Paul Maycock, former director of the Department of Energy's photovoltaic program, estimates that by the mid-1990's the worldwide photovoltaic market could well be $1 billion. Already, projects dot the globe—for example, in Upper Volta, a system for grain grinding; in Saudia Arabia, a salt water desalinization plant; and in Niger, an irrigation pumping system—in which the power is supplied by photovoltaic cells.[74]

However, in order to penetrate the broader markets and perhaps one day compete with conventional fuels in the utility market, a reduction in cost to less than a tenth of present levels is necessary (to one dollar per peak watt). Few experts are willing to stake their reputations that this level will be reached soon.

But if the utility power generation cost barrier is crossed, the potential for photovoltaics would be very large indeed. The cells could be used on site, like solar heating. But photovoltaics as a generator of electricity would have greater effect than solar heating on the role of utilities, for if on-site power generation by photovoltaics became widespread, the utility industry may have to purchase power from on-site installations, mark it up, and distribute it. Unless low-cost means of electrical power storage were developed, the utilities would still supply conventional backup power with especially large capacities being needed at night.

One can certainly say that photovoltaics thus far constitutes a success story. With the help of only relatively small volumes of sales, costs have dropped to less than one percent of original costs. Moreover, advances can come quickly, for as one specialist has put it, photovoltaics are "embedded in what has been one of the most fertile environments for innovation in the twentieth century—the semiconductor industry."[75] As has been the case in that industry, increased volume will bring increased experience, improved processes, and reduced costs. But unlike the semiconductor industry, technological progress in the photovoltaic industry will not come from the design of smaller-area, higher-yield devices but from material savings from thinner devices of the same area, and from simpler, lower-cost processes and new "photovoltaic" grade semiconductor materials. But the same ingenuity that slashed transis-

tor prices and created the integrated circuit can now be expected
to innovate within the new rules provided by the sun. Investments
in research will produce fundamentally new cell production techniques that will lead to sharply lower costs.

Policy for photovoltaic devices should have two objectives:
First, to create a market by federal purchases to drive present
technology to lower costs; second, to fund R&D for thin-film
amorphous semiconductors and other high-risk proposals. The
payoff in either case could be very large.

CONCLUSION |

How much of America's energy needs could be derived from solar
energy by the year 2000? Estimates vary over a very wide range
and comparative analysis is difficult, because different analysts
work with different definitions of solar.[76] Some begin and end
with solar heating, whereas others include all the solar options
except hydropower. Recently, however, many analysts have begun
to converge on a definition similar to the one presented at the
beginning of this chapter, which includes all the "recent" solar
cycles.[77] Even after adjusting predictions to our definition of solar
energy, a selection of high-quality projections still ranges from 7
to 23 percent by the year 2000. The variation is demonstrated in
Table 7-1.

Two studies published within a few weeks of each other in
1980 illustrate the problem. The National Academy of Sciences
concluded that unless there is massive government intervention,
solar, including hydropower, would contribute no more than 8–9
percent to energy supply in this century. On the heels of this
four-year, $4 million study involving some 250 people, the Union
of Concerned Scientists (UCS) published a book-length analysis
that included a high-solar scenario in which solar would contribute
35 percent of the energy needed by the year 2000; even the lowest
UCS scenario is 50 percent higher than the most likely scenario
projected by the National Academy of Science.

The truth is that *no one really knows what the contribution
from solar energy will be in the year 2000.* Solar's contribution

TABLE 7·1
SOLAR CONTRIBUTION BY YEAR 2000 †

	Solar Energy (oil equivalent mbd)	Total Energy Consumption (oil equivalent mbd)	Solar as a Percent of Total
President's Council on Environmental Quality (CEQ)[78]	12	50	23%
Stanford Research Institute 1* (Business as Usual)	5	73	7%
Stanford Research Institute 2* (Low Solar Cost)	10	70	13%
Stanford Research Institute 3* (High Fuel Cost)	6	45	12%
National Academy of Science[79a] ** (CONAES)	4	50	8%
Union of Concerned Scientists[79b] *** (Maximum demand)	10	50	20%
Union of Concerned Scientists[79b] *** (Intermediate demand)	10	40	25%
SERI Study****	8.7	32	27%

†Calculations based on quads given in original sources.

*The Stanford Research Institute developed three scenarios.[80] The first is a business-as-usual scenario. The two remaining scenarios are renewable emphasis scenarios. In case 2, the emphasis is achieved by lowered renewable costs, whereas in scenario 3, the change comes primarily from increased prices of competing fuels.

**Figures for the year 2000 linearly extrapolated from CONAES Scenario II, 3% GNP growth. Includes hydropower. Since publication of the CONAES study some of the participants have indicated a larger contribution from solar energy may be possible by the year 2000.[79c]

***The Union of Concerned Scientists report gave ranges rather than individual numbers. In both cases the midpoint of their ranges was used in the table. The 20 percent estimate was actually given as 12–28 percent while the 25 percent estimate is the centerpoint of a 15–35 percent range.

****The SERI Study also gave ranges and the midpoint was also used. The renewable contribution ranged from 19–35 percent.

depends on at least six other complex and uncertain variables, each difficult to forecast.

1. Prices of competing energy sources
2. Overall levels of domestic energy consumption
3. Level of federal support for involvement in solar energy
4. Rate of advancement of solar technologies
5. Rate at which institutional barriers to solar will be overcome
6. Reliability of conventional energy sources.

In this context of uncertainty, not uncommon for new technologies, predictions are fraught with risk. To have a high probability of being correct one can only speak in terms of ranges. For instance, it is relatively safe to predict that renewables by the year 2000 will account for 10–30 percent of the nation's energy supply.

On the other hand, it is difficult to motivate people toward a range of goals. For this reason, managements and governments set specific goals. To be effective, goals must be difficult to reach but achievable. It is in this spirit that we believe that a goal of achieving one-fifth of the nation's energy from solar by the year 2000 is a sensible goal for our country. This does not mean that uneconomic solar technologies should be espoused, but it does mean that the portfolio of solar technologies includes alternatives which, if given a fair chance against conventional sources and an initial stimulus, may contribute up to 8 to 10 mbd of oil equivalent by the turn of the century.[81]

Presently solar energy in the form of wood and hydropower contributes 7 percent of the national energy supply. To achieve a 20-percent contribution from solar by the end of the century, a commitment must be made now to existing technologies. The only realistic two options for the short-term are wood and wood waste, and on-site solar technologies, such as solar heating, small hydropower, and small wind. The short-term challenge is not developing new technology, but accelerating diffusion. As stated before, we recommend continued incentives to get these technologies through the early sluggish phase of commercialization, combined with measures to overcome the institutional barriers.[82] Incentives would not only stimulate demand, they would encourage private firms to make larger commitments and take greater risks.

The legal and institutional impediments toward renewables have already been discussed and surely no facile remedy exists for dealing with this inertia factor. How to best amend tens of thousands of building codes and local laws that discourage renewables? The traditional route—professional journals, graduate schools, trade shows—are all worth pursuing, but here also funding and leadership are required to generate momentum.

As we progress toward a greater reliance upon renewables, one of the few certainties upon which we can rely is that unanticipated environmental problems will appear. Just as evidence now mounts that acid rain and the "greenhouse effect" pose constraints upon coal use, we can also expect that noise problems may affect the growth of wind power or that residential wood burning can raise indoor and outdoor pollution problems. Such constraints must be recognized and addressed quickly if renewables are to sustain high growth rates over the long term.

On this page is a rough guide to the breakdown of solar sources, assuming total U.S. energy consumption of 45 mbd of oil equivalent in the year 2000.[83]

Energy Source	Oil Equivalent (mbd)
1. Solar Space and Hot-Water Heating (Including Active and Passive)	1
2. Other On-Site Technologies*	2
3. Wood and Waste	4
4. Hydropower (Large Installations)[84]	2
TOTAL	9

*See Reference 10

Although our illustration resembles other recent estimates, it differs in two key respects. Unlike others, ours does not envision significant contribution from the Big Solar research technologies. Any contributions made by high-technology sources, including photovoltaics, would be a bonus. Nonetheless, we believe that a significant contribution can be expected from photovoltaics by the year 2000, perhaps .5 mbd of oil equivalent. We have not, however, included this contribution in our projection because we wanted to highlight the potential of those technologies that do *not* require technological breakthroughs. Thus photovoltaics, and any early contribution from the research technologies, is a buffer in case of a shortfall from any of the more mature solar technologies. Also assumed in our projection, and not in most of the others, is an aggressive program to spur commercialization of the on-site solar technologies.

For the longer term, the technological alternatives are less distinct. It is not even clear in some cases, such as in the case of solar satellites, whether the concept is feasible. In other areas, such as in ocean thermal power, technological feasibility is promising, but there is great uncertainty about size, cost, operating efficiency, and timing. A solid ten to fifteen years of research and development will be required of the research technologies before final priorities can be assigned and some possibilities ruled out. Congress should, in the meantime, be prepared to proceed incrementally, with a diversified research-and-development program; that is, to fund prototype versions of the centralized electric technologies (power towers, solar satellites, ocean thermal, large wind machines), and to commit substantial funds to photovoltaics and energy plantation research and development. By the early 1990's, when technological risks have been satisfactorily reduced (at least for some of the technologies), it should be possible to decide what to commercialize.

During the late 1970's, renewables received noteworthy support from the federal government, of both a symbolic and substantive nature. The federal budget for renewables increased to $561 million in 1980, part for research and development and part for other programs. In addition, two acts of Congress—the aforementioned PURPA and renewable tax credits—provided strong incentives for renewables.

The election of Ronald Reagan marked a sharp change in the federal attitude toward renewable energies. The Reagan Administration's 1983 budget proposals, for instance, were only 10 percent of the 1980's expenditure levels. Much of the research and development effort, as well as most of the information and educational programs, were eliminated. This redirection has crippled the effort to identify and develop realistic near-term and longer-term renewable energy sources.

A realistic program to implement solar energy would consist of three phases: First, short-term incentives for a rapid commercialization of existing technologies. Second, a ten-year research-and-development program to identify the best of the new alternatives. And finally, commercialization by private industry of the alternatives identified in the second phase, leading toward a gradual transition to an increasingly Solar America in the twenty-first century, when hydrocarbons would be reserved for premium uses.

Admittedly, what has been described here is a vision—but an eminently practical one. At the very least, it deserves a fair chance.

8 | ENERGY WARS

ROBERT STOBAUGH
DANIEL YERGIN

The fundamental purpose of U.S. energy policy, we have argued, should be to manage a transition from a world of cheap imported oil to a more balanced system of energy sources. It is clear that the total output of conventional domestic resources—oil, gas, coal, and nuclear—cannot be vastly increased during the next decade. It is equally clear that these sources cannot be ignored. America needs all of them. Broadly speaking, however, the nation has only two major alternatives for increased energy supplies during the next decade—to import more oil or to accelerate the development of conservation and solar (renewable) energy. This is the nature of the choice to be made. Conservation and solar energy, in our view, are much to be preferred.

For a number of years, an important blinder obscured reality and impeded America's ability to confront its energy problem. The blinder was simple ignorance. Although U.S. oil imports grew from 3.4 million barrels a day (24 percent of consumption) in 1970 to 8.4 million (almost 50 percent of consumption) in 1978, there was an extraordinary lag in appreciating the dimensions of the increases. Even opinion polls taken in 1979 and 1980 found that half the American people were not aware of the high level of U.S. oil imports.

This simple ignorance, in turn, contributed heavily to the

search for a domestic villain on whom to blame the problem. The adversary character of the American political system, the never-ending welter of charge and countercharge, the regulatory confusion, the cacophony of contradictory expert opinions—all reinforced the tendency to embark upon an energy witch hunt. Various groups argued that the villain was the government, environmentalists, or both. But much more pervasive was the belief that the "oil companies" were the villain. More than half the people in a poll in October 1979 asserted that the oil companies had fabricated the energy shortage, and one-quarter thought that the government should take over the companies and run them.[1] Here too was an example of time lag—the belief that the oil companies were as powerful in 1980 as they were in 1960; when in fact one of the causes of the problem we face today is the waning power of the oil companies in the face of the growing assertiveness of OPEC producers.

Indeed, one noteworthy result from the rise of the Ayatollah Khomeini was the greater realization that America was dependent on imported oil and that there were serious limitations to the power of any U.S. entity, even the U.S. government. Thus, OPEC —as the villain—moved onto center stage. But then, in late 1981 and early 1982, public perception shifted abruptly as the "oil glut" appeared. U.S. consumers, encouraged by some unknowing writers and economists, began to believe that the OPEC members were no longer able to hold up oil prices and that all of America's energy problems were over. This misperception, which was encouraged by the desire for a simple view and a simple solution, obscured the nature of the energy situation.

The character of the basic choice also has been obscured by a long series of bitter political battles and confrontations in Congress, the regulatory agencies, the courts, and the press. Because the nation's energy problems will persist for some time, these energy wars are likely to continue as well. For they involve enormous sums of money, competing perceptions of the nation's interests, environmental and other social costs not easily quantifiable, disagreement over the nature of the technical facts, and conflict over basic values. Although battles over energy cannot be averted, they can be settled with lesser harm to the participants and the nation than in the past. Because the lessons of the past should help us reach better settlements in the future, we present herewith a brief history of the energy wars.

MONEY |

The amount of money involved is in itself a major obstacle in the path of clear comprehension of the issues. Some of the energy battles were going on in the United States before the 1973 OPEC price revolution, but compared to what happened after the price hike, they were only minor skirmishes. OPEC, of course, imposed very heavy costs—in effect, very heavy taxes—on U.S. energy consumers.

But OPEC also increased the value of U.S. oil and gas reserves. The initial OPEC price hikes in 1973 and 1974 increased the value by some $800 billion of the proved U.S. reserves of crude oil and natural gas. By January 1, 1983, the value of those reserves (even after depletion) had increased, at OPEC prices, to more than $2 trillion—a ten-fold increase, or $25,000 for every American family.[2] Quite naturally, the sudden and dramatic increases in the value of domestic reserves raised the question of how the "windfall" would be distributed. Who was to benefit? Consumers, through price controls that prevented energy prices from rising to world levels? The federal government, through taxation? Producers, through higher prices for domestic oil and gas? And how would the windfall be split among producing and consuming regions?

Indeed, the income-distribution questions raised by the "windfall" ignited the most visible fight in the attempt to formulate a U.S. energy program. And the failure to achieve a national consensus proved to be one of the greatest obstacles to a rational energy policy. So intense and heated was the debate that participants were led to make exaggerated statements that weakened their credibility and contributed to polarization. Congress, which by and large wanted the consumers to get the windfall, pretended that there was no energy crisis and ignored the problems posed by imported oil. The Carter Administration, which wanted much of the windfall collected in taxes, argued that the supply of natural gas would increase if the price went up to $1.75 per mcf., but above that price, supply would increase only slightly. Meanwhile, the oil and gas companies, who wanted the windfall for themselves, contended that the decontrol of prices would give them the money and incentives to find the new supplies required to solve U.S. energy problems. Indeed, some industry spokespersons implied that, with price decontrol, the United States could substantially increase its oil output, a scenario quite at variance with the experience of the petroleum industry, especially in the years since 1973. For while the dramatically increased cash flows and higher prices for new oil and gas have engendered a sharp jump in exploration and development activity, domestic production and reserves have either fallen or barely stayed level.

Finally, two other groups helped to confuse and obscure the energy picture.

One group consisted of those economists and engineers who used information gathered under one set of conditions, primarily pre-1973, to make projections of what would occur under another, radically different set of conditions, post-1973. The result: highly optimistic projections and estimates of how easily the United States could increase its domestic energy supplies and how difficult it would be for OPEC to sustain prices as high as even $12 a barrel. This group of technicians generally tended to support, at least implicitly, the oil companies' position; that is, if U.S. prices were deregulated, U.S. oil production would increase dramatically.

The other group laid heavy blame on what they perceived as the oligopolistic structure of the petroleum industry. They tended to favor the congressional position—to give most of the windfall to the consumers by keeping prices low. Their "solution" to U.S. energy problems was to break up the oil companies—although there is little reason to think that divestiture would bring forth more oil from the ground. And there is good reason to think that the oil companies have made a positive contribution to modernizing the coal industry.

To be sure, our description of the debates and the participants is simplified. There are many nuances and variations, and even some dissenters, within each camp. But the essential outlines are correct. Of course, one could hardly expect that there would not be a major political war, for an $800 billion or $2 trillion bounty is well worth fighting for.

The issue of price is so important—and so emotional—that the terms of the debate must be clarified. True, the decontrol of oil prices was a major step forward. But price controls on natural gas still remain. This vexing issue of price controls on gas is usually argued in terms of equity versus efficiency (just as it was on oil). Keeping price controls on gas is said to be more equitable than decontrol because the poor suffer unduly from higher prices; that is, relatively more than the well-to-do. The rewards are said to be given to one set of the well-to-do—stockholders.

On the other side of the debate, letting prices rise to whatever level the market sets is said to be more efficient because the higher prices encourage greater efficiency in energy usage. And many of those who favor decontrol believe in equitable treatment just as strongly as those who support price controls. Their prescription is to achieve a more efficient economy and then split up the extra income in an equitable way, thereby increasing everyone's income, including that of the poor. Thus, these people would let the price system allocate supplies and then tax the well-to-do and give to the poor. Indeed, controlling prices produces a "shotgun effect," a very inefficient way to help the poor. In fact, given overall consumption levels, price controls actually provide more of a subsidy to the rich than the poor. In absolute terms, the rich use more energy than the poor, and, some studies indicate, in relative terms the rich use almost as much (Table 8-1).* There are more direct ways to aid the poor, such as grants for home insulation or fuel purchases.[3]

Finally, as the second oil shock should have demonstrated, the net result of price controls on oil almost surely was higher oil prices than would have been the case if controls had not existed. Low prices encouraged consumers to use more oil than they otherwise would. This increased consumption, in turn, made the world oil market tighter than it would have been otherwise. The tighter

---

*This relationship does not hold for the very poor.

TABLE 8·1
HOUSEHOLD EXPENDITURES AND ENERGY USAGE,
UNITED STATES

Household Expenditures (thousands of 1980 dollars)	Energy Usage (millions of BTUs)	Increase in Energy Usage with a 100-percent Increase in Household Expenditures
7	270	—
14	510	89%
28	940	84%
56	1700	81%

Source: R. Herendeen and J. Tanaka, "Energy Cost of Living," *Energy* (June 1976). The original data are in 1961 dollars, which we converted to 1980 dollars using the GNP deflator. The original source applies to household expenditures, which we believe are highly correlated with income; although some persons, such as retirees, have spending patterns not strongly related to current income.

world oil market resulted in disastrously higher oil prices. Higher prices for imported oil resulted in even further loss of GNP because of the deflation of domestic economic activity due to large flows of money out of the United States, combined with the difficulty of stimulating the economy during periods of high inflation, partially induced by higher oil prices. Dollars that might have been invested in the United States instead went overseas to oil producers, who did not reinvest or "recycle" all such dollars in the United States. Price controls on natural gas (or other energy forms) also result in over consumption in the present and a tighter market in the future.

Thus our own view is clear. We believe that the system of price controls on domestic natural gas is doing all American consumers a great disservice—a policy of penny wisdom and pound foolishness, just as the oil price controls were. Those who have argued for continued price controls, or who advocate the reimposition of controls, assume that America is economically self-sufficient—an energy island unto itself. This is a dangerous delusion for a country that imports 30 to 40 percent of its oil and is the largest buyer of OPEC oil.

MIRACLES |

Although we stress the importance of decontrolling prices, it would be a mistake to regard decontrol as a miracle solution. Indeed, the drive to find *the* answer—be it nuclear power, cheap gas, price decontrol, Mexican oil, Chinese oil, Alaskan gas, Athabascan tar sands, synthetic fuels, the opening up of public lands—has been a blinder. It is always possible that a *deus ex machina* will arrive just in time. However, it is, to say the least, not prudent to base energy policy on faith, and all the miracles proffered to date have been tightly circumscribed. While some of the technical fixes will make significant contributions, they will do so only at the end of very long lead times—ten or fifteen years— and then only perhaps in limited amounts. Undue emphasis here diverts attention from the immediate problem and responses that can have much greater impact in much shorter times. Yet appeals for another Manhattan Project or another man-in-space program seem almost a constitutionally mandated requirement for Presidential energy speeches and White House policy.

The first major post-embargo initiative, taken at a time when Richard Nixon was concerned about his own political survival, was Project Independence. Invoking the spirit of the Manhattan Project and the man-in-space program, President Nixon, three weeks after the embargo in 1973, announced the goal "that by the end of the decade we will have developed the potential to meet our own energy needs without depending on any foreign energy sources." The emphasis was very much on substantially increasing domestic supplies through conventional techniques, primarily through higher prices and a rapid expansion of atomic energy. That commitment continued into the Ford Administration. In January 1975, President Ford envisaged the construction within 10 years of 200 major nuclear power plants (that would have been 20 a year), 250 major new coal mines, 150 major coal-fired power plants, 30 major new oil refineries, and 20 major new synthetic fuels plants.[4]

This strategy proved wholly unrealistic for a combination of technological and political reasons. It was impossible to decontrol prices in the way those administrations advocated. It was not at all clear that significant increments of oil and gas, above current production levels, could be called forth from the ground, or indeed whether production could even be maintained at current levels. To expect so much from nuclear energy when a virtual moratorium had already descended upon the industry represented wishful thinking. Environmental issues and resulting political restraints, which had retarded coal and nuclear energy, could not simply be rolled back. In fact, the arms control community had entered into energy policy formulation in the Ford Administration, successfully slowing down a commitment to the "plutonium economy." Both Nixon and Ford had talked about conservation but, in policy terms, conservation was a minor concern. Moreover, solar energy appeared virtually not at all in the plans of the two administrations. When all was said, the effort to find an alternative to imported oil through an accelerated conventional production strategy was an obvious failure.

The Carter Administration, taking office in January 1977, mounted a much more sustained drive to develop a realistic energy program. The National Energy Plan presented a shift in priorities and emphasis from the previous administration and embodied what might be called a transitional strategy. It drew upon a trend of thought that really defined itself in opposition to the high-production strategies, an alternative set of ideas that had been partly affected by the growth of environmental concerns. More central, however, was the conception that the United States needlessly expended—wasted—vast amounts of energy, and since the world value of oil had increased sharply, perhaps the most effective way to "produce" new energy was by saving it. Attention also was directed toward the "renewables"—solar energy. Finally, this approach tended to play down the advisability of accelerated nuclear development. The latter point was reinforced by members of the arms control community, who opposed the uncontrolled development of a plutonium economy and, citing the dangers of proliferation, argued for deferring reprocessing and the breeder reactor.[5]

It could be seen that this set of ideas powerfully influenced the Carter program when it finally emerged in April 1977. Indeed, the Carter program marked a significant difference from the previous administrations. The President emphasized that a major transition was at hand—no less significant than that from wood to coal at the beginning of the Industrial Revolution and from coal to oil and gas in the twentieth century. Carter raised conservation from the bottom of the priority list, where it had been languishing, to the top: "the cornerstone of our policy . . . our first goal . . . the cheapest, most practical way to meet our energy needs and to reduce our growing dependence on foreign supplies of oil." But other elements of the program leaned heavily on the promise of increased production. For one thing, foreign oil was to be replaced with domestic coal, and the program proposed to double coal production to 1.2 billion tons by 1985. The plan also called for the development of renewable energy. Finally, the Administration sought mechanisms to raise energy prices so that "the price of energy should reflect its true replacement cost as a means of bringing supply and demand into balance over the long run."[6]

Thus, the initial Carter program represented a substantial shift from the proposals of the previous administrations. In the most striking departure, Carter had made conservation the highest priority. He had discounted the feasibility of increased production of domestic oil and gas, and stressed the inevitability of a move away from these fuels, whether foreign or domestic. And for the first time, a national administration had characterized solar energy as a serious, near-term energy source. And, while calling for a streamlining of the nuclear power licensing procedures in order to increase the contribution from atomic energy, the President still characterized the source as an unpleasant necessity, "a last resort." He did, however, project a quadrupling of nuclear power by 1985 (from 1 million barrels a day of oil equivalent to 3.8 million). Any increase would only come from the light water reactor, for on April 7, two weeks before his energy message, the President officially took a stand against reprocessing and the breeder.[7]

Two key goals were set—to reduce growth in energy demand to less than 2 percent a year and to bring imports in 1985 down to six million barrels a day, as opposed to a potential level, if unchecked, of 10 to 14 million barrels a day. The National Energy Plan was, at heart, a tax and pricing program. The goal, as then

Energy Secretary James Schlesinger expressed it, was "to establish a pricing and tax framework within which decisions can be made, rather than the jerry-built structure that was constructed after the 1973 embargo."[8]

The centerpiece of the program was the crude oil equalization tax, which was to bring domestic oil prices up to the world level. Further, the price of all newly discovered natural gas, whether interstate or intrastate, would be regulated, but at higher prices, equal to the energy equivalent of oil priced at the world market. There would also be taxes on industrial users of oil and natural gas to get them to convert to coal; and tax credits for conservation and solar energy. New cars that did not meet fuel-efficiency standards would be hit with a "gas guzzlers tax." A standby authority to tax gasoline would be available if certain consumption targets were exceeded. Utility rates were to be reformed to discourage increasing electricity consumption.

The National Energy Plan comprised an immense and complicated range of proposals. Yet the provisions to implement the conservation and solar energy features of the program were rather minor when compared to the declaratory stress laid on them by the President in his speeches. Indeed, the actual conservation measures were not very different from those proposed by Gerald Ford, and the bureaucratic follow-through was slight. Meanwhile, the programmatic commitment to nuclear energy was greater than the declaratory commitment. And, curiously, the plan assumed no increase in the real price of oil on the world market.[9]

On balance, certainly, Carter's energy program was constructive and sensible. It was introduced as the "moral equivalent of war," but it failed to capture the imagination of the public or the experts. At about the same time as the President's speech was delivered, the Central Intelligence Agency released a prescient and pessimistic study of the world oil market. Critics immediately dismissed it as merely a tactical political document, and unfortunately, the critics carried the day. There was lots of oil in the world, the critics said, and oil producers would produce it rapidly to maximize profits.

The ensuing complacency took on a momentum of its own. In an influential article in 1978, for example, when world oil prices were just $12.50 a barrel, then Congressman David Stockman dismissed the argument for a national energy policy as "reminiscent of Chicken Little's defective logic." He announced with considerable assurance, "The global economic conditions necessary for another major unilateral price action by OPEC are not likely to re-emerge for more than a decade—if ever." Writing at the end of 1978, one energy analyst announced that with oil at $12.50 a barrel, by 1983 "the world production of oil should be causing one of the greatest oil gluts that we have seen," and dismissed the oil crisis as "largely a media event."[10]

All of these analyses shared a common thread—they looked at the oil market in narrow, abstract economic terms. They assumed an underlying stability and exaggerated production potentials, portraying the producing countries as simple profit-maximizing firms.

Amid such optimism, it was not surprising that the President's energy plan was painfully mauled by Congress. The crude oil equalization tax was killed by the Senate at an early stage. And in October 1978, after an arduous struggle, Congress passed the Natural Gas Policy Act, which raised what had been artificially low and misleading prices for natural gas. But actual decontrol, and then only for new gas, is not scheduled to take place until 1985.

When the second shock hit in 1979, President Carter's decision to decontrol oil prices gradually, between June 1979 and September 1981, led to another bitter money battle—this time over the windfall tax; that is, over whether the extra money paid by the consumers would go to the producers or to the government. As with pricing, the debate in Congress broke largely along regional, producing-consuming lines. It was not until early 1980 that the Senate and House conferees finally agreed on the amount of the tax—$227 billion over a ten-year period. A fight then broke out between the majors and independents within the oil industry over how the tax burden was to be allocated. Unfortunately, in the final settlement, Congress decided that the tax would apply to revenues obtained from the sale of newly found oil, which we believe was a major mistake given the need to encourage the supply of all energy sources.[11]

The decision to decontrol oil prices fully recognized the need for increased conservation. But, beyond that, the Carter Administration had little taste for going down the path it had traveled in 1977 and 1978. It, too, was ready for a miracle. In this case the miracle was to be synthetic fuels.

The full political impact of the 1979 gasoline crisis hit while President Carter was in Tokyo for the economic summit. In a memorandum later disclosed, one of his closest advisers, Stuart Eizenstat, warned, "We have a worsening short-term domestic energy crisis. Congress is growing more nervous each day over the energy problem. . . . Nothing else has so frustrated, confused, angered the American people—or so targeted their distress at you personally." It was in the mood of near-panic reflected in the memorandum that, on his return from Tokyo in July, President Carter retired to Camp David, where he conferred with about a hundred prominent leaders and reviewed his energy options.

The plan with which the President finally emerged was built around a crash program for synthetic fuels—primarily liquids and gas from coal, and liquids from shale. The program's roots lay in a campaign that had been mounted in Washington in the spring. Particularly influential was a memo circulated by three prominent Washington figures. Citing the experience with synthetic rubber, aluminum, and other materials during World War II and the Korean War, the three argued that (1) the United States could produce 5 million barrels a day of synthetic fuels—more than a quarter of then-current U.S. oil consumption—within five to ten years; (2) the technologies in question were "proven"; and (3) the capital cost would be $20 billion to $40 billion for each million barrel a day. The three advocates added that the program "would give us all the psychological lift of 'doing something' instead of just doing without."[12]

That last proposition was of obvious interest to an Administration that had been bitterly attacked for emphasizing "doing without"—conservation—two years earlier in the first Carter energy program. Administration interest was made even more intense because the House of Representatives, frightened by the political effect of the gas lines, had just rushed to approve a synthetic fuels bill. The Administration thought it was moving in the direction that was popular on Capitol Hill.

Thus, on July 15, 1979, President Carter unveiled an $88 billion proposal for a crash synthetic fuels program—to be financed mostly out of the proceeds from the windfall tax on oil. The proposal launched a vigorous debate. Even some who had been strong advocates of an accelerated synthetic fuels program argued that such a massive program was unmanageable in anything like the President's time frame. Each of the proposed plants would be as large or larger than the largest industrial plant project ever built at one time in the United States. Together, the construction would constitute a huge undertaking that would strain skills and infrastructure to a great and unknown degree. Nor was it correct to say that the technology was "proven." There was neither enough experience nor knowledge to scale up rapidly from pilot plants to a host of full-sized plants. By way of analogy, it was as if a man who had built only doll houses was about to commence immediately a tract of forty full-sized houses—having never before built one full-sized house.

The cost estimates of the program obviously were highly uncertain. As late as 1974, the best estimate of the production costs for oil from a synthetic fuel plant was (in 1979 dollars) about $10 a barrel. By 1980, those estimates were in the $40–50 plus range. Meanwhile by 1980, estimates of individual plant costs had risen from $2 billion to as high as $4 billion; and, of course, until a commercially sized plant has been completed, these cost estimates remained highly speculative. What did seem certain was that a crash program would create tremendous inflationary pressures, as it bid away available workers and materials from other activities. (North Sea oil drilling costs tripled between 1973 and 1978). Fiscal conservatives worried about shielding such a large undertaking from market forces, while others concerned themselves with the diversion of attention and resources from the immediate problems of the 1980's to partial solutions that *might* become available in the 1990's.

Certainly, the logic of an accelerated synfuels effort was compelling. The President rightly insisted that the United States should develop this capability. Indeed, the effort should have begun earlier. But a manageable program, critics asserted, should be less ambitious and structured to proceed step by step from pilot plants to demonstration units, scaling up on the basis of experience. In that spirit, the Congress, in effect, took the President's program as a rough first draft, reworked it, and finally, in November 1979, came up with an alternative. Twenty billion dollars were allocated for synthetic fuel development, with the program and further funding to be reviewed after four years. Some officials in the Administration hoped that only a relatively meager portion of the government funds would have to be spent to develop an industry, since a number of observers thought that the high prices of oil and gas meant that only a small subsidy would be necessary. Managing the synfuels project was to be the task of a newly created government-owned Energy Security Corporation.

The debate on synthetic fuels at least reduced the President's initial proposal very greatly. Unfortunately, however, the amount of time devoted to the matter diverted attention and funds away from the fundamental and continuing issue of energy conservation.

During 1979 the Congress began to take conservation seriously for the first time. In the late summer and early fall of that year, a number of measures were introduced in Congress that would have put conservation on an economic par with conventional sources. These bills were stimulated by the perception of crisis and, more directly, by the Administration's synthetic fuel program. Many in Congress felt that conservation deserved at least the same degree of financial support as synthetic fuels, especially since, by the President's own program, a barrel of conservation energy cost only about a tenth in federal funds of what a barrel of synthetic fuels cost.[13] Moreover, the conservation would be available almost immediately to help the United States get through the 1980's, while the first drop of synthetic fuel from a commercial plant would not be processed until the late 1980's. The bold imagery of a synthetic fuels program—equivalent to another man-in-space program—was apparently considered more attractive politically than that of conservation.

In some cases the Carter Administration had to battle entrenched congressional leaders to gain any support for conservation and renewables; but in the Senate especially, sentiment for these two "sources" increased dramatically during 1979. Moreover, in 1979, existing federal conservation programs expended only $1.5 billion. To make matters worse, when the windfall tax proceeds were apportioned in early 1980, conservation measures were grossly neglected. The windfall tax was allocated as follows: 60 percent for income-tax reductions, 25 percent for low-income assistance, and 15 percent for energy and transportation programs. So at the insistence of the House conferees, the legislation did not expand the present 15-percent credit on conservation investments. True, the subsidy for solar energy installations on residences was increased to 40 percent, but for business the subsidy was set at only 15 percent.

Overall, the total share of windfall-tax proceeds estimated to be spent between 1980 and 1990 was only $600 million for residential energy tax credits and $8.1 billion for business energy tax incentives. In other words, the measure calls for spending less than 4 percent of the windfall tax for conservation and renewable energy sources. An "energy bank" was also set up to provide up to $2.75 billion in low-interest loans and grants for conservation and solar between 1980 and 1987. In short the new expenditures planned for conservation and solar (renewable) would approximate $1.0 and $1.5 billion per year, respectively. To put the two numbers in perspective, America's bill for imported oil was running in early 1980 at the rate of $90 billion per year.

As for imports, in early 1980 the President took another step to raise the price of gasoline to the American motorist, this time by 10 cents a gallon. Imposed was an oil import fee of $4.62 a barrel, which would be administered by the Department of Energy so that gasoline purchasers would pay the entire amount. The Congress overwhelmingly overturned the President's action.

Another part of Carter's policy called for the formation of an Energy Mobilization Board, which was to be empowered to cut through environmental barriers for a selected number of important non-nuclear projects. Environmentalists opposed it. There was also considerable controversy over states' rights—whether the board could override state and local laws and regulations. And there was considerable fear by some of the energy-producing companies that the board might become yet another layer of bureaucracy, which would slow rather than speed new projects. A coalition of congressmen, representing these diverse interests, defeated the board in June 1980.

REAGAN'S "FREE MARKET" |

President Reagan brought his own miracle solution to the White House. He also chose the production path, but instead of Ford's emphasis on nuclear and coal and Carter's emphasis on synthetic fuels, Reagan focused on domestic oil and gas production. Domestic oil and gas was to be increased sufficiently to solve America's energy problem. Reagan's transition team complained that the Carter Administration had "tucked energy away like a rare bottle of wine" instead of encouraging its development. In effect, the Reagan Administration proceeded on the premise that the geological base of the United States was still in the same condition that it had been a quarter-century earlier—a view quite at variance with the real world.[14]

President Reagan's overwhelming ideological commitment to a "free market" has dominated his Administration's energy policy. According to this view, the major reason for the energy problem was simply the federal government itself. Thus, the "free market" should be allowed to determine the levels and types of energy to be consumed, produced domestically, imported, and exported. To be sure, some members of the Administration, such as Budget Director David Stockman, recognized that a number of imperfections existed in energy markets. But these members believed strongly that the government was not capable of picking winners among so many different energy sources. In other words, they preferred obviously impaired energy markets—in which they would hope over the long run to eliminate imperfections—rather than have the government intervene in the short term in an attempt to counteract imperfections until the imperfections could be removed.

The import of this rationale was to encourage the overconsumption of energy. Consider, for instance, the Reagan Administration's actions on the decontrol of oil and natural gas prices. The Administration clearly preferred to decontrol prices rather than to grant financial incentives to encourage oil and gas users to insulate their houses. Reagan's speeding up of oil-price decontrol in early 1981 was consistent with this principle. But this decision was easy, especially given the "oil glut" that commenced in 1981—an oil glut caused primarily by the 1979–80 price runup and a business recession rather than by Reagan's speedup of oil price decontrol. The issue of natural gas price regulations was much more complicated and difficult than the oil price issue. Faced with the natural gas issue in early 1982, the Administration chose not to push, at least for the time being, for a speedup in the deregulation. But when confronted with the arguments of Republican Senator Howard Baker, Senate majority leader from Tennessee, Reagan agreed to continue subsidizing the Clinch River Breeder Reactor, even though many pro-nuclear advocates considered this to be a waste of resources. Hence, it became obvious during 1981–82 that gross market imperfections would continue to encourage the overuse of energy, thereby penalizing energy efficiency, solar energy, and other new energy sources in the marketplace for many, many years.

All this the Reagan Administration ignored. It set out to kill all sorts of energy programs; those it could not kill quickly by eliminating from the budget were to be allowed to die slowly through a "non-implementation" treatment.

The Administration wanted to eliminate the Department of Energy, the Synthetic Fuels Corporation, financial incentives to conservation and solar energy, and federal authority for instituting emergency measures during any future oil crises. Congressional pressure kept alive the Department of Energy and the Synthetic Fuels Corporation, and forced the retention of a very meager part of the financial incentives passed by the Carter Administration to aid conservation and solar energy. As of mid-1982, the DOE and Synthetic Fuels Corporations were staffed by officials with a "go-slow" attitude, and the various energy programs were being subjected to either a "go-slow" treatment or outright "non-implementation."

Whatever the exact shape of the final outcome of the Reagan Administration's energy policy, it became clear that financial incentives for conservation and new energy sources would drop substantially, excessive energy consumption would still be encouraged by market imperfections, and the public would continue to be given the message that the nation's energy problems were over. This latter message was reinforced when Reagan vetoed a bill giving him standby authority to deal with any emergency arising from a breakdown in the world oil market—such as had occurred during the 1973–74 and 1979–80 oil crises.

This neglect of the nation's energy problems, the propensity to overconsume energy, and the unwillingness to accept powers to deal with an oil emergency baffled the United State's allies. Indeed, it represented a breakdown between the domestic and international sides of the Administration. While Defense Secretary Caspar Weinberger was declaring "our dependence on foreign oil sources" to be one of America's most important geopolitical realities, DOE Secretary Edwards was declaring that "market principles" would suffice and implied that there was no reason for the United States to make special efforts to reduce its oil imports.

All in all, Reagan's actions represented another shift in U.S. energy policy, veering from the panic that had led to Carter's synthetic fuel proposals to a stance of overcomplacency based on the belief that the adjustment process was more or less complete. Thus, the major themes of U.S. energy policy continued: a belief in easy answers; a disagreement over the basic nature of the energy problems and the roles of various actors; sharp shifts in perceptions of shortage or glut conditions; and an inability to tie domestic energy, national security, and foreign policy considerations into one coherent package. Unfortunately, the energy problem remains one of the most parochial issues in the country, with any single government policy likely to result in important costs or benefits to every man, woman, and child in the nation.

Where, then, does the United States now stand in developing a coherent energy program, and what still needs to be done? Our conclusion is that the legislation passed in 1978–1981, coupled with the decontrol of oil prices, brought the country to the halfway point. The decontrol of prices of new natural gas by 1985, provided it stands, is an essential element in such a program.

Yet the prospects for achieving a substantial permanent reduction in American oil imports remain uncertain; and the economic and political consequences of continued major U.S. dependence on imported oil can only become progressively more serious. True, the surplus in OPEC capacity that existed in mid–1982 is a positive sign. But almost all the other potential developments abroad now point in a negative direction. Political instability in the Middle East—especially in Saudi Arabia—could result in the repetition of the experience of 1979–1980 brought on by the Iranian revolution.

The public should not be misled by the easing of oil prices from the peaks reached at the end of the 1979–81 price runup. Indeed, we hope that cries of "oil glut" will not lull the nation into the complacency that prevailed in 1978. The United States must continue to push ahead to create what is needed—a balanced energy program.

9 | CONCLUSION: TOWARD A BALANCED ENERGY PROGRAM

ROBERT STOBAUGH
DANIEL YERGIN

The battles over energy have been so intense, the field so littered with charges and countercharges, that the most important point has been obscured. However, the two trillion dollars is finally apportioned, the United States might well face zero growth in conventional domestic energy sources in the 1980's.

There are two possible responses to the problem. One is to import more oil. More imports would likely lead to higher oil prices, which would result in periods of slow economic growth punctuated by recessions. More foreign oil would also accentuate America's political and strategic vulnerability. The second response is to accelerate energy efficiency and to bring renewable energy sources more swiftly into play. Such a program would allow and even encourage higher rates of economic growth.

How constrained are the conventional domestic energy sources?

Quite constrained. In fact, there is little likelihood of a substantial increase in the production of domestic oil and gas. U.S. oil production will almost surely decline, and the nation will be fortunate if natural gas output remains at current levels. Entrepreneurs have searched the continental United States for so long (more than 120 years), and so thoroughly (over 2 million wells), that it would be foolish to base a national policy on the supposition, advanced by some forecasters, that the absolute quantity of U.S. production of oil and gas will increase beyond what it is today.[1]

True, at the margin, more new oil and gas will be found at higher prices than at lower prices, and these extra finds will make up for some of the inevitable decline in production from existing wells. For these reasons, the move toward having consumers pay higher prices to producers makes good economic sense, although the extra output will be less than has often been advertised.

There are two other conventional domestic sources proffered as solutions to imported oil—coal and nuclear. Of course, coal and nuclear power have obvious benefits—to the users of electricity, to people who find employment (a job in a boom town is better than no job at all), to the companies that mine coal and uranium, and to those who profit from the economic activity associated with these industries. But coal and nuclear are also embroiled in controversy, although of a different kind than oil and gas. The conflicts over coal and nuclear have tended to bring out, rather than hide, the fact that only a modest contribution in increased energy can be counted on with reasonable certainty from these sources. Moreover, the conflict over coal and nuclear has been less about the distribution of huge sums of money than about the distribution of side effects, that is, the externalities, or costs, indirectly borne by the members of society at large rather than paid for directly in cash by the consumers of the energy.[2]

External costs, in the form of environmental and health problems, are rung up at every step in coal's journey from the mine along the railroad to the boiler where it is burned. When an economist or engineer says that the cost of electricity produced from coal is five cents a kilowatt hour, he or she is ignoring a number of important externalities. In the mining and transportation stage, the costs include acid drainage from mines and the disruption of life in Western communities by noisy trains hauling coal. The costs are even greater when coal is burned, for it releases sulfur dioxide and a host of other pollutants. The costs include smoggy skies, acid rain, emphysema, and the (unknown) consequences for future generations of increasing the temperature of the atmosphere by producing carbon dioxide.

There is another question. To what extent should external costs be "internalized" as a cost of coal production, transportation, and consumption? Internalization costs money—for the installation of scrubbers by utilities to remove sulfur dioxide, for the building of overpasses above railway tracks, and for the return of strip-mined land to its original contour and condition. But even after a number of such costs are internalized, many external costs still remain, and different people quite naturally place different values on them. A person with a large inheritance might well ascribe a greater value to blue skies than to overall economic activity, while an unemployed person might have the reverse preference, even though both live in the same city. The problem is accentuated when people live in different cities. New Yorkers do not want to risk increased chances of lung disease so that coal can be burned in Ohio to provide Cleveland with electricity. And the problem is accentuated even more when people live in different countries. Canadians certainly do not want to risk increased chances of lung disease, nor do they want acid rain ruining Canadian lakes and forests, in order for Clevelanders to have electricity available.

Because environmental and health problems have increasingly become issues in the political process, and because the cost of building new coal-fired electric generating plants has ballooned, the outlook for coal is not as bullish as has often been projected. In fact, it would be unwise for the nation to plan that the conventional use of coal will increase between 1981 and 1991 by an amount greater than the oil equivalent of 3.0 million barrels daily —which would still amount to a 40–percent growth, a substantial amount. In addition, some coal will be used to produce synthetic fuels—oil and gas—but by 1990, the likely quantity will still be negligible.

Nuclear energy has a set of external costs even more controversial than coal. Bitter disagreements about reactor safety have been a major cause for the many delays around the country in the completion of nuclear power plants. In turn, the delays, along with the increasingly stringent safety requirements, have caused such dramatic cost escalations that a second major controversy has erupted: Does it cost more, the same, or less to generate electricity from nuclear power than from coal? The question is difficult enough to answer when only the direct costs carried by the utility are considered. It is virtually impossible to answer when an effort is made to measure the relative external costs of coal and nuclear.

Furthermore, what makes nuclear power unique among the energy sources are the pervasive external costs it imposes on future generations—generations that will inherit caches of spent fuel that will emit radioactive rays for many centuries.[3] Some of the technical problems of managing this dangerous material might be simplified if it were "reprocessed" to recover uranium or plutonium, both of which are potentially useful. But reprocessing leads to new problems. Plutonium, a material that can also be used to make atomic bombs, would become more readily accessible. Thus, the promotion of reprocessing technology might lead to the proliferation of nuclear weapons.

In the 1960's, the nuclear advocates rushed ahead to attempt one of the most massive technological innovations in history— seeking to convert the world's electric generating system from fossil fuels to nuclear. In so doing, they confused dreams with reality. Utilities made their decisions to install billions of dollars of generating plants on the basis of costs *estimated* by the manufacturers without an adequate base of relevant experience. The proponents also ensured an increasing supply of dedicated enemies by the manner in which they dismissed the opposition, attacking them as revolutionaries, Luddites, and misguided children. In general, the advocates failed to conceive of nuclear power generation as an overall system, one that starts with the mining of uranium and ends with a satisfactory disposal of spent fuel. Meanwhile, nuclear critics fought a war of attrition in fish and game commissions, county commissioners' offices, state regulatory agencies, and the federal courts. Wherever the critics went, they asked one question: "How safe is safe enough?"

Today, the nuclear industry faces shutdowns of some operating plants in this decade unless the problem of handling spent fuel can be resolved. Space limitations make the current method of storing spent fuel in pools of water at the nuclear power plants unsatisfactory for any substantial period of time. A workable solution will have to satisfy a wide cross section of the public, including at least some of those normally considered to be nuclear opponents. The safety questions highlighted by Three Mile Island could, obviously, force shutdowns at any time, especially of those units located near large cities.

At the most, during the next ten years, nuclear energy might add a million and a half barrels a day of oil equivalent to the million and a quarter barrels a day it provides now, thus reaching a production level of slightly under 3 million barrels per day of oil equivalent. That level would require the continued operation of all existing nuclear capacity, plus the completion and operation of much of the new capacity currently under construction or on order. That, we stress, is a very bullish scenario. Indeed, we regard the nuclear condition to be far more uncertain, and believe that the energy generated by nuclear power could actually undergo an absolute decline within ten years. It is, therefore, unwise to rely on nuclear to make any substantial contribution to reducing dependence on imported oil for the rest of this century. It would be equally unwise, however, to foreclose the possibility of a longer term contribution by nuclear energy. It is, after all, pretty clear that our major objective should be to create realistic energy options, not to deny them.

In other words, the prospect for dramatic *increases* in domestic supplies from the total of the four conventional fuels—oil, gas, coal, and nuclear—is bleak. But the country certainly cannot afford to ignore measures that *might* marginally increase domestic supplies. Thus we favor:

1. The leasing of offshore oil and gas properties, under strict environmental regulations, and in a manner to promote rapid development.

2. Continuation of the current thrust to decontrol the price of domestic gas, including the "old gas" that is not slated for decontrol under the current legislation. In conjunction, however, there should be programs targeted to help lower-income people weatherproof their dwellings in order to adjust to these higher prices.

3. Elimination of the windfall profits tax on *newly found* oil.

4. Government assistance for technologies that could provide new supplies—such as coal gasification and liquefaction, and shale

oil. The instability in the Arab/Persian Gulf argues in particular, on security grounds, for continued and consistent research, development, and demonstration efforts on synthetic fuels.

5. A major attempt by the government to find an acceptable method to dispose of spent fuel from nuclear reactors and to ensure reactor safety.

Unless measures such as these are pursued, there could be an absolute decline in output from the four traditional sources, potentially making the United States even more dependent on imported oil than current forecasts indicate.[4] But whether the four domestic sources increase somewhat, remain constant, or decline, the broad choice before the United States is the same—increased dependence on imported oil, or a transition to a more balanced energy system in which conservation and solar play large roles.

THE PROBLEMS OF IMPORTED OIL |

The problems flowing from increasing quantities of imported oil are so large that they deserve some reiteration here.[5] There is the obvious risk of a supply interruption because of the politics of the Middle East. The United States can help protect itself by having an adequate amount of oil-storage capacity, perhaps a volume equal to six months of imports. Such a program is inexpensive compared with the possible economic losses from another embargo. As of this writing, the United States had in storage the equivalent of about two months of imports.

The greatest single matter of concern posed by increasing U.S. oil imports is their potential link to world oil prices: The higher U.S. oil imports, the higher will be world oil prices. There is no accepted theory about the exact nature of the link. But the role of U.S. imports is crucial, for if the United States does not act to dampen imports, Europe and Japan will find it harder to restrain their own demand. For example, lags in the development of such energy sources as nuclear or solar, or an inattention to conservation in the United States, will contribute to similar conditions in Europe and Japan.

It is difficult to predict world oil prices with much certainty because one cannot answer the question of how much, at any given time, Saudi Arabia can dominate OPEC and thus the setting of the world price. No one can say for sure exactly how the Saudis set price. But it is reasonable to assume that the most fundamental goal of the present ruling family is survival, that is, to keep themselves in power. There are forces pushing them in different directions. On the one hand, they desire good relations with the United States, and want to avoid creating economic conditions in Western Europe that would lead to left-wing governments. They fear that higher prices will augment the arms-buying potential of their neighbors, such as Iran. On the other hand, they are not anxious to sell their only real asset—oil—at too low a price. Furthermore, they are becoming increasingly wary of producing substantially greater quantities of oil in order to pay for massive industrial development, especially with Iran as an object lesson. Also, the Saudis are under pressure from other producers on price and production policies. During the second shock, the Saudis lost control over the market, making price prediction even more difficult.

Thus, predicting oil prices is as much art as it is science, requiring sensitivity to political nuance as much as dexterity in mathematical analyses. Our estimates should be viewed accordingly. The reader will recall from Chapter 2 our illustration of how costly imports might be in the future. The experience of 1979–81 suggests that marginal barrels of oil probably cost the United States $65 to $100 a barrel. Higher U.S. imports make for a tighter world oil market, and a tighter market makes for higher prices.[6]

Higher oil prices, in turn, result in national income being lower than would otherwise be the case. And if the history of 1973–75 and 1979–82 is any guide, an economic slowdown might be accentuated by policies adopted by governments to combat inflation and balance-of-payments deficits. Even without sharply higher prices, the United States and other governments could still feel forced to adopt deflationary policies because of higher oil imports. In any case, increasingly high imports from OPEC result in increased tension and suspicion among the nations of the West.

A FAIR CHANCE

What to do? We favor reliance on the marketplace. We do not think an ever-more-regulated system is the answer to the problems posed by energy. But if the market is to resolve the problems, its distortions must be corrected so that all energy sources, including conservation and solar, will be able to compete on an equal economic footing. Some might think that we are proposing a transformation of the market. On the contrary, we argue that without a transition to a more balanced energy program, the market system itself in the years ahead will inevitably return to a pattern of increased constraints—by regulation and disruption. Although both incentives and sanctions have a role to play in the process of equilibration, the emphasis should be placed on incentives. The pursuit of profit has, after all, served American society well in the past, and clearly the carrot makes for better politics and more acceptable change than does the stick.[7]

That last point is crucial, because a politically acceptable program that can make a significant contribution to a solution of the energy problem is better than one that might theoretically solve it altogether but which has no chance of being adopted. Indeed, given the elusive nature of true costs, the uncertainty generated by using GNP to indicate how well-off the country is, and the difficulty of making accurate predictions as to what effects different policies would have, we do not think it is useful to think in terms of an "economically optimum" energy policy.[8] An improved policy, yes. But an economic optimum, no.

Of course, it is not a new idea to intervene in the marketplace to correct distortions that come under the heading of market imperfections (such as lack of information) and market failures (such as the externalities of a polluting smokestack). Because of continuing imperfections and failures, it is unrealistic to expect an uncorrected "free" market to solve U.S. energy problems.[9]

The U.S. price structure for energy has been heavily distorted. In addition to the distortion brought about because the price of imported oil fails to represent its true cost, American consumers have received enormous price subsidies to use domestic sources of conventional energy. Although we have not made a detailed study of these subsidies, it appears that they exceed $100 billion a year or more. Controls are keeping the prices of domestic gas far below their economic values, although "new" natural gas is scheduled to be decontrolled in 1985. Moreover, regulations hold electricity prices at only a fraction of the replacement cost of power plants. This has given consumers large indirect subsidies to use coal and uranium (as well as that oil and gas used to generate electricity.) In addition, coal and nuclear power bear external costs of sufficient importance to cause major political controversies.[10]

The cornerstone of our thinking is that conservation and solar energy should be given a fair chance in the market system to compete with imported oil and the other traditional sources. Of course, a straightforward alternative, and one sometimes suggested by economists, would be to impose a tariff on imported oil and let all other energy prices rise to whatever level market forces take them. Since Congress overwhelmingly rebuffed President Carter's attempt to impose a gasoline tax of ten cents a gallon via a $4.62 per barrel tariff on imported oil, we judge that a tariff high enough to offset the true costs of oil would not be politically acceptable; neither would the proposal to let the prices of all other domestic energy rise to such a high level. And President Reagan, while contemplating a modest tariff on imported oil, has been reluctant to propose one.

Accordingly (and this follows our preference for the carrot rather than the stick), we favor financial incentives to encourage consumers to use conservation and solar energy, not because there is anything intrinsically virtuous about these energy sources, but because they make good economic sense.[11] Of course, an important variation on this alternative is theoretically possible—that is, to take our principle of the "fair chance" with imported oil and apply it to conventional domestic resources by giving financial incentives to producers of oil, gas, coal, and nuclear power. But we have serious doubts that this program would be politically acceptable. For some years the government did not allow finders of new oil—and still does not allow finders of new gas—to obtain even the world prices; to obtain a large premium over world prices would seem impossible, at least for many years to come. One must recognize that many people question whether even world prices, much less a financial incentive in addition to world prices, would be justified by the incremental domestic energy forthcoming—especially given the lack of success in keeping U.S. oil and gas reserves from declining even after the dramatic price jumps that have occurred since 1973, and also given the environmental costs and resultant political barriers associated with coal and nuclear power.

Thus, it appears to us that the only viable program that would consistently reduce U.S. dependence on imported oil in the 1980's would be for the government to give financial incentives to encourage conservation and solar energy.[12] It is worth noting, however, that analyses—albeit of a preliminary nature—suggest that conservation and some forms of solar energy are cheaper for an additional ten million barrels per day of oil equivalent than are conventional energy sources.

We do not claim to know exactly the appropriate level of financial incentives. But the fact that the true costs of imported oil are at least two and perhaps three times its current U.S. market price suggests an incentive payment or other form of offsetting subsidy as high as two-thirds of the cost of implementing conservation and solar energy. We do not, however, recommend this large an incentive, for we acknowledge readily that our calculations are only crude approximations. Furthermore, for the most part we would think somewhat lower incentives would probably be sufficient to encourage a substantial increase in investment in conservation and solar energy.[13]

Three questions must be answered at this point: What kind of program is needed? How can the program be financed? What would be the likely consequence? We answer each of these questions in turn.

Of the two "new" energy sources, the most immediate priority is conservation, which can reduce America's dependence on imported oil until solar energy can make a substantial contribution. The conservation measures depend on the nature of the sector.

- In transportation, an obvious form of subsidy would be to experiment with free public transportation in some municipalities, and much greater emphasis should be placed on ride-sharing—particularly vanpooling to and from the workplace. In any case, the automobile is unlikely to be displaced as a central part of American life, so increased fuel efficiency is a number-one priority. The mandatory requirements setting higher miles-per-gallon standards seem to be especially attractive because the government need only regulate and monitor a few companies. Even higher mpg standards—but standards that do not hamper flexibility and experimentation and that do give some stability to the planning horizon and capital problems of auto companies—should be set for the post-1985 period. Still, with all this in place, the likely prospects of a difficult oil market during the 1980's provides a compelling rationale for a strong gasoline tax.

- In the industrial sector, there are many decisionmakers, but they generally have better information than most private citizens about the real costs of alternative energy choices. To give them appropriate signals and incentives, we suggest offsetting payments in the form of investment tax credits and accelerated depreciation up to 40 percent of capital costs.

- The residential-commercial sector is highly fragmented. While the potential savings from retrofit of existing dwellings can be very great, market imperfections, in particular poor information and limited access to capital, currently present great barriers. Under these circumstances, we suggest tax credits of up to 50 percent of retrofit costs, with rebates for lower income groups. Because it is desirable to use existing organizations where possible, electric utilities should be encouraged to deliver energy conservation and, along with other organizations, to arrange financing. This, of course, means continuing to change regulations to make the conditions attractive enough for them to do so. The new building market can be reached through revised building codes and through the mortgage requirements of loan agencies.

• • •

Solar energy presents a different set of problems. A wide variety of technologies are involved, some of them well known, some used in the past but made uneconomic by cheap conventional sources, and some of them on the technological frontier. What is called "solar" includes many forms of renewable energy —not only the active hot-water systems, but also photovoltaics, wood, and other plant material, hydroelectric, wood, and passive solar design. It has long been recognized that the benefits to society of the diffusion of technology exceed the benefits that accrue to the entrepreneur. Individuals and companies are more risk-averse than society as a whole, and information generated by an installation that does not work is often of less use to the innovator who failed than it is to society.[14] Therefore, solar energy deserves and needs greater governmental assistance than conservation. Solar users might receive an offsetting payment equal to about 60 percent of installation costs.

In order for conservation and solar incentives to work, certain additional barriers must be broken. At present, for instance, an industrial firm wanting to cogenerate electricity and steam can face a regulatory obstacle in selling electricity to its utility. Solar energy is hampered by lack of standardized building codes, confusion over the right of a person to prevent others from blocking the sun, utility regulations that deny a solar house all-electric rates, and property taxes.

Our recommendations for conservation and solar energy are rough guides. It is impossible to determine precisely how large various subsidies should be, nor do we know what subsidies at any given time that Congress and the Administration would approve. We do know, however, that the subsidies should be larger than those that have been approved so far. The meager financial incentives given to conservation, and the attempts of the Reagan Administration to reduce these, have been especially disappointing.

If the nation is to make the transition to a more balanced energy system, the government must be the champion of solar and, especially, conservation for several reasons. First, the conventional energy sources have a host of allies, witting and unwitting, in those analysts who understate the external costs generated by these sources. They not only tend to underestimate the disadvantages of imported oil, but also tend to underestimate the environmental costs of conventional energy. Studies, for example, often equate the health costs of pollution with lost wages plus medical expenses. Presumably, in such a formulation it "costs" society very little for a non-working wife to contract lung cancer from emissions, provided that she dies quickly, so that large medical bills are avoided. Conservation, in particular, has no obvious constituency. Moreover, the conservation and solar energy industries do not have as many companies and workers involved in them as do other energy sources. Imported oil, for example, has a powerful constituency among those who produce, refine, and distribute it. The international oil majors take in more money in a few hours than the entire solar industry does in a year. And these companies, their workers, and their customers have a natural tendency to favor their ongoing activities.[15]

The government must lead, for the only thing that is going to happen "automatically" in the years immediately ahead is the stream of imported oil. Some of the most efficient large enterprises in history manage that process in a way to make it seem quite easy, transporting oil halfway around the world and then refining it, all for just a few pennies per gallon.* But government leadership does not mean government management. Rather, it means correcting market defects in a way to create more jobs and more business opportunities for both large established companies and small new firms with a stake in conservation and solar energy.

Are we not talking about a great deal of money? No—not when compared to America's bill for imported oil, which came to $80 billion in 1981. The Reagan program is obviously inadequate when measured against this number. The Administration's budget requests for conservation for the next fiscal year at the beginning of 1982 were $22 million—equivalent in value to two hours of American oil imports at the time.

How to pay for this kind of program? The obvious answer would be: "Out of the windfall tax on old oil and gas." As it is,

---

*Most of the price paid at the pump goes in the form of payments to the governments of the producing and consuming countries. The "few pennies" refers to profit.

however, less than 10 percent of the windfall tax on oil is designated for residential and business energy tax credits. The failure to use a more substantial part of these revenues to correct the under-investment in conservation and solar is a dramatic case of misplaced priorities.

Another way to finance conservation and solar energy would be through the revenues from an increased gasoline tax. (Alternatively, a gasoline tax could be rebated directly to consumers or be used to reduce other taxes.) Further, conservation and solar energy should be encouraged by the same approach proposed for synthetic fuels. That is, a number of large-scale trials should be inaugurated in different settings in the United States in order to determine the best method for achieving results.

We also wish to stress the need for greater understanding among normally warring parties. For instance, public interest groups must understand the substantial and complex difficulties faced by utilities as they try to adapt to the new energy era. Utilities should be partners in the promotion of conservation and solar.

THE CONSEQUENCE OF A BALANCED PROGRAM |

What pattern of energy use will result from the move to a more balanced system? No one knows with a high degree of certainty, for the base of experience with incentives for conservation and solar energy is inadequate for detailed predictions. But the urgency of adopting a balanced program giving greater emphasis to conservation and solar energy is clear. The dangers of not doing so are highlighted in Table 9-1, which shows how U.S. imports could *grow* in the 1980's and early 1990's unless different policies are adopted.

Many energy analysts expect that U.S. consumption of energy will rise from about 36 mbdoe in 1981 to about 42 mbdoe in 1991, an annual growth rate of 1.5 percent.[16] This rate of growth, when combined with a modest 1 to 1.5 percent annual increase in energy efficiency, would allow an economic growth rate of 2½ to

TABLE 9·1
U.S. ENERGY SUPPLY, ACTUAL 1981
AND PRUDENT ESTIMATE FOR 1991
(MILLIONS OF BARRELS DAILY OF OIL EQUIVALENT)

	1981 Actual	1991 Prudent Estimate
Domestic (excluding U.S. exports)		
Oil	9.6[b]	7.0[d]
Natural Gas	9.2	7.7
Coal	7.4	10.4[e]
Nuclear	1.4	2.5
Subtotal, Non-renewables	27.6	27.6
Renewables[a]	2.4	3.2
Total Domestic	30.0	30.8
Imports		
Oil	6.0[c]	5.0
Gas	0.4	0.8
Subtotal	6.4	5.8
TOTAL	36.4	36.6
Conservation Needed	—	5.4
TOTAL	36.4	42.0

[a]Includes for 1981 and 1991, respectively, 1.5 mbd and 1.7 mbd combined total for hydroelectric and geothermal and 0.9 and 1.5 mbd for biomass. Biomass is not part of statistics published by Department of Energy, Energy Information Administration.

[b]Domestic production of oil and natural gas liquids was 10.2 mbd; but exports were 0.6 mbd, thereby leaving 9.6 mbd for domestic consumption.

[c]Excludes imports of 0.3 mbd for Strategic Petroleum Reserve.

[d]This assumes production at 7.6 mbd, with 0.6 exports.

[e]Excludes estimated exports of 1.7 million barrels per day of oil equivalent.

Sources: 1981, from Department of Energy, Energy Information Administration, Monthly Energy Report (Washington D.C.: Government Printing Office), expect renewables which are from Securing America's Energy Future: The National Energy Policy Plan (Washington, D.C.: Government Printing Office, July 1981), p. 22. The 1991 estimates are based on Chapters 2–7 of this book, except estimate for renewables is from same source as 1981 figures. For a list of various projections, see reference 17 in Reference Notes for this chapter.

3 percent. Unfortunately, there is a great deal of controversy about where this quantity of energy could be obtained. In 1981, domestic supplies of "conventional" energy (i.e., energy from depletable sources) was about 28 mbdoe. By 1991, this could be any number between 28 and 32 mbdoe. There is especially a high degree of uncertainty surrounding domestic oil and natural gas. Exxon, for example, estimated in 1979 that the domestic production of oil would be 6.1 mbd in 1990; a year later, Exxon raised this estimate to 7.1 mbd. At about the same time, Conoco was estimating 10 mbd. Given the continuing rundown of U.S. oil and gas reserves even after the substantial price hikes, it seems prudent for the nation to adopt policies that would be satisfactory in case some of the lower estimates turn out to be accurate. We present just such a prudent estimate of supply for 1991 in Table 9–1. It shows U.S. energy supply from non-renewable sources as being about 28 mbd in 1991—in other words, zero growth in such domestic energy supplies between 1981 and 1991.

These quantities, along with the modest growth in renewable energy supplies expected if the Reagan Administration policies are adopted, would result in a total domestic energy supply of about 31 mbd. Gas imports are not expected to exceed one mbd. Thus, oil imports would have to be about 10 mbd. It is highly questionable whether this quantity of imported oil will be available to the United States in 1991. Indeed, any attempt to import such levels would entail serious economic, political, and security costs for the United States, Western Europe, and Japan.

A reasonable (but not necessarily satisfactory) import target for 1991 might be half that quantity, or 5 mbd. There is a danger that still higher oil prices will close this gap of 5 mbd by inducing a mix of "unproductive" conservation as occured in the early 1980's—the shutting down of factories, higher unemployment, offices and houses being too warm or too cold for efficient work or comfortable living, and a choice for some between food or fuel. In other words, we would experience economic recessions interspersed with periods of slow economic growth, both accompanied by inflation and monetary dislocations—and intensified political conflict, both domestically and internationally.

This 5 million barrels per day can be thought of as a policy gap. Constructive public policies are required to fill it. The synthetic fuels program, of course, was expected by its advocates to play a major role in doing so. But it is now clear to all that the contribution of synthetic fuels will be inconsequential in 1991, and perhaps to the end of the century. Thus, we need a much greater stimulation of conservation and renewable energy sources. In that way, the nation can adapt successfully, and with minimal disruption, to this situation in which there is likely to be an overall zero energy growth in conventional fuel sources.

We come to two inescapable conclusions: Conservation is the principle additional energy source for the 1980's. And creative public policies are needed to correct market imperfections.

Our whole industrial system is like a vehicle built to operate on $4 oil, puffing along with an inefficient engine leaking vast amounts of energy. Each BTU wasted drives higher the price of future oil purchases, which in turn makes it easier for OPEC to cut production and raise prices even more. Now that we have $30-plus oil, correcting this situation is the nation's first order of business.

Can this be done? We think it can, with substantial investments in conservation measures encouraged by federal financial incentives. The result will not only be a higher GNP but much less inflation than if we send the same dollars abroad to pay for oil at ever-increasing prices.

At the very least, our aim should be to have substantial economic growth with zero energy growth. Some economic analysts relying on historical relationships might dismiss this notion as fanciful. We say it is not. Practical experience is proving that the flexibility is considerable. AT&T is hardly a fanciful dreamer. On the basis of its own experience, the company has set an internal goal of negative energy growth—to use less energy in 1985 than in 1973—even though business is projected to more than double.[18] In this case, what is good for AT&T is also good for the United States.

The matter can be viewed thusly: Our conventional energy production—oil, gas, coal, and nuclear—may be thought of as well-explored producing regions. We favor continuing and augmenting production in these terrains. But in terms of allocating resources and effort for further major increments of energy, the evidence strongly suggests that the nation would be better served by concentrating more exploratory and development "drilling" in the partially proven acreage of conservation, and the promising but still largely untested domain of renewable energy.

What is still missing is an energy policy to guide the transition. What we propose would make possible an economically sound and politically workable transition away from ever-growing dependence on imported oil. No other nation has so great an impact on the international energy system. Now is the time for the United States to come to terms with the realities of the energy problem, not with romanticisms, but with pragmatism and reason. And not out of altruism, but for pressing reasons of self-interest.

APPENDIX: LIMITS TO MODELS

SERGIO KOREISHA
ROBERT STOBAUGH

The oil crisis of 1973 attracted intense attention from specialists —econometricians and technologists—who build formal models in order to make predictions about the future.

Econometricians build and operate models which consist of mathematical equations based upon relationships derived from economic theory and estimates based on historical statistical relationships. The use of such models is often characterized as "looking forward through a rearview mirror." Usually developed with the aid of a computer, these models are used primarily to make forecasts about *existing* energy systems: How much coal will be produced at such and such a price? How much oil will be consumed if the price goes up two dollars a barrel?

The technologists, meanwhile, base their analyses mostly on engineering cost estimates. Such models are used extensively to forecast energy supplies that might be forthcoming from *new* sources: What, for example, is the likely cost of gasifying coal or utilizing shale oil? They are also used to estimate supplies from conventional energy sources: What, for example, are the chances of finding new oil reserves? The results of both types of formal models—econometric and technological—are often modified by personal judgment to make the results correspond more closely to the specialist's understanding of the real world.[1]

A systematic survey of all published formal models is not possible here, for they number in the dozens, perhaps even in the hundreds. But a very important point can still be made. The major studies since 1973 have given us predictions about the U.S. energy situation that have consistently been more optimistic than the reality has proved to be, especially in regard to energy supplies. Some of the models were published without receiving much notice and had virtually no lasting impact. Nevertheless, it seems abundantly clear that some of the optimistic forecasts issued did influence—and mislead—both the energy policymakers and the informed public about the causes and possible solutions for the energy problem.

In a world of contradictory assertions, it is not surprising that, as one leading econometric modeler put it, "Public officials increasingly fall back on the computer model as their ultimate authority." *Fortune* magazine, with some hyperbole perhaps, summarized the situation as follows: "When the history of economic policymaking in the turbulent late 1970's is written, an important part of the story will be about the ever-widening impact of econometric models on federal policy decisions. The wondrous computerized models—and the economists who run them—have become new rages on the Washington scene. These days, it seems, every spending and tax bill is played into mathematical simulations inside a computer. The model managers themselves are star witnesses before the congressional committees whose members seek to divine the future. And what these machines and their operators have to say has come to have a significant bearing on what Washington decides to do."[2]

Although other factors, such as the judgments of consultants and industry executives, obviously also affect energy estimates, our discussions with government officials, as well as published evidence, provide support for a conclusion that energy policy indeed has been affected to an important extent by formal models. In November 1974, for example, the federal government released a study that showed how the United States could become self-sufficient in energy by 1985. A *New York Times* article, in reporting the study, quoted an anonymous Administration official, who, citing a large computer model, said, "We expect oil prices to level out between $4 and $6 a barrel."[3] At the time, OPEC prices were about $10 a barrel. In January 1975, Secretary of State Henry Kissinger stated that discoveries of oil and new sources of energy would make it "increasingly difficult for the cartel to operate," and that this would begin to "occur within two or three years." And in order to encourage the development of domestic energy sources in the major industrial nations, Kissinger spent much time trying to arrange a floor price on oil of $7 a barrel.[4]

Models have also had similar impact on some decision-makers in the private sector. In early 1979, Henry Ford II expressed a hope that the federal government "would give up" on efforts to get tighter post-1985 fuel economy standards. He was asked, "Aren't you going to have to develop something in the 1985 period that really copes with the likelihood of oil becoming more and more scarce?" Ford replied, "I thought so once, but I'm not sure I do now. In late 1974 we asked the Stanford Research Institute to study this problem. They said we don't see that as a worry. If it doesn't come out of the ground, it will come from conversion of coal or shale or what Occidental is doing, or gasohol or God knows what."[5]

What went wrong with the models is a question that obviously needs to be pursued. In general, the modeling enterprise needs to be demystified so that a better understanding of both the utility and the limitations of models can be obtained. To try to answer the question of what went wrong with some of the specific predictions, we will show the critical importance of the various assumptions made by the modelers, for these assumptions, in effect, determine the results of the models. And these assumptions are all too often overlooked.

We also hope to encourage a recent tendency wherein model builders state explicitly, even highlight, what the limitations of their studies are.[6]

From the innumerable studies made about energy prospects, we selected three for detailed examination, precisely because of the authors' extraordinarily high degree of competence and sense of responsibility. We know of no one who could have done better using the tools of the craft. The studies also happened to be three of the most prominent published. They are as follows:

- The Kennedy-Houthakker World Oil Model
- The MIT Energy Self-Sufficiency Study
- The Federal Energy Administration's Project Independence Report

The very word *model* can confuse people. Here it means a representation of some phenomenon or observable system in the real world. Thus, the builder must seek to balance his or her model between two extremes. It must be complex enough to be a reasonable representation of the phenomenon, but it must also be simple enough to be constructed and used.

To fit the complexities of the real world into the variables that can be handled in a model, the builders of energy models are forced to make a number of simplifying assumptions that can lead to inaccuracies. For convenience, we refer to these simplifying assumptions as *red flags*, items to which the model builder and the user of the model's results should pay special attention. The first three red flags discussed are relevant for both econometric and technological models, whereas the last two apply mainly to econometric models.

1. *Exclusion.* The influence of any factor not included in the model is assumed to be unimportant in affecting the conclusions.

In an econometric model, the builder seeks to measure the impact of one or more economic variables on another variable in order to predict future events or to explain some economic process. For example, a very simple econometric model could be constructed on the supposition that demand for oil this year is dependent solely on this year's oil price. In such a case, the model builder would be assuming that natural gas prices had no effect on oil consumption. But in fact, in the real world, one expects that higher natural gas prices lead to increased oil consumption by encouraging consumers to use oil instead of natural gas.

In a technological model, the model builder typically studies the current state of technology, estimates the costs of individual elements that make up the total investment and operating costs, and then estimates the cost of these elements for commercially sized plants. For example, a technological model could be constructed in order to forecast the cost of producing oil from shale rock. One element that would be included in the cost of the plant would be the interest costs incurred during the construction period, costs that would be partially dependent on the number of years needed for construction. If a prototype plant had already been built and was in operation, the model builder might estimate the time period needed to build the commercial plant by extrapolating from the experience obtained during the construction of the prototype. If the prototype plant had not experienced delays due to objections raised by environmentalists, the model builder might make the assumption that environmentalists would not delay the commercially sized plant.

2. *Aggregation.* Data on different subprocesses are often combined, or aggregated, as if they were just one process in order to reduce the number of variables to manageable proportions, or because it is not possible or convenient to measure them separately. For example, U.S. onshore and offshore oil production clearly have different cost structures, yet many econometricians lump them together as though they constituted just one large field. Similarly, for technological models, although workers with different skills have different costs and productivities, cost estimators sometimes lump them together as though they were one homogenous group of workers.

3. *Range.* The data put into an equation used to make forecasts are calculated from observations made within a range of prior experience. If there is no change in the underlying economic behavior, then logic dictates that such data should be useful in making forecasts within this range of prior experience. But if the data are used to make projections outside this range, the logical underpinning of the estimates deteriorates. As one moves further outside the range, the potential for error increases dramatically.[7]

For forecasting purposes in an econometric model, some of the input data consist of economic statistics known as elasticities. In the context of supply and demand, the term *elasticity* can be defined as the responsiveness of the demand or supply of a commodity to changes in factors which influence that demand or supply. The price elasticity of supply relates to the extent to which supplies respond to changes in the price of a commodity. Similarly, the price elasticity of demand is a measure of the extent to which the quantity demanded responds to a change in the price of the commodity. To be more explicit, the price elasticity of demand is the percentage change in the demand that would result from a one-percent change in price. For example, a coefficient of − .5 for the price elasticity of demand for oil means that if the *price* of oil were to rise by one percent, the *demand* for oil would fall by half a percent. That is, the elasticity can be viewed as the percentage change in demand (or supply) divided by the percentage change in price.

Percentage Change in Price	*Percentage Change in Demand*	*Elasticity*
↑1%	↓.5%	− .5

If a − .5 elasticity was found to exist when the price of oil rose from $2.90 to $3.00 a barrel, one might assume with some confidence that the same elasticity would apply if the price of oil were to rise from $3.00 to, say, $3.15. But there is no real basis for assuming that the same elasticity also would apply if the price were to rise from $3.00 to $10.00. It would be as though one were predicting the outcome of a marathon among runners whose track record was limited to the 100-yard dash.

The range issue also figures in technological models, as, for instance, when the cost of a commercially sized plant is estimated from the experience gained in building and operating a prototype. Although there is both theory and empirical evidence to suggest that a chemical processing plant twice as large as another plant with identical technology would cost only about 1½ times as much to build, the extrapolation of experience upward by a factor of 10 or 100 produces much more uncertainty.[8]

4. *Reversibility.* This red flag applies primarily to econometric models. For example, if the elasticities used to make forecasts are derived during a demand process in which *reduced* prices are accompanied by *increased* consumption, then, under the reversibility assumption, it is assumed that forecasts can also be made using these elasticities for periods when *increased*

prices are expected to be followed by *reduced* consumption.

5. *Time lag.* This also applies primarily to econometric models. Data are seldom available to enable the modeler to make an accurate estimate of the time lag required for the change in one variable, such as price, to achieve any given effect. True, econometric models (using "distributed lags") could take into account slow adjustments to price changes, such as retrofitting furnaces, making cars smaller, and changing commuting habits. But in many cases there are no historical data on which to measure how fast and effective the response is likely to be. This problem is sometimes handled by using two elasticity estimates: a short-term elasticity to indicate those effects that will appear in a short period of time (often less than a year), and a long-term elasticity to indicate the full effects that will occur (often requiring many years). Thus, estimates of lags generally require considerable personal judgment.

In light of the foregoing, it is not surprising that estimates of similar elasticities can differ significantly from model to model. Table A–1, for example, shows the disparity in agreement for the

TABLE A · 1
ESTIMATES FOR THE PRICE ELASTICITY OF CRUDE OIL SUPPLY

Study	Estimate
Kennedy-Houthakker World Oil Model[a]	
"Pessimistic" Case	.15
"Optimistic" Case	.50
MIT Study (Erickson-Span Model)[b]	.87
Project Independence[c]	.78

[a]Hendrik S. Houthakker, *The World Price of Oil: A Medium-Term Analysis* (Washington, D.C.: American Institute for Public Research, 1976), p. 19.

[b]The Policy Study Group of the MIT Energy Laboratory, "Energy Self-Sufficiency: An Economic Evaluation," *Technology Review,* May 1974, p. 34.

[c]Derived from data in Federal Energy Administration, *Project Independence Report* (Washington, D.C.: Government Printing Office, November 1974).

price elasticity of crude oil supply among the three studies analyzed in this Appendix. The crude oil supply that would result with an elasticity of .87 is very different from the supply that would be forthcoming from an elasticity of .15. The high elasticity implies that a 100 percent increase in price would increase supply by 87 percent, compared with an implied increase of only 15 percent with the lower elasticity.

THE KENNEDY-HOUTHAKKER WORLD OIL MODEL|

The World Oil Model, formulated by Michael Kennedy and Hendrik Houthakker* in 1973 and 1974, was the first attempt of which we are aware to set up an analytical structure that could systematically predict long-run levels of consumption, production, and price of oil in various regions of the world based on flexible sets of assumptions.[9] The model consists of four sectors: crude oil production, transportation, refining, and consumption of products. It distinguishes six regions: United States, Europe, Japan, Canada, Latin America, and the Middle East. It uses five commodities: crude oil and four refined products—gasoline, kerosene, distillate fuel, and residual fuel.

The model contains the assumption that the Persian Gulf and North African members of OPEC determine the world oil price, which they do by announcing the revenues that they will receive per barrel and then selling whatever oil is demanded at this revenue plus production costs. (Hereinafter, we refer to this revenue as a "tax."[10]) The other members of OPEC are assumed to hold their production constant at 1972 levels; the output of the rest of the world is fixed by the user of the model.

The detailed assumptions made by Kennedy and Houthakker

---

*The model was constructed by Kennedy for his doctoral thesis in economics at Harvard University. He is now at the Rand Corporation. Hendrik Houthakker, a member of Kennedy's thesis committee, is a professor of economics at Harvard University and a world-renowned expert on elasticities and their uses in econometric models; he was formerly a member of the President's Council of Economic Advisors.

are of particular interest, for they can be used to illustrate some of the red flags discussed above.

First, take the *exclusion* assumption. None of the other energy supply sectors, such as coal, natural gas, and nuclear, were incorporated into the model.[11] Consequently, the model cannot explicitly quantify the effects that changes in the other sectors would have on the oil market.

Second, in order to estimate price and income elasticities, the authors *aggregated* available data for industrialized countries and assumed that these applied for all regions of the world.[12] Furthermore, in three of the four products, data for the United States—consumer of one third of the world's oil—were deficient and hence not included.

Third, let us recall that when elasticity figures are used far outside the *range* of values of the observations used to calculate them, the potential for error is large. In the Kennedy-Houthakker model, data covering the pre-embargo period of 1962 to 1972 were used to estimate the post-embargo period, when prices were several times those of the pre-embargo period. In other words, the historical experiences observed when prices changed from $1.75 to $2.00 a barrel were used to estimate the effects of changing price from $2.00 a barrel up to $10.00 a barrel.

Fourth, the modelers assumed that the processes being modeled were *reversible:* that is, the extent to which reduced oil prices were accompanied by increased consumption would be an accurate guide of the extent to which increased oil prices were accompanied by reduced consumption.

Although this reversibility assumption sounded plausible, in fact we believe that it was not justified. The principal reason is that a fall in the "real" price of oil (that is, the price corrected for inflation) helped oil to replace coal in the 1950's and the 1960's. But energy users could not be as responsive to the 1973–74 rise in oil prices as they had been to the earlier drop—that is, they could not switch from oil back to coal as readily as they switched from coal to oil, for a variety of reasons. Many consumers who were allowed to burn coal in earlier years were prevented or discouraged from returning to coal in the 1970's because of laws designed to protect the environment. Whereas the replacement of coal-handling equipment by oil was relatively inexpensive, the reinstallation of the dismantled coal-handling equipment was costly. A boiler designed to burn coal requires a larger firebox per unit of output than one designed to burn oil, so a boiler conversion from coal to oil could be done without any loss of capacity. But if a boiler designed to burn oil was converted to coal, the capacity loss would be substantial. In other words, many factors not included in Kennedy's and Houthakker's equations affected the outcome and undercut the potential reversibility of the economic processes.

Fifth, consider the *time-lag* red flag. The model builders assumed that the full effects predicted by the model would occur by 1980—that is, that six years would be sufficient time for the long-run elasticities to apply. A lag structure had to be *assumed* rather than derived. The model was not constructed to trace the pattern of events leading to the conclusions—it was a static model.

Given this list of red flags, it is not surprising that many of the elasticities calculated by the authors differed significantly from what such elasticities were generally believed to be. Consequently, following a practice sometimes used by econometricians, the authors made "some substantial modifications to the . . . [elasticities] for projection purposes."[13]

The projections made by Kennedy and Houthakker for 1980 were very optimistic. For example, Kennedy stated (in 1974) that "price hikes of crude which occurred in late 1973 are not likely to persist in the future." The results of simulations from the model suggested that a host government tax of about $3.50 a barrel, which represented less than one half the then-current tax of about $9.00, was most likely to occur in the long run. But Kennedy used his judgment to select a different scenario as the most likely one: "Changing the assumptions behind the simulations to make them reflect conditions more favorable to a high price *implied* that a value closer to $5.00 was easier to maintain, and thus more likely to occur." (All monetary figures in the Kennedy-Houthakker study were in constant 1972 dollars. Five dollars in 1972 was equivalent to $7.95 in early 1979, when the OPEC price was $13.34.)[14]

Table A–2 shows some of the results on which Kennedy based his conclusions. Note that in all cases revenues from oil exports by the Persian Gulf and North African governments are maximized when the tax lies between $3.50 and $5.25 per barrel, and that the *United States becomes an oil exporter* in the "high-supply elasticity case" when the host-government tax reaches $8.75 (or $13.90 in early 1979 dollars).

Noticeably lacking in the model's projections are the likely boundaries, or ranges, associated with each forecast. The absence is actually not too surprising, for it is extremely difficult to make a calculation of likely boundaries for the type of model used by Kennedy and Houthakker.[15] To get around the problem, modelers often construct scenarios typifying the worst and best situations that can occur within reason. These scenarios can be viewed as boundary limits for the forecasts. The wider the range is between the limiting cases, the higher the chances are for the actual figure to fall between the boundary values. Ideally, one would like to specify narrow ranges and still have the actual figures fall within those boundaries.

With these thoughts in mind, we proceed to select two different scenarios as the upper and lower boundaries for the forecasts. We assume that the high-supply elasticity case in Table A–2 represents the *lower limit* for the forecasts of oil exports and oil revenues of the Persian Gulf and North African OPEC members. The reason for our assumption is that a high-supply elasticity implies a large U.S. oil supply and hence relatively low OPEC exports. Similarly, we assume that the high-income elasticity case represents the *upper limit* of that range. The reason for this assumption is that a high-income elasticity implies a strong demand for oil products, resulting in relatively high U.S. oil imports and OPEC oil exports. We then note that in these limiting cases, as values for the host-government tax increase, the forecasts for Persian and North African exports and revenues become quite low. At a time when the host-government tax approximated $8.75 (1972 dollars), the boundary limits of forecasts at a tax of this level indicated that the oil exports of the Persian Gulf and North African countries would be in the range of 3 to 8 million barrels daily; at the time of the forecasts, such exports were approximately 23 million barrels daily.[16]

One can question whether it was reasonable to believe even

TABLE A.2
KENNEDY-HOUTHAKKER WORLD OIL MODEL PROJECTIONS FOR 1980 FOR THREE CASES
(ALL MONETARY FIGURES ARE IN 1972 U.S. DOLLARS)

Host Government Tax at Persian Gulf (dollars per barrel)	High-Supply Elasticity Case			Base Case			High-Income Elasticity Case		
	Persian Gulf & N. Africa		U.S.	Persian Gulf & N. Africa		U.S.	Persian Gulf & N. Africa		U.S.
	Exports (millions of barrels daily)	Revenues (billions of dollars yearly)	Imports (millions of barrels daily)	Exports (millions of barrels daily)	Revenues (billions of dollars yearly)	Imports (millions of barrels daily)	Exports (millions of barrels daily)	Revenues (billions of dollars yearly)	Imports (millions of barrels daily)
$1.75	31	$22	13	31	$22	13	40	$29	n.a.
3.50	19	26	9	21	28	9	27	36[a]	n.a.
5.25	13	26[a]	4	15	29[a]	6	19	36	n.a.
7.00	8	20	1	11	29	4	13	34	n.a.
8.75	3	10	-2	7	24	2	8	26	n.a.

[a]Maximum revenue for respective case
n.a.: not available

Source: Constructed from information in Michael Kennedy, "An Economic Model of the World Oil Market," *The Bell Journal of Economics and Management Science,* Autumn 1974, pp. 540–577.

Notes:
1. One dollar in 1972 is equal to $1.59 in early 1979 dollars.
2. The above table represents only part of the information presented by Kennedy. The host-government tax presented by Kennedy ranged from a low of $.80 to a high of $8.75 per barrel.
3. Kennedy refers to the host-government tax as an "export duty"; see Reference 6, this Appendix.
4. Numbers are rounded from those in original source.

back in 1974 that forecasts of Persian Gulf and North African exports so much lower than then-existing conditions were likely to prevail in 1980. An observer might conclude either that the assumptions used for these cases were so unreasonable as to preclude the cases from being reported as evidence for what could occur if the supply or income elasticities were at the boundary limits, or that the model was not sufficiently robust so as to be able to handle situations that even then would seem reasonable to consider.

Indeed, in a talk before the Conference Board in April 1974, Houthakker recognized that the results of the model "are subject to a wide margin of error because there is much uncertainty about the exact response of production and consumption to the unprecedently high price levels of the moment." Although Houthakker still made lower estimates of OPEC prices than eventually proved to be the case, he did begin to raise his estimates. The *Wall Street Journal* reported that an "eminent economist" (Houthakker) was relatively optimistic about the world oil situation: "Running his data through a computer, he [Houthakker] came up with a tentative future price of something around $6 a barrel based on 1972 dollars" ($9.50 in early 1979 dollars), a figure lower than in fact proved to be the case, but higher than Kennedy's earlier estimate of $5 a barrel.[17]

Two years later Houthakker published the results of model simulations that contained much greater variations in elasticities for the different regions of the world. He presented two different cases:

1. An "optimistic" case, in which there was considerable response to higher prices in terms of both increasing crude oil production outside of OPEC and decreasing product consumption in the industrial world.

2. A "pessimistic" case, in which the opposite was assumed —that is, neither crude oil production outside of OPEC nor product consumption was very responsive to higher prices.

The results of these simulations differed from the results of the simulations of the earlier model in two important ways. First, the optimum host-government tax, and resulting host-government revenues, for the Middle East and African exporters were substantially higher than in the earlier results.* In the optimistic case, the optimum tax was $7.50 per barrel, while the pessimistic case shows the optimum tax as $20.00 (with Middle East and African annual revenues of $35 billion and $75 billion, respectively, for the two cases). Second, the resulting ranges were much wider than those presented earlier. If we assume, as in the earlier simulations, that the two extreme cases represented the upper and lower bounds of a "reasonable" range, then the range of optimum host-government taxes was from $7.50 to $20.00 per barrel, as shown in Table A-3, instead of the $3.50 to $5.25 per barrel in the two earlier cases that represented the upper and lower bounds (or, in early 1979 dollars in round numbers, $12 to $32 instead, of $6 to $8).

Although it is desirable to recognize the width of the range for the estimates of the later simulations, the question arises as to the usefulness of such a model to policymakers. Take the case of U.S. imports. With a host-government tax of $7.50 per barrel, imports are shown as zero for the optimistic case and 10 million barrels daily for the pessimistic case.

In any event, Houthakker ultimately used his judgment instead of the results of the model in order to make a prediction. After explaining the problem of determining the production level of each OPEC country if OPEC's output were to drop substantially, he stated that the optimum export levels shown in Table A-3 "are probably academic. Perhaps an uneasy equilibrium at a total output level not much below that of 1975 [22 million barrels daily of exports from the Middle East and Africa] is the most likely outcome for the next several years." Houthakker used his judgment for this volume estimate because the model does not contain a theory of cartels, and he thought that the Middle East and African OPEC members would need at least 20 million barrels daily of output in order for the cartel to hold together. His volume estimates based on this judgment proved to be close—only about 10 percent low—to the actual figures for the next two years.[18]

---

*The earlier model simulation included "Persian Gulf and North African OPEC," whereas the later simulation included "Middle East and African OPEC"; the difference is insignificant for our purposes.

TABLE A.3
KENNEDY-HOUTHAKKER WORLD OIL MODEL RESULTS FOR 1980 FOR "OPTIMISTIC" AND "PESSIMISTIC" ELASTICITY CASES (ALL MONETARY FIGURES ARE IN 1972 DOLLARS)

Host-Government Tax at Persian Gulf (dollars per barrel)	Optimistic Case			Pessimistic Case		
	Middle East & Africa		U.S. Imports (millions of barrels daily)	Middle East & Africa		U.S. Imports (millions of barrels daily)
	Exports (millions of barrels daily)	Revenues (billions of dollars)		Exports (millions of barrels daily)	Revenues (billions of dollars)	
$ 5.00	22	$34	3	29	$46	12
7.50	15	35[a]	0	24	57	10
10.00	10	29	−1	20	65	9
12.50	n.a.	n.a.	n.a.	18	70	9
15.00	n.a.	n.a.	n.a.	15	73	8
17.50	n.a.	n.a.	n.a.	14	75	7
20.00	n.a.	n.a.	n.a.	12	75[a]	7
22.50	n.a.	n.a.	n.a.	11	74	7

[a]Maximum revenue for respective case

n.a.: not available

Source: Constructed from information in Hendrik S. Houthakker, The World Price of Oil, pp. 21, 26.

Notes:
1. One dollar in 1972 is equal to $1.59 in early 1979.
2. The above table presents only part of the results presented by Houthakker. For example, the host-government tax presented by Houthakker ranged from a low of $1.25 to a high of $22.50 per barrel.
3. Houthakker refers to the host-government tax as a "royalty"; see Reference 6, this Appendix.
4. Numbers are rounded from those in the original source.

THE MIT ENERGY SELF-SUFFICIENCY STUDY |

In May of 1974, The Policy Study Group of the MIT Energy Laboratory* released a major report, the MIT Energy Self-Sufficiency Study. The study focused on "the question of whether the goal of energy independence [for the United States by 1980] could be achieved and, if so, the price its achievement might entail for the nation." The focus was on price rather than imports, because the study was based on the key assumption that the United States could meet *all* its energy demands from internal sources by 1980.[19]

The group conducted the study in a remarkably short time— in the first few months of 1974—so it was forced to rely mainly on already existing information, much of which was work done earlier at the MIT Energy Laboratory. The group used both econometric and technological models, but to arrive at a final judgment they checked the results of the models with "judgmental forecasts" that were made separately from the formal models. Such forecasts were made by an expert (or a group of experts) after taking into account past trends and relationships and expected future events that might affect the variables being predicted. The experts included a number of distinguished academicians, consultants, and industry specialists.

The group made estimates of supply and demand at three levels of energy prices—the equivalent of oil prices of $7, $9, and $11 per barrel in 1973 dollars (or, $10.50, $13.50, and $16.50 in early 1979 dollars).

They estimated the supply of energy for each of five major sources—oil (including natural gas liquids), natural gas, coal, hydroelectric and uranium, and new technology (such as synthetic

---

*Some of the principal members of the Policy Study Group included Morris A. Adelman, professor of economics and author of *The World Petroleum Market;* Paul W. MacAvoy, then professor of management and later a member of the President's Council of Economic Advisors; Henry D. Jacoby, professor of management; David C. White, professor of engineering and director of the laboratory. Much of the group's work was based on studies made by Edward Erickson, Dale Jorgenson, Robert Spann, National Petroleum Council experts, and the staff of National Economic Research Associates.

crude oil, synthetic gas, and shale oil). They then totaled the figures for each of the five energy sources to obtain estimates of total U.S. energy supply at each price level.

They derived demand figures by using a large econometric model of the U.S. economy in conjunction with another econometric model of production and consumer behavior, a model that in turn predicted demand for the output of four sectors—private consumption, private investment, government expenditures, and net exports. The energy input required per unit of output was determined as a function of price by the use of an input-output model. These estimates of energy requirements per unit of output were then multiplied by estimates of the output of each of the four sectors to obtain an estimate of total energy demand.

Using these results to define points on their approximate supply-and-demand curves for total energy, the modelers looked for the point of intersection of the curves—that is, the point where domestic supply and demand were in balance. The price associated with this point was then used as the econometric forecast for what the price of oil would have to be in 1980 for the United States to become energy self-sufficient.

Although the MIT group did not publish as much detail about their models as did Kennedy and Houthakker, sufficient information was available to indicate some of the problems likely to be caused by some of the five red flags.

To illustrate the possible problem encountered with the second red flag, the *aggregation* assumption, we discuss only one issue —the utilization of an econometric model of oil supply that does not make an explicit distinction between onshore and offshore production of oil (that is, onshore and offshore fields are treated as one source).

Within physical limitations, the supply of oil obtained from both offshore and onshore fields should increase as the price for that commodity increases. But start-up costs are generally higher for offshore production. Hence, the threshold price required for production to begin is higher for offshore oil. Further, there is no reason why the rates at which production increases with price would be the same offshore as onshore; in other words, the slopes of the supply curves for the two areas likely would differ. Thus, up to the threshold level of price required for offshore production to begin, the total supply curve would reflect onshore conditions. Beyond that level, the total supply curve would reflect a mixture of onshore and offshore supply curves and hence would differ from that of the onshore curves—that is, it has a kink at the threshold price required for offshore production to begin. Estimating the price elasticity of oil supply using such an aggregated curve is like fitting a straight line through a kinked curve.

We have no way of knowing how much of an error this one aggregation assumption might have caused in the projections. It is possible that the aggregation of onshore and offshore areas into one area may have been an important cause for the grossly overestimated price elasticity value of .87 for the supply of oil. This high elasticity figure, of course, is crucial to the group's conclusion that "crude oil sources are forecast to produce more from onshore and offshore domestic wells in 1980 than at the present [1974], because the incentives of increased price more than compensate for depletion of inground reserves."[20]

Of course, the MIT group faced the same fundamental problem as did Kennedy and Houthakker. They were forced to rely on data obtained under one set of conditions and assumed that it could be used to predict the outcome of processes operating under radically different conditions—the assumptions regarding the applicability of the *range* of the data and the *reversibility* of the supply-and-demand processes.[21]

Although the MIT group indicated, correctly, that energy from new technology would make no contribution to U.S. energy supplies by 1980, their estimates of the prices required for the commercialization of new technologies to produce energy turned out to be much too low. These estimates, which were based primarily on published information, indicated, for example, that synthetic crude oil from shale would become feasible when the price of oil reached $6.80 per barrel (or $10.20 in early 1979 dollars). In contrast, reports in mid-1980 indicated that oil prices of at least $30 a barrel (in early 1979 dollars) were required for production of shale oil to be economic.[22] The MIT group projected $7.70 per barrel for synthetic crude from coal ($11.60 in early 1979 dollars). In late 1978, the U.S. Department of Energy was projecting about

2½ times that amount—the equivalent of about $30 in 1979 dollars.[23] Indeed, discussions with industry experts suggest that probably all of the estimates in Table A-4 will eventually prove to be too low by a factor of at least two and sometimes three.

That the engineering cost estimates used for new technologies by the MIT group were much too low is not surprising. Indeed, for years a narrow focus on technology has resulted in too optimistic a picture of energy supplies that might be forthcoming from new technologies.[24] Some of the lessons of the nuclear story in Chapter 5 of this book are relevant—especially the importance of conflicting political interests, the level and distribution of external costs, and the problems encountered in massive scale-ups of complex systems when working outside of a prior range of experience.[25]

Although the MIT group correctly estimated no energy in 1980 from the new technologies, their estimates of U.S. domestic supplies for 1980 seem high, primarily because of overestimation of new supplies of crude oil, natural gas, and nuclear. As shown

TABLE A · 4
ESTIMATES BY MIT ENERGY POLICY STUDY GROUP OF WHAT THE PRICE OF OIL WOULD HAVE TO BE FOR SOME "NEW TECHNOLOGY" FUELS TO BECOME ECONOMICAL

Fuel	Cost per Barrel (oil equivalent)	
	(1973 dollars)	(early 1979 dollars)[a]
Synthetic Crude from Oil Shale	$6.80	$10
Synthetic Crude from Coal	$7.70	$12
Synthetic Natural Gas from Coal		
Old Technology	$9.05	$14
New Technology	$7.30	$11
Methanol from Coal	$10.00	$15

[a]Rounded to nearest dollar. One 1973 dollar equals $1.50 in early 1979 dollars.

Source: The MIT Policy Study Group, "Energy Self-Sufficiency."

in Table A-5, the econometric models (supplemented by judgmental forecasts when econometric models were not available) predicted 38 million barrels daily of oil equivalent at $7.00 per barrel of oil (or $10.50 in early 1979 dollars), and 43 million barrels at $9.00 per barrel (or $13.50 in early 1979 dollars). In fact, United States domestic production did not even reach 30 million barrels daily of oil equivalent in 1980.

True, most of the econometric models used by MIT—with some natural gas projections the principal exception—contain an implicit or explicit assumption that prices would be based on the interplay of market forces rather than controlled by the government; in fact, neither U.S. oil nor natural gas prices have been substantially free of price controls since the time of the MIT study. And even though it is true that by 1978 the price of newly found oil had been allowed to rise to about $9.00 a barrel and newly found gas to a little over $7.00 per barrel of oil equivalent (both values in 1973 dollars), it is possible that the mere existence of price controls might have affected supply and demand independently of the effect on the price level.

Price controls add uncertainty, for example, which might have reduced investment for new supplies below the level that would otherwise have resulted at the uncontrolled price identical to the controlled price. On the other hand, producers might have expected price controls to be eased or removed, thereby allowing prices to rise toward or to the world level. Such an expectation, of course, might have increased investment for new supplies above the level otherwise expected at the controlled price. Thus, it is impossible to say with a high degree of certainty whether the MIT domestic supply estimates were optimistic, given the assumptions of the MIT group.

On the other hand, their rough estimate that the world's productive capacity for oil in 1980 would be 87.4 million barrels daily was clearly too optimistic. This estimate was based on a host-government tax of about $7.00 a barrel in 1973 prices (or $10.50 in early 1979 dollars) and on the group's judgments of the price elasticities of supply. And though recognizing "that the range of conceivable values for the world oil price over the next decade is very large," the group concluded that "it is unlikely—

TABLE A · 5
ESTIMATES BY MIT ENERGY POLICY STUDY
GROUP OF ENERGY EQUILIBRIUM IN 1980 USING
SUPPLY FORECASTS
BASED ON ECONOMETRIC MODELS SUPPLEMENTED BY
JUDGMENTAL FORECASTS
(monetary figures in 1973 dollars)

| Fuel | Source of Estimate | Millions of Barrels per Day of Oil equivalent, at prices per barrel of oil | | |
		$7.00	$9.00	$11.00
Crude oil and natural gas liquids[a]	Econometric models of Erickson-Spann (crude oil) and MIT (natural gas liquids)	10[b]	13	15
Natural gas	MIT econometric model	15	16	17
Coal	Judgmental from MIT analysis	7	8	8
Uranium and hydroelectric	Judgmental from equipment survey	6	6	6
New technology	Judgmental from MIT analysis	0	0	neg.
Total supply		38	43	46
Forecasts of total demand	Econometric model of Hudson-Jorgenson	44	42	41

[a]Estimates for natural gas liquids are 2.1, 2.2, and 2.4 for the three respective prices.

[b]Rounded from 10.5 in the original source, in order to present it closer to, rather than farther from, actual.

Numbers rounded from those in original source.
neg.: negligible.

Source: Constructed from information in The MIT Policy Study Group, "Energy Self-Sufficiency."

Note: A 1973 dollar equals $1.50 in early 1979 dollars.

though certainly not impossible—that the price of world oil to the U.S. will rise above this level in the next few years."[26]

The MIT group, of course, recognized shortcomings in their studies. Among other things, they declared that "until more experience is gained at these high price levels, the uncertainty over this range of prices will remain," and "there may be some doubt about the completeness of the reversibility" assumed to exist.[27] And they explicitly stated that the econometric estimates of supply "are very probably optimistic." Indeed, they concluded that the market clearing price required for U.S. energy independence of $9.00 ($13.80 in late 1979 dollars), as indicated by the econometric models, was "extremely optimistic." In contrast, the judgmental forecasts, based principally on estimates from industry, showed a lower supply estimate and a higher demand estimate than the econometric models. Thus, the judgmental forecasts indicated a far higher market clearing price than did the econometric models. Therefore, the MIT group backed off from the results of the econometric analyses and stated that, on balance, in order for the United States to achieve self-sufficiency in energy in 1980, "the results point to the conclusion that the price of energy would be from $10.00 to $12.00 a barrel" (or $15.00 to $18.00 in early 1979 dollars).[28]

Fortunately for U.S. imports, U.S. demand in 1980 almost surely will be lower than forecast either by the econometric models or by the judgmental approach—but not so low as to make actual imports as low as the zero to 7 million barrels daily indicated for the $7.00 to $9.00 price range ($10.50 and $13.50 in early 1979 dollars).[29]

PROJECT INDEPENDENCE
EVALUATION SYSTEM

The 1974 Project Independence Evaluation System (PIES-74) constitutes a set of models that culminated a colossal effort directed by the Federal Energy Administration to model the U.S. energy system. In fact, it is the most complex, sophisticated set of models yet developed for this purpose. PIES-74 represents the national energy system as a multiregional network that links the producing, refining, processing, converting, distributing, transporting, and consuming sectors of the system. Myriads of models and submodels are interlinked to generate forecasts for the years 1977, 1980, and 1985 under different sets of supply-and-demand scenarios. For explanatory purposes these various submodels have been grouped into four categories: supply, demand, integration, and assessment.

Price-sensitive *supply* curves have been developed for each geographical region by various intergovernmental task groups of eight different energy sources: oil, natural gas, coal, nuclear, synthetic fuels, shale oil, geothermal, and solar. These curves have been developed in order to determine how much production could be achieved for each source of energy at different prices under two alternative policy strategies: Business-as-Usual (BAU) and Accelerated Development (AD). Table A-6 contrasts the assumptions made for each energy source under the two strategies. The supply data provided by the government task groups also contain the requirements for materials, equipment, investment, and manpower associated with the production levels of the various energy sources.

Price-sensitive *demand* forecasts for the entire nation have been generated by an econometric simulation model developed by the FEA but based on work done by Data Resources Incorporated (DRI). This model predicts quantities demanded by the major consuming sectors of the economy and by fuel type, conditioned upon expected energy prices and key economic and demographic variables, such as population, employment, GNP, and growth in housing stocks.[30]

The *integration* of the supply-and-demand components of the U.S. energy system has been accomplished by determining the prices and quantities at which supply and demand are in equilibrium for each energy source for each region. To accomplish this integration, the modelers have derived production levels and prices that meet at minimum cost the demand indicated by the econometric simulation model. The production levels and prices are obtained from a linear programming model that contains resource and economic constraints.[31]

TABLE A·6
COMPARISON OF BUSINESS-AS-USUAL AND ACCELE-
RATED DEVELOPMENT ASSUMPTIONS OF PROJECT
INDEPENDENCE ENERGY MODELS

Energy	Business-as-Usual (BAU)	Accelerated Development (AD)
Oil	Moderate outer continental shelf leasing program (1–3 million acres per year); Prudhoe Bay developed with one pipeline	Accelerated OCS leasing program, including Atlantic and Gulf of Alaska; expanded Alaskan program, assuming additional pipeline and authority to develop Naval Petroleum Reserve No. 4
Natural Gas	Phased deregulation of new natural gas; liquefied natural gas facilities in Alaska	Deregulation of new natural gas; additional gas pipelines in Alaska; gas produced in tight formations
Coal	Some federal coal land leasing; phased implementation of Clean Air Act with installation of effective stack gas control equipment; moderate strip mining legislation	Same as BAU, with additional leasing and larger new mines
Nuclear	No change in licensing or regulations; added enrichment and reprocessing capability	Streamlined siting and licensing to reduce lead times; increased reliability; additional uranium availability; material allocation
Synthetic Fuels	No change from current policies	Streamlined licensing and siting; financial incentives; increased water availability
Shale Oil	No change from existing policies	Additional leasing of federal lands; modification of Colorado air-quality standards; financial incentives; increased water availability

Geothermal	Continued R&D and federal leasing programs	Leasing of federal lands; streamlined licensing and regulatory procedures; financial incentives
Solar	Continued R&D program	Additional R&D expenditures and financial incentives

Source: Federal Energy Administration, *Project Independence Report,* pp. 64–65.

Now, for the *assessment* category: Several models were built to assess the impact that the equilibrium solutions would have on the environment, economy, and international scene. These evaluations were incorporated into the final PIES-74 report in order to help policymakers judge the energy strategies in terms of their influence on other national priorities. Results of the various assessment models, however, were not used as feedback for the other sectors of PIES-74 to refine estimates and reassess forecasts.

More effort has already been made in critiquing this model than perhaps any other in history,[32] and the complexity of PIES-74 precludes a detailed critique here. We do, however, think it worthwhile to comment on PIES-74 in relation to the five red flags mentioned earlier.

PIES-74 handles three of the five issues raised by the red flags more effectively than either the Kennedy-Houthakker model or the MIT study. It includes many more factors—hence the assumption that the effects of factors *excluded* from the model are less likely to cause error. However, the exclusion of factors, such as sulfur levels in coal, and different types of crude oil and certain other fuels, may also, the report states, "make conclusions which appear correct in the aggregate impractical in reality. In particular they may overstate the ability of the supply system to shift to certain domestic fuel sources. For example, anti-pollution standards may preclude the use of coal with high sulfur level."[33] Further, PIES-74 uses data that are not as *aggregated* as those used in the other models; also, PIES-74 estimates *time lags* more formally than do the others. However, the integrating sector of PIES-74 is not dynamic; that is, it presents solutions for given years—1977, 1980, 1985—but does not guarantee that the time paths of supply developments or their costs are feasible or efficient. Even though time lags were included in the derivation of price elasticities to approximate major economic changes, nothing in the model assures that a facility found to be economically feasible and hence built in 1980, will be even in operation in 1985. PIES-74 modelers state that "judgment and careful scrutiny are needed to assure that major shifts between periods do not occur or are not relevant to the conclusions being drawn." Unfortunately, the handling of these three issues raises another problem—the problem of scale and complexity. As one model analyst says about complicated, large-scale models in general, they "may contain much that is not fully understood and substantiated. The very magnitude of these models may diminish their helpfulness to policymakers."[34] We do not know the extent to which this warning applies to PIES-74, but it is a complicated, large-scale model, as shown in Figure A-1.

PIES-74, as did all other energy models formulated at that time, contained the problems associated with the other two red flags—the assumptions that *range* of prior experience is relevant and that the processes are *reversible*. The authors of PIES-74 readily state their concerns about these problems. In fact, William Hogan, who directed the PIES-74 project, has been quite articulate in pointing out the limitations of econometric models.[35]

Problems associated with all the red flags led to the determination of several elasticities that were contrary to what theory would presume. For example, the equations, which were derived by fitting curves to historical data, showed that in the household-commercial sector the demand for natural gas would fall as the price of oil increased. According to theory, however, the opposite should be true—that is, the demand for natural gas should rise because higher oil prices should encourage consumers to switch to natural gas. Many other such unexpected elasticities were also obtained.[36] Also, some elasticities declined with time, whereas one would expect responsiveness (and hence elasticity) to increase

FIGURE A·1
ORGANIZATIONAL STRUCTURE OF THE TASK FORCE
THAT FORMULATED PIES—74

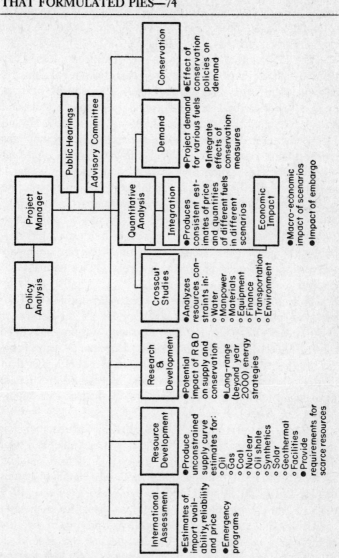

Source: Federal Energy Administration, *Project Independence Report,* p. 410.

over time. Furthermore, some elasticities were considered too high. Consequently many judgmental modifications and adjustments were made. Such adjustments, observed the General Accounting Office, "raise questions regarding the accuracy of all elasticities developed by the system."[37]

The PIES authors raised another list of uncertainties. They pointed out that sensitivity analyses on potential rates of domestic oil production "show that, within a range of reasonable assumptions, different values regarding discount rates, financial costs, and finding rates could affect the quantities produced at $4, $7, and $11 per barrel in 1985 by 10 to 40 percent. Other assumptions about drilling costs, effective depletion rates, and co-product prices would affect production levels at these prices by as much as 15 percent . . . The uncertainties inherent in estimating future petroleum production (especially uncertainties having to do with the magnitude of undiscovered resources in as yet totally unexplored provinces and the finding rate per foot of exploratory drilling) are so great that numerical estimates of this type are highly speculative."[38] Similar observations were made for natural gas.

The published projections of U.S. energy supplies made by the Project Independence Group were quite optimistic. Take 1980, for example. With a $7.00 oil price in 1973 dollars (or $10.50 in early 1979 dollars), domestic supply was projected to be the equivalent of 35 million to 36 million barrels of oil daily (Table A-7). Because their consumption estimates also were higher than is likely to be the case, their projections of 1980 oil imports are much closer to current expectations for 1980 than are their supply figures.

Turning to 1985, one finds that the PIES-74 estimates of U.S. supply also seem quite optimistic. As shown in Table A-8, total domestic supplies were estimated as 39 million to 45 million barrels daily at a $7.00 oil price and 46 million to 49 million barrels daily at an $11.00 oil price (or $10.50 and $16.50 in early 1979 dollars). Not only do the PIES oil and gas estimates seem especially high, but so do the nuclear projections—presumably because of the *exclusion* of the political forces affecting this issue.

In addition, their projections were too optimistic for the quantity of synthetic fuel production and for the prices at which

TABLE A·7
PROJECTIONS BY PROJECT INDEPENDENCE STUDY
GROUP OF U.S. ENERGY SUPPLIES IN 1980
*(millions of barrels of oil daily, with oil prices
in 1973 dollars per barrel)*

| | $7 Oil | | $11 Oil | |
	Business as Usual	Accelerated Development	Business as Usual	Accelerated Development
Domestic supply	35	36	37	39
Imports	9	8	4	3
Total	44	44	41	42

Source: Federal Energy Administration, *Project Independence Report,* p. 61
and AI-37–48.

Notes:
1. Quads in original table were converted to millions of barrels daily of oil
   equivalent by dividing by 2.1, and then rounded.
2. A 1973 dollar equals $1.50 in early 1979 dollars.

these fuels could be economically produced. One case, for example, suggested that it would be possible in 1985 to produce 1
million barrels daily of oil from shale alone and 1.5 million daily
in total from shale, tar sands and heavy oils, and coal liquefaction[39]—projections that now seem virtually impossible.

THE DILEMMA OF MODELS |

Everyone uses models to predict the future, even if the models are
only implicit mental ones—such as judgmental forecasts. There is
no doubt that in many instances formal models, such as econometric models, have advantages over implicit mental models, for the
formal models provide an explicit, organized framework for the
forecaster and thus help to clarify assumptions. They also improve
communication between model builders and users, and aid in the
accumulation of knowledge and the making of forecasts under
different assumptions. Furthermore, formal models can help un-
cover counter-intuitive results and thus promote deeper under-

TABLE A · 8
PROJECTIONS BY PROJECT INDEPENDENCE STUDY
GROUP OF DOMESTIC FUEL PRODUCTION BY SOURCE
AND IMPORTS, 1985
*(millions of barrels of oil daily equivalent, with oil prices
in 1973 dollars per barrel)*

| | $7 Oil | | $11 Oil | |
Fuel Source	Business as Usual	Accelerated Development	Business as Usual	Accelerated Development
Domestic				
Oil	11	15	15	18
Gas	11	12	12	12
Coal	9	9	11	10
Nuclear	6	7	6	7
Hydro & Geoth	2	2	2	2
Synthetics	—	—	—	neg.
Subtotal	39	45	46	49
Imports	12	8	3	0
Total	52	53	49	50

neg.: negligible

Source: Federal Energy Administration, *Project Independence Report,* p. 23,
and Appendix A-1, pp. 37, 39, 45, 47.

Notes:
1. A 1973 dollar equals $1.50 in early 1979 dollars.
2. Some columns do not total, due to rounding.
3. Quads in the original table were converted to millions of barrels daily of oil equivalent by dividing by 2.1, and then rounded.
4. "Oil" apparently includes shale, tar sands, and heavy oil; see *Project Independence Report,* pp. 46–47.

standing.[40] In fact, some model builders state explicitly that the production of individual answers is only a minor element of the contribution of models, and that the purpose of energy modeling should be "insight, not numbers."[41]

The problem with formal models, however, is that the scientific aura surrounding them encourages those who use the results of models to expect much more than this.[42] And such expectations at times are encouraged by model builders who get so enthralled with their own models that they promise much more. As we shall show, a model incorrectly used can do more harm than good.

By now it should be clear that the predictions derived from energy models are subject to a great deal of imprecision. The derivation of coefficients that are necessary to generate forecasts often requires the modeler to make assumptions that cannot be completely substantiated, or to make simplifications that may obscure the representation of the system being analyzed. Furthermore, dramatic changes and trend reversals in certain economic processes in the course of the last few years may well mean that assumptions used today, though valid prior to these changes, may no longer apply. The lack of experience with these new economic processes contributes to the general imprecision of results generated by models.

Yet precise—and highly misleading—estimates concerning energy keep appearing. For example, Robert Pindyck, a professor of economics at MIT, writing in the *Wall Street Journal* in late 1977, stated that "OPEC's best price today is between $12.50 and $13.00—slightly below the actual posted price. . . . In real (constant dollar) terms, this price should grow by no more than 2% per year over the next ten years."[43] How did Pindyck obtain such precise estimates? He used, as he explained, "a small computer model that quantitatively describes the characteristics of total world oil demand (and its response to income growth and price changes), non-OPEC oil supply (and its response to price changes as well as resource depletion), resource depletion within OPEC and the different levels of reserves and different rates of time discounting among OPEC members."[44]

The margin of error for each of those variables is so large that one must question how anyone could suggest, let alone self-confidently state, that OPEC's best price is between $12.50 and $13.00 or that the price should grow by no more than 2 percent per year over the next ten years. In fact, the self-confidence of the assertion seems quite surprising given the uncertainty that exists. Another professor of economics at MIT, M. A. Adelman, states that the optimum price for OPEC is very much above 1977 prices—

perhaps more than double—and that if the OPEC "monopoly holds together, then we [can] . . . predict that the real price of oil (i.e., adjusted for general price-level changes) must rise substantially over the next ten years."[45]

But even though a model's predictions may be quite imprecise and therefore not as useful for policymakers, they still can be helpful in "organizing the information base and guiding the decisions," as Hogan stated.[46] But even for this purpose, models must be used with great care. When present conditions are far different from the historical experience, it is possible that the models can do more harm than good by directing attention to inappropriate concerns. For example, most models of energy demand until very recently showed, incorrectly, an "iron link" between GNP and energy consumption, thereby focusing undue attention on the trade-off between energy production and loss of GNP. This focus was accentuated by models that, incorrectly, showed high responses of energy supplies to prices. These were no mere intellectual debates. They had serious effects on U.S. energy policy, for these models helped shore up the potential of traditional sources at the expense of conservation and solar energy.[47]

There is also a tendency for those working with technological models to concentrate too heavily on technology. An almost comical example of *exclusion* was provided by a recent headline in *Chemical Week:* "Oil from Coal: It could be a gusher by the 1990s."[48] But the opening sentences of the article read, "The technology is now available. The only barriers are political, social and economic."

When facing a future that is likely to be quite a bit different from the past, detailed studies of politics, institutions, and markets are needed along with economics and technology in order to provide the adequate base of data required for plausible answers and realistic frameworks for discussion. In energy, politics is a crucial factor, yet an explicit consideration of it is typically omitted in most formal models. Although the MIT group's report did include a number of suggestions about changing governmental policies, it contained little or no political analysis indicating the extent to which these suggestions were feasible, stating, "Behind every energy bottleneck and in every future decision stand serious societal issues—nuclear power plant safety, environmental protection, and many others. Such issues, though both appropriate and important to the debate which is now in progress throughout the nation, are beyond the scope of this report."[49]

True, one could argue that an exclusion of national politics might be justified if the goal is to help national policymakers comprehend the outcomes of different national policies. But even so, the exclusion of issues such as nuclear safety and environmental protection almost guarantees unrealistic projections and offers solutions that are much further from a theoretical optimum than model builders often acknowledge. In addition, the decentralized nature of political decisions makes it even more imperative to consider the likely actions of regulatory agencies, courts, states, and other local bodies if realistic estimates, especially of energy supplies, are to be obtained. Even if the United States had had no price controls on oil and gas, the actions of different political bodies would still have been especially important in affecting energy supplies from offshore oil, coal, nuclear, and new technologies.*

The actual extent to which the results generated by mathematical models influenced decisions is, of course, impossible to tell. But since it is becoming apparent that policymakers are using

---

*We have been discussing why the predictions of energy models often give unrealistic results. Still unanswered is an important question: Why does there seem to be this upward bias in predictions of future energy supplies that is not borne out by subsequent experience? One reason, which we have highlighted throughout the book, is the effect of the political barriers, especially those raised by concerns about environmental issues and income distribution. Another reason, no more than a tentative hypothesis at this point, is consistent with the disappointing results in finding new oil and gas in the United States in spite of the substantially increased exploratory and development activities that resulted from the higher financial incentives. The hypothesis relates to natural resources as a special case. It is this: The relatively slow rate of technological progress normally encountered in older industries does not offset the increasing difficulty of exploitation that results from the fact that the reserves easier to develop are exploited first. This slowdown in technological progress, combined with the increasing difficulty of exploitation, could cause a downward-sloping cost curve to change direction and thereby move upward. Any econometric model fitted as a straight line from historical data, as many are, would not pick up the change of direction. A model fitted with a curvilinear equation would show a change in direction. But it would probably not show the change until quite some time after it had occurred.

models to an increasing extent to help them make decisions, it is imperative that the officials find out what lies behind the assumptions made by the modelers before they start using the results. They should also test the validity of the predictions by asking what would happen when certain plausible changes are made to key parameters. Do the predictions remain plausible or do they change so much as to become totally ludicrous? A substantial change may indicate possible faults in the structure of the model. At the same time, of course, the modeler has the burden of thinking of ways to make the model both useful and understandable to the decision-maker.

Once it has been ascertained that the model adequately depicts the situation being analyzed, the results derived from the model should be used in conjunction with the decision-makers' own knowledge of the problem, which often contains factors not explicitly accounted for by the model.

As a final note, we would like to reiterate what we said at the outset of this Appendix: namely, that models can be extremely useful in the formulation of energy policy. They provide a framework for decision-makers to make intelligent choices. They facilitate the evaluations of the influences of the various factors that affect the decision. Furthermore, they allow decision-makers to test their ideas "on paper" without manipulating the actual system. *But a model is not reality.*

REFERENCES

Chapter 1 | *The End of Easy Oil*

1. The price of oil in the Arab/Persian Gulf at the end of the 1960's was $1.00 to $1.20 per barrel. See M. A. Adelman, *The World Petroleum Market* (Baltimore: Johns Hopkins University Press, 1972), pp. 183, 191. The U.S. message was first presented in a meeting of the Oil Committee of the Organization for Economic Cooperation and Development in Paris at the end of 1968 by James Akins, then director of the Office of Fuels and Energy in the State Department.
2. Of course, there is no reason why over the long run an increase in oil prices should necessarily affect the dollar's equilibrium point in the foreign exchange markets. But with over $300 billion held in the Eurodollar market, the expectations of foreign traders and psychological elements can have an important effect on exchange rates. And our discussions with European government officials, bankers, and business executives lead us to conclude that the dollar was weakened by rising U.S. oil imports in the late 1970's.
3. For a further discussion of unemployment and its impact, see Daniel Yergin and Martin Hillenbrand, eds., *Global Insecurity: A Strategy for Energy and Economic Renewal* (Boston: Houghton Mifflin, 1982).

   For the $800 billion figure, see Department of Energy, Energy Information Administration, *Annual Report to Congress, Volume III, 1977* (Washington, D.C.: Government Printing Office, May 1978), especially p. 61. The $800 billion represents an increase, in 1979 dollars, of $10 per barrel of the 84 billion barrels of crude oil equivalent that were in U.S. proved reserves of crude oil, natural gas, and natural gas liquids at the end of 1973. Proved reserves are the estimated quantities that geological and engineering data demonstrate with reasonable certainty to be recoverable in future years from known reservoirs under existing economic and operating conditions. This estimate overstates the value because future income was not discounted to obtain a present value; but it understates the eventual value of all oil and gas in the ground because additions will be made to proven reserves.

4. *New York Times,* June 6, 1978, sec. D, p. 15, and Sunday magazine, p. 20.

5. The $120 billion estimate is from Battelle Memorial Institute, *An Analysis of Federal Incentives Used to Stimulate Energy Production* (Springfield, Va.: National Technical Information Service, March 1978). Two things seem clear: (1) The estimates are controversial, and (2) federal subsidies to existing energy sources have been very substantial. The consumer subsidies resulted mostly at the expense of the owners of "old" oil and "old" gas, and from average pricing for electricity, which masks the incremental costs of electricity from new coal, nuclear, and hydroelectric power plants.

6. For an example of studies that assume away many of the problems that we discuss and regard as most important, see Energy Modeling Forum, *Coal in Transition: 1980–2000, EMF Report 2,* vol. 1, Stanford University, Energy Modeling Forum, July 1978. A series of models analyzed by this forum generally supported the conclusion that President Carter's goal of almost doubling coal production between 1977 and 1985 could be met. But the models specifically excluded a number of environmental, political, and productivity constraints that are important barriers.

Chapter 2 | *After the Peak: The Threat of Hostile Oil*

1. Now most observers agree with the sentiment in this paragraph. But several years ago, interviews with executives of the major international oil companies revealed that some saw fewer problems in relying on imported oil than I did.

Of course, if U.S. import controls had not existed, imports would have become significant a decade earlier. See *The Energy Industry: Organization and Public Policy* (Washington, D.C.: Government Printing Office, 1974).

2. For histories of the U.S. oil industry, see Alfred D. Chandler, Jr., *The Visible Hand* (Cambridge: Harvard University Press, 1977); Ralph W. Hidy and Muriel E. Hidy, *Pioneering in Big Business, 1882–1911* (New York: Harper and Row, 1955); Harold F. Williamson and Arnold R. Daum, *The American Petroleum Industry* (Evanston: Northwestern University Press, 1959); M. A. Adelman, *The World Petroleum Market* (Baltimore: John Hopkins University Press, 1972); Anthony Sampson, *The Seven Sisters* (New York: Viking, 1975); Benjamin Shwadran, *The Middle East, Oil and the Great Powers* (New York: John Wiley and Sons, 1973); Raymond Vernon, ed., *The Oil Crisis* (New York: W. W. Norton, 1976); William N. Greene, "Strategies of the Major Oil Companies," Unpublished Ph.D. thesis, Harvard University; Lorenzo Meyer, *Mexico and the U.S. in the Oil Controversy, 1917–1942* (Austin: University of Texas Press, 1977); Mira Wilkins, *The Emergence of Multinational Enterprise* (Cambridge: Harvard University Press, 1970) and *The*

Maturing of Multinational Enterprise (Cambridge: Harvard University Press, 1974); U.S. Senate, *Hearings before the Subcommittee on Multinational Corporations of the Committee on Foreign Relations, Multinational Petroleum Companies*, 93 Cong., 2 sess., 1974 (Washington, D.C.: Government Printing Office, 1975), hereafter referred to as *MNC Hearings;* and U.S. Senate, *Hearings before the Subcommittee on Multinational Corporations of the Committee on Foreign Relations, Multinational Petroleum Companies: Multinational Oil Corporations and U.S. Foreign Policy, Report Together with the Individual Views to the Committee on Foreign Relations*, 93 Cong., 2 sess. (Washington, D.C.: Government Printing Office, 1975), hereafter referred to as *MNC Report.* The modern oil industry was born when oil production began in Canada, but the Canadian industry was soon overtaken by the U.S. industry.

3. For statistical sources, see various issues of the British Petroleum Company's *BP Statistical Review of the World Oil Industry;* of U.S. Bureau of Mines, *Minerals Yearbook* (Washington, D.C.: Government Printing Office); of Department of Energy, *Monthly Energy Review;* and of *International Petroleum Encyclopedia* (Tulsa: Petroleum Publishing). See also Energy Information Administration, *Annual Report to Congress;* American Petroleum Institute, *Facts About Oil* (New York: API, 1977) and *Petroleum Facts and Figures* (Washington, D.C.: API, 1971); Leonard M. Fanning, *American Oil Operations Abroad* (New York: McGraw-Hill, 1974); and Central Intelligence Agency, *International Energy Statistical Review.*

4. The change of the United States to a net import position in 1948 was, of course, recognized within the oil industry. The United States now is a permanent importer of oil in the sense of this being likely for the foreseeable future. The Cabinet (advisory) Committee on Energy Supplies and Resources Policy concluded in 1955 that if the ratio of oil imports to domestic production rose above 1954 levels (of about 10 percent), national defense would be endangered, although many observers believe that the politically powerful domestic oil producers played an important role in getting imports restricted. Voluntary controls were instituted in 1957, when the plans of sixty importing companies indicated that imports would reach 17 percent of domestic production for the last half of 1957. Mandatory controls were established in 1959. See Douglas R. Bohi and Milton Russell, *Limiting Oil Imports* (Baltimore: Johns Hopkins University Press, 1978), chaps. 2 and 3.

5. *BP Statistical Review of the World Oil Industry,* Central Intelligence Agency, *International Energy Statistical Review.* Consumption does not equal production plus imports, because exports are omitted. The U.S. Bureau of Mines reports consumption figures higher by 1 to 3 percent, presumably because of processing gains.

6. Adelman, *The World Petroleum Market.*

7. Between 1900 and World War I, U.S. companies purchased oil leases in Japan and Rumania, and explored for and found oil in Mexico; Hidy and Hidy, *Pioneering in Big Business,* pp. 498, 516–520; Wilkins, *The Maturing of*

Multinational Enterprise, pp. 14–15. The Lansing quote is from *MNC Report*, p. 49; the quote by the director of the U.S. Geological Service is from *New York Times*, quoted in *MNC Report*, p. 33. The underlying motivations of the government and the companies, of course, were different. The U.S. government wanted oil in American hands because of security reasons; the companies wanted profits. Throughout this chapter, the comapnies' names are as of 1978. Of course, Exxon was at one time Standard Oil of New Jersey. For an explicit statement about the State Department's beliefs on the control of oil by U.S. companies, see *MNC Report*, p. 41.

The story that follows mirrors an important thread in history: the rise and fall of American oil power. Two other important threads also exist. First, the major oil companies continued to seek stability in the industry; for example, the big oil companies, Exxon and the foreign-based ones, agreed that non-U.S. market shares that each had in 1928 would be maintained in subsequent years more or less "as is." Second, in keeping with the American sentiment for the division of power, the U.S. government typically adopted policies that would ensure the survival of the so-called "independent" oil companies. Thus, since the independents felt that they gained by the market stabilization agreement of 1928, the U.S. government made no effort to reject the agreement even though it went against its earlier Open Door policy. Furthermore, at times— especially when conditions were tranquil—the U.S. government seemed to ignore the world oil business. These two themes, along with the theme that I emphasize, are discussed in Raymond Vernon, "The Influence of the U.S. Government Upon Multinational Enterprises—The Case of Oil," in *The New Petroleum Order* (Quebec: Les Presses de l'Université Laval, 1976).

8. *MNC Report*, p. 41.
9. France eventually obtained a 6 percent interest in the Iranian consortium, as discussed later in the chapter. True, the Middle East nations did bargain with the oil companies, but which companies were allowed to begin the bargaining was often decided by the Great Powers and not the host governments (Kuwait is one example).
10. *MNC Hearings*, part 7, pp. 497–500; and Shwadran, *The Middle East, Oil and the Great Powers*, p. 409.
11. *MNC Hearings*, part 7, pp. 84–86.
12. The payments actually were based on pounds sterling—£50,000 and £10,000, respectively—and the £50,000 was an advance against future royalties. See Shwadran, *The Middle East, Oil and the Great Powers*, pp. 304–311. Socal originally operated in Saudi Arabia as owner of the California–Arabian Standard Oil Company, and it was this company in which Texaco bought half interest, in December 1936, for $3 million cash and a promise to pay $18 million out of the oil produced. Also in 1936, Socal put up Bahrain and Texaco put up its marketing facilities east of the Suez to form a fifty-fifty joint venture, the California Texas Oil Company (Caltex). *MNC Report*, p. 37, and Shwadran, pp. 303–312.
13. "Desperate" is a quote by the Socal vice-president in *MNC Report*, p. 37.

"American hands" in a quote in Daniel Yergin, *Shattered Peace* (Boston: Houghton Mifflin, 1977), p. 446. In fact, the U.S. government attempted to buy 100 percent of Aramco in 1943, but Socal and Texaco refused to sell. See *MNC Report*, pp. 39–41.

14. This was the Red Line Agreement, so named because of a red line drawn on a map to indicate the territories in which the owners of IPC agreed not to explore on their own for oil. Saudi Arabia was within the red line. The owner of the French share of IPC and Calouste Gulbenkian, who owned 5 percent, sued Exxon and Mobil for violating the Red Line Agreement. The case was settled out of court. See *MNC Report*, pp. 50–55.

15. The State Department's suggestion was consistent with the American concern over the concentration of power and the resulting desire to ensure the survival of the independents; see Reference 7. *MNC Hearings*, part 8, pp. 72–76. The companies received a credit on U.S. tax bills for the taxes paid to Saudi Arabia. Thus, for every dollar paid in income taxes to Saudi Arabia, a dollar could be subtracted from income taxes owed the U.S. government.

16. The Cold War information is from Yergin, *Shattered Peace*, p. 179. This account of the Iranian nationalization crisis comes primarily from Robert B. Stobaugh, "The Evolution of Iranian Oil Policy, 1925–1975," in George Lenczowski, ed., *Iran Under the Pahlavis* (Stanford, Ca.: Hoover Institution, 1978). Also, see the histories in Reference 2. See Adelman, *World Petroleum Market*, chap. 3, for production statistics by company.

17. In a related development, on January 12, 1953, President Truman, acting on General Omar Bradley's assurance that national security called for the action, requested that the Justice Department terminate a grand jury investigation of the U.S. majors for possible criminal violation of the U.S. antitrust laws because of their alleged activities as part of a world oil cartel. Truman's instructions were in accordance with the recommendation of the Departments of State, Defense, and Interior, which had concluded in a report that any attack on the oil companies would be viewed in Europe and the Middle East as a fundamental attack on the whole American system and would pose great potential danger in both Venezuela and the Middle East, which were the only sources from which the free world's import requirements of oil could be supplied. Truman emphasized, however, that he wanted the case pursued vigorously in civil courts. This was done, and the case was settled years later by consent degrees. See *MNC Report*, pp. 60–74.

18. *MNC Hearings*, part 7, p. 297.

19. The Shah expressed his resentment of the market power of the consortium to me in an interview in April 1976. The quote is from *Wall Street Journal*, August 10, 1960, p. 2. See also Sampson, *The Seven Sisters*, pp. 156–158.

20. See Paul Swain, "Discounts Break Middle East Prices," *Oil and Gas Journal*, August 15, 1960, p. 84.

21. *New York Times*, August 10, 1960, p. 41.

22. The words are those of Senator J. W. Fullbright, quoted in Zuhayr Mikdashi, "The OPEC Process," in Vernon, ed., *The Oil Crisis*, p. 214. Some oil

executives have told me that OPEC would likely have been formed eventually, and without the price cuts, as Europe and Japan became increasingly dependent on imported oil. But it is not surprising that a price cut triggered the move, because a threat to an established position can be an important galvanizer of action. See Raymond Vernon, *Sovereignty at Bay* (New York: Basic Books, 1971), p. 71.

23. From the author's interviews with Faud Rouhani in Tehran in April 1976 and with Perez Alfonzo in Caracas in February 1974. For a history of OPEC and its methods of operations, see Mikdashi, "The OPEC Process," in Vernon, ed., *The Oil Crisis*, and Mikdashi, *The Community of Oil Exporting Countries* (Ithaca: Cornell University Press, 1972). As of 1982 OPEC membership included Algeria, Ecuador, Gabon, Indonesia, Iran, Iraq, Kuwait, Libya, Nigeria, Qatar, Saudi Arabia, United Arab Emirates, and Venezuela. The reader will recall that BP and Royal Dutch/Shell were international majors along with the U.S. majors. The loss of control by the U.S. majors, of course, was accompanied by a loss of control by BP and Royal Dutch/Shell. See also U.S. Senate, Committee on Interior and Insular Affairs, *United States—OPEC Relations, Selected Materials*, 94 Cong., 2 sess. (Washington, D.C.: Government Printing Office, 1976); Dankwart A. Rustow and John F. Mugno, *OPEC Success and Prospects* (New York: New York University Press, 1976); and *Wall Street Journal*, March 22, 1982, p. 3.

24. The information on Libya is from *MNC Report*, pp. 121–140. The estimate of 1969 oil prices came from Adelman, *The World Petroleum Market*, pp. 183 and 191. Because of lower investment per barrel, however, the return on investment of the companies does not seem to have declined. See Citibank's *Energy Newsletter*, various issues. For a discussion of the difficulty in measuring return on investment, see Thomas R. Stauffer, "Measurement of Corporate Rates of Return and Marginal Efficiency of Capital," Unpublished Ph.D. thesis, Harvard University, 1971.

25. Some oil executives speculate that because Europe seemed to need Libya's oil, whereas Libya had several years of savings in banks, Qaddafi might have still been able to obtain higher prices even if there had been only majors in Libya. Of course, there is no way of determining what would have happened. The Occidental executive is quoted in Daniel Yergin, "The One-Man Flying Multinational: Armand Hammer Wheels and Deals," *Atlantic Monthly*, June 1975, p. 32.

26. Descriptions of the events between 1970 and mid-1973 are given in a number of places. See, for example, chapters by Robert B. Stobaugh in Lenczowski, ed., *Iran Under the Pahlavis*, and in Vernon, ed., *The Oil Crisis*. Also see chapters in *The Oil Crisis* by Edith Penrose and Mira Wilkins; Sampson, *The Seven Sisters*, pp. 182–184; and *MNC Report*, pp. 121–140. U.S. oil imports, after increasing by 800,000 barrels daily between 1967 and 1970, increased by 2,835,000 barrels daily between 1970 and 1973.

27. Information about Aramco's cushion is from interviews with executives of major oil companies. The U.S. import quota system was abandoned during

1973, and U.S. imports rose 1.5 million barrels daily during 1973, compared with a rise of 800,000 barrels during 1972. For a discussion of market conditions in mid-1973, see Penrose, "The Development of Crisis," in Vernon, ed., *The Oil Crisis.*

28. *MNC Hearings,* part 7, p. 509.

29. For information on the embargo period, see Stobaugh, "The Oil Companies in Crisis," in Vernon, ed., *The Oil Crisis;* and *MNC Report,* pp. 144–150.

30. Quoted from Stobaugh, "The Oil Companies in Crisis," in Vernon, ed., *The Oil Crisis,* p. 189. An intermediate meeting of OPEC in October agreed to a unilateral raise in prices that would raise the government income to $3.08 a barrel; but this raise was not agreed to by the companies. For a summary, see Lenczowski, "The Oil Producing Countries," *The Oil Crisis;* and *MNC Report.*

31. Some of the companies that bid very high prices eventually refused to take delivery of the oil and pay such prices. The quote by the refiner is in *Petroleum Intelligence Weekly,* December 3, 1973, p. 3. The majors, through their actions in allocating oil among nations so as to "equalize suffering" during the embargo, helped avoid an unmanageable crisis. See Stobaugh, "The Oil Companies in Crisis," in Vernon, ed., *The Oil Crisis.* The OPEC meeting in Tehran was reported in a number of places, including *New York Times,* December 24, 1973, p. 1. For a discussion of the realization that the problem was one of price, not supply, see *The Oil Crisis.*

32. Libya did not lift its 1973–74 embargo until later, nor was the embargo against countries other than the United States lifted until later. See Lenczowski, "The Oil-Producing Countries," and Appendix A in Vernon, ed., *The Oil Crisis,* pp. 67 and 284.

There was considerable confusion in the world oil market in 1974, and, in fact, the OPEC take never did settle at the $7.00-per-barrel figure announced for January 1, 1974. Negotiations during the year resulted in the following estimated prices—obtained from oil-company files—for Arab Light (also see Reference 26, Appendix):

Carter's toast, *Wall Street Journal,* January 4, 1979, p. 1; disappointments of oil producers about industrial development, Walter J. Levy, "The Years that the Locust Hath Eaten: Oil Policy and OPEC Development Prospects," *Foreign Affairs,* Winter 1978, pp. 287–305; Sheik of Kuwait, *New York Times,* March 11, 1979, p. F17; President of France, *Newsweek,* July 3, 1979, p. 30.

Quote by Sheikh Yamani in *Financial Times,* April 21, 1981, p. 1. Also see, "Why the Saudis want an oil glut," *Financial Times,* Thursday, April 23, 1981; OPEC output agreement, quote by Youssef M. Ibrahim, "OPEC Members Agree to Pare Output Levels," *The Wall Street Journal,* Monday, March 22, 1982, p. 3. For information on changing structure in world oil markets, see Dr. Ian M. Torrens, *Changing Structures in the World Oil Market* (Montclair, N.J.: Allanheld, Osmun & Co., 1981); also the Atlantic Institute for International Affairs, and Dr. Fariborz Ghadar, *Petroleum Prospects in Developing Nations: Opportunities for Investment in the 1980s* (The George Wash-

Date	Average Acquisition Cost, Aramco Partners (including buy-back and equity oil)	Prices Paid by non-Aramco Companies to Saudi Arabia	Prices Paid by non-Aramco Companies to Aramco Companies	Spot Prices
1-1-74	$9.35	$10.83	—	$11.05 (1st Q. avg.)
4-1-74	9.35	10.83	$10.20 (2nd Q. avg.)	10.80 (2nd Q.)
7-1-74	9.45	10.46	10.40 (3rd Q.)	10.20 (3rd Q.)
11-1-74	10.24	10.46	10.30 (4th Q.)	10.40 (4th Q.)
1-1-75		10.46	—	
10-1-75		11.51	—	

ington University, Graduate School of Business, Washington, D.C., April 30, 1982).

33. Statistics on Saudi Arabia's shares of OPEC production and reserves are from the Department of Energy, *Monthly Energy Statistics*, various issues. "Ease of exploitation" refers to the low costs and very large output per well, and hence to the relatively few wells needed. In fact, the geological structure is quite complex, according to geologists I have interviewed. Population estimates vary widely, depending upon the source. Many experts believe that the official statistics overstate the population. The oil reserves estimate is from Harold J. Haynes, chairman of Socal, who stated that "in each year of its operations, Aramco had added more liquid hydrocarbons to Saudi reserves than it has produced," reaching 151 billion barrels in 1976, in "The Changing Role of Multinational Oil Firms," *Oil and Gas Journal, Petroleum 2000: 75th Anniversary Issue*, August 1977, p. 500. For an explanation of some earlier confusion about a possible decline in Saudi reserves, see *Oil and Gas Journal*, February 14, 1977, p. 62.

Financial reserves figures are from Morgan Guaranty Trust, *World Financial Markets*, various issues and interviews with U.S. officials and banks. Also, see David Ignatius, "Even With World Oil Glut, Saudi Arabia Has Enough Income for Domestic Needs," *The Wall Street Journal*, Wednesday, April 7, 1982, p. 29.

The Department of Energy's *Monthly Energy Review* of August 1978 (p. 88) shows excess capacity held by OPEC nations, some of which has been shut in for internal political reasons and not for lack of a market. Kuwait is an example of a nation that shut in some of its capacity prior to 1973 when it could have sold more oil. From 1974 to 1975 production was reduced from 8.35 to 6.97 million barrels, or 17 percent, per day in Saudi Arabia, and from 6.06 to 5.39 million barrels, or 11 percent, per day in Iran; see *BP Statistical Review of the World Oil Industry*, 1976. On a monthly basis, the Saudi cut was as deep as 35 percent, falling from a peak of 9.05 million barrels daily in October 1974 to 5.92 million daily in April 1975, and in 1982 Saudi output was cut to 5.5 mbd from its 1981 peak of 10–10.3 mbd.; see *Petroleum Economist*, various issues.

Some analysts point out that although Saudi Arabia is clearly the leader within OPEC, it must be joined by others in adjusting output over the long run; see M. A. Adelman, "Constraints on the World Oil Monopoly Price," *Resources and Energy*, 1 (1978), pp. 1–39. Although the OPEC countries determine crude oil prices, the companies typically set product prices, but the OPEC countries, by processing their own crude oil or having others process it for them, are playing an increasingly important role in product markets; also, see Fereidun Fesharaki and David T. Isaak, *OPEC Downstream Processing —A New Phase of the World Oil Market* (Resource Systems Institute, East-West Center, October 1981).

34. I am aware of over 100 studies of the world oil outlook. Unless otherwise noted, my conclusion about the world oil outlook came from a review of the better-known ones listed below and from studies by some of the leading consulting firms. A recent reference is in my chapter in Yergin and Hillenbrand, *Global Insecurity.* For a good summary of the best-known studies, see *Energy: An Uncertain Future,* prepared by Herman Franssen at the request of the Senate Committee on Energy and Natural Resources, publication no. 95–157, December 1978 (Washington: Government Printing Office, 1978). Perhaps the most extensive study was the one by Workshop on Alternative Energy Strategies, *Energy: Global Prospects 1985–2000,* Sponsored by the Massachusetts Institute of Technology (New York: McGraw-Hill, 1977); other well-known studies include: Energy Modeling Forum, *World Oil—Summary Report* (Stanford, California: Stanford University, February 1982); Office of Technology Assessment, *World Petroleum Availability 1980–2000* (Washington D.C.: U.S. Government Printing Office, October 1980), #052-003-00781-9; Fereidun Fesharaki and T. Milo Johnson, *Short Term and Medium Term Outlook for Oil: A Review and Analysis of Recent Studies,* Revised February 1982; Exxon Background Series, *World Energy Outlook,* December 1980, and Exxon, *U.S. Energy Outlook,* December 1980, Prepared by the Corporate Planning and the Public Affairs Departments of Exxon Corporation; Organization for Economic Cooperation and Development, *World Energy Outlook* (Paris: OECD, 1977); Marcello Colitti, "The Energy Supply Problem Up to and After the Year 2000," Paper presented at the Second International Conference on Environmental Policy and the Fuel Crisis, Turin, April 26–29, 1977; A. Benard, "Prospects for Oil and Gas to the End of the Century," Address to the Commission of the European Communities, Brussels, Novem-

ber 29, 1977; Richard Nehring, "Giant Oil Fields and World Oil Resources," Prepared for the Central Intelligence Agency (Santa Monica, Calif.: The Rand Corporation, June 1978). Estimates for the Soviet Union and its allies (Eastern Europe, Mongolia, Cuba, and Vietnam) vary widely; for examples, see Central Intelligence Agency, *Prospects for Soviet Oil Production: A Supplemental Analysis*, ER77-10425, Washington, July 1977; and *International Herald Tribune*, September 14, 1978, p. 4. The North Sea estimate is from D.D.F. Laidlaw, a BP executive, in his "A Global View of the Prospects of the European Oil and Gas Industry in All Its Phases," Paper delivered at the European Petroleum and Gas Conference, Amsterdam, May 1978. Note that these studies consider the subject of "oil proliferation"—discoveries of new fields in non-OPEC areas. Information on Venezuelan heavy oil from private correspondence with Venezuelan official.

35. See George W. Grayson, "Mexico's Opportunity: The Oil Boom," *Foreign Policy*, Winter 1977/1978, pp. 65–89; "Mexico: A Survey," *The Economist*, April 22, 1978; David Ronfeldt, Richard Nehring, Arturo Gandara, *Mexico's Petroleum and U.S. Policy: Implications for the 1980s* (Santa Monica, Calif.: Rand, June 1980); Congressional Research Service, *Mexico's Oil and Gas Policy: An Analysis* (Washington: Government Printing Office, December 1978). Secretary of Energy Schlesinger predicted that Mexico could be producing 4 to 5 million barrels per day by 1985, and the CIA suggested that Mexico could produce 10 million barrels daily by 1990. Saudi Arabia's proven reserves of gas are about 16 billion barrels of oil equivalent; *Oil and Gas Journal*, December 25, 1978, p. 102. But any comparison of the ultimate size of Mexico's hydrocarbon reserves with those of Saudi Arabia is highly speculative, since estimates of potential reserves of Saudi Arabia have not been released.

36. See Reference 35. The estimates of Mexico's production and exports were obtained in a confidential interview from a knowledgeable source, but they should be regarded merely as educated speculation.

37. Central Intelligence Agency, *China: Oil Production Prospects* (Washington, D.C.: Library of Congress, 1977), p. 11. For a discussion of the theory supporting a gradual decline in the oligopolistic control of multinational corporations in raw-material industries and of the rise in the power of host governments, see Raymond Vernon, *Sovereignty at Bay*, chap. 2; Fariborz Ghadar, *The Evolution of OPEC Strategy* (Lexington, Mass.: Lexington Books, 1977); Daniel Fine, "Multinational Oil, The Energy Crisis, and Government Control in Kenya," Unpublished mimeograph paper, 1978; Irving Kuczynski, "British Off-Shore Oil and Gas Policy," Unpublished D.B.A. thesis, Harvard University, June 1978; Stobaugh, "The Evolution of Iranian Oil Policy," in Lenczowski, ed., *Iran Under the Pahlavis;* and Louis Turner, *Oil Companies in the International System* (London: George Allen and Unwin, 1978). For more optimistic reports, see Selig S. Harrison, "China: The Next Oil Giant, Time Bomb in East Asia," *Foreign Policy*, Fall 1975, p. 25; Choon-ho Park and Jerome Alan Cohen, "The Politics of the Oil Weapon," *Foreign Policy*, Fall

1975, pp. 33, 40; Wang Kung Ping, *The People's Republic of China—A New Industrial Power with a Strong Material Base* (Washington, D.C.: U.S. Bureau of Mines, 1975, p. 38); and *Review of Sino-Soviet Oil*, March 1978, p. 70. The CIA and Commerce Department estimates on China were reported in *International Petroleum Finance*, March 29, 1982, p. 1. Also, see Thomas Fingar, *Energy and Development: China's Strategy for the 1980s* (Stanford, Calif.: Northeast Asia–United States Forum on International Policy, Stanford University, October 1980).

38. For example, a princess was executed on orders of her grandfather for attempting to elope with a man not approved of by her family. The official charge against her was adultery, and her "husband" was stoned to death. See *New Orleans Times Picayune*, January 22, 1978, sec. 1, p. 17. The late King Abdul Aziz Ibn Saud is known in Saudi Arabia as King Abdul Aziz rather than King Ibn Saud, as he was called in the West. For a history of Saudi Arabia, see David Holden and Richard Johns, *The House of Saud* (London: Sidgwick and Jackson, 1982); Charles M. Doughty, *Travels in Arabia Deserta* (New York: Random House, 1946); H. St. John B. Philby, *Saudi Arabia* (London: Been, 1955); Benoist-Mechin, *Ibn-Seoud: Le loup and le léopard* (Paris: Albin Michel, 1955); and for more leisurely reading, parts 4 and 5 of the *Aramco Handbook* (Dhahran: Arabian American Oil Company, 1968), and "A Survey of Saudi Arabia—Filling a Void," *The Economist*, February 13, 1982.

39. For an alternative view, which assumes that all OPEC nations are profit maximizers, see Basil Kalymon, "Economic Incentives in OPEC Oil Pricing Policy," *Journal of Development Economics* (December 1975), pp. 357–362; Nabil Chartouni, "Optimal Pricing/Investment Decisions for Natural Resources Production," Unpublished D.B.A. thesis, Harvard Business School, June 1978; and Robert A. Marshalla, "An Analysis of Cartelized Market Structures for Non-Renewable Resources," Unpublished doctoral thesis, Stanford University, August 1978. M. A. Adelman states, "Saudi Arabia will produce as much or as little oil as to maximize its revenues," but also recognizes that nations have political objectives. He maintains, however, that "political objectives are served perfectly by economic gain. There is no sacrifice or tradeoff of one for the other." Both of these quotes are in his "Need for Caution Over Prices," *Petroleum Economist*, September 1977, pp. 359–360. He also recognizes the need for current income: see his "Constraints on the World Oil Monopoly Price," *Resources and Energy*. For a discussion of how to make decisions to meet several goals simultaneously, see D. Bell, R. Kenney, and H. Raiffa, eds., *Conflicting Objectives in Decisions* (New York: John Wiley and Sons, 1977). For an explicit discussion of an example of France's not maximizing its income in order to meet international political goals, see *International Herald Tribune*, July 28, 1978, p. 4. Also, see David J. Teece, *A Behavioral Analysis of OPEC: Monopolization with Limited Collusion*, Research Paper No. 578, Stanford University.

My view is consistent with Yamani's, who said, "The political aspect of the decision [to limit the price increase to 5 percent] was obvious to everybody concerned." Interview in *Al-Medina*, July 10, 1977. My view also is consistent with the fact that the Saudi government for some time earned a negative profit (in real terms) on its investments outside the nation, and has a goal of minimizing what would probably be a steady real loss, whereas its leaders state that they believe that the price of oil will rise more rapidly than inflation. For the first point, see the statement of James Akins, former U.S. ambassador to Saudi Arabia, in a footnote in Theodore H. Moran, *Oil Prices and the Future of OPEC* (Washington: Resources for the Future, 1978), p. 19. For second point, see Yamani's statement in *Oil and Gas Journal*, July 3, 1978, p. 28.

40. Some experts on Saudi Arabia have said that King Khalid is enjoying his job more now than he initially did. The press carried a report that Prince Abdullah has asked for a meeting of the full family of perhaps 5,000 to decide the issue, but my interviews with persons who, I believe, have more reliable information indicate that this is not correct. See *The Economist*, July 16, 1977, p. 76, and September 17, 1977, p. 79.

41. For a report on the 1969 attempted coup, see *New York Times*, September 9, 1969, p. 1. The *Petroeconomic File* has contained reports of as many as six attempted coups in the last decade (see, for example, their October 1977 issue), but U.S. company and government officials with substantial experience in Saudi Arabia believe these reports to be highly exaggerated. See also Peter Mansfield, *The Arab World* (New York: Thomas Y. Crowell, 1976). Ian Smart believes that a replacement government might well have the same economic and political goals as the present government; see his "Patterns of Middle East Politics in the Coming Decade," in J. C. Hurewitz, ed., *Oil, the Arab-Israel Dispute, and the Industrial World* (Boulder, Colo.: Westview, 1976).

42. Given to me in interviews.

43. A Libyan cabinet officer told me the story about Qaddafi in Tripoli in 1974.

44. For an analysis of the U.S.S.R.'s aspirations, see John C. Campbell, "The Soviet Union in the Middle East," *The Middle East Journal*, 32 (Winter 1978). The remainder of the information in this paragraph came from interviews with U.S. and European government officials, and Arab individuals and government officials. For an account of a recent assassination of a president of North Yemen, see *New York Times*, June 25, 1978, p. 1.

45. From interviews, as in Reference 44. But recently, Iraq has seemed less pleased with its Soviet connection. For a broad discussion of Middle East politics, see Paul Y. Hammond and Sidney S. Alexander, eds., *Political Dynamics in the Middle East* (New York: American Elsevier, 1972); and Dale R. Tahtinen, *National Security Challenges to Saudi Arabia* (Washington: American Enterprise Institute, 1978).

46. *International Herald Tribune*, March 27–28, 1982, p. 1; and *Wall Street Journal*, April 1, 1982, p. 31, for statement of Saudi Ministry of Interior.

47. Quote from Richard C. Steadman, *Report to the Secretary of Defense on the National Military Command Structure*, Department of Defense, July 1978, p. 11. Also, see C. K. Ebinger, *The Critical Link: Energy and National Security in the 1980s* (Cambridge: Ballinger Publishing Co., 1982) and Pan Heuristics,

Report on Persian Gulf Oil and Western Security (Marina del Rey, Calif., 1980); Committee on Energy and Natural Resources, *The Geopolitics of Oil —Staff Report,* Publication No. 96-119 (Washington, D.C.: Government Printing Office, December 1980); and Christopher Van Hollen, "Don't Engulf the Gulf," *Foreign Affairs,* Summer 1981.

48. The world-oil-outlook studies are listed in Reference 34.

49. The 60 percent and 230 percent increases in energy demand for the period 1977–2000 is based on the ratio between the annual rate of growth of energy usage to annual rate of growth of the world's economy, estimated to range between .82 and 1.12, and the annual rate of the world's economic growth, estimated to range between 2.5 and 4.5 percent; see studies in Reference 34. By 1982 these estimates seemed unrealistically high; see my chapter in Yergin and Hillenbrand, *Global Insecurity.*

50. *Wall Street Journal,* January 6, 1978, p. 22, and November 28, 1978, p. 2. As of January 1978, Aramco—Saudi Arabia's only producer other than in the Neutral Zone, which is owned jointly with Kuwait—was producing a little over 8 million barrels daily from only fifteen of Aramco's thirty-seven fields. An expansion to 14 million barrels daily would require very major capital expenditures. The estimate of 16 million to 20 million barrels daily is disputed by some in the oil industry, but it comes from discussions with petroleum engineers familiar with the Saudi Arabia oil fields.

51. For a description of Saudi relations with the U.S. government, see the discussion of the issues of selling jet fighters to Saudi Arabia in *Wall Street Journal,* March 13, 1978, p. 1. For a description of U.S. aid to Saudi Arabia, see press reports, such as *New Orleans Times Picayune,* February 9, 1978, sec. 2, p. 12.

52. Some observers have suggested that the U.S. government was encouraging Saudi Arabia to raise prices gradually so as to avoid a sharp upward break later; for speculation in the press on this point, see *Forbes,* March 20, 1978, pp. 31–32, and *Washington Post,* July 10, 1977, p. 1. But U.S. government officials have denied this in interviews with me. In fact, in 1978 the Saudis reduced their projected development plans; see *Wall Street Journal,* January 6, 1978, p. 22, and November 28, 1978, p. 2. Some authors have an opposite view and assume that Saudi Arabia will increase expenditures in geometric progression each year. For an example of an assumption of 50 percent annual increases at current prices in imports for the rest of the 1970's, see James Bedore and Louis Turner, "The Industrialization of the Middle Eastern Oil Producers," *The World Today,* September 1977, pp. 326–334. Also see Theodore H. Moran, "Why Oil Prices Go Up? The Future: OPEC Wants Them," *Foreign Policy,* Winter 1976–77, pp. 58–77, and his *Oil Prices and the Future of OPEC.*

53. From interviews with U.S. individuals and government officials knowledgeable about Saudi Arabia, and with Saudi government officials.

54. In economic terms, this represents a problem of income distribution across generations. For a discussion of the difficulties in handling the problem, see

Robert M. Solow, "The Economics of Resources or the Resources of Economics," *American Economic Review,* 64 (May 1974), pp. 1–14.

55. The quote on profit-maximizing is from Adelman, "Need for Caution Over Prices," *Petroleum Economist.* Also see his "Constraints on the World Oil Monopoly Price," *Resources and Energy;* page 16 of this latter reference contains a scenario with a Saudi daily production of 20 million barrels. Both these articles state that current OPEC prices seem to be far below the level that would maximize OPEC revenues. The statement of the Department of Energy official is in *Forbes,* March 20, 1978, p. 32, in response to a suggestion that Saudi Arabia might produce 19 million barrels daily. A recent book disputes the widely held belief that firms maximize profits, stating instead that "firms set a 'comfortable' price in terms of their capacity to survive." The author believes that the fundamental difference between his theory and conventional theory is the fact that decisions are made by agents whose motivations differ from those of an ideal profit-maximizing firm. See Harvey Leibenstein, *Beyond Economic Man* (Cambridge: Harvard University Press, 1977), pp. 216, 271.

56. From confidential reports of a well-known oil consultant, a research institute, and two high-level U.S. governmental officials. This view also has been reflected in a number of studies in Reference 34.

57. Those believing in a gradual price increase generally place heavy emphasis on the effects of the economic growth of industrial nations on the demand for oil and hence on oil prices; see Adelman in References 2 and 39. Some observers say a fourth "accident" had occurred—the replacement of Libya's King Idris by Colonel el-Qaddafi. They speculated that if Idris had remained in power, then U.S. political influence (exemplified by the Wheelus Air Force Base) would have deterred him from raising prices; see, for example, Dankwart A. Rustow, "Political Factors Affecting the Price and Availability of Oil in the 1980's," in Petroleum Industry Research Foundation, *Outlook for World Oil into the 21st Century* (Palo Alto, Ca.: Electric Power Research Institute, June 1978), app. A. Others say nonsense, because all OPEC nations always maximize their profits; thus Idris would have taken the same action as Qaddafi.

58. Daniel Yergin, "Killjoy of the Western World," *New Republic,* February 25, 1978, pp. 18–21; Yergin, "West Ready for Another Oil Embargo," *The Boston Globe,* March 21, 1978. There is no legislative authority, however, requiring the United States to live up to its commitments, and some government officials feel that the progress thus far has been "inexplicably slow" (private correspondence). A program to provide 500 million barrels of strategic storage (or 3 months' supply of 6 million barrels daily of imports) has been underway for some time. In mid-1978, the Department of Energy decided to double the capacity to a billion barrels by 1985; see its *Energy Insider,* July 10, 1978, p. 1.

59. Yergin and Hillenbrand, *Global Insecurity,* Chapter I. Also see J. Plummer, ed., *Energy Vulnerability* (Cambridge, Mass.: Ballinger Publishing Co., 1982) and R. G. Hubbard and R. C. Fry, Jr., "The Macroeconomic Impacts of Oil

Supply Disruptions," discussion paper E-81-07 (Energy and Environmental Policy Center: John F. Kennedy School of Government, Harvard University), revised June 1982. William D. Nordhaus, "Energy and Economic Growth," in Hurewitz, ed., *Oil, the Arab-Israel Dispute and the Industrial World*, p. 280. Also see estimates in Edward R. Fried and Charles L. Schultze, eds., *Higher Oil Prices and the World Economy* (Washington, D.C.: Brookings Institution, 1975), chaps. 1 and 2; and J.R.B. Associates, Inc., "Estimation of the Short-term Macroeconomic Impacts of Energy Price Changes on the U.S. Economy," Mimeograph report prepared as an account of work sponsored by the U.S. government and Brookhaven National Laboratory, McLean, Va., June 1978. The U.S. share of the economic loss almost surely exceeds $100 billion, with some estimates running into the hundreds of billions of dollars. One study reported that "the large increase in the price of energy in 1974 permanently reduced economic capacity, or the potential output of the U.S. economy, by four to five percent"; see Robert H. Rasche and John A. Tatom, "The Effects of the New Energy Regime on Economic Capacity, Production, and Prices," *Review of Federal Reserve Bank of St. Louis* (May 1977), p. 2. Analyses by the Wharton Econometric Forecasting Associates, Inc., show that the post-1972 increases in world oil price reduced real GNP (and real consumption) by 2 percent in 1978, with the reduction forecast to reach 5 percent by the mid-1980's; private correspondence December 11, 1978. Some economists have told me that economic losses could have been far fewer with proper management by the U.S. government, and that next time the United States might manage the problem much better. For a discussion of why a large change in the price of oil tends to retard economic growth and create inflation at the same time, and of the difficulty of avoiding these conditions, see Nicholas Kaldor, "Inflation and Recession in the World Economy," *The Economic Journal*, 86 (December 1976), pp. 703–714. For a lucid description of the difficulties in managing the U.S. economy, see Lester C. Thurow, "Economics 1977," *Daedalus*, Fall 1977, p. 80. He points out that "the economy is widely perceived as out of control."

60. See Charles Bartlett, "Dollar Decline Now is Nose of the Wolf," *New Orleans Times Picayune*, February 10, 1978, p. 12. Of course, factors in addition to oil imports are causing the U.S. balance-of-payments deficit, and the extent to which a balance-of-payments deficit represents a fundamental weakness in the U.S. dollar is questionable because of the build-up of U.S. assets abroad and other factors. See Raymond Vernon, "A Skeptic Looks at the Balance of Payments," *Foreign Policy*, Winter 1971–72.

61. A discussion with almost any European political leader reveals the fears listed here, and by 1978 some Europeans were beginning to issue public warnings to the United States. See the statement by British Prime Minister Callaghan that reduction in U.S. oil imports was an "essential ingredient" for success at the forthcoming summit at Bonn in *International Herald Tribune*, June 7, 1978, p. 3. For a discussion of the European view, see Guy de Carmoy, *Energy for Europe: Economic and Political Implications* (Washington, D.C.: Ameri-

can Enterprise Institute, 1977); Horst Mendershausen, *Europe's Changing Energy Relations* (Santa Monica, Ca.: Rand Corporation, 1976); *International Energy Supply: A Perspective from the Industrial World,* Rockefeller Foundation, May 1978; Romono Prodi and Alberto Clo, "Europe," and Stobaugh's article in Vernon, ed., *The Oil Crisis;* and Louis Turner, "The European Community: Factors of Disintegration—Politics of the Energy Crisis," *International Affairs,* February 1978, pp. 39–49.

62. For example, see Petroleum Industry Research Foundation, *The Outlook for Oil to 1990 and After* (New York: PIRC, 1978).

63. The first two solutions are shown in numerous places. For examples, see statements by Senator Russell Long in the *National Journal,* November 5, 1977, p. 1717; Texaco senior vice-president Alfred C. DeCrane, Jr., "United States Energy Policy, Programs, and Prospects: An Appraisal," Speech, American Bar Association, August 8, 1978; and investment banker John A. Hill, "In Fact, We Do Have an Energy Policy," *New York Times,* May 28, 1978, sec. 3, p. 12. The last-mentioned solution—divestiture—is in John M. Blair, *The Control of Oil* (New York: Pantheon, 1976). A central theme of Blair's book is the alleged withholding of oil production, both domestically and abroad, in order to keep prices high. The estimated OPEC-induced increase for 1973–74 and 1979 is for about 35 billion barrels of proved reserves of crude oil and natural gas liquids at an increase of about $29 a barrel. As discussed in Chapter 3, the value of U.S. natural gas reserves also increased dramatically.

64. In fact, this is an indeterminate issue. But what does appear to be true is that the supply elasticity in some major oil areas of the world can be quite low with respect to price. A recent estimate indicates that a 33-percent higher price for North Sea oil would result in increased output of 3.2 and 2.3 percent in 1980 and 1985, respectively. See Paul L. Eckbo, Henry D. Jacoby, and James L. Smith, "Oil Supply Forecasting: A Disaggregated Process Approach," *Bell Journal of Economics* (Spring 1978), p. 233. Not only were regulations apparently confusing, but some companies stated that the Department of Energy was basing claims on a retroactive interpretation of government rules that differed from the interpretation of rules in effect at the time of the transactions in question. The matter is being litigated in the courts. See Columbia Broadcasting System, News Release, June 17, 1978; *Wall Street Journal,* June 13, 1978, p. 1; and *New York Times,* January 6, 1978, p. 1. The reader should not confuse the cases of retroactive interpretation of rules with the alleged cases of oil-price manipulation by middleman firms; see *Wall Street Journal,* September 22, 1978, p. 1.

65. This conclusion about U.S. production levels does not imply that oil supply is insensitive to price, for without substantially higher prices, oil output would decline even more because of normal annual depletion. Earlier projections indicated much higher domestic production rates, but more recent estimates are much lower. See Exxon's *Energy Outlook 1980–2000* (December 1980). For years the oil companies have been anxious to explore these virgin territories, the property of the federal government. Until a Supreme Court decision

in early 1978, lawsuits had prevented drilling on the only East Coast outer continental shelf territory for which leases had been granted (off South Carolina, in August 1976); see *Wall Street Journal,* January 27, 1978, p. 17. And in early 1978 lawsuits brought by the state of Massachusetts and groups of environmentalists and fishermen asking for additional safeguards for the environment and fishing industry prevented the Department of the Interior from granting leases to oil companies to explore on the outer continental shelf off New England. Congress might well pass legislation providing for additional environmental safeguards. The result would be extensive exploration of offshore territories, especially off the East Coast, although the new environmental safeguards might slow the ongoing exploration in the Gulf of Mexico.

    The U.S. production estimates are based on interviews with company officials, an analysis of literature in Reference 34 and Exxon's *Energy Outlook 1980–2000* (December 1980). The number of wells drilled is from John P. Henry, Jr., "Energy: A World Perspective," Paper presented to the Stanford Research Institute Council, March 3 and 4, 1977, fig. 8.

66. The quote of the oil executive is from an interview with the author.
67. Conventional, or secondary, recovery consists of allowing the natural pressure in the oil field to force the oil out, then installing pumps at the bottom of the well to pump the oil out, and finally, injecting high-pressure natural gas or water into the field to force the oil out.

    Even an increase in production from enhanced recovery would require higher oil prices; see U.S. Congress, Office of Technology Assessment, *Enhanced Oil Recovery Potential in the United States* (Washington, D.C.: Government Printing Office, 1978), pp. 7, 19. Also see National Petroleum Council, *Enhanced Oil Recovery* (Washington, D.C.: NPC, 1976).
68. Guy Elliott Mitchell, "Billions of Barrels of Oil Locked Up in Rocks," *The National Geographic Magazine,* February 1918, p. 205.
69. Some observers stated, however, that it was economic at prices existing even prior to the 1979–80 explosion. Occidental Petroleum Chairman Dr. Armand Hammer has stated that his company would earn a 15-percent return on Occidental's investment in a shale-oil project in Colorado, based on the U.S. price paid for OPEC oil in early 1978. Some other companies—Cities Service and Continental Oil, for example—thought that Dr. Hammer's estimates of required price are too low. The latter re-estimates Occidental's costs as $16 to $26 a barrel. A study indicated required prices of $23 to $29 per barrel in early 1979 prices for surface retorting. Edward W. Merrow, *Constraints on the Commercialization of Shale Oil* (Santa Monica, Calif.: Rand, September 1978), p. vii. For earlier estimates of the production costs of shale oil, see Federal Energy Administration, *Project Independence, Potential Future Role of Oil Shale: Prospects and Constraints,* U.S. Department of Interior, November 1974 (Washington, D.C.: Government Printing Office, 1974); Other Energy Resources Subcommittee of the National Petroleum Council's Committee on U.S. Energy Outlook, *An Initial Appraisal by the Oil Shale Task Group: 1971–1985* (Washington, D.C.: NPC, 1972); and various issues of

Oil and Gas Journal, Chemical Engineering, and *Chemical and Engineering News.* For Exxon's study, see Exxon U.S.A., *The Role of Synthetic Fuels in the United States' Energy Future* (Houston: 1980); "Exxon Scuttles Oil Shale Project with Tosco Corp," *The Wall Street Journal,* May 3, 1982, p. 3; "Alsands Failure Is Major Loss for Canada, May Force It to Revise Economic Strategy," *The Wall Street Journal,* May 3, 1982; and "Synfuels: Bringing Costs Into Focus," *Rand Research Review,* Winter 1981–82 (Santa Monica, Calif.: The Rand Corporation).

70. Although I judge that shale oil is unlikely to make a major contribution to the U.S. supply of oil by the turn of the century, individual companies might earn a good profit from it.

71. For information on the finding of reserves in the last thirty years, see *Energy: An Uncertain Future,* p. 58, plus more recent data from the American Petroleum Institute.

72. This is my conclusion after studying the available literature. For those sources tending to support divestiture, see Fred Allvine and James M. Patterson, *Competition, Ltd.: The Marketing of Gasoline* (Bloomington: Indiana University Press, 1972); Blair, *The Control of Oil;* Paul Davidson's statement in *Chemical Engineering Progress,* 73 (April 1977), pp. 14–32; Paul Davidson, "Divestiture and the Economics of Energy Supplies," and Walter S. Measday, "Feasibility of Petroleum Industry Divestiture," in David J. Teece, ed., *R&D in Energy: Implications of Petroleum Industry Reorganization* (Stanford: Institute for Energy Studies, Stanford University, 1977); and Federal Trade Commission proposal to break up oil companies. For those tending not to support divestiture, see Treasury Department analysis of break-up of large oil companies, *Implications of Divestiture* (Washington, D.C.: Superintendent of Documents, 1976); Donald C. Baeder, "Divestiture and the Impact on Pioneering Research in Energy," Thomas Baron, "Consequences of Divestiture for R&D and the Development of Alternative Energy Sources," F. A. L. Holloway, "A View of the Effect of Oil Industry Divestiture on Science and Technology," and David J. Teece and Henry O. Armour, "Innovation and Divestiture in the U.S. Oil Industry," all in Teece, ed., *R&D in Energy;* Edward J. Mitchell, ed., *Vertical Integration in the Oil Industry* (Washington, D.C.: American Enterprise Institute, 1976); David J. Teece, *Vertical Integration and Vertical Divestiture in the U.S. Oil Industry* (Stanford: Institute for Energy Studies, Stanford University, 1976); Frank N. Trager, ed., *Oil, Divestiture and National Security* (New York: Crane, Russak, 1977); W. A. Johnson, R. E. Messick, S. Van Vactor, and F. R. Wyant, *Competition in the Oil Industry,* Energy Policy Research Project, George Washington University, 1976; Edward W. Erickson, "The Energy Crisis and the Oil Industry," Statement before the U.S. Senate, Committee on the Judiciary, Subcommittee on Antitrust and Monopoly, January 27, 1976; Barbara Hobbie and Richard Mancke, "Oil Monopoly Divestiture: A Clash of Media Versus Expert Perceptions," *Energy Policy,* September 1977; Exxon, "Competition in the Petroleum Industry," Submission before the Senate Judiciary Subcommittee on Antitrust and Monopoly,

January 21, 1975. The estimate of the tank of gasoline per capita is about one-half the extreme estimate appearing in print; an executive of one major estimated a loss (with no strong evidence for the statement) in GNP of $6 billion yearly (or about 2½ cents per gallon of oil used). On the other hand, independent refiners have estimated that, based on their experience, they can compete with the majors when their crude oil costs do not exceed the major's costs by 50 cents to $1 a barrel (or about 1¼ to 2½ cents a gallon), thereby implying a greater efficiency than that of the majors; see Robert Yancey, president of Ashland Oil, in U.S. Congress, Senate, *Hearings Before the Subcommittee on Antitrust and Monopoly of the Committee on the Judiciary of United States Senate, S.1167, Part 8,* August 6–9, 1974, p. 5918. For other testimony on this subject, see *S.1167, Part 9,* January 21, 22 and 30, 1975; *S.2387* and related bills *S.739, S.745, S.756, S.1137,* and *S.1138* in *Part 1,* September 23, 26, October 29, 31, November 12, 19, 1975, and *Part 3,* January 21, 22, 27, 28, 30, and February 3, 18, 1976. The text discusses divestiture from the standpoint of domestic supply. There are also arguments in the above sources about the extent to which the majors help OPEC maintain price; but as indicated in the text, I believe Saudi Arabia's position is by far the dominant influence.

73. Quote from Trager, ed., *Oil, Divestiture, and National Security,* back cover. Some members of the financial community suggest that the shareholders of at least some of the majors would be financially better off if management dismantled the company by selling the individual operations. As one analyst wrote, "As preposterous as it sounds, the idea of voluntary self-liquidation by Exxon Corporation is not without economic and strategic logic insofar as the shareholders' interest is concerned." (William L. Randall, "A Case Study in the Limits to Corporation Growth," Pamphlet published by Blyth Eastman Dillon and Company, June 1978, p. 6.) John S. Herold, Incorporated, in *Petroleum Outlook,* June 1978, reports that Exxon shares were selling at a 46-percent discount from the value as appraised by Herold. Many other oil companies, including a number of majors, were selling at comparable discounts; and the takeover of Marathon by U.S. Steel and Conoco by DuPont in 1981 were indicative of larger discounts at which oil shares were being sold. But I doubt whether purchasers could absorb a number of liquidations simultaneously without a substantial fall in value, although the shares of the individual operations could be spun off to existing shareholders.

74. A number of polls have shown that Americans place heavy blame for energy problems on the oil companies. For evidence that a positive noneconomic effect could result just from the mere fact of breaking up a concentration of power, see Richard Hofstadter, *The Paranoid Style in American Politics and Other Essays* (New York: Alfred A. Knopf, 1966), p. 205; R. A. Dahl, *Pluralist Democracy in the United States: Conflict and Consent* (Chicago: Rand McNally, 1967), p. 24; S. P. Huntington, "Political Modernization: America vs. Europe," *World Politics* (April 1966), pp. 378–414; Bernard Bailyn, *Ideological Origins of the American Revolution* (Cambridge: Harvard University

Press, 1967), pp. 53–93, 273–301; and Raymond Vernon, "The Influence of the U.S. Government Upon Multinational Enterprises: The Case of Oil," in *The New Petroleum Order* (Quebec: Les Presses de l'Université Laval, 1976). For literature stressing the benefits of more equal income distribution, see Tibor Scitovsky, *The Joyless Economy* (New York: Oxford University Press, 1976); and Fred Hirsch, *Social Limits to Growth* (Cambridge: Harvard University Press, 1978). Those readers doubting that this is a serious issue should read the description by Daniel Yergin of a meeting in the United Kingdom in "The Great Fritter Debate," *New Republic*, August 5–12, 1978, pp. 16–17.

75. U.S. imports of crude oil, products, and natural gas liquids were 9 million barrels daily in 1977. As Alaskan production began in late 1977, imports declined by about a million barrels daily but began to climb again in mid-1978. The rise was cut short in early 1979 because of the combination of higher prices as well as gasoline lines and fear of future shortages. Imports in 1979 were 8.4 million daily; see Department of Energy, *Monthly Energy Review*. An Administration official was quoted as saying, "We expect oil prices to level out between $4 and $6 a barrel"; see *New York Times*, November 13, 1974, p. 1. Also see Federal Energy Administration, *Project Independence*. The price of newly found oil, adjusted by the GNP deflator to correct to 1973 dollars, was $9.94 in 1975, $9.16 in 1976, $8.22 in 1977, and about $8.26 in 1978; see Federal Energy Administration, *Monthly Energy Review*, July 1978, p. 61; and *International Financial Statistics*, July 1978, pp. 380–381. These prices were far above the $3.89 that existed in 1973, or the $3.60 in 1972 (in 1973 dollars); see Federal Energy Administration, *Annual Report to Congress*, p. 39.

76. See Reference 58. Anthony Copp, vice-president, Energy and Resource Development Group, Salomon Brothers, estimates that the investment cost of the oil storage for the United States for 500 million barrels will be some $10.7 billion, or almost 35 percent greater than anticipated in 1977 by the Federal Energy Administration; see his "Strategic Oil Storage Requirements and Costs for the United States: Some Economic Observations," Unpublished mimeograph paper, April 14, 1977. Dr. Copp says that is "peanuts" compared with the possible damage to the U.S. economy of an Arab oil boycott. The estimate of $5 billion annually is based on the assumptions that the U.S. imports 6 million barrels daily, priced at $35 a barrel, the cost of capital for the U.S. Government is 10 percent, storage costs are $1/barrel annually, and there will be no increase in the value of the oil. M. A. Adelman had recommended strategic storage for the Eastern Hemisphere noncommunist countries in 1967; see his "Security of Eastern Hemisphere Fuel Supply," Unpublished mimeograph paper M.I.T. Economics Department, December 1967.

77. The $23 billion estimate is based on the difference between the price of imported crude oil acquired by refiners ($21.67 in 1979) and the price for domestic oil ($14.27) times the annual production of domestic oil (8.5 million barrels daily of crude oil, ignoring crude oil quality and 1.6 mbd of natural gas

liquids), or $7.40 × 8.5 × 365 = $23 billion. Consumption data are from the Department of Energy, *Monthly Energy Review,* various issues.

78. For recommendations on decontrolling oil prices, see Stobaugh, "Comments on Recovery and Beyond," Interview on energy outlook in *Saturday Review,* July 12, 1975, pp. 28–30; "Gas Rationing is No Panacea," *Wall Street Journal,* January 4, 1974, p. 4; "The Hard Choice on Energy," *Wall Street Journal,* December 9, 1974, p. 22; and "For Oil and Gas Compromises," *New York Times,* December 2, 1977, p. A27.

79. *Crude Oil Profit Tax Act of 1980,* Conference Report, 96th Congress, 2d session, March 7, 1980 (Report No. 96-817); and *The Crude Oil Windfall Profit Tax* (New York: Price Waterhouse, 1980). Richard N. Cooper, undersecretary of state, stated that "reducing energy demand . . . should be judged by a test of cost-effectiveness" without giving any indication that the world price of oil does not reflect the risks associated with its use; see *Department of State Bulletin,* February 1978, p. 29. Many opponents of the Carter Administration's energy plan held, of course, that the world price of oil is too high for the United States.

80. For a discussion of externalities and social costs, see Chapter 9.

81. Other than our efforts at Harvard Business School, the only attempt that I had seen to quantify the incremental costs of imported oil are in a series of unpublished memoranda by Harvard economist Thomas Schelling as part of his activities as a member of the project entitled "Energy: The Next Twenty Years," of the Resources for the Future. (I also was a member of this project.) I am grateful for discussions with Schelling and other members of the RFF project, although I am solely responsible for my estimates. Since these early efforts at quantification, there have been numerous subsequent studies; see Harry Broadman (in reference 86) and Stanford Energy Modeling Forum, *World Oil—Summary Report* (Stanford, Calif.: Stanford University, February 1982) and William W. Hogan, "Oil Gluts and Oil Tariffs," discussion paper H-82-04, May 1982 (John F. Kennedy School of Government, Harvard University: Energy and Environmental Policy Center); and James Plummer in reference 59.

82. A recent OECD study assumes a positive and direct relationship between U.S. oil imports and other OECD oil imports, with a variation in U.S. imports of 8 million barrels daily being accompanied by a variation in the remainder of OECD of 7 million daily. See OECD, *World Energy Outlook.* Also, see William W. Hogan, "Oil Stockpiling: Help Thy Neighbor," discussion paper H-82-02, March 1982 (John F. Kennedy School of Government, Harvard University: Energy and Environmental Policy Center); and Mason Willrich and Bijan Mossavar-Rahmani, "Oil on Troubled Waters: The Industrial World and the OPEC Middle East," *ORBIS,* Vol. 23, No. 4, Winter 1980 (Foreign Policy Research Institute).

83. If it is assumed that the 2.5 mbd of imports are before the effects of the price, rather than after, as I assume here, the cost of marginal imports still exceeds $54 a barrel. For ease in exposition, I ignored the effect of the higher prices

on U.S. demand, the small element of price (perhaps 2 percent) representing profits earned by U.S. companies that might be returned to the United States, and the fact that transportation costs, which are about 10 percent of total costs, might not increase proportionately, because only a proportion of transport costs are fuel-related. Any error caused by these assumptions would not affect the basic conclusion that incremental oil imports might be very costly to the United States.

84. See References 59 and 60. The exact amount of lost economic activity would depend on (1) whether oil prices rose gradually throughout the period, rose in several larger steps, or rose in one giant step reminiscent of 1973–74; (2) the fiscal and monetary responses of other governments to higher oil prices; and (3) the fiscal and monetary response of the U.S. government to (1) and (2). I am grateful for discussions with Professor Francis Bator on this subject, although I am solely responsible for my estimates. Also, see W. Nordhaus, "Oil and Economic Performance in Industrial Countries," BPEA 2, 1980.

85. The Japanese are especially dependent on imported oil, having less domestic coal than the European countries. The Japanese (uncharacteristically) leveled their sharpest criticism at the United States since World War II, expressing "severe disappointment" with U.S. leadership: see *International Herald Tribune*, July 11, 1978, p. 7; *The Economist*, July 8, 1978, p. 67.

86. Although these costs can be thought of as "external costs" in the sense of the phrase as used here, economists sometimes refer to direct payments for the oil as pecuniary costs. For more explicit discussions of disruption costs and security issues, see Harry Broadman, "Review and Analysis of Oil Import Premium Estimates," Discussion Paper D-82-C (Washington, D.C.: Resources for the Future, 1981); "The Social Costs of Imported Oil: Theoretical Issues and Empirical Estimates" in *Energy Modeling IV: Planning for Energy Disruptions* (Chicago: Institute of Gas Technology, 1982); IGT Symposium, "Planning for Energy Disruptions," Washington, D.C., May 10–12, 1982; William W. Hogan, "Energy and Security Policy," discussion paper, E-81-09, September 1981 (J.F. Kennedy School of Government, Harvard University: Energy & Environmental Policy Center); and Benjamin S. Cooper, "Current Policy for Petroleum Supply Disruptions," Remarks to the California Energy Commission, Los Angeles, Calif., March 18, 1982.

87. Estimating the likelihood of different events occurring during different time periods, the costs associated with the events and the risk-averseness of U.S. society as a whole are not easy tasks; neither is estimating an appropriate discount rate for consumption for society as a whole. See Solow, "The Economics of Resources or the Resources of Economics," *The American Economic Review*.

88. This assumes, of course, that the consumer is basing investment decisions on current costs—an assumption in line with analyses that I have seen on conservation and solar energy. Companies, on the other hand, are likely to be assuming some rise in costs, but nothing that can approach the estimate of the incremental costs to the nation of imported oil. For discussions of why

innumerable small decisions might result in a different outcome for society than the decision-makers would want, see Thomas Schelling, "On the Ecology of Micromotives," in Robin Marris, ed., *The Corporate Society* (London: Macmillan, 1974), pp. 19–64; and Alfred E. Kahn, "The Tyranny of Small Decisions: Market Failures, Imperfections, and the Limits of Economics," *Kyklos* (1966), pp. 23–46. For studies of possible long-run response to higher prices, see Harry Broadman and Stanford Energy Modeling Forum, *World Oil —Summary Report.*

89. This seems obvious, since for years political forces held oil prices in the domestic market below the world price.

90. Many observers, including some environmental experts with whom I have spoken at universities, believe that current environmental rules are satisfactory. Also see Reference 66.

91. In theory, new oil should be priced substantially above the deregulated price (that is, substantially above the imported price) in order to give domestic oil an equal chance with imported oil. I judge that this would not be acceptable politically. (See Reference 89.) It must be recognized that many observers question whether even world prices, much less a financial incentive in addition to world prices, would be justified by the incremental domestic energy forthcoming. This is especially so given the lack of success in keeping U.S. oil and gas reserves from declining even after the dramatic price jumps that have occurred since 1973.

Chapter 3 | *Natural Gas*

1. U.S. Department of Energy, *Monthly Energy Review,* April 1982, pp. 4, 49, and 50. Also, *The Wall Street Journal,* March 26, 1980, p. 10. For background on regulation, see Stephen G. Breyer and Paul W. MacAvoy, "Regulating Natural Gas Producers," in Robert J. Kalter and William A. Vogely, eds., *Energy Supply and Government Policy* (Ithaca: Cornell University Press, 1976), pp. 161–192; U.S. Senate, Committee on Interior and Insular Affairs, *Natural Gas Policy Issues,* 92 Cong., 2 sess. (Washington, D.C.: Government Printing Office, March 1972); and Department of Energy, Energy Information Administration, *The Current State of the Natural Gas Market* (Washington, D.C.: Government Printing Office, December 1981). Newspapers carried reports of $100 billion at stake in the debate over decontrol of natural gas prices in 1978. Our estimate of $1 trillion is based on a notion of economic values of natural gas at world energy prices rather than value with prices controlled by law or long-term contracts. For example, U.S. proved reserves of natural gas were 250 trillion cubic feet (tcf), or 44 billion barrels of crude oil equivalent, at the end of 1973. The OPEC price rises of 1973–74 increased the world oil prices, in round numbers, by about $30 a barrel (in 1980 dollars). Thus, the value of U.S. proved reserves of natural gas increased, based on a world oil price, by some $1 trillion. This has not been corrected by discounting future cash flows to obtain present vlue, nor does it consider enlargement of

reserves. See Department of Energy, Energy Information Administration, *Annual Report to Congress, Volume III, 1977* (Washington, D.C.: Government Printing Office, May 1978), p. 61. We recognize that the economic value of gas, when compared with the price of world oil, would be more than this in some cases and less in others, depending upon a number of factors, including the comparative costs of delivering gas versus oil products, the particular oil product in question, and the premium value of gas because of its cleanliness. Regardless of assumptions, the main conclusion is clear: U.S. consumers are receiving a large subsidy, at the expense of producers, in using natural gas approximating $80 billion in 1980. Interview with U.S. Senator by authors.

2. Proved reserves were 293 tcf at the end of 1967 and 216 tcf at the end of 1978; see *Annual Report to Congress,* pp. 53, 61; American Gas Association, *Gas Facts 1978* (Arlington, Va.: AGA, 1979), sections 2 and 3. The reserve estimates are by *Oil and Gas Journal,* December 31, 1979, and December 25, 1978. By 1980, reserves were estimated at 199 tcf.: F. Murphy, R. O'Neill, and M. Rodekohr, *An Overview of Natural Gas Markets,* reprinted in *Monthly Energy Review* (Washington, D.C.: Government Printing Office, December 1981); and U.S. Department of Energy, *Monthly Energy Review,* January, 1980, p. 52. For information about possible U.S. production rates, see Paul W. MacAvoy and Robert S. Pindyck, *Price Controls and the Natural Gas Shortage,* National Energy Study 7 (Washington, D.C.: American Enterprise Institute for Public Policy Research, 1975), pp. 4 and 5; U.S. Department of Energy, Office of Policy, *Energy Projections to the Year 2000* (Washington, D.C.: Government Printing Office, July 1981), pp. 6–1 through 6–10; and U.S. Senate, Committee on Interior and Insular Affairs, *Natural Gas Policy Issues and Options, A Staff Analysis,* 93 Cong., 1 sess. (Washington, D.C.: Government Printing Office, 1973). But even on the decline of reserves, some critics dispute published estimates. See Bethany Weidner, "What Natural Gas Shortage?" *The Progressive,* April 1977, pp. 19–23.

3. This account of the history of the American manufactured gas business draws heavily on Paul J. Garfield and Wallace F. Lovejoy, *Public Utility Economics* (Englewood Cliffs, N.J.: Prentice Hall, 1964), chap. 4.

4. See National Economic Research Associates, "The Natural Gas Industry: An Overview," Aide-mémoire submitted to the U.S. Senate Committee on Energy and Natural Resources, June 16, 1977; "The Natural Gas Pipeline Industry," in Salamon Brothers' *A Quarterly Review,* March 29, 1977; U.S. Congress, Committee on Commerce Hearings, *U.S. Senate Hearings on Interstate Pipelines and Transmission Companies,* 94 Cong. (Washington, D.C.: Government Printing Office, 1975); and James T. Jensen, *Energy Company Strategies for the 1970s* (Cambridge, Mass.: Arthur D. Little, 1969). Useful articles on various aspects of the natural gas industry appear regularly in the *Bell Journal of Economics,* published in New York. Additional industry data appear regularly in the *Oil and Gas Journal,* published in Tulsa, Okla. See generally, American Gas Association, Policy Evaluation and Analysis Group,

A Forecast of Capital Requirements of the U.S. Gas Utility Industry to the Year 2000: 1982 Update (January 6, 1982); also American Gas Association Policy Valuation and Analysis Group, *Comparison of Initial Capital Investment Requirements for New Domestic Energy Supplies: 1982 Update* (January 6, 1982).

5. Garfield and Lovejoy, *Public Utility Economics*, chap. 4. While this chapter primarily focuses on price control, regulations also include certification and dedication of reserves.

6. *Phillips Petroleum Co.* v. *Wisconsin*, 347 U.S. 622, 1954. The 1954 decision traced back to the 1877 decision in *Munn* v. *Illinois*, which allowed state legislatures to fix the maximum price for grain storage, and to *Nebbia* v. *New York* in 1934, which allowed legislatures to impose price controls on any business within their jurisdiction, "where in their judgment it would serve the public interest, provided only that they did not do so in an utterly capricious or discriminatory manner." Quoted in Garfield and Lovejoy, *Public Utility Economics*, p. 113.

7. *New York Times*, February 7, 1956, pp. 1, 22, and February 18, 1956, p. 1.

8. Breyer and MacAvoy, in *Energy Supply and Government Policy*, pp. 161–192; and MacAvoy and Pindyck, *Price Controls and the Natural Gas Shortage*, p. 12. Most observers believe that this decision helped speed the development of the transcontinental pipelines because it facilitated financing of the lines by ensuring them low-priced, long-term supplies (dedicated reserves were an item regulated), just as the 1938 Natural Gas Act had helped their development by giving them public-utility status. In doing so, the Federal Power Commission used various formulas. During the first few years after the 1954 Supreme Court decision, the FPC tried to control wellhead prices for individual producing companies in much the same way that individual electric utility companies have been controlled—with a price intended to cover the costs of production, including an adequate return on investment. The large numbers of producers and gas fields led to an administrative nightmare. By the late 1950's, the commission had become inundated with some 2,900 applications for price review—a logjam that would have taken decades to free. In 1961 the agency switched to area rate regulation. On the basis of historical average production costs in five gas-producing regions, the FPC set a ceiling price for gas within each one. Although the switch to area rates hardly settled the question of what a "just and reasonable" price for gas should be, the technique did prove administratively workable. See Breyer and MacAvoy, "Regulating Natural Gas Producers," pg. 174, in Robert J. Kalter and William A. Vogely, eds., *Energy Supply and Government Policy* (Ithaca: Cornell University Press, 1976).

9. It is possible to calculate that the difference was about 27 cents per mcf in 1977. The 27 cents represents the difference between the average interstate price of 69 cents per mcf in Table 3-1 and an estimated average price of 96 cents for intrastate gas, which is the price intrastate gas had to sell at in order for the average price of all gas to be 78 cents. Interstate is approximately

two-thirds and intrastate one-third of the total $[(1/3 \times 96) + (2/3 \times 69) = 78]$, which is reported in *Annual Report to Congress*, Vol. III, p. 59.

10. Subcommittee on Energy and Power, Committee on Interstate and Foreign Commerce, House of Representatives, *Long-Term Natural Gas Legislation*, 94 Cong., 2 sess. (Washington, D.C.: Government Printing Office, 1976), p. 469.

11. Federal Energy Administration, *Annual Report to Congress, Volume II, 1977: Projections of Energy Supply and Demand and Their Impacts* (Washington, D.C.: Government Printing Office, 1978), p. 166.

12. U.S. Department of Energy, *Monthly Energy Review*, January 1980, p. 91. Texas governor and New York commissioner, *Natural Gas Pricing Proposals of President Carter's Energy Program*, 95 Cong., 1 sess. (Washington, D.C.: Government Printing Office, June 1977), pp. 113 and 150.

13. Many studies have been done about the cost of gas production. For a particularly lucid discussion on the various viewpoints, see Clark A. Hawkins, *The Field Price Regulation of Natural Gas* (Florida: Florida State University Press, 1969), chap. 3; for Joskow and Steele, see Hawkins, pp. 88–90.

14. In the 1950's and early 1960's, a much greater percentage of gas was associated with oil than in the 1970's. For an excellent discussion of the complicated problem of "joint costs," see Alfred E. Kahn, *The Economics of Regulation: Principles and Institutions*, Vol. 1 (New York: John Wiley and Sons, 1970), pp. 77–83. For alternative studies placed in evidence before FPC, see National Academy of Sciences, National Resource Council, *Panel on Gas Reserve Estimation*, Washington, D.C., 1975; also F. Murphy, R. O'Neill, and M. Rodekohr, *An Overview of Natural Gas Market*.

15. James W. McKie, "Market Structure and Uncertainty in Oil and Gas Exploration," *Quarterly Journal of Economics* 16 (September 1972), pp. 543–571.

16. Jackson quote is in *Natural Gas Pricing Proposals of President Carter's Energy Program*, p. 506.

17. Quote from O'Leary in *Natural Gas Pricing Proposals of President Carter's Energy Program*, p. 160.

18. In 1974, two M.I.T. economists, Paul W. MacAvoy and Robert S. Pindyck, constructed an econometric model that predicted that if the government stopped controlling the wellhead price of interstate gas, domestic discoveries would climb to 33 tcf per year by 1980 at a price of $1.00/mcf. (At the time of their estimate, the national average of controlled prices for new discoveries was $.54/mcf.) See MacAvoy and Pindyck, *Price Controls and the Natural Gas Shortage*, p. 57. For ERDA study, see Energy Research and Development Administration, *Market Oriented Program Planning Study—1* (Washington, D.C.: Government Printing Office, 1976). Also, see U.S. Senate, *Hearings before the Committee on Energy and Natural Resources: Market Oriented Program Planning Study*, 95 Cong., 1 sess. (Washington, D.C.: Government Printing Office, June 23 and 27, 1977), p. 95; and Comptroller General of the United States, Report to the Committee on Government Operations, House of Representatives, *Implications of Deregulating the Price of Natural*

Gas (Washington, D.C.: General Accounting Office, January 14, 1976).

19. The U.S. Geological Survey conducts periodic studies to update natural gas supplies. A summary of 1975 estimates appears in the *U.S. Geological Survey Circular*, 725, 1975; also see U.S. Central Intelligence Agency, *The International Energy Situation: Outlook to 1985* (Washington, D.C.: Library of Congress, April 1977), p. 6. A recent USGS estimate indicates recoverable gas reserves of some 330 to 660 tcf, or the equivalent of 16 to 33 years at a consumption rate of 20 tcf. These estimates include the 205 tcf of proven reserves existing at the end of 1978. The USGS estimate is in *Energy: An Uncertain Future*, prepared by Herman Franssen at the request of the Senate Committee on Energy and Natural Resources, Publication 95-157 (Washington, D.C.: Government Printing Office, December 1978), p. 59; see also U.S. Department of Energy, *Energy Projections to the Year 2000*, pp. 6-1 through 6-10.

20. Since the 1973 oil embargo, many of the major oil companies have published reserve estimates of oil and gas in the United States. Most of the estimates are revised periodically and appear in the firms' annual reports. One of the more comprehensive sets of estimates is in *Energy Outlook 1976–1999* and *Energy Outlook 1980–2000*, published by the Exxon Corporation. Other similar estimates are published periodically by the American Gas Association in Arlington, Va., and the Independent Petroleum Association of America in Washington, D.C.

21. See "Independents Vital to U.S. Petroleum Supply," *Oil & Gas Journal*, October 24, 1977, reprint; "Natural Gas Pipeline Industry," *A Quarterly Review;* and *Annual Report to Congress, Volume III*, p. 51.

22. Interview with Ben Cubbage, June 1978.

23. Interview with Jim Daugherty, president, Weal Drilling Company, June 1978. Other interviews with producer companies indicate that besides objections to the regulated price, companies cite instances of long delays in FERC's licensing processes.

24. This section is based heavily on interviews by the authors with officials of several interstate pipeline companies, particularly Mr. Hayward Coleman and his associates at the Southern Natural Gas Company, and Mr. Ed Najaiko and his associates of El Paso Natural Gas. Also, see *Natural Gas Pricing Proposals of President Carter's Energy Program*, p. 62.

25. Testimony of John F. O'Leary, administrator, Federal Energy Administration, *Natural Gas Pricing Proposals of President Carter's Energy Program*, p. 45ff.

26. Information on transfer of wealth is given in Department of Energy, Energy Information Administration, "An Evaluation of Natural Gas Pricing Proposals," Analysis memo AM/IA, 7802, June 14, 1978. Lee White quote from *Natural Gas Pricing Proposals of President Carter's Energy Program*, pp. 517–518.

27. Interview by authors with the Gallup Poll firm, Princeton, N.J., July 1978.

28. U.S. Congress, Senate Conference Report 95 1126 (to accompany House Report 5289), 95 Cong., 2 sess., 1976. See also U.S. Congress, U.S. House of

Representatives, Committee on Interstate and Foreign Commerce, and U.S. Senate, Committee on Energy and Natural Resources, *Natural Gas Pricing Agreement Adopted by the Conferees on H.R. 5289,* 95 Cong., 2 sess. (Washington, D.C.: Government Printing Office, June 1978), and "The Natural Gas Policy Act of 1978," Public Law 95-621, November 9, 1978, in United States Senate, Committee on Energy and Natural Resources, *The National Energy Act,* 96 Cong., 1 sess. (Washington, D.C.: Government Printing Office, January 1979).

29. Interview with Ellen Berman.

30. *New York Times,* September 6, 1981, Section 3, p. 1; *Wall Street Journal,* December 7, 1981, p. 33. For a comprehensive discussion of NGPA-78 and its related problems, see Department of Energy, Energy Information Administration, *The Current State of the Natural Gas Market* (Washington, D.C.: Government Printing Office, December 1981).

31. Edward W. Erickson, *Natural Gas and the Natural Gas Policy Act: A Pragmatic Analysis* (Washington, D.C.: Natural Gas Supply Association, January 1981), chapters 3 and 4, and appendix C, p. 89; Department of Energy, Energy Information Administration, *Background Information on the Natural Gas Market* (Washington, D.C.: Government Printing Office, March 1982).

32. Interviews with executives of various pipeline companies.

33. Department of Energy, Energy Information Administration, *The Current State of the Natural Gas Market* (Washington, D.C.: Government Printing Office, December 1981), pp. 71–85.

34. Interviews with executives of Transco Energy Company.

35. Interviews with executives of pipeline companies.

36. Department of Energy, Office of Policy, Planning, and Analysis, *A Study of Alternatives to the Natural Gas Policy Act of 1978* (Washington, D.C.: Government Printing Office, November 1981), and *Monthly Energy Review.*

37. American Gas Association, *Gas Facts 1980* (Arlington, Va.: American Gas Association, 1980); also, see Department of Energy, Energy Information Administration, *The Current State of the Natural Gas Market* (Washington, D.C.: Government Printing Office, December 1981), pp. 21–36.

38. For Canada, see *Annual Report to Congress, Volume III,* p. 51; *Annual Report to Congress, Volume II: Projections of Energy Supply and Demand and Their Impacts,* pp. 161–171. Also, *Wall Street Journal,* March 26, 1980, p. 10, and March 31, 1980, p. 7. An unpublished report from Stanford Research Institute, December 1978, contains estimates for Canada and Mexico. Also, for Mexico see "Supplemental Natural Gas Sources: Factors and Policy Issues," Report prepared by the Congressional Research Service, Library of Congress, for the use of the Subcommittee on Energy and Power, Committee on Interstate and Foreign Commerce, U.S. House of Representatives, June 1978, p. 11, and *New York Times,* September 22, 1979. For 1981, see Department of Energy, Energy Information Administration, *Monthly Energy Review* (Washington, D.C.: Government Printing Office, April 1982), p. 50; and Department of Energy, Energy Information Administration, *The Current*

State of the Natural Gas Market (Washington, D.C.: Government Printing Office, December 1981), pp. 53–58.

39. Department of Energy, Energy Information Administration, *Background Information on the Natural Gas Market* (Washington, D.C.: Government Printing Office, March 1982).

40. U.S. Department of Commerce, *Natural Gas from Unconventional Geologic Sources* (Washington, D.C.: National Academy of Sciences, 1976), sec. IV; "Amoco Makes Tuscaloosa Find in S. Louisiana," *Oil and Gas Journal*, March 3, 1980, p. 85; "FERC Sets Special Incentive Price for Tight Gas," *Oil and Gas Journal*, February 18, 1980, p. 70; U.S. Department of Energy, *National Gas Survey*, Report on Natural Gas Resources to the Federal Energy Regulatory Commission (Washington, D.C.: GPO, June 1978); and *Wall Street Journal*, March 27, 1980, p. 46. True, geopressured brine can be found at depths less than 15,000 feet, but the geologists we interviewed believe that most of it is likely to be found at depths greater than 15,000 feet.

41. Richard P. O'Neill, "The Interstate and Intrastate Natural Gas Markets," *Monthly Energy Review*, January 1982, pp. i–ix.

42. See chapter 4 of this book, and National Petroleum Council, *U.S. Energy Outlook—Coal Availability* (Washington, D.C.: NPC, 1973).

43. Speech appearing in Sonya Marchand, ed., "Energy—The Global Challenge," Proceedings of a conference sponsored by California State University at Northridge, May 6–7, 1977.

44. The most authoritative study that we have seen is U.S. Congress, Office of Technology Assessment, *Transportation of Liquefied Natural Gas* (Washington, D.C.: Government Printing Office, 1977); our account of the LNG situation draws heavily on this source. Also see Edward K. Fariday, *LNG Review: 1977* (Energy Economics Research Limited, 1978). Ironically, the oldest operating marine LNG project in the United States is one from which Phillips Petroleum and Marathon Oil export Alaskan LNG to Japan. This project started operation in 1969. Prediction of OPEC prices are from interviews by the authors with executives of interstate pipeline companies. Information on the Energy Regulatory Agency's El Paso refusal comes from a news release, Office of Public Affairs, Department of Energy, Washington, D.C., December 21, 1978, and from interviews with officials of the Department of Energy.

Chapter 4 | *Coal: Constrained Abundance*

1. Gordon Young, "Will Coal be Tomorrow's 'Black Gold,' " *National Geographic*, August 1975, pp. 234–259. "The Great Black Hope: Coal," *Colorado Business*, September/October 1976, pp. 33–34. "Old girl" is from Edmund Faltermayer, "Clearing the Way for the New Age of Coal," *Fortune*, May 1974, pp. 215–338. The idea of coal as a "transition" or "swing" fuel is widespread: see, for instance, R. L. Gordon, "Coal—Swing Fuel," in R. J. Kalter and W. A. Vogely, eds., *Energy Supply and Government Policy* (Ithaca:

Cornell University Press, 1976); D. Meadows and J. Stanley-Miller, "The Transition to Coal," *Technology Review*, 75, No. 1 (October/November 1975), pp. 19–29; A. Ford, "Environmental Policies for Electricity Generation: A Study of the Long-Term Dynamics of the SO$_2$ Problem," *Energy Systems and Policy*, 1 (1975), pp. 287–304.

2. The President's Address, "National Energy Program," *Presidential Documents: Jimmy Carter*, 13, No. 17, Delivered before a joint session of Congress, April 20, 1977; Executive Office of the President, *The National Energy Plan*, April 29, 1977. The 1976 coal production figure comes from Energy Information Administration, *Annual Report to Congress, Volume III-77* (Washington, D.C.: Government Printing Office, May 1978), p. 77.

3. David J. Goerz, "Coal: Presentation to Harvard Energy Seminar," Speech, May 1, 1978; Federal Energy Administration, *Final Task Force Report on Coal, Project Independence* (Washington, D.C.: Government Printing Office, November 1974); *1977 Keystone Coal Industry Manual* (New York: McGraw-Hill, 1977), pp. 777–778; *Demonstrated Reserve Base of Coal in the United States on January 1, 1979* (Washington, D.C.: U.S. Department of Energy, May, 1981).

4. For President's Coal Commission see *Recommendations and Summary Findings* (Washington, D.C.: The President's Commission on Coal, March 1980). For the government's new coal conversion plan see "DOE Plans Would Add 300 Million tpy of Coalby 1990," *Coal Age*, February, 1980, p. 41; *Wall Street Journal*, February 27, 1980, p. 1. The Administration's coal-conversion plan was subsequently reduced in Senate committee to a \$3.6 billion plan in a "phase I" for mandatory coal conversion for a smaller number of power plants than the Administration had proposed. The targeted plants were primarily in the eastern part of the country, relatively near the coal fields. Many of the plants in the Southwest that currently were using natural gas were eliminated from the phase I coal-conversion list. See Christopher Madison, "Backing Off the Backout Bill," *National Journal*, Vol. 12, No. 25 (June 21, 1980), p. 1023. For 1979 and 1980 total coal export figures, see U.S. Department of Energy, *Monthly Energy Review* (Washington, D.C.: U.S. Government Printing Office, April 24, 1981), p. 58. For steam coal shares, see U.S. Department of Commerce, Bureau of Census, EM522, January 28, 1981. For the World Coal Study, see World Coal Study, *Coal-Bridge to the Future* (Cambridge, MA: Ballinger, 1980) and World Coal Study, *Future Coal Prospects: Country and Regional Assessments* (Cambridge, MA: Ballinger, 1980). For the text of the declaration of the Venice economic summit meeting, see *The New York Times*, July 24, 1980, p. A7. For the Reagan Administration's energy policy, see "The Fiscal Year 1983 Budget Request for the Federal Fossil Energy R&D Program," Prepared Statement of Jan Mares, Assistant Secretary of Energy for Fossil Energy, to the U.S. Senate Subcommittee on Energy Research and Development, Committee on Energy and Natural Resources, March 17, 1982. For various estimates for 1985 coal production, see Earl T. Hayes, "Energy Resources Available to the United States, 1985 to

2000," *Science*, vol. 203, January 19, 1979, p. 236; for 800 million tons 1985 estimate, see *Wall Street Journal*, February 21, 1979, pp. 1, 35. For "there is a lot of it" quote, see General Accounting Office, *U.S. Coal Development —Promises, Uncertainties*, EM-77-43, September 22, 1977, p. 1.1. For factors working to stimulate the use of coal in the short term, see "New Developments Revealed in Moves to Hike U.S. Coal Use," *Oil and Gas Journal*, January 22, 1979, p. 40; U.S. Department of Energy news release, "National Energy Act to Conserve Energy, Accelerate Shift to Coal and Reduce U.S. Oil Import Needs," R-78-413, October 20, 1978.

5. For coal-consumption patterns for the 1950–73 period, see Energy Information Administration, *Annual Report to Congress, Volume III-77*, pp. 78–79; National Electric Reliability Council, *7th Annual Review*, July 1977, p. 8; General Accounting Office, *U.S. Coal Development*, chap. 2; Gordon, "Coal —Swing Fuel," *Energy Supply and Government Policy;* and *1977 Keystone Coal Industry Manual*. For ESECA, see Stuart M. Rosenblum, "The Future of the Coal Substitution Option," *Duquesne Law Review*, 3 (1975), pp. 581–622; Ronald F. Ayres, *Coal: New Markets/New Prices—Ramifications of the Federal Coal Conversion Program* (New York: McGraw-Hill, 1977).

6. General Accounting Office, *U.S. Coal Development*, chap. 2; and ICF, Inc., *Final Report: Production and Consumption of Coal, 1976–1980*, May 1976. For an expression of the Reagan Administration's reliance on the decontrol of oil and natural gas deregulation to increase coal production, see "Coal— The Refocused Federal Program," address by Roger W.A. Le Gassie, Acting Assistant Secretary for Fossil Energy, San Antonio, Texas, June 15, 1981, DOE Release # CONF-810658-1.

7. National Electric Reliability Council, 10th *Annual Review*, August, 1980, p. 11. For statistics and reasons for decline in growth rates of electricity, see Federal Energy Regulatory Commission, *Status of Coal Supply Contracts*, p. 1; *Electrical World*, September, 1981, p. 79; *Coal Week*, April, 1982, p. 1. Energy Information Administration, *Annual Report to Congress, Volume II-77*, p. 215. For the need for managerial innovation in the environmental area see: Marc J. Roberts and Jeremy S. Bluhm, *The Choices of Power: Utilities Facing the Environmental Challenge* (Cambridge, Mass.: Harvard University Press, 1981).

8. U.S. Energy Information Administration, *Impact of Financial Constraints on the Electric Utility Industry*, # DOE/EIA-0311 (Washington, D.C.: Government Printing Office, December, 1981).

9. National Electric Reliability Council, *7th Annual Review*, July 1977, pp. 1, 6–7; *Electrical World*, September 15, 1976, p. 54. Planner in "Planning for Uncertainty," *EPRI Journal*, May, 1978, pp. 6–11.

10. National Electric Reliability Council, "The Coal Strike of 1977–78: Its Impact on the Electric Bulk Power Supply in North America," 1978. Analysts' comments in A. D. Rossin and T. A. Rieck, "Economics of Nuclear Power," *Science*, August 18, 1978, p. 583; National Coal Association, *Study of New*

Mine Additions and Major Expansion Plans of the Coal Industry and the Potential for Future Coal Production, November 1977.

11. For information on the rise of and causes for long-term coal delivery contracts, see ICF, Inc., *Final Report: Coal Mine Expansion Study,* May 1976; General Accounting Office, *U.S. Coal Development,* chap. 4, pp. 1.41–1.42; Federal Power Commission, *Status of Coal Supply Contracts for New Electric Generating Units, 1976–1985,* Staff Report by the Bureau of Power, January 1977; Marvin H. Kahn and Robert Hand, *Implications of Ownership Patterns of Western Coal Reserves and their Impact on Coal Development* (McLean, Va.: The Mitre Corp., 1976); Richard L. Gordon, *U.S. Coal and the Electric Power Industry* (Washington: Resources for the Future, 1975). For 1980 estimates, see *New York Times,* May 16, 1982, p. 28F.

12. For the geographic distribution of coal and for statistical trends according to coal production methods, see *Demonstrated Reserve Base of Coal in the United States on January 1, 1979,* p. 7; Energy Information Administration, *Annual Report to Congress 1980, Volume II,* pp. 127–135. But uncertainty exists over coal reserve and "heat value" estimates; see Francis X. Murray, ed., *Where We Agree: [Final] Report of the National Coal Policy Project* (Boulder: Westview Press, 1978), pp. 76–99; General Accounting Office, *Inaccurate Estimates of Western Coal Reserves Should Be Corrected,* EM-78-32, July 11, 1978.

13. For 1981 domestic coal distribution figures by transportation mode, see U.S. Department of Energy, *Coal Distribution—1981* (Washington, D.C.: Government Printing Office, April, 1982), p. 16. Federal Power Commission, *Status of Coal Supply Contracts for New Electric Generating Units, 1976–1985.*

14. Federal Energy Regulatory Commission, *Status of Coal Supply Contracts,* pp. 31–37.

15. Congressional Research Service, *National Energy Transportation: Issues and Problems,* vol. 3, March 1978, pp. 473–476. For the conflict over high freight rates and level coal prices see "Freight Rate Stakes: Playing For Keeps," *Coal Age,* October 1979, p. 11; "White House Seeks Coal Transportation Policy Agreement," *Coal Age,* February 1980, p. 19; *New York Times,* March 25, 1980, p. A18.

16. National Coal Association, *Coal News,* No. 4403, January 20, 1978, p. 2; U.S. Congress, Office of Technology Assessment, *A Technology Assessment of Coal Slurry Pipelines* (Washington, D.C.: OTA, March 1978); "Why Coal Gasification is Leaving the West," *Business Week,* September 13, 1976, pp. 76J–76K; "Coal Transporters Face Challenge," *Coal Age,* January 1977, pp. 13–15, *Coal Week,* April 19, 1982, p. 1. One coal slurry pipeline clearly was a deterrent to high rail rates. In 1957 Consolidation Coal Company built a 108-mile coal slurry pipeline in Ohio. But in 1963 Consolidation stopped operation of the slurry pipeline after the railroads lowered their freight rates. Today in the West the railroads are attempting to capitalize on their seeming monopoly position in coal transportation. But again, the threat of coal slurry

pipelines, along with other factors, such as the inertia of the regulatory process, tends to keep rail rates lower than they otherwise would be. See Martin B. Zimmerman, *Rent and Regulation in Unit-Train Rate Determination: Regional Discrimination and Inter-Fuel Competition,* MIT Energy Laboratory Working Paper, MIT-EL 78-010WP, revised June 1978.

17. *Coal Age,* August 1978, p. 45; *Oil and Gas Journal,* July 21, 1978, newsletter; "Slurry Line Clears Kansas Right-of-Way Hurdle," *Oil and Gas Journal,* March 5, 1979, p. 71; General Accounting Office, *Coal Slurry Pipelines: Progress and Problems For New Ones,* CED-79-49, April 20, 1979; *New York Times,* May 16, 1982, p. 28F; *Coal Week,* March 29, 1982, p. 1.

18. Private communication, Harry Perry to author, July 1978; "Revised Air Standards Will Influence Coal Mining and Burning," *Coal Age,* September 1978, p. 9; "EPA Proposes Strict New Sulfur Curbs." *Oil and Gas Journal,* September 18, 1978, p. 69; "Rep. Luken (D.–Ohio) Pushes for Amendments to Clean Air Act," *Coal Age,* February 1982, p. 9; "While Congress Lags, the EPA Forges Ahead With Clean Air Act," *Coal Act,* May, 1982, p. 9; *Coal Outlook,* May 10, 1982, pp. 1, 4. For leasing, see U.S. Department of Energy, Leasing Policy Development Office, *Federal Coal Leasing and 1985 and 1990 Regional Coal Production Forecasts,* June 1978; Congressional Research Service, *The Coal Industry: Problems and Prospects—A Background Study* (Washington, D.C.: Government Printing Office, 1978), pp. 67–81; "Bureau of Land Management Offers Largest Coal Lease Sale Ever," *Coal Age,* April, 1982, p. 11; "Interior Department Proposals Would Slash Coal Lease Legislation," "OSM Proposes Enforcement Changes," "The West Striving for Overcapacity," *Coal Age,* February, 1982, pp. 17, 29, and 65.

19. For the environmental effects of coal, see General Accounting Office, *U.S. Coal Development;* Richard L. Gordon, "The Hobbling of Coal: Policy and Regulatory Uncertainties," *Science,* April 14, 1978, pp. 153–158; *Report of the Committee on Health and Environmental Effects of Increased Coal Utilization,* December 27, 1977 (henceforth called *The Rall Committee Report,* after the committee's chairman, David P. Rall, director of the National Institute of Environmental Health Sciences); C. E. Chrisp, G. L. Fisher, and J. E. Lammert, "Mutagenicity of Filtrates from Respirable Coal Fly Ash," *Science,* 199 (January 6, 1978), pp. 73–75. For a comparative study that emphasizes the uncertainty and complexity in surface mine land reclamation, see Daniel Philip Wiener, *Reclaiming the West* (New York: Inform, Inc., 1980).

20. For the need for better data on acid rain, see "Acid Rainfall Arouses Public Interest in U.S. and Europe," *Coal Age,* November 1979, p. 13.

21. For information on carbon dioxide emissions from coal (and other fossil fuels) see National Academy of Sciences, *Energy and Climate: Outer Limits to Growth?* (Washington, D.C.: NAS Geophysics Board, 1977); *New York Times,* June 10, 1977, p. A28; *New York Times,* July 25, 1977, pp. 1, 37; George M. Woodwell, "The Carbon Dioxide Question," *Scientific American,* January 1978, pp. 34–43; Richard A. Kerr, "Carbon Dioxide and Climate:

Carbon Budget Still Unbalanced," *Science*, September 30, 1977, pp. 1352–1353; U. Sigenthaler and H. Oeschger, "Predicting Future Atmospheric Carbon Dioxide Levels," *Science*, January 27, 1978, pp. 388–395; "Energy Agency to Study Carbon Dioxide," *Chemical and Engineering News*, December 5, 1977, p. 4; William W. Kellogg, "Is Mankind Warming the Earth," *The Bulletin of the Atomic Scientists*, February 1975, pp. 10–19; *New York Times*, June 9, 1979, p. 12; Department of Energy, *Status Report: Carbon Dioxide Effects Research and Assessment Program*, Vol. 1, No. 1 (July 1979) and Vol. 1, No. 2 (January 1980). For an informed nuclear advocate's views see Alvin M. Weinberg, "Is Nuclear Energy Necessary?" *Bulletin of Atomic Scientists*, March 1980, pp. 31–35. For doubts on the catastrophic effects of CO_2 see "Making the Most of the CO_2 Problem," *Science News*, April 14, 1979; Luther J. Carter, "Panel Says Synfuels Pose No CO_2 Hazard for Now," *Science*, Vol. 205, August 31, 1979, p. 884.

22. *The Rall Committee Report.* For the Massachusetts utility, *The Boston Globe*, May 21, 1978, p. 21. However, the Federal Energy Regulatory Commission estimated in 1978 that 43 percent of new coal-fired generating capacity between 1977 and 1981 will use scrubbers to meet air-quality standards. See Federal Energy Regulatory Commission, *Status of Coal Supply Contracts*, pp. 38–42.

23. For the early twentieth century history of labor relations in the U.S. coal industry, see United Mine Workers of America, *It's Your Union, Pass It On*, September 1976; Hoyt N. Wheeler, "Mountaineer Mine Wars: An Analysis of the West Virginia Mine Wars of 1912–1913 and 1920–1921," *Business History Review*, 50 (Spring 1976), 69–91; Alicia Tyler, "Dust to Dust," *Washington Monthly*, January 1975, pp. 49–58; Melvyn Dubofsky and Warren Van Tine, *John L. Lewis: A Biography* (New York: Quadrangle, 1977).

24. Figures on the U.S. coal industry employment and union membership come from the following sources: *1977 Keystone Coal Industry Manual*, p. 550; United Mine Workers of America, *It's Your Union, Pass It On; Wall Street Journal*, October 5, 1977, p. 44; and *New York Times*, February 26, 1978, sec. III, pp. 2, 16. The "new breed" in *New York Times*, September 1, 1977, pp. 33, 39; for attraction of skilled labor, see *Wall Street Journal*, November 10, 1978, p. 1. For 1980, UMW production contribution and median age figures, see personal communication with Bituminous Coal Operators Association, May 17, 1982. For threat of wildcat strikes in 1982, see *New York Times*, May 16, 1982, p. 28F.

25. General Accounting Office, *U.S. Coal Development*, chap. 4; U.S. Department of Labor/U.S. Department of Energy, *Determinants of Coal Mine Labor Productivity Change*, DOE/IR/0056 (Washington, D.C.: U.S. Government Printing Office, November 1979). For recommendations to improve coal workforce productivity, see John Short and Associates, *A Study to Determine the Manpower and Training Needs of the Coal Mining Industry*, #PB80-164742 (Springfield, VA: NTIS, December 1979). For 1980–1981

productivity increases, see Merrill Lynch, Pierce, Fenner and Smith, Inc., *Coal Industry Quarterly*, August, 1981, p. 33.

26. For an in-depth discussion on the results and implications of the diverse attempts by certain representative coal companies to innovate in the area of management organizational structure, personnel, and labor relations, see Balaji Chakravarthy, *Managing Coal: A Challenge in Adaptation* (Albany, N.Y.: State University of New York Press, 1981). For the overall need and opportunities for improving the management of the coal work force, see Congressional Research Service, *The Coal Industry*, chap. 7.

27. *Kentucky Coal Mining Corporation (A-C)*, ICH 9-678-101-103 (Boston: Intercollegiate Case Clearinghouse, 1977). For the mixed success of an attempt in the mid-1970's to restructure the workforce organization in a unionized coal mine see, "Rushton 'Quality of Work' Experiment: Mixed Results," *Coal Age*, January 1980, pp. 19–21.

28. For observers stressing coal's negative social effects, see Harry M. Caudill, *Night Comes to the Cumberlands* (Boston: Atlantic, Little, Brown, 1962); Dick Kirschten, "Troubles of the 'Eastern Tilt,' " *National Journal*, 10, No. 12 (March 25, 1978), pp. 461–464; Kai T. Erikson, *Everything in Its Path: Destruction of a Community in the Buffalo Creek Flood* (New York: Simon and Schuster, 1976). For the positive and adaptive aspects of the communities in the Eastern coal-field regions, see the review of *Everything in Its Path* by Dwight Billings and Sally Maggard in *Social Forces*, vol. 52:2, December 1978, pp. 722–723; and Harry K. Schwarzweller, James S. Brown, and J. J. Mangalam, *Mountain Families in Transition* (University Park: The Pennsylvania State University Press, 1971). For the miners' new prosperity, see *Wall Street Journal*, November 10, 1978, p. 1.

29. Information on petroleum-firm activity in the U.S. coal industry comes from the following sources: U.S. Bureau of Mines, *The State of the U.S. Coal Industry*, Information Circular IC 8707, 1976; *Note on the U.S. Coal Industry*, ICH 9-676-133 (Boston: Intercollegiate Case Clearinghouse, 1976); U.S. Congress, Senate, *Interfuel Competition: Hearings Before the Subcommittee on Antitrust and Monopoly of the Committee on the Judiciary* (Washington, D.C.: Government Printing Office, June 17, 18, 19, July 14, October 21 and 22, 1975); U.S. Congress, Senate, *Petroleum Industry Involvement in Alternative Sources of Energy*, Prepared at the request of Frank Church for the Subcommittee on Energy Research and Development of the Committee on Energy and Natural Resources, Publication No. 95-54, September 1977; *Submission of Exxon Company, U.S.A., before the House Judiciary Committee on Monopolies and Commercial Law*, September 11, 1975.

30. For arguments in favor of divestiture, see Herbert S. Sanger, Jr., and William E. Mason, *The Structure of the Energy Markets: A Report of TVA's Antitrust Investigation of the Coal and Uranium Industries, and Appendices A-H*, June 14, 1977; Walter Adams, "Horizontal Divestiture in the Petroleum Industry: An Affirmative Case," in Edward J. Mitchell, ed., *Horizontal Divestiture in the Oil Industry* (Washington, D.C.: American Enterprise Institute for Public

Policy Research, 1978), pp. 7–19; *Coal Patrol,* 33 (August 5, 1977), pp. 8–10.

31. Evidence against divestiture can be found in U.S. Federal Trade Commission, *Concentration Levels and Trends in the Energy Sector of the U.S. Economy,* March 1974; Jesse W. Markham, Anthony P. Hourihan, and Francis L. Sterling, *Horizontal Divestiture and the Petroleum Industry* (Cambridge, Mass.: Ballinger, 1977), p. 105; U.S. Department of Treasury, *Implications of Divestiture,* June 1976; Donald Norman, *The Performance of Oil Firm Affiliates in the Coal Industry,* American Petroleum Institute, Research Study #004, March 1977; National Coal Association, *Implications of Investments in the Coal Industry by Firms from Other Energy Industries,* September 1977; General Accounting Office, *The State of Competition in the Coal Industry,* EMD-78-22, December 30, 1977; *Oil and Gas Journal,* April 10, 1978, newsletter. Actually, economists usually measure market concentration rather than concentration of production. But in the case of coal, production and market concentration are so congruent that production concentration is an accurate indicator of market concentration and can be substituted as the measure used. For data on control of reserves, see Hossein G. Askari, Timothy W. Reufli, and Michael P. Kennedy, *Horizontal Divestiture of Energy Companies and Alternative Policies* (Austin: Graduate School of Business, The University of Texas at Austin, undated), p. 13. For data on control of production, and on coal-company shares, see American Petroleum Institute, *Market Shares and Individual Company Data for U.S. Energy Markets: 1950–1980* (Washington, D.C.: API, October 9, 1981), pp. 120, 130. For oil-company share of total research and development, see Norman, *The Performance of Oil Firm Affiliates in the Coal Industry.*

32. A recent case suggests that the threat or possibility of legal or legislative considerations like horizontal divestiture may already be influencing the actions of top management at coal companies. In early September 1978 Amax rejected an offer to merge with Standard Oil of California (Socal), the fourth largest U.S. petroleum company. Socal, which already owned 20 percent of Amax's common stock, proposed acquiring an additional 25 to 39 percent of Amax's common stock. But Amax claimed that the offer raised "serious and substantial antitrust questions." Its chairman added that such antitrust considerations "raise grave doubt as to the feasibility of any such proposal and would in any event involve long delays and great uncertainties." On the other hand, Socal's chairman commented that it was "unfortunate" that the Amax board "had taken refuge in supposed antitrust problems." See *Wall Street Journal,* September 8, 1978, p. 10.

33. For ways to preserve competition short of divestiture, see *New York Times,* April 23, 1977, pp. 25, 27; Askari *et al., Horizontal Divestiture of Energy Companies; Oil and Gas Journal,* April 10, 1977, newsletter. For the estimate of the federal share of Western coal reserves, see "Major Decisions Near on Federal Leasing," *Coal Age,* November 1978, pp. 11–12. For leasing program in Reagan Administration, see note 18 above.

34. For General Electric, utilities, and U.S. Steel, see National Coal Association,

Implications of Investment in the Coal Industry; 1981 *Keystone Coal Industry Manual,* p. 714; Louis Kraar, "General Electric's Very Personal Merger," *Fortune,* August 1977, pp. 187–194. For FERC Study, see *Coal Week,* March 1, 1982, p. 1.

35. For the establishment of the Peabody Holding Company and on the members of this holding company, see *1977 Keystone Coal Industry Manual,* pp. 546, 770; "Splicing Together the Peabody Deal," *Business Week,* November 1, 1976, p. 24; Carol J. Loomis, "Down the Chute with Peabody Coal," *Fortune,* May 1977, pp. 228–248; *New York Times,* June 8, 1977, pp. 47, 56; "FTC Approves Sale of Peabody," *Coal Age,* July, 1977, p. 27; Western Gasification Company, *Coal Gasification: A Technical Description,* revised April 1, 1974. The composition of the shares in the Peabody Holding Company was as follows: Newmont Mining Corporation—27.5 percent, Williams Company—27.5 percent, Bechtel Corporation—15 percent, the Boeing Company—15 percent, Fluor Corporation—10 percent, and Equitable Life Assurance—5 percent. For a chronology of DuPont's takeover of Continental Oil, see: Appendix 1 in Richard S. Ruback, "The Conoco Takeover and Stockholder Returns," *Sloan Management Review,* Winter, 1982, pp. 25–29.

36. Multiorganizational and multisector enterprises are discussed in Mel Horwitch and C. K. Prahalad, "Managing Technological Innovation: Three Ideal Modes," *Sloan Management Review,* Winter 1976, pp. 77–89; and Mel Horwitch, "Uncontrolled Growth and Unfocused Growth: Unsuccessful Life Cycles of Large-Scale, Public-Private, Technological Enterprises, With Special Reference to the United States SST Program and the United States Attempt to Develop Synthetic Fuels from Coal," Paper presented at the Symposium on the Management of Science and Technology, in Rio de Janeiro, June 22–23, 1978, to be published in *Interdisciplinary Science Reviews;* Mel Horwitch, "Designing and Managing Large-Scale, Public-Private, Technological Enterprises: A State of the Art Review," *Technology in Society,* Vol. 1 (1979), pp. 179–192.

37. For large-scale mining/synthetic fuels projects in the West, see Federal Energy Administration, *Western Coal Development Monitoring System,* Summer Quarter, FEA/G-77-306, August 1, 1977; *1977 Keystone Coal Industry Manual; Pacific Lighting: Wesco,* ICH 9-377-889 (Boston: Intercollegiate Case Clearinghouse, 1977); *The ConPaso Coal Reserve Project,* ICH 4-678-152 (Boston: Intercollegiate Case Clearinghouse, 1978); "Two Gas Companies Plan Commercial Coal-Gas Plant," *Coal Age,* May 1977, p. 17.

38. For the traditional technological innovation process in the coal industry, see E. Mansfield, "Firm Size and Technological Change in the Petroleum and Bituminous Coal Industries," in Thomas D. Duchesneau, ed., *Competition in the U.S. Energy Industry* (Cambridge, Mass.: Ballinger, 1975), pp. 317–345; *Coal Mining: Research and Development,* Society of Mining Engineers, February 28, 1978; N. P. Chironis, "Consol's Record Production Runs Give Impetus to Use of Shield Supports for U.S. Longwalls," *Coal Age,* August 1976, pp. 92–97; "Productivity Perspective," "Underground Mining," and

"Surface Mining" in *Coal Age,* July 1976, pp. 63–169. For fluidized-bed combustion, see "Energy Department Will Emphasize Direct Coal Combustion," *Coal Age,* January 1979, p. 9; U.S. Department of Interior, Office of Coal Research, *Clean Energy from Coal Technology* (Washington, D.C.: Government Printing Office, 1974), p. 41; U.S. Energy Research and Development Administration, Office of Fossil Energy, *Power and Combustion,* October-December 1975 (Washington: ERDA, 1976), pp. 1–13, 25–33, 51–53; U.S. Federal Power Commission, *The Status of Flue Gas Desulfurization Applications in the United States: A Technological Assessment,* a Staff report by the Bureau of Power, July 1977, pp. III–56 to III–65; U.S. Department of Energy, *International Coal Technology Summary Document* (Washington, D.C.: Office of Technical Programs Evaluation, December 1978), pp. 19–29; General Accounting Office, *How to Burn Coal Efficiently and Economically, and Meet Air Pollution Requirements—The Fluidized Bed Combustion Process,* EMD-80-12, November 9, 1979; "Dirty Coal Burns Clean in Fluidized Bed," *Coal Age,* November 1979, pp. 88–93. Walter C. Patterson and Richard Griffin, *Fluidized-Bed Technology: Coming to a Boil* (New York: Inform, Inc., 1978).

39. For South Africa, see Roger Vielvoye, "South Africa's Optimistic Outlook," *Oil and Gas Journal,* January 15, 1979, p. 41; "Liquid Coal Looks Good as Hunt Heats Up for Other Oils," *Financial Times World Business Weekly,* February 26, 1979, pp. 9–11; "U.K., South Africa Boosts Oil-from-Coal Work," *Oil and Gas Journal,* March 5, 1979, p. 78; *New York Times,* March 8, 1979, pp. D1, D4. For the history of pre-1960 U.S. synthetic fuels policy, see Richard E. Vietor, "The Synthetic Liquid Fuels Program: Energy Politics in the Truman Era," *Business History Review,* Vol. LIV, No. 1 (Spring 1980), pp. 1–34. The brief history of U.S. synthetic fuels development in the sixties comes from the following sources: *Chemical Week,* April 13, 1963, p. 69; August 3, 1963, pp. 63–64; November 18, 1964, p. 23; May 28, 1966, p. 110; December 3, 1966, p. 76; December 30, 1967, p. 40; March 2, 1968, p. 50; March 23, 1968, p. 67; May 11, 1968, p. 59; June 15, 1968, p. 41; June 29, 1968, p. 13. *Coal Age,* April 1965, p. 55; January 1966, pp. 64–71; April 1966, p. 46; January 1967, pp. 90–92; March 1967, p. 48; September 1967, pp. 64–68; March 1968, pp. 40–42; December 1968, pp. 26–27; May 1969, p. 50; July 1969, p. 44. For an overview of U.S. synfuels policy and decision making between 1944 and 1980, see Mel Horwitch and Richard Vietor, "The Political Management of Synthetic Fuels: A Retrospective Appraisal," submitted for publication July, 1980.

40. For synthetic gas cost estimates, see Roger Detman, C. F. Braun and Company, *Preliminary Economic Comparison of Six Processes for Pipeline Gas from Coal,* Presentation to the Eighth Synthetic Pipeline Gas Symposium, Chicago, Illinois, October 18–20, 1976; *Chemical Week,* December 23, 1970, p. 23. For synthetic crude estimates, see Earl T. Hayes, "Energy Resources Available to the United States, 1985 to 2000," *Science,* vol. 203, January 19, 1979, p. 238. For Coalcon, see Luther J. Carter, "Synfuels: Data Gap Imperils

'Coalcon' Demonstration," *Science*, vol. 195, January 7, 1977, p. 38; General Accounting Office, *First Federal Attempt to Demonstrate a Synthetic Fossil Energy Technology—A Failure*, EMD-77-59, August 17, 1977. For the need for a liquefaction capability, see L. E. Swabb, Jr., "Liquid Fuels from Coal: From R&D to an Industry," *Science*, vol. 199, February 10, 1978, pp. 619–622. For the shifts in government coal technology strategies, see "Carter Budget Cuts Coal, Oil Outlays," *Oil and Gas Journal*, January 29, 1979, pp. 94–96; "Coming This Spring: Son of National Energy Plan" and "Energy Department Will Emphasize Direct Coal Combustion," *Coal Age*, January 1979, p. 9; U.S. Department of Energy news release, "DOE Authorizes Both Competitors to Proceed with Coal-to-Gas Demonstration Plant Designs," R-79-035, January 23, 1979.

41. By 1979, certain recent studies had already indicated that the cost of high-BTU synthetic gas may be economically competitive with the delivered cost of coal-fired electric residential heating; see Patrick Crow, "Prospects Seem Brighter for U.S. LNG and SNG," *Oil and Gas Journal*, January 16, 1978, pp. 23–28; William F. Hederman, Jr., *Prospects for the Commercialization of High-BTU Coal Gasification*, R-2294, Rand Corp., April 1, 1978, pp. 23–25, append. D. For the status of the U.S. synfuels effort in early 1979, see U.S. Senate, Committee on Energy and Natural Resources, *Synthetic Fuels from Coal: Status and Outlook of Coal Gasification and Liquefaction*, Publication No. 96-17 (Washington, D.C.: Government Printing Office, June 1979). For a comparison of the various 1979 synfuels proposals, see Congressional Research Service, *The Pros and Cons of a Crash Program to Commercialize Synfuels*, report prepared for the House Subcommittee on Energy Development and Applications of the House Committee on Science and Technology (Washington, D.C.: Government Printing Office, February 1980), Appendix I, pp. 66–76. For the synfuel interest in the House in the spring of 1979 and for the House synfuels proposal, see U.S. House, Committee on Banking, Finance, and Urban Affairs, Subcommittee on Economic Stabilization, *To Extend and Amend the Defense Production Act of 1950*, Hearings on March 13, 14, April 4, 25, and May 5, 1979 (Washington, D.C.: Government Printing Office, 1979). For the high-level private lobbying for synfuels in Washington in the spring of 1979, see the *Washington Post*, June 10, 1979. For the large, high-BTU gasification project, see DOE news release # FE-747, "FERC Grants Approval to Great Plains Coal Gasification Project," November 15, 1979. For the new large liquefaction projects, see "Interest Building in Coal-Based Synfuels," *Oil and Gas Journal*, March 10, 1980, pp. 50–51. For various warnings and expressions of caution about a crash, massive synfuels effort, see *Helping Insure Our Energy Future: A Program for Developing Synthetic Fuel Plants Now* (New York: Committee for Economic Development, July 29, 1979); Edward W. Merrow, Stephen W. Chapel, and Christopher Worthing, *A Review of Cost Estimation in New Technologies: Implications for Energy Process Plants* (# R-2481-DOE) (Santa Monica, California: Rand Corporation, July 1979); Luther J. Carter, "Synfuels Crash

Program Viewed as Risky," *Science*, Vol. 205 (September 7, 1979), pp. 765–979; Mel Horwitch, *Statement on the Proposed Energy Security Corporation*, *Congressional Record—Senate*, October 31, 1979, pp. 15591–92; *New York Times*, July 6, 1979, pp. A1, D3; *New York Times*, August 8, 1979, p. D13. On the other hand, for reports that downplay immediate adverse environmental impacts of a crash effect, see Luther J. Carter, "Panel Says Synfuels Pose No CO_2 Hazard Now," *Science*, Vol. 205 (August 31, 1979), p. 884; U.S. Department of Energy, *Environmental Analysis of Synthetic Liquid Fuels*, #DOE/EV-0044 (Washington, D.C.: U.S. Department of Energy, July 12, 1979). For the intensive synfuels lobbying in 1980, see the *Wall Street Journal*, February 25, 1980, pp. 1, 31. For the emerging shape of the synfuels program, see *New York Times*, March 5, 1980, p. A1; *Wall Street Journal*, February 27, 1980, p. 1; "Conferees Break Deadlock, Approve Synfuels Bill," *Oil and Gas Journal*, March 10, 1980, pp. 54–55. For passage of the bill that created the U.S. Synthetic Fuels Corporation, see *The New York Times*, July 1, 1980, pp. D1, D4. For the Reagan Administration's synfuels policies, see *New York Times*, May 5, 1982, pp. D1, D2; "The U.S. Government Program and Policies for Coal Liquefaction," remarks by Roger W.A. Le Gassie, Deputy Assistant Secretary for Fossil Energy, to the Coal Liquefaction Symposium, October 21, 1981.

42. Federal R&D in U.S. Congress, Senate, *Energy Research and Development —Problems and Prospects*, Prepared at the request of Henry M. Jackson, chairman, Committee on Interior and Insular Affairs, Serial No. 93-21 (92-56), (Washington, D.C.: Government Printing Office, 1973); General Accounting Office, *U.S. Coal Development*, app. III; National Coal Association, *Special Analysis: Federal Funding for Activities Concerned with Coal—Fiscal Years 1979 and 1980*, June 18, 1979; "The Fiscal Year 1983 Budget Request for the Federal Fossil Energy R&D Program," prepared Statement of Jan Mures. Industry R&D in Markham, *et al.*, *Horizontal Divestiture and the Petroleum Industry*; Norman, *The Performance of Oil Firm Affiliates in the Coal Industry*; and U.S. Congress, Senate, *Petroleum Industry Involvement in Alternative Sources of Energy*. Synthetic fuels projects are identified in U.S. Bureau of Mines, *Projects to Expand Fuel Sources in Western States*, IC 8719, 1976.

43. For the recent history and various forecasts of the world coal trade, see U.S. Department of Energy, *[Draft] Interim Report of the Interagency Coal Export Task Force*, #DOE/FE-0012 (Washington, D.C.: Department of Energy, January 1981). For 1979–1981 U.S. coal export figures, see U.S. Department of Energy, *Monthly Energy Review*, March 1982 (Washington, D.C.: U.S. Government Printing Office, March 24, 1982), p. 58; National Coal Association, *International Coal Review*, February 12, 1982. For the issue of dedging coal ports, see U.S. Office of Technology Assessment, *Coal Exports and Port Development: A Technical Memorandum*, (Washington, D.C.: Office of Technology Assessment, April, 1981); Christopher Madison, "Money for Deeper U.S. Coal Ports—Needed or Just More Pork Barrel?" *National Journal*, February 7, 1981, pp. 225–228. For corporate strategy and managerial

factors related to coal exports, see Harry Bruce, Mel Horwitch, and Pedro Nueno, "The Evolution of the International Coal Trade: A Strategic and Decision Making Perspective," Paper presented at the Academy of International Management–European International Business Association, December 17–19, 1981, *Journal of International Business Studies,* forthcoming.

44. For the National Coal Policy Project, see *Where We Agree: [Draft] Report of the National Coal Policy Project,* February 9, 1978, p. 2 (the final report of this group is Francis X. Murray, ed., *Where We Agree: Report of the National Coal Policy Project*); *The Boston Globe,* February 10, 1978, p. 23; Tom Alexander, "A Promising Try at Environmental Détente for Coal," *Fortune,* February 13, 1978, pp. 94–102; National Coal Association, *Coal News,* no. 4451, December 22, 1978, p. 2; private communication between Francis X. Murray and author in March 1980; and various personal interviews in 1978.

Chapter 5 | *Nuclear Power: The Promise Melts Away*

1. For Project Independence, see U.S. Federal Energy Administration, *Project Independence Report* (Washington, D.C.: Government Printing Office, 1974). Chirac's statement was part of his remarks opening the First Conference of the European Nuclear Society, held in Paris, April 1975. See also the Energy Policy Project of the Ford Foundation, *A Time to Choose: America's Energy Future, Final Report* (Cambridge, Mass.: Ballinger, 1974); and U.S. Atomic Energy Commission, Office of Planning and Analysis, *Nuclear Power Growth, 1974–2000,* WASH-1139(74) (Washington, D.C.: Government Printing Office, February 1974).

2. This, of course, is a highly simplified account of some very complex circumstances. For a detailed, book-length account of Three Mile Island see: Daniel Martin, *Three Mile Island: Prologue or Epilogue* (Cambridge, Mass.: Ballinger Publishing Co., 1980). See also Harold W. Lewis, "The Safety of Fission Reactors," *Scientific American,* March 1980, pp. 53–65. For an account by a prominent anti-nuclear activist, see: Daniel F. Ford, *Three Mile Island* (Penguin Books, Baltimore, 1982).

3. The "anti-nuclear" literature is enormous. One of the best books is McKinley C. Olsen's *Unacceptable Risk* (New York: Bantam, 1976). See also Joel Primack and Frank von Hipple, "Challenging the Atomic Energy Commission on Reactor Safety," in *Advice and Dissent: Scientists in the Public Arena* (New York: New American Library, 1974). For a more complete set of references to the literature, see Irvin C. Bupp and Jean-Claude Derian, *Light Water: How the Nuclear Dream Dissolved* (New York: Basic Books, 1978); and Amory B. Lovins, *Soft Energy Paths* (San Francisco: Friends of the Earth, 1977).

4. Calculated as follows:
   a. Operation at 100 percent of capacity = (624 million barrels per year of oil, most residual fuel oil ÷ 365 days per year) ÷ (358,000 GW hours per year

via oil ÷ 8,760 GW hours per year of potential output per each GW of capacity) = 42,000 barrels of oil per day

b. At actual 1977 operating rate = 42,000 barrels of oil per day per each GW operating at 100 percent of capacity × (2,125,000 GW hours per year total actual ÷ 515 GW × 8,760 hours possible output per year) = 42,000 × .47 = 20,000 barrels of oil per day

Source: U.S. Department of Energy, *Monthly Energy Review*, June 1978, pp. 33–34. For 1979 operating statistics, see U.S. Department of Energy, *Monthly Energy Review*, November 1979.

5. David Bodansky, "Electricity Generation Choices for the Near Term," *Science*, Vol. 207, February 15, 1980, pp. 721–727. See also National Research Council, *Energy in Transition: 1985–2010; Final Report of the Committee on Nuclear and Alternative Energy Systems* (National Academy of Sciences, Washington, D.C., 1979) And: Hans H. Landsberg, *et al.*, *Energy: The Next Twenty Years;* Report by a Study Group sponsored by the Ford Foundation and administered by Resources for the Future (Cambridge, Mass.: Ballinger Publishing Co., 1979), chap. 2.

6. This section draws heavily on Bupp and Derian, *Light Water.* See also Richard G. Hewlett and Francis Duncan, *Atomic Shield 1947–1952; A History of the USAEC,* vol. 2 (University Park: Pennsylvania State University Press, 1969); and Richard G. Hewlett and Francis Duncan, *Nuclear Navy, 1946–1962* (Chicago: University of Chicago Press, 1974).

7. "The Jersey Central Report," *Atomic Industrial Forum Memo,* 11, no. 3 (March 1964).

8. See, for example, *Nuclear News* (formerly *Atomic Industrial Forum Memo*), 11 (January 1968). For Weinberg quote, see U.S. Congress, Joint Committee on Atomic Energy, *Nuclear Power Economics—1962 through 1967,* 90 Cong., 2 sess. (Washington, D.C.: Government Printing Office, February 1968), p. 5.

9. Irvin C. Bupp, "Priorities in Nuclear Technology: Program Prosperity and Decay in the United States Atomic Energy Commission, 1956–1971," Ph.D. thesis, Harvard University, 1971.

10. Harold P. Green and Alan Rosenthal, *Government of the Atom: The Integration of Powers* (New York: Atherton Press, 1963).

11. U.S. Congress, Joint Committee on Atomic Energy, *AEC Authorizing Legislation Fiscal Year 1968,* 90 Cong., 1 sess. (Washington, D.C.: Government Printing Office, March 1967), part 2, pp. 660–662, 667–900, and throughout.

12. Bupp and Derian, *Light Water,* chap. 1.

13. Bupp and Derian, chap. 9. See also Spurgeon Keeny *et al., Nuclear Power: Issues and Choices* (Cambridge, Mass.: Ballinger, 1977); and U.S. Congress, Committee on Government Operations, *Nuclear Power Costs,* 95 Cong., 2 sess. (Washington, D.C.: Government Printing Office, April 1978). For an industry defense of nuclear power's recent economic performance, see A. D. Rossin and T. A. Rieck, "Economics of Nuclear Power," *Science,* vol. 201, no. 18, August 1978, pp. 582–589.

14. David L. Bodde, "Regulation and Technical Innovation: A Study of the Nuclear Steam Supply System and the Commercial Jet Engine," Doctoral thesis, Graduate School of Business Administration, Harvard University, 1975.

15. H. E. Van, M. J. Whitman, and H. I. Bowers, "Factors Affecting the Historical and Projected Capital Costs of Nuclear Plants in the USA," *Proceedings of the Fourth International Conference on the Peaceful Applications of Atomic Energy,* vol. 2 (Geneva: September 1971), pp. 21–43.

16. William E. Mooz, "Cost Analysis of Light Water Reactor Power Plants," Rand Corp., R-2304-DOE, June 1978. See also Bupp and Derian, chap. 9; Duncan Burn, *Nuclear Power and the Energy Crisis* (London: Trade Policy Research Centre, 1978), chap. 4; U.S. Nuclear Regulatory Commission, "Coal and Nuclear: A Comparison of the Cost of Generating Baseload Electricity by Region," NUREG-0480 (Washington, D.C.: U.S. Government Printing Office, December 1978); U.S. Congress, Committee on Government Operations, *Nuclear Power Costs,* 23rd report, April 1978.

17. Personal communication with the author. I am indebted to Professor Brooks for his advice and comments on this chapter. Naturally, this does not imply that he necessarily agrees with all of the analyses or conclusions.

18. This proposition, stated rather badly here, is the central theme of Bupp and Derian, *Light Water.*

19. *The Risks of Nuclear Power Reactors: A Review of the Nuclear Regulatory Commission's Reactor Safety Study* (Cambridge, Mass.: The Union of Concerned Scientists, August 1977).

20. This argument is developed at length in Bupp and Derian, *Light Water,* chap. 9.

21. State of Wisconsin, Public Service Commission, *Advance Plans for Construction of Facilities—Findings of Fact, Conclusion of Law and Order,* August 17, 1978, p. 15; also, considerable quantitative support for this finding is contained in the appendix to the order. See also State of New York, Public Service Commission, Case 26974, "Proceeding on Motion of the Commission as to the Comparative Economics of Nuclear and Fossil Generating Facilities," Recommended decision by Administrative Law Judge Reed, Albany, December 18, 1978, p. 171; see also pp. 175–181.

22. In 1981, nuclear critic Charles Komanoff published the results of several years of research on the comparative economics of nuclear power: *Power Plant Construction Costs,* published by Komanoff Energy Association, 333 West End Avenue, New York, N.Y. 10023. Komanoff's analysis rests on a comprehensive data base of actual construction and operating costs for nuclear and coal-fired power plants. Although it is possible to disagree with the conclusions he draws, no serious student of nuclear economics can ignore his data or his analytic methods. I am personally indebted to Mr. Komanoff for several stimulating discussions on nuclear economics.

23. Mason Willrich, "Prospects for Nuclear Power in the United States," Paper for the Sixth Annual Symposium of the Uranium Institute, Washington,

D.C., September 1981. Available from the author at Pacific Gas and Electric Co., San Francisco.

24. Alan Jakimo and Irvin C. Bupp, "Nuclear Waste Disposal: Not in My Backyard," *Technology Review*, March/April 1978. See also Charles L. Hebel, *et al.*, *Report to the American Physical Society* by the Study Group on Nuclear Fuel Cycles and Waste Management (Washington, D.C.: American Physical Society, 1977); and Richard G. Hewlett, "Federal Policy for Disposal of Radioactive Wastes from Commercial Nuclear Power Plants," U.S. Department of Energy, March 1979.

25. See Amory Lovins, *et al.*, "Nuclear Power and Nuclear Bombs," *Foreign Affairs*, July 1980. See also Theodore B. Taylor and Mason Willrich, *Nuclear Thefts: Risks and Safeguards* (Cambridge, Mass.: Ballinger, 1975); John McPhee, *The Curve of Binding Energy* (New York: Farrar, Straus and Giroux, 1974); and Daniel Yergin, "The Terrifying Prospect: Atomic Bombs Everywhere," *Atlantic Monthly*, April 1977.

26. Michael Brenner, *Splicing the Atom: The Remaking of U.S. Non-Proliferation Policy* (New York, Cambridge University Press, 1980).

27. Testimony to the U.S. House of Representatives, Committee on Government Operations, Subcommittee on Environment, Natural Resources and Energy, September 22, 1977.

28. Statement of A. Z. Roisman and S. J. Scherr on behalf of the Natural Resources Defense Council before the House Committee on Interior and Insular Affairs, January 25, 1979.

29. Executive Office of the President, Office of Science and Technology Policy, *Report of the Subgroup on Alternative Technology Strategies*, Interagency Review Group on Nuclear Waste Management, August 7, 1978.

30. Daniel S. Metlay and Gene I. Rochlin, "Radioactive Waste Management in the United States"; a paper prepared for the RESOLVE Nuclear Waste Management Press Review Workshop, Palo Alto, Ca., December 1979. See also Office of Science and Technology Policy, *Alternative Technology Strategies for the Isolation of Nuclear Wastes: Report of Subgroup One*, September 8, 1978; see also U.S. Department of Energy, *Final Report of the Task Force for Review of Nuclear Waste Management*, March 1979.

31. Keeny, *et al.*, *Nuclear Power: Issues and Choices*, chaps. 8, 11, and 12.

32. "Message from the President of the United States Transmitting a Report on his Proposals for a Comprehensive Radioactive Waste Management Program" (Washington, D.C.: U.S. Government Printing Office).

33. Bupp and Derian, *Light Water*, op. cit., chap. 8, pp. 132–134. See also Calvert Cliff's Coordinating Committee v. USAEC, 449 F.2d 1109 (1971).

For an excellent summary of these issues, see "Statement of Position of the California Energy Commission in the Matter of Proposed Rulemaking on the Storage and Disposal of Nuclear Wastes," California Energy Commission, Sacramento, CA, July 1980.

34. This section draws heavily on: Wm. Walker and Mans Lonnroth, "Survival and Leadership in the World Nuclear Industry: The Impact of Recession and

Structural Change on Nuclear Trade Relations," December 1981, draft (to be published in 1982 by the Rockefeller Foundation).

35. It is an open question whether the worldwide slowdown in the rate of growth of nuclear power significantly lessens the problem of nuclear weapons proliferation. The temptation, of course, is to see the slowdown as "good news" in this regard. But many analysts correctly point out that slowdowns or even cancellations of large-scale reactor development programs have no necessary effect on clandestine nuclear weapons acquisition by countries using small-scale, non-power-producing facilities.

Indeed, one can logically regard the pattern of a couple of hundred nuclear power plants spread thinly across thirty-five to forty countries as a sort of "worst of all possible" outcomes: greatly diminished potential for significant contribution to energy supply, combined with undiminished potential for weapons proliferation or even the occurrence of catastrophic accidents.

For a cogent statement of this position see: Pierre Lellouche, "Breaking the Rules Without Stopping the Bomb," Institut Français des Relations Internationales, Paris, 1980.

36. This particular phrase has been used by Amory Lovins.

37. Charles Komanoff, *Power Plant Construction Costs*, op. cit. Much of Komanoff's avowedly partisan work is supported by analysts who are not anti-nuclear. See, for example, William E. Mooz, "A Second Cost Analysis of Light Water Reactor Power Plants," RAND, R-2504-RC, December 1979. It is clear that the cost of electricity from nuclear power plants continues to skyrocket. But, I personally remain agnostic on whether coal is the better bargain. For quantitative support for this position, see Hans H. Landsberg, *et al.*, *Energy: The Next Twenty Years*, op. cit., chap. 12.

38. U.S. Department of State, Office of the U.S. Trade Representative, "International Trade Issues of the U.S. Nuclear Power Industry," paper prepared for CCCT Working Group on Nuclear Equipment, August 1982.

39. *Report of the President's Commission on the Accident at Three Mile Island* (Washington, D.C.: U.S. Government Printing Office), October 1979.

40. *Wall Street Journal*, January 25, 1980, p. 1. See also M. Rogovin, *et al.*, *Three Mile Island: A Report to the Commissioners and to the Public* (Washington, D.C.: U.S. Nuclear Regulatory Commission), 1980, Vol. 1.

41. The fraction cannot be much more than an educated guess. The problem lies in trying to estimate exactly what would happen to the oil-fired generating capacity that some new nuclear plants would replace. Few, evidently, would shut down completely, at least for a few years. Instead, they would probably be used as load-followers. The U.S. Department of Energy estimates that those nuclear plants *scheduled* (as of December 1979) to begin operating in 1980, 1981, and 1982 would, respectively, actually displace about 60,000, 170,000 and 240,000 barrels of oil per day.

It is true that on a strict energy-equivalent transformation, one nuclear power plant can, in principle, supply the equivalent of approximately 40,000 barrels of oil per day. But the nuclear critics are correct in arguing that for policy-making purposes, this is a very misleading number. Many government and business leaders have, indeed, been misled by such transformations into the conclusion that nuclear power can provide a large and rapid substitute for oil. For a provocative quantitative challenge to this proposition, see Vince Taylor, "Energy: the Easy Path," 1979; available from the Union of Concerned Scientists, 1208 Massachusetts Avenue, Cambridge, Mass. 02138.

42. Brian Flowers, "Nuclear Power: A Perspective of the Risks, Benefits, and Options," *Bulletin of the Atomic Scientists*, vol. 34, no. 3, March 1977, pp. 21ff.

43. Harold P. Green, "On the Kemeny Commission," *The Bulletin of the Atomic Scientists*, March 1980, pp. 46–47.

Chapter 6 | *Conservation: The Key Energy Source*

1. For general surveys on conservation, see Marc A. Ross and Robert Williams, *Our Energy: Regaining Control* (New York: McGraw-Hill, 1981); John H. Gibbons and William V. Chandler, *Energy: The Conservation Revolution* (New York: Plenum, 1981); Solar Energy Research Institute, *A New Prosperity: Building a Sustainable Energy Future* (Andover: Brick House, 1981); Robert Socolow, "The Coming Age of Energy Conservation," *Annual Review of Energy: 1977*, vol. 2, pp. 239–289; Lee Schipper and Joel Darmstadter, "The Logic of Energy Conservation," *Technology Review*, January 1978, pp. 41–50; Schipper, "Raising the Productivity of Energy Utilization," *Annual Review of Energy: 1976*, vol. 1, pp. 455–517. One of the most important of all energy studies conducted so far is that of the MIT Workshop on Alternative Energy Strategies, which concluded, "Energy conservation may well be the very best of the alternative energy choices available." Carroll Wilson, ed., *Energy: Global Prospects 1985–2000* (New York: McGraw-Hill, 1977). The toast example is borrowed from Grant Thompson. The 30 percent range would bring the United States close to the energy intensities of other advanced industrial nations, which might also, in turn, become more efficient. For instance, in a major appraisal of energy technologies prepared by Britain's Department of Energy, it is estimated that "good housekeeping and technological breakthroughs apart, technically feasible improvements in energy use could save at least 25 to 35 percent" in all the major energy-consuming sectors in the United Kingdom. Department of Energy, *Energy Technologies for the United Kingdom: An Appraisal for R D & P Planning*, Energy Paper Number 39 (London: Her Majesty's Stationery Office, 1979), p. 24.

2. The often ignored but indeed substantial job creating potential of conservation is discussed in U.S. Congress, Joint Economic Committee, *Creating Jobs Through Energy Policy: Hearings*, 95 Cong., 2 sess. One of the most detailed efforts to investigate job-creating potential of various energy sources was carried out for Long Island. Its findings: A six-billion-dollar investment in conservation and solar provided twice as much energy for end use as a seven-billion-dollar investment in nuclear power. Over a thirty-year period, the

conservation and solar package created 178,000 jobs, as opposed to 72,000 jobs created by the nuclear investment; *Creating Jobs Through Energy Policy*, pp. 28–39. A more detailed analysis is found in Steven Buchshaum and James W. Benson, *Jobs and Energy: The Employment and Economic Impacts of Nuclear Power, Conservation and other Energy Options* (New York City: Council on Economic Priorities, 1979).

3. President Reagan quoted in Daniel Yergin and Martin Hillenbrand, eds., *Global Insecurity: A Strategy for Energy and Economic Renewal* (Boston: Houghton Mifflin, 1982), p. 110. For Schipper and Darmstadter quote, see their "The Logic of Energy Conservation," p. 42.

4. A Massachusetts poll found that half of the respondents expected a technological production fix to solve the problem. Letter from Henry Lee, director, Massachusetts Energy Office, to author, July 24, 1978.

5. The proceedings of the conference are in Sonja S. Marchand, ed., "Energy —The Global Challenge," Proceedings of a Conference sponsored by California State University of Northbridge, May 6–7, 1977. The senator's aide's comment is from an interview with the author. At a recent national governor's conference, there were six energy panels. Only two governors bothered to show up at the single panel concerned with conservation. The other forty-eight hurried off to hear about supply.

6. Scientist is Socolow, "The Coming Age of Conservation," in *Annual Review of Energy: 1977*, p. 252. For a critique of the lack of support for applied research on conservation, see Terry Grew, George W. Sutton, and Martin Zlotnick, "Fuel Conservation and Applied Research," in *Science*, April 14, 1978, pp. 135–142. Roger Sant, Remarks to the Conference Board, FEA release, September 30, 1975.

7. The first prominent statement encouraging energy conservation was the Ford Foundation's Energy Policy Project, *A Time to Choose: America's Energy Future* (Cambridge, Mass.: Ballinger, 1974). The reader is advised to note the searing dissents of those associated with supply on the advisory committee. As visible has been Amory Lovins, "Energy Strategy: The Road Not Taken?" *Foreign Affairs*, October 1976, pp. 65–96. For Carter's April 1977 program, see U.S. Congress, Senate, Energy Committee, *The President's Energy Program: A Compilation of Documents*, 95th Congress, 1st Session (Washington: GPO, 1977), pp. 2–10.

8. See, for instance, Bernard A. Gelb, "U.S. Energy Price and Consumption Changes in the Mid-1970s," Conference Board Information Bull. No. 38, March 1978; Eric Hirst et al., *Energy Use from 1973 to 1980: The Role of Improved Energy Efficiency*, ORNL/CA 79 (Oakridge National Laboratory, 1981). The inadequacies—and great social strains—of trying to depend exclusively upon price signals to stimulate conservation are stressed in Massachusetts Energy Office, *The New England Policy Alternatives Study: Final Report*, October 1978, pp. 41–44.

9. *Energy Report from Chase*, September 1976. Oil company in an internal memorandum. The Texas Railroad commissioner was quoted in *Newsweek*,

April 18, 1977, p. 73. The Federal Energy Agency's 1976 outlook assumed that the connection between energy consumption and economic activity was relatively fixed for industry, which may be one of the reasons conservation was so low a priority in the Nixon and Ford administrations. Federal Energy Agency, *National Energy Outlook: 1976* (Washington, D.C.: Government Printing Office, 1976), p. 27.

10. Energy to GNP data is from John G. Myers, "Energy Conservation and Economic Growth—Are They Incompatible?" *The Conference Board Record,* February 1975, pp. 27–32. Also see Sam H. Schurr and Joel Darmstadter, "Some Observations on Energy and Economic Growth," Resources for the Future, 1977. Some of the factors that have to be considered in evaluating how elastic the energy-GNP link has become since 1973 include economic recession, weather, differential growth in electricity demand among different countries, structural shifts in industry, rate of investment in capital stock that embodies energy savings, and so on and on. No wonder the task is so difficult. Thus, at a conference the chief economist of one major oil company postulated energy savings per unit of GNP in the OECD countries during the period 1973–77 as 4 percent; another oil company economist with no less certainty more than doubled the estimate to 9 percent.

11. For 1972 data (though slightly revised since then), see Joel Darmstadter, Joy Dunkerley, and Jack Alterman, *How Industrial Societies Use Energy: A Comparative Analysis* (Baltimore: Johns Hopkins University Press, 1977), p. 5. For an in-depth study of Sweden, see Lee Schipper and A. J. Lichtenberg, "Efficient Energy Use and Well-Being: The Swedish Example," *Science,* December 3, 1976, pp. 1001–1013.

12. The complexities involved in these comparisons have been much illuminated in the study by Darmstadter, Dunkerley, and Alterman, *How Industrial Societies Use Energy.* Some have leaped upon this work to argue, as *The Oil and Gas Journal* of March 6, 1978 (pp. 30–31) did in a headline, "Study Explodes U.S. Energy-Waste Myth." On the contrary, it does not. Despite the rather cautious conclusions by the authors of *How Industrial Societies Use Energy,* their evidence and arguments do affirm that the United States is more intensive in its energy use.

13. The similarities are noted in Socolow, "The Coming Age of Conservation," *Annual Review of Energy: 1977,* p. 247. Also, see Joy Dunkerley, ed., *International Comparison of Energy Consumption* (Washington, D.C.: Resources for the Future, 1977). One might ask why the correlation between energy and GNP should be any more fixed than that between GNP and the size of the labor force. Increased productivity of labor—not just a growing labor force—has been a major source of economic growth. See Robert Solow, "Technological Change and the Aggregate Production Function," *Review of Economics and Statistics* 39 (April 1957), pp. 312–320. The same might be true, to some degree, for an increasing "productivity" of energy. Although some might reply that energy is a trade-off for human labor, the evidence suggests otherwise: that even in industry, most energy is used for process and space heat, not

power. Darmstadter, Dunkerley, and Alterman, *How Industrial Societies Use Energy*, pp. 116–117.

14. S. M. Lambert of Shell U.S.A., quoted in *New York Times*, February 11, 1978. W. W. Rostow has pointed out that a radical change in the price of a commodity such as oil sets off a dynamic process that has far-reaching consequences difficult to capture in conventional models—direct income effects that differ by regions, changing investments and population flows, and alterations in the pace and character of development. "Energy-economy models are substantially misleading," he observes, because "these models mask out by assumption the critical features" in the current U.S. situation. Rostow, "Energy, Full Employment, and Regional Development," Paper delivered at the American Association for the Advancement of Science, February 14, 1978. Suddenly, the economic life of the entire capital stock is foreshortened. Jean Saint-Geours *et al.*, *In Favour of an Energy Efficient Society*, study prepared for the European Communities, D.G. XVII-235 (79) EN (Brussels: June 1979).

15. The discussion of the Los Angeles Plan draws on three Rand Corporation studies: Jan Paul Acton and Ragnhild Mowill, "Regulatory Rationing of Electricity under a Supply Curtailment." P-5624; Acton and Mowill, "Conserving Electricity by Ordinance: A Statistical Analysis," R-1650-FEA; and Acton, M. H. Graubard, and D. J. Weinschrott, "Electricity Conservation Measures in the Commercial Sector: The Los Angeles Experience," R-1592-FEA. Interview with Harold Williams by author in January 1975; Harold Williams, "Why We Must Break the OPEC Cartel: A Response to President Ford's Energy Program," Statement, October 10, 1974. (Williams, now chairman of the Securities and Exchange Commission, was Los Angeles' energy coordinator during the crisis.) U.S. Congress, Joint Economic Committee, Subcommittee on Energy, *Energy Conservation: Hearings*, 94 Cong., 2 sess., p. 272; and *Los Angeles Times*, various articles, November–December 1973 and January 1974. Philip Hawley speaks with considerable practical experience, since he is chief executive officer of one of the nation's largest retailing companies. His observations are in U.S. Congress, Senate, Committee on Energy and Natural Resources, Subcommittee on Energy Regulation, *Mandatory Energy Conservation and Gasoline and Diesel Fuel Rationing*, 96th Congress, 1st session, pp. 499–507.

16. *Monthly Energy Review*, March 1982.

17. For number of workers and turnover, see *Motor Vehicles Facts and Figures '79*, pp. 38, 69. In the 1950's, "gasoline costs of the order of one to three cents per mile were marginal costs in owning an automobile. Consequently, once a family was able to purchase a car its use added negligibly to the overall cost. There was little incentive for efficient utilization of the vehicle." Richard Michaels, "Alternative Strategies for Energy Conservation in Highway Transportation," in Daniel Yergin, ed., *The Dependence Dilemma: U.S. Gasoline Consumption and America's Security* (Cambridge, Mass.: Center for International Affairs, 1980). Forty percent of all car miles were devoted to commuting

in 1970. Three quarters of all workers drive to work, and four-fifths did so alone. See Dorothy Newman and Dawn Day, *The American Energy Consumer* (Cambridge, Mass.: Ballinger, 1975), p. 78.

18. U.S. Federal Task Force, *Motor Vehicle Goals Beyond 1980*, vols. 1 and 2 (Washington, D.C.: Energy Resources Council, 1976), chap. 8.

19. Society of Automotive Engineers, *Passenger Car Fuel Economy Trends Through 1976*, Paper 750957, October 1975; Newman and Day, *The American Energy Consumer*, p. 72; Robert Williams, ed., *The Energy Conservation Papers* (Cambridge, Mass.: Ballinger, 1975), pp. 23, 312–314; U.S. Congress, Senate, Finance Committee, *Energy Conservation and Conversion Act of 1975: Hearings*, 94 Cong., 2 sess., p. 465; John Tien, Ray W. Clark, and Mahendra K. Malu, "Reducing the Energy Investment in Automobiles," and Joseph Kummer, "The Automobile as an Energy Converter," both in *Technology Review*, February 1975, pp. 26–43. Between 1968 and 1973, pollution standards may have imposed as much as 12 percent penalty on efficiency on a sales-weighted average. However, improvements in emissions-control devices had reduced the penalty by 1975.

20. A senior executive with one of the top three manufacturers recalled, "The low priority assigned to fuel efficiency before 1973 was associated with ever-rising world oil reserves and a real decline in the price of gasoline when measured in minutes of labor at the average wage rate" (private communication with author). And the minutes of a meeting involving senior officials of another of the top three manufacturers in 1972 point to some suspicion of the oil industry: "We must evaluate realistically the basic energy supply data and energy demand data. Almost all studies are based on [American] Petroleum Institute statistics, an unneutral body. It is likely safe to say that proven reserve statistics are not overstated; the question is to evaluate how much they are understated."

21. Ward and Paulhus, *Suburbanization and Its Implication for Urban Transportation Systems;* James J. Mutch, *Transportation Energy Use in the United States: A Statistical History: 1955–71*, Rand Corporation, R-1391-NSF, December 1973; Eric Hirst, "Transportation Energy Conservation: Opportunities and Policy Issues," in U.S. Department of Transportation, *Energy Primer*.

22. Milton Russell, "Energy," Resources for the Future reprint, No. 145, p. 331. *Monthly Energy Review*, October 1978, p. 65.

23. Darmstadter, Dunkerley, and Alterman, *How Industrial Societies Use Energy*, pp. 92–93; General Accounting Office, *U.S. Energy Conservation Could Benefit from Experiences of Other Countries*, ID-78-4, January 10, 1978, pp. 10–11; Organization for Economic Cooperation and Development, *Energy Conservation in the International Energy Agency: 1976 Review* (Paris: OECD), pp. 42–43.

24. Woodcock in U.S. Congress, Senate, Finance Committee, *Energy Conservation and Conversion Act of 1975: Hearings*, 94 Cong., 1 sess., p. 473. For down-sizing, see Tien, Clark, and Malu, "Reducing the Energy Investment in Automobiles," *Technology Review*, February 1975, pp. 38–43; U.S. Congress, Senate, Finance Committee, *Energy Conservation and Conversion Act*

of 1975: Hearings. 94 Cong., 2 sess., pp. 173–174. Three quarters of GM's weight reduction came from resizing and engineering improvements, between 10 and 15 percent from smaller engines, drivetrains, and accessories, and the rest from use of premium materials. *Automotive News,* August 28, 1978, p. 43.

25. For possible effects on market share, see William Abernathy, and Balaji S. Chakravarthy, "Technological Change in the U.S. Automobile Industry: Assessing the Federal Initiatives," Paper prepared for the Department of Transportation, December 1977, pp. 1, 45. For the competing demands, see Abernathy and Chakravarthy, p. 59; Raymond E. Good, "The Automobile: Interaction of Energy, Safety, Environment and the Economy," in U.S. Department of Transportation, *Regulation and Transportation: Report of the Third Workshop on National Transportation Problems* (Washington, D.C.: DOT, 1975). "One element of uncertainty is the success of specific technology we are now developing," said Henry Duncombe, chief economist for General Motors in 1977. "However, the range of this uncertainty is relatively small. Technical feasibility is not the key issue here today—cars on the market already exceed 27.5 mpg. The major uncertainty will be the potential losses of auto sales caused by fuel economy standards." Cited in Richard John, Philip Coonley, Robert Ricci, and Bruce Rubinger, "Mandated Fuel Economy Standards as a Strategy for Improving Motor Vehicles' Fuel Economy," Paper presented at Symposium on Technology, Government, and the Future of the Automobile Industry at the Harvard Business School, October 19, 1978, p. 29.

26. General Motors in *Energy Conservation and Conversion Act of 1975: Hearings,* p. 139; Henry Ford II, Speech to the White House Conference on Balanced National Growth and Economic Development, January 30, 1978.

27. Frank Von Hippel, "Forty Miles a Gallon by 1995 at the Very Least," in Daniel Yergin, ed., *The Dependence Dilemma: Gasoline Consumption and America's Security* (Cambridge, Mass.: Center for International Affairs, 1980); Milstein, "Energy Conservation and Travel Behavior," p. 3; Richard Strombotne, "Transportation: Energy Outlook," Speech at Conference Board, December 7, 1977; *Ward's Automotive Yearbook: 1976,* p. 20. The cumulative fuel savings in Richard John, *et al.,* "Mandated Fuel Economy," p. 4. On light vans, see Robert F. Hemphill, Jr., "Energy Conservation in the Transportation Sector," in John Sawhill, ed., *Energy Conservation and Public Policy* (New York: Prentice-Hall, 1979).

28. For importation of technology and $80 billion capital estimate, see Richard John *et al.,* "Mandated Fuel Economy." The $5 billion to $10 billion figure is from U.S. Federal Task Force, *Motor Vehicle Goals Beyond 1980,* vol. 1, p. 29, and vol. 2, pp. 6–6, 6B–1–2. Also see Abernathy and Chakravarthy, "Technological Change in the U.S. Auto Industry," p. 60; "Machine Tools: Uproar over a Bottleneck," *New York Times,* February 26, 1978; Robert Irvin, "Big Four Spending Jacked Up Again," *Automotive News,* June 5, 1978, p. 1.

29. For the technical practicality, see Richard R. John, "Transition to the Post-

1985 Motor Vehicle," paper, October 31, 1979; for the "cucumber on wheels," see Transportation Task Force, *Conservation and Alternative Fuels in the Transportation Sector* (draft) (Golden, Co: SERI, March 11, 1980). For future mileage, see Charles Cohn, "Improved Fuel Efficiency for Automobiles," *Technology Review*, February 1975, pp. 45–53; *Economist*, January 20–27, 1978, pp. 76–77; Charles Deutsch, *Economies d'Energie par la Conception des Voitures Particulières, Les Dossiers de l'Energie* 10 (Paris: Ministry of Industry and Commerce, 1977); *Motor Vehicle Goals Beyond 1980;* and Joan Claybrook, "The Snail's Pace of Innovation," Speech at *Automotive News* World Conference, June 13, 1977; Marion Meader, *Seminar on Automobile Fuel Efficiency: Proceedings*, vol. 2 (McLean, Va.: Mitre Corp., 1978), p. 64; Gerald Leach *et al.*, *A Low Energy Strategy for the United Kingdom* (London: Science Reviews, 1979), pp. 156–164. The innovation problem, as well as fuel economy potentials, is discussed in Abernathy and Chakravarthy, "Technological Change in the U.S. Auto Industry," pp. 28–29, 60–65, and in Richard John *et al.*, "Mandated Fuel Economy."

30. Statements of F. G. Seacrest and Douglas A. Fraser before the House Ways and Means Committee, Subcommittee on Trade, March 7, 1980; *Automotive News*, April 5, 1982, p. 6.

31. "A Conversation with Henry Ford II," *Los Angeles Times*, January 21, 1979; Frank Von Hippel, "Automotive Fuel Economy: Why the Market Can't Do It Alone."

32. Richard John, "Transition to the Post-1985 Motor Vehicle."

33. Average fuel economy loss has been estimated in one study at between 4 and 6 percent. J. L. Duda *et al.*, *Program Evaluation Support for the Motor Vehicle: Diagnostic Inspections, and Demonstration Program, Volume 2, Costs and Benefits*, Department of Transportation Report HS-802406 (Falls Church, Va.: Computer Science Corporation, 1977); Ted Baylor and Leslie Eden, *Fuel Economy Improvement through Diagnostic Inspection*, DOT-NHSTA Report HS 802284, March 1977. Other studies put the penalty because of improperly inflated tires alone at 5 percent. Synthetic motor fuel oils can improve miles per gallon by more than 4 percent. J. A. C. Krulish, H. B. Lowthen, and B. J. Miller, "An Update on Synthesized Engine Oil Technology," Paper prepared for Fuels and Lubricants Meeting, Society of Automotive Engineers, June 1977. Also see Daniel Yergin, "France's Tough Energy Program Puts the Heat on the Admen," *Fortune*, June 17, 1978, pp. 106–112. For speed limits see General Accounting Office, *Speed Limit 55: Is it Achievable*, CED-77-27, 1977. Low-grade tires may impose a 15 percent penalty on fuel economy. *Ward's Automotive Reports*, December 18, 1978, p. 404. Richard Michaels observes: "Most studies have shown that work travelers find only a few simple paths through urban highway networks. These are rarely the shortest or least congested. This is the case simply because drivers do not have information about alternative routes or the knowledge to locate them. . . ." In "Alternative Strategies for Energy Conservation in Highway Transportation," op. cit.

34. See Fred Salvucci's report in Daniel Yergin, ed., *The Dependence Dilemma:*

Gasoline Consumption and America's Security, op. cit.; Jeffrey S. Milstein, "Energy Conservation and Travel Behavior," Department of Energy paper, October 1977, pp. 3–4; letter from Henry Lee, Director, Massachusetts Energy Office, to author, July 24, 1978.

35. See Jerry Ward and Norman Paulhus, *Suburbanization and Its Implications for Urban Transportation System* (Washington, D.C.: Department of Transportation, 1974). For a survey of mass transit issues, see "Transportation Agenda for the 1980s," Department of Transportation Working Paper, January 31, 1980. For various demonstration projects and innovative experiments in transit, see Department of Transportation, *Service and Methods Demonstration Program: Annual Report,* (Report #UMTA-MA-06-0049-79-8) (Washington, D.C.: DOT, August 1979). For criticism of the energy content in mass transit, see Alan Altshuler with James P. Womack and John R. Pucher, *The Urban Transportation System: Politics and Policy Innovation* (Cambridge: MIT Press, 1979), pp. 170–71, 430–34. For the discrimination against mass transit, see *ibid.,* pp. 31–33. Also on the energy budget of mass transit, see Congressional Budget Office, *Urban Transportation and Energy: The Potential Savings of Different Modes* (Washington, D.C.: GPO, 1977), pp. 42–57; Charles A. Cave, "The Mass Transit Panacea," *Atlantic Monthly,* October 1979, pp. 39–43.

36. The subject of gasoline taxes and rationing is discussed in Daniel Yergin, ed., *The Dependence Dilemma: Gasoline Consumption and America's Security* (Cambridge, Mass.: Center for International Affairs, 1980). An overview of the major proposals is provided by William Chandler and Holly Gwin, "Gasoline Conservation in an Era of Confrontation." Thomas Schelling analyzes the similarities between tax and rationing in "Alternatives to Gasoline." He writes: "Once people get used to the idea that their weekly ration is a kind of 'entitlement' that has a cash value, and that the 'cost' of every gallon consumed is the pump price plus the coupon price, people may come to recognize that the system is not much different from a weekly cash benefit coupled with a gasoline tax. Thus the system is, except for appearance, exactly equivalent to a . . . gasoline tax on every gallon sold with a rebate system in which all the tax proceeds are distributed precisely in accordance with what would have been a rationing scheme." Robert Williams, in "A $2 a Gallon Political Opportunity," presents a program for a heavy gasoline tax combined with a tax shift and rebate. Al Alm argues for a windfall tax rather than rationing as a response in an emergency in his paper, "Coping with Petroleum Supply Interruptions." One concern about a tax is that it would encourage sales of imported cars at the expense of American-built cars. Less oil and more Toyotas. However, Detroit is now much better equipped than a few years ago to meet increased demand for more efficient cars. Public opinion analyst William Schneider, in his remarks at the symposium reported in the volume, suggested that the American people may need to experience rationing to decide they prefer a gas tax.

37. On inattention to materials-saving innovation in the United States in the

postwar years, see William H. Davidson, "Patterns of Factor-Saving Innovation in the Industrialized World," *European Economic Review 8* (1976), pp. 207–217. Aluminum, in John Myers and Leonard Nakamura, *Saving Energy in Manufacturing: The Post-Embargo Record* (Cambridge, Mass.: Ballinger, 1978), p. 122. The energy-intensive paper industry gets a growing part of its fuel needs from burning "hog fuels"—that is, such wastes as sawdust, chips, barks and "black liquors"—and in the process reducing environmental pollution. Gas costs quote from *Wall Street Journal*, February 12, 1982, p. 14.

38. *Energy User News*, April 10, 1977, June 13, 1977, and February 27, 1978.

39. Industrial energy consumption in *Monthly Energy Review*, February 1980. Industrial production from *Economic Indicators*, Department of Commerce. Energy-GNP ratio (thousand BTUs per 1972 dollar of GNP) from Table 2-2 in John G. Myers, "Industrial Energy Demand 1976–2000," Draft study prepared for the U.S. General Accounting Office, January 31, 1979. The qualifications are stressed in this paper and in an earlier paper by Myers, "Energy Conservation in Manufacturing Since the Embargo," Paper presented at Conference on the Economic Impact of Energy Conservation, July 1978. For criticism of the voluntary industrial energy use reporting scheme, see Myers and Nakamura, pp. 11–13, and *Energy User News*, June 20, 1977, October 17, 1977, and October 30, 1977. Obviously, associations and firms eager to avoid further regulation will tend to put the best interpretation on ambiguous data. Another rather critical energy audit, this with twenty major industrial firms, also found a gap between claims and results. See General Accounting Office, *Federal Agencies Can Do More to Promote Energy Conservation by Government Contractors*, EMD-77-62, September 30, 1977, pp. 5–19. A more recent report points to the confusion between energy saving and production runs. General Accounting Office, *The Federal Government Should Establish and Meet Conservation Goals*, EMD-78-38, June 30, 1978, p. 32.

40. Myers and Nakamura, *Saving Energy in Manufacturing*, pp. 7–9, 24, 121–23; Robert C. Marlay, *Working Paper on Industrial Energy Use and Conservation*, Dept. of Energy, September 1979. The 1973–80 analysis is in Eric Hirst et al., *Energy Use from 1973 to 1980*, pp. 28–33. For the shift in product mix throughout the OECD, see Claire Doblin, *The Growth of Energy Consumption and Prices in the USA, PRG, France, and the UK, 1950–80* (Luxembourg: IIASA, 1981), pp. 26–29.

41. Goodyear in *Energy User News*, November 28, 1977. See also Neil DeKoker, "Energy Conservation in Management," *Industrial Engineering*, December 1977; Allied Chemical, "Energy Conservation Program," Unpublished paper, June 1978. The absolute requirement of senior management commitment is stressed by the chairman of British Petroleum and an executive of Courtaulds. David Steel, Speech, and J. R. S. Morris, "Implementing an Energy Management Policy," Paper, both presented at National Energy Management Conference, Birmingham, England, October 1978. As Morris said, "Everything starts from the top." For a study of the need for commitment of senior management and methods used to induce organizationwide change in activi-

ties that often do not impact heavily on profits, see Robert Ackerman and Raymond Bauer, *Corporate Social Responsiveness: The Modern Dilemma* (Reston, Va.: Reston, 1976). For Armco, see Henry Miller, "User Requirements and Conservation," Speech at Conference Board, December 7, 1977, p. 2, 8. TWA's energy manager in *Energy User News*, April 12, 1982, p. 1.

42. Henry Miller, "User Requirements and Conservation"; *Energy User News*, April 11 and 25, 1977. G. N. Hatsopoulos, E. P. Gyftopoulos, R. W. Sant, and T. F. Widmer, "Capital Investment to Save Energy," *Harvard Business Review*, March–April 1978, pp. 111–122. Also Roger Sant to author, October 26, 1978. Courtaulds, an international chemical company with major operations in the United States, initially established a three-year payback criteria, then shortened it to two. This was partly because there were "ample opportunities" at two years—apparently much in excess of the allocated capital. J. R. S. Morris, "Implementing an Energy Management Policy." Many companies fail to note the "insurance valve" of conservation. See Robert C. Lind, "The Rationale for Federal End Use (Conservation and Solar) Programs; Inplications for Policy and Program Evaluation," Draft of paper prepared for Office of Conservation Planning and Policy, Department of Energy, pp. 5–6, 10–11. For a survey of how different firms calculate returns on conservation investments, see Barnaby J. Feder, "Energy Paybacks Draw More Attention," *Energy User News*, November 27, 1978, p. 1.

43. Michael Tenebaum, "Reflections on Steel's Energy Maze," Speech to the American Iron and Steel Institute, May 25, 1977.

44. Pan Am president in *Wall Street Journal*, March 27, 1982, p. 27. Letter from Henry Lee to author, July 24, 1978; Massachusetts Energy Office, "Survey of New England Business Attitudes Toward Energy and Energy Conservation," Mimeograph memo; National Federation of Independent Business, "Fifth Energy Report for Small Business," June 1977, p. 30; General Accounting Office, *Federal Agencies Can Do More to Promote Energy Conservation by Government Contractors*, pp. 19–22, 40; "Carpet Firms on Fuel Crisis: Is it Real, Can We Cope?" *Energy User News*, December 1977, p. 7; Samuel I. Doctors, Liam Fahey, and G. Richard Patton, "The Response of Small Manufacturers to the Energy Environment," Working Paper 248, Graduate School of Business, University of Pittsburgh. A detailed survey of potential for industrial conservation in Texas pointed out several constraints that "will reduce the impact of economics as a stimulus for conservation." In larger firms, conservation projects must compete with other often higher-priority activities for investment capital. In smaller firms, the requisite knowledge for economic and engineering analysis may be lacking. "Another disincentive for conservation is that in industries where competition is low or demand is insensitive to price increases, the increased cost for energy can be passed on to the consumer through increased product price. In many cases also, the costs of energy are only a small fraction of the total production costs. In this case small savings may be ignored." William Cepeda, *Potential for Energy Conservation in Texas: Report to Governor's Energy Advisory Council*, Number 77-001, April

1977, pp. 67–8. Here we see numerous examples of Alfred Kahn's "tyranny of small decisions"; see "The Tyranny of Small Decisions: Market Failures, Imperfections, and the Limits of Economics," *Kyklos* (1966), pp. 23–46. A survey of small business in New England indicated that lack of information and capital constraints stand as even greater barriers to energy conservation for smaller businesses than for larger firms. Daniel Yergin, Taia Ergueta, and Julie Rogers, "Energy and Small Business in New England," paper prepared for White House Conference on Small Business, September 1979. In an innovative approach to the capital problem, some consulting firms will put up the capital needed for a company's conservation efforts and then split the resulting dollar savings with the company. *Energy User News*, November 5, 1979, p. 1; January 14, 1980, p. 4.

45. *Energy User News*, May 14, 1978, p. 9.

46. Thermo-Electron, *A Study of Inplant Electric Power Generation in the Chemical, Petroleum Refining and Paper and Pulp Industries: Final Report*, Prepared for the Federal Energy Administration, Contract CO-04-50224-00.

47. Kjell Larsson, "District Hearing: Swedish Experience of an Energy Efficient Concept"; Commission of the European Community, *Rational Use of Energy, Second Periodical Report of Sub-Group G: Conversions in Power Stations*, pp. G-33-36; U.K. Department of Energy, *District Heating Combined with Electricity Generation in the United Kingdom*, Energy Paper No. 20; Robert Williams, *The Potential for Electricity Generation as a Byproduct of Industrial Steam Production in New Jersey* (Princeton: Center for Environmental Studies, 1977), p. 24. For the possibilities for district heating in St. Paul and Minneapolis, see Minnesota Energy Agency, District Heating Institutional Study: Draft Final Report, September 7, 1979; Minnesota Energy Agency, A Proposal to Develop a Plan to Implement District Heating in Minnesota, Draft, September 19, 1979; Oak Ridge National Laboratory, *District Heating/ Cogeneration Applications: Studies for the Minneapolis St. Paul Area*, ORNL-/TM-6830/P3, October 1979. The Oak Ridge study concluded "that district heating on a regional basis in the Twin Cities area is technically feasible, that large quantities of the potentially scarce and expensive fuels (natural gas and oil) can be saved, and that air quality can be improved. The economics are judged to be viable provided a suitable method of refinancing is used for the transmission and distribution system."

48. In the 1920's and early 1930's, several major paper companies went into the electricity business via cogeneration. And a very profitable business they found it. In the 1930's, the Justice Department took an interest in their activities, and in a series of court suits the companies were forced to decide whether they were in the paper business or the electric power business. They chose paper. See Charles Berg, "Conservation in Industry," *Science*, April 19, 1974, p. 268.

49. U.S. Congress, Senate, Energy Committee, Subcommittee on Conservation, *Status of Federal Energy Conservation Programs: Hearings*, 95 Cong., 1 sess., p. 196.

50. Williams, *The Potential for Electricity Generation as a Byproduct of Industrial Steam Production in New Jersey*, pp. 2–4; Thermo-Electron, *A Study of In-plant Electric Power Generation*, p. 2–2; U.K. Department of Energy, *District Heating Combined with Electricity Generation in the United Kingdom*, p. 3; Federal Energy Agency, *Comparison of Energy Consumption Between West Germany and the United States*, Conservation Paper No. 33.

51. Dow Chemical, *Energy Industrial Center Study*, June 1975; Thermo-Electron, *Summary Assessment of Electricity Cogeneration in Industry*, March 15, 1977; Hatsopoulos, Gyftopoulos, Sant., and Widmer, "Capital Investment to Save Energy," *Harvard Business Review*, p. 115; Williams, *The Potential for Electricity Generation as a Byproduct of Industrial Steam Production in New Jersey*, pp. 14–15. For Massachusetts, see Resource Planning Associates, *The Potential for Cogeneration Development in Six Major Industries by 1985: Executive Summary*, December 1977, p. iv; and Robert Elgin, "Some Implications for Cogeneration in New England from the Resource Planning Associates Study," Paper prepared for Governor's Commission on Cogeneration, 1978. These studies discuss return on investment.

52. The author, having sat for a year on the Governor's Commission on Cogeneration in Massachusetts, speaks from experience on the difficulties in analyzing the problem. The Massachusetts study, intended as a guide for the rest of the country, is a thorough investigation of the economic, regulatory, environmental, and market potential for cogeneration in New England. Governor's Commission on Cogeneration, *Cogeneration: Its Benefits to New England* (Boston: Commonwealth of Massachusetts, 1978). The report and its preparations provide the background for the discussion of cogeneration. It is a basic study of the real-world implementation for cogeneration. Also see John Belding, "Alternatives to Oil and Gas Through Energy Management," Paper prepared for New Options in Energy Technology Conference of the American Institute of Aeronautics and Astronautics, 1977.

Increasing attention is now being focused on proposals to free potential cogenerators from federal and state utility regulations and to ensure that utilities take their surplus power. The cogeneration question can be seen as part of what has been called "the great rate debate" (W. Donald Crawford, "An Electric Utility Perspective on Rate Design Revision," *Public Utilities Fortnightly*, September 14, 1978, pp. 15–19). The 1978 National Energy Act, as well as some state regulatory bodies, seeks to change utility-pricing systems to encourage conservation through such measures as peak-load pricing and the phasing out of declining block rates. Very significant energy and capital cost savings could result, for instance, from peak-load pricing. See Jan Paul Acton, Bridger M. Mitchell, and Willard G. Manning, *Projected Nationwide Energy and Capacity Savings from Peak-Load Pricing of Electricity in the Industrial Sector*, Rand Corporation, R-2179-DOE, June 1978.

The shift of emphasis represented in such measures involves "a basic change in the electric utility industry from one of supplying energy to one of encouraging conservation and efficiency in its use while, at the same time, maintaining reliable service and meeting the energy needs of its customers. This is a demanding challenge," (Hamilton Treadway, "Energy Conservation Rates for an Effective Conservation Program," *Public Utilities Fortnightly*, August 17, 1978, pp. 16–20). A case study of utility fears about cogeneration is in Tom Alexander, "The Little Engine That Scares Con Ed," *Fortune*, December 31, 1978, pp. 80–84. A contrary case is that of Southern California Edison, which is working with customers and regulatory agencies to promote cogeneration. "It's a new ball game," observed Arthur Blake, the utility's supervisor of the load management project. Rising marginal cost for new capacity and uncertain and expensive energy supplies encouraged the utility to welcome cogeneration as a "means to defer construction of expensive new generating plants as well as conserve natural resources"; Arthur J. Blake, "Utility Looks at Cogeneration to Manage Peaks," *Energy User News*, October 30, 1978, pp. 22–23.

An example of the kind of cooperative exchange required of normally warring parties if such problems are to be sensibly resolved for a reasonable transition, is provided in an admirable document, New England Energy Congress, *New England Blueprint for Energy Action* (Somerville: 1979). As is evident from the coal and nuclear chapters in this book, utilities now find themselves trying to make long-term decisions in a very uncertain environment. Coping with the energy transition certainly does impose heavy burdens on utilities, forcing them to face several competing demands at once, and could well bring about substantial changes in their role and orientation. The question of their future role is one of the most important in the entire energy field, but is one that has only begun to be addressed by research.

For an example of a utility's seeking to substitute conservation and load management for new generating capacity, see New England Electric's innovative *NEESPLAN: 1980–1995* (Westborough, Mass.: 1979). In the utility's own words, "NEESPLAN is a new way to accomplish an old job."

53. Hatsopoulos, Gyftopoulos, Sant, and Widmer, "Capital Investment to Save Energy," *Harvard Business Review*, pp. 111–122; Thermo-Electron, *Summary Assessment of Electricity Cogeneration in Industry*, p. 2–3.

54. Hatsopoulos, Gyftopoulos, Sant, and Widmer, "Capital Investment to Save Energy," *Harvard Business Review;* letter from Roger Sant to author, October 26, 1978.

55. For Union Carbide, see R. S. Wishart, "Energy R&D Priorities and Decentralized Electricity and Cogeneration Options, paper at Aspen Institute Seminar, July 1979. Also, letter from Wishart, May 26, 1982. Wishart, noting the "surprising results in the industrial sector," quotes an eighteenth-century American minister: "Experience must be our only guide; reason may mislead us." Gillette, from interviews with Cameron Beers. Gillette has an aggressive program that seeks to build energy awareness throughout the firm, reward those who come up with ideas, and diffuse new concepts and techniques throughout the company. AT&T information from AT&T, Energy and Environment Group, Energy Conservation in the Bell System, paper of June 1,

1980. William Ellinghaus, "The Energy Efficient Network of Tomorrow," speech, November 28, 1979.

56. Myers and Nakamura, *Saving Energy in Industry*, p. 45; Myers, "Conservation in Manufacturing Since the Embargo," p. 7.

57. William Sneath, speech given at the Harvard Business School, reprinted in *Energy User News*, October 8, 1979. A similar point has been made by the associate director of energy for Kaiser Aluminum, who has argued that the first level of conservation savings—about 10 percent of total consumption—is being made. "Our studies also indicate in the energy-intensive process industries such as ours, there is another 15-percent conservation potential which could be obtained with existing technology but which requires substantial capital investments. These projects will be implemented sometime in the future, but they are not being undertaken today. In our judgment, the main reason why these projects are not proceeding today is because of the large capital requirements needed to implement them and, in many cases, they are not cost effective to industry, i.e., the return on investment is not adequate." Clement Gomes, statement, September 11, 1979. For the reporting system, see General Accounting Office, *The Federal Government Should Establish and Meet Energy Conservation Goals*, p. 34. The 2500 copies are reported in Dept. of Energy, *Industrial Energy Efficiency Program: Annual Report, July 1977–December 1978* (Washington, D.C.: Dec. 1979). The report also notes a reduction in the share of energy provided by natural gas and an increase in the share provided by petroleum products.

58. The discussion about Dow is based on interviews with several Dow executives. Also see J. C. Robertson, "Energy Conservation in Existing Plant," *Chemical Engineering*, January 21, 1974, pp. 104–22; W. A. Rollwage, "Energy Conservation in Chemical Plants," *Chemical Engineering Progress*, October 1975, pp. 44–49; Gerald Decker, "Energy Conservation in Industry," Unpublished paper, September 27, 1976, and Decker, "Energy Conservation at the Dow Chemical Company," Unpublished paper, December 1976; *New York Times*, February 5, 1978, sec. 3.

59. The data on residential energy use (in 1975) from Eric Hirst and Jane Carney, *Residential Energy Use to the Year 2000: Conservation and Economics*, Oak Ridge National Laboratory/Con 13, September 1977. Also Fred Dubin, "New Energy Conservation Ideas for Existing and New Buildings," *Specifying Engineer*, January 1976; U.S. Congress, Senate, Interior Committee, *Energy Conservation Act of 1976: Hearings*, 94 Cong., 2 sess., p. 109. New York office building information is cited in Richard G. Stein, *Architecture and Energy* (New York: Doubleday, 1977), pp. 60–61. For the trend in private dwellings, see Eric Hirst and Jerry Jackson, "Historical Patterns of Residential and Commercial Energy Uses," *Energy* 2 (June 1977). Also see Newman and Day, *The American Energy Consumer*, pp. 39–43. Of course, new sealed buildings have one advantage: Dirt does not blow in the window.

60. Stein, *Architecture and Energy*, pp. 215, 292.

61. IBM in Claire Stegmen, "Not Bad, But Still Not Good Enough," *Think*,

October-November 1976; U.S. Congress, Joint Economic Committee, Subcommittee on Energy, *Energy Conservation: Hearings*, pp. 67–74; U.S. Congress, Senate Interior Committee, *Energy Conservation Act of 1976: Hearings*, p. 182; and Letter, John Honeycomb, IBM, to author, August 4, 1978.

62. GSA in Fred Dubin, "Energy Management for Commercial Buildings," Paper presented at Lawrence Berkeley Laboratory, July 1976, p. 25; and Dubin, "Energy Conservation Studies," *Energy and Buildings*, vol. 36, 1977. Ontario Hydro in *Energy User News*, March 20, 1978.

63. H. C. Fisher *et al.*, *The Annual Cycle Energy System: Initial Investigations*, Oak Ridge National Laboratory ORNL/TM-5525, October 1976. For a practical viewpoint from inside the construction industry, see Ray Harrell, "Can We Build a More Efficient House?" in Paul Hendershat, ed., *Energy Conservation and Development* (Murfreesboro, Tenn.: Middle Tennessee State University, 1977). The comparison described in Ralph A. Johnson, "The Performance of an Energy Efficient Residence versus a Conventional Comparison home," paper presented to the ASHRAE/DOE Thermal Performance of the Exterior Envelopes of Building Conference, December 3–5, 1979. For the 50 Canadian houses, see R. S. Dumont, H. W. Orr, C. P. Hendlin, and J. T. Makohon, "Measured Energy Consumption of a Group of Low-Energy Houses," paper presented at Solar Energy Society of Canada, August 1980; Yergin and Hillenbrand, *Global Insecurity*, pp. 134–36.

64. This viewpoint is eloquently expressed by Stein in *Architecture and Energy*.

65. City of Seattle, Energy Office, *First Quarter's Report*, January–March 1978. For a description of the process whereby HUD is tightening standards, see *New York Times*, March 18, 1978, p. 25.

66. Newman and Day, *The American Energy Consumer*, pp. 40, 42; Robert Rosenberg, "Energy Usage in the Home—Consumption and Conservation," in George Morganthaler and Aaron N. Silver, eds., *Energy Delta: Supply vs. Demand* (Tarzana, Calif.: American Astronautical Association, 1974), pp. 76–77.

67. U.S. Congress, Senate, Commerce Committee, *Energy Conservation Act of 1976: Hearings*, 94 Cong., 2 sess., p. 126; U.S. Congress, Senate, Interior Committee, *Energy Conservation Act of 1976: Hearings*, pp. 667–668; Harold B. Olin, "Put Some Sunshine into Your Mortgage Portfolio," *Savings and Loan News*, January 1977; "Energy Loan Programs Square Off against the Elements," *Savings and Loan News*, October 1977.

68. U.S. Congress, Senate, Interior Committee, *Energy Conservation Act of 1976: Hearings*, p. 117.

69. Interview with John Honeycomb; letter from Honeycomb, May 21, 1982. Energy Programs Department, "IBM's Energy Conservation Program," manuscript, January 1980; U.S. Congress, Joint Economic Committee, Subcommittee on Energy, *Energy Conservation: Hearings*, p. 70; IBM Annual Report: 1977, p. 33. In IBM world-trade countries, the energy reduction over preconservation levels in 1973 to 1979 was 40 percent per square foot. Between 1973 and 1979, AT&T reduced its energy use per square foot by 35 percent, also

with very little investment. See AT&T, "Energy Conservation in the Bell System," June 1, 1980.

70. For 3M, see U.S. Congress, Joint Economic Committee, Subcommittee on Energy, *Energy Conservation: Hearings*, pp. 74–104; U.S. Congress, Senate, Interior Committee, *Energy Conservation Act of 1976: Hearings*, pp. 174–77; 3M, "Plant Energy Optimization Guidelines," January 14, 1977, and "Engineering Energy Conservation Standards," Mimeographed papers, July 14, 1977. Ashland case described in letter from Paul Chellgren to author, April 28, 1978. Bell Telephone, in its effective conservation program, also found outside air to be one of the biggest villains. AT&T, "Energy Conservation in the Bell System," Unpublished paper, December 1977, p. 8. These various cases stand out more as examples of what is possible than of what is being generally done. While the design of new commercial buildings emphasizes energy saving, there is a considerable body of evidence that conservation energy in the existing commercial stock is not being tapped anywhere near its potential. One major reason is that a two- to three-year payback is often considered too long. Also, expenditures for improvement in management and maintenance of buidings lag when the economy is uncertain or weak. These are the conclusions of a DOE-sponsored study of the commercial building sector. See Joseph H. Newman, "Commercial Buildings: Retrofit and Other Energy Opportunities and Strategies," in Richard F. Hill, ed., *Energy Technology V: Challenges to Technology* (Washington, D.C.: Government Institutes, 1978).

71. W. R. Godwin, "Energy Conservation," *National Journal*, April 3, 1976, p. 456; General Accounting Office, *National Standards Needed for Residential Energy Conservation*, RED 75 377, June 20, 1975; Ralph Johnson, "Retrofit: a New Business Opportunity for Remodelers and Homebuilders," Speech at National Association of Home Builders Convention, January 22, 1975; Federal Energy Agency, "Retrofitting Homes for Energy Conservation," Energy Conservation Paper No. 23, pp. 3–4; Rosenberg, "Energy Usage in the Home—Consumption and Conservation," in Morgenthaler and Silver, eds., *Energy Delta: Supply vs. Demand*, p. 72; U.S. Department of Commerce, *Annual Housing Survey: 1975*, sec. A, p. 1.

72. *Monthly Energy Review*, March 1976, pp. 4–6; George A. Tsongas, *Home Energy Conservation Demonstration Project: Final Report for Chevron USA*, August 1977. Johns-Manville came to similar conclusions in applying a basic retrofit package to a standard ranch-style home in Belleville, Illinois. See Johns-Manville, "Residential Energy Savings: Retrofit," and John C. Moyers, *The Value of Thermal Insulation in Residential Construction: Economics and the Conservation of Energy*, ORNL-NSF-EP-9. So did the TVA: W. C. Whisenant, to author, May 23, 1977.

73. U.S. Congress, Senate, Commerce Committee, *Energy Conservation Act of 1976: Hearings*, 94 Cong., 2 sess. (Washington, D.C.: Government Printing Office, 1974), pp. 69–70; Donald C. Navarre, Washington Natural Gas, "Conservation and Utility Marketing," Mimeographed paper, November 1,

1977. The company estimates that its Super Heat Keeper package reduces by 70 percent the energy that an uninsulated house would consume for space heating.

74. Letter from W. C. Whisenant, TVA, to author, May 23, 1977. This is true for other utilities as well. See U.S. Congress, Senate, Energy Committee, *Energy Conservation Provisions of President Carter's Energy Program*, 95 Cong., 1 sess., p. 216. Conservation as an alternative to new capacity is discussed in Willey, "Alternative Energy Systems for Pacific Gas and Electric Co.: An Economic Analysis." Also see Willey, Prepared testimony submitted to the Arkansas Public Service Commission, on behalf of Attorney General Bill Clinton, May 15, 1978. "It is our hope," Attorney General Clinton notes, that the Arkansas Public Service Commission "will decide to embark on this innovative path to meeting Arkansas' power and energy needs for the 1980's." Letter to author, June 16, 1978.

75. Robert Socolow, ed., *Saving Energy in the Home: Princeton's Experiments at Twin Rivers* (Cambridge, Mass.: Ballinger, 1978), pp. 63–64, 100. But it is still doubtful whether the skills and knowledge represented in the Twin Rivers study would have become part of the repertoire of the typical insulation contractor. An excellent guide available for the homeowner is John Rothchild, *Stop Burning Your Money: The Only Home Energy Guide You'll Ever Need* (New York: Penguin, 1982).

76. Robert Williams and Marc Ross, "Drilling for Oil and Gas in Our Houses," *Technology Review*, March/April 1980, pp. 25–36. Moyers, *The Value of Thermal Insulation in Residential Construction: Economics and The Conservation of Energy*; NAHB, "Retrofitting Homes for Energy Conservation," p. 4; Johns-Manville, "Residential Energy Savings: Retrofit."

77. General Accounting Office, *National Standards Needed for Residential Energy Conservation*, p. 17.

78. Moyers, *The Value of Thermal Insulation in Residential Construction*, p. 1. For mobility, see Newman and Day, *The American Energy Consumer*, p. 45. There may, however, be a growing perception that the cost of energy-saving investments can be passed on to the buyer.

79. Florence Leyland discusses her case in U.S. Congress, Joint Economic Committee, Subcommittee on Energy, *Energy Conservation: Hearings*, p. 26.

80. Cepeda, *Potential for Energy Conservation in Texas*, p. 148. The serious effects of lack of knowledge are discussed, on the basis of a series of studies, in Lind, *The Rationale for Federal End-Use (Conservation and Solar) Programs*, p. 9. The institutional and political problems faced by the Energy Extension Service are perceptively analyzed by Robert Reisner, "The Federal Government's Role in Supporting State and Local Conservation Programs," in John Sawhill, ed., *Energy Conservation and Public Policy*. For survey data, Roger Seasonwein Associates, "The Conservation Decision: American Attitudes About Energy-Saving Programs," conducted for Union Carbide, March 1980.

81. Ralph Johnson, "Retrofit: A New Business Opportunity," Speech to NAHB Convention, January 22, 1975.

82. One method to involve the utilities is through the Michigan Plan, where utilities take responsibility for retrofit. See William G. Rosenberg, "Conservation Investments by Gas Utilities as a Gas Supply Option," *Public Utilities Fortnightly,* January 26, 1977; Detroit Edison, "Detroit Edison: Home Insulation Finance Man," brochure; Joel Sharkey, "Report to the Michigan Public Service Commission on the Home Insulation Promotion and Financing Program," Mimeographed paper.

83. Tennessee Valley Authority, Division of Energy Conservation and Rates, Program Summary, June 1981, Dan G. Ozenne and Robert A. F. Reisner, *The TVA Home Insulation Program: An Evaluation of Early Program Impact: Report Prepared for the TVA by ICF Inc.* (Washington, D.C.: April 1980).

Charles Luce's remarks are in Steven Westley, ed., *Energy Efficiency and the Utilities: New Directions* (San Francisco: California Public Utilities Commission, July 1980). This volume, based upon a symposium sponsored by the CPUC, provides an excellent overview of the prospects and problems of utilities in dealing with energy conservation. It includes a summary by CPUC president John Bryson of the many initiatives taken by one public utility commission in the face of "the profound changes of the past several years in the economics of energy supply."

The "house doctor" is discussed in Robert Williams and Marc Ross, "Drilling for Oil and Gas in Our Houses," *Technology Review,* March/April 1980, pp. 25–36.

84. Leon R. Glicksman, "Heat Pumps: Off and Running . . . Again," *Technology Review,* June/July 1978, pp. 64, 70; General Accounting Office, *The Federal Government Should Establish and Meet Energy Conservation Goals,* pp. 60, 88–89. Industrial applications of the heat pump are discussed in R.L.J. McLaren, "Heat Pumps," Paper presented at National Energy Management Conference, Birmingham, England, October 1978.

The concern with making homes energy-efficient has led to the first concentrated attention to indoor air quality. Recent research indicates possible pollution problems in very tight houses from four indoor contaminants—carbon monoxide and nitrogen dioxide from gas appliances and tobacco smoke; formaldehyde from particleboard, plywood, urea-formaldehyde foam insulation, and gas appliances; and radon from building materials, soil, and ground water. Various of these problems may have been long-standing in some homes, but only recently noticed—an example of the low level effort in research on energy conservation. Reduced infiltration and ventilation increase concentrations of the pollutants. It appears highly likely that the problem can be eliminated simply through the use of mechanical ventilation systems with air-to-air heat exchanges. For discussion see C.D. Hollowell, J.V. Berk, M.C. Boegel, R. R. Miksel, W. W. Nazaroff, and G. W. Traynor, "Indoor Air Quality in Residential Buildings," Lawrence Berkeley Laboratory-10391 Dev., EEB-Vent-80-3; W. W. Nazaroff, M. C. Boegel, D. C. Hallowell, and G. D.

Roseme, "The Use of Mechanical Ventilation with Heat Recovery for Controlling Radon and Radon-Daughter Concentrations," Lawrence Berkeley Laboratory-10222, E EB-Vent-80-6; D. C. Hallowell, J. V. Berk, C. Lin, W. W. Nazaroff, and G. W. Traynor, "Impact of Energy Conservation in Buildings in Health," Lawrence Berkeley Laboratory-9379, EEB-Vent 79-9; R. J. Budnitz, J. V. Berk, C. D. Hallowell, W. W. Nazaroff, A. V. Nero, A. H. Rosenfeld, "Human Disease from Radon Exposure," *Energy and Buildings* 2(1979):209–15.

85. Eric Hirst and Robert Hoskins, "Residential Water Heaters: Energy and Cost Analysis," *Energy and Buildings I* (1977–78), pp. 393–400; Hoskins, Hirst, and W. S. Johnson, "Residential Refrigerators: Energy Conservation and Economics," *Energy,* 3 (August 1978), pp. 43–49; Socolow, ed., *Saving Energy in the Home,* pp. 3, 13; C. Franklin Montgomery, "Product Technology and the Consumer," *Scientific American,* December 1977, pp. 47–53.

86. Eric Hirst, Janet Carney, Dennis O'Neal, "Feasibility of Zero Residential Energy Growth," *Energy,* 3 (August 1978).

87. For temperature settings, see General Accounting Office, *The Federal Government Should Establish and Meet Conservation Goals,* pp. 60–61; and Robert Socolow, ed., *Saving Energy in the Home,* pp. 207, 232. Some aspects of the behavioral issues are surveyed, including a warning against coercion, in Paul C. Stern and Eileen M. Kirkpatrick, "Energy Behavior," *Environment,* December 1977, pp. 10–15. Psychological issues involved in energy conservation are surveyed in "Motivating the Troops for the Energy War," a special section in *Psychology Today,* April 1979, pp. 14–33.

88. For limitation of economic models in this regard, see Otto Eckstein and Sara Johnson, "Forecast Summary," in Federal Energy Administration, *1976 National Energy Outlook;* also see William Hogan, ed., *Energy and the Economy,* vol. 1 (Stanford, Calif.: Energy Modeling Forum, 1977), for the difficulty of including "non-market behavior: . . . The effects of regulation, industrial organization, or the expectations created by government's future role are not well understood . . . nor the impacts of unexpected embargoes." Information on "Low-Cost/No Cost" from Lynn Collins, Department of Energy, Office of Buildings and Community System, *An Evaluation of the Low Cost/No Cost Conservation Program in New England* (Washington, 1980 draft). The booklet, written by John Rothschild, was distributed in 1979. The poll data are Cambridge Reports, October 1979, for the Alliance to Save Energy. For a succinct summary of the new consensus on energy conservation, see *The Dynamics of Energy Efficiency* (Alliance to Save Energy: Washington, 1980), a report on a symposium held at Dumbarton Oaks in October 1979 under the joint sponsorship of the Alliance to Save Energy and Harvard University.

89. The results are reported in Demand and Conservation Panel of the Committee on Nuclear and Alternative Energy Systems, "U.S. Energy Demand: Some Low Energy Futures," *Science,* April 14, 1978, pp. 142–152. The four scenarios projected total primary energy consumption in 2010 of 58, 74, 94, or

136 quads. Consumption in 1975 was 71 quads. Price assumptions were a quadrupling in real terms of 1975 prices in the first two scenarios, a doubling in the third, and unchanged in the last. The panel stressed the important conceptual point—that energy conservation is, in effect, a source of energy: "A major slowdown of demand growth can be achieved simultaneously with significant economic growth by substituting technological sophistication for energy consumption." In other words, after capitalizing on the relatively simple steps that can save considerable energy, conservation technologies can compete with supply technologies for the energy "services" market.

90. This study was undertaken by Marc Ross and Robert Williams, and is reported in "The Potential for Fuel Conservation," *Technology Review*, February 1977, pp. 49–57. See Marc Ross and Robert Socolow, eds., *Efficient Use of Energy, American Institute of Physics Conference Proceedings, No. 25* (New York: AIP, 1975). The date of substitution was very generalized, and they emphasized physical possibilities, without attempting to calculate a cost. The purpose was to stake out a potential.

91. *Monthly Energy Review,* May 1977, p. 44.

92. Indeed, one of the most compelling pieces of evidence challenging the need for reprocessing of nuclear waste during Britain's Windscale Inquiry was a physical modeling effort similar to the American Physical Society study. Its conclusions for Britain paralleled the American study. See Gerald Leach, "Written Evidence to the Windscale Inquiry on Behalf of Friends of the Earth Limited," Mimeographed paper, 1978. Also see his "Energy for the Built Environment," Paper to the Social Science Research Council Seminar on Energy Utilisation, April 26, 1978.

93. General Accounting Office, *U.S. Energy Conservation Could Benefit from Experience of Other Countries;* International Energy Agency, *Energy Policies and Programs of IEA Countries: 1977 Review* (Paris: OECD, 1978). Daniel Yergin, "France's War on Energy Waste," Energy Research Project paper, June 1978; German Information Center, *Economic Reports,* June 23, 1978. For Canada, see Ministry of Energy, Mines, and Resources, *A Synopsis of Federal Initiatives in Conservation and Renewable Energy,* January 1982. For the strong effort in Japan, see Yergin and Hillebrand, *Global Insecurity,* chapters 5–6.

94. Henry Lee, "The Role of Local Governments in Promoting Energy Efficiency," draft paper, March 1980. Lee notes three ingredients for a successful program: First, strong leadership on senior elected officials, a need analogous to that, as already noted, required of corporate leaders. Second, "a pervasive belief" that energy efficiency would be in the long-run economic interests of the city. Third, an extensive participatory process that legitimized the undertaking. For a survey of community energy efforts, see James Ridgeway, *Energy Efficient Community Planning* (Erasmus, Penn.: J. G. Press, 1979); also see Seattle Energy Office, "The Seattle Energy Code Proposal: An Analysis of Its Development, Policies, and Cost-Effectiveness," paper, February 14, 1979; Minnesota Energy Agency, *Energy Policy and Conservation Report* (St. Paul,

1978); Franklin County, *Energy Goals and Policy Development: 1980–85* (Greenfield, Mass.: October 30, 1979). Franklin County's plan aims to reduce energy consumption in absolute terms in that area of Northwestern Massachusetts by 6.4 percent by 1985.

95. Roger Sant, "A Preliminary Assessment of the Potential to Adjust Capital Stock to Higher End Use Efficiencies," Paper at American Association for the Advancement of Science, February 14, 1978. The caveat against conservation is in *Citibank Energy Newsletter* 4 (1978), p. 4. The value of conservation as a way to buy time and promote flexibility is stressed in a paper by a very shrewd energy analyst: Mons Lönnroth, "Nuclear Power in the Swedish Energy Futures—Commitments and Alternatives," Paper presented at Bellerive Conference, February 1979. He makes the additional point that distribution systems should be designed "so that different long-term technologies are adaptable."

96. The rationale and strategy for information and public education on conservation is set out in MIT Center for Policy Alternatives, *The Impact of Advertising, Marketing, and Other Market Information on Consumer Energy Use: A Workshop Report*, June 30, 1978, FTC Contract L0304. Another analysis that, like this chapter, points to the advantages of incentives for promoting conservation is Lind, *The Rationale for Federal End Use (Conservation and Solar) Programs*.

97. Incentives can, in many instances, be politically more acceptable than regulations in our society. If all homes at the time of sale were required to be brought up to certain conservation standards, the nation's realtors would oppose it. Tax credits for insulation would not call up such organized opposition. Public opinion analysts who carried out one of the major energy attitude surveys concluded: "Positive economic incentives—those that can help the consumer save money—may be more efficient than either behavioral regulation or price regulation." William H. Cunningham and Sally Cook Lopreato, *Energy Use and Conservation Incentives: A Study of the Southwestern United States* (New York: Praeger, 1977), p. 100.

Chapter 7 | *Solar America*

1. Sun Day's Denis Hayes, however, is not optimistic about reaching these levels of solar contribution, since they would require "a World War II style mobilization"; Denis Hayes, personal communication. R. W. Scott, *World Oil*, June 1978. Mr. Hayes is the former Director of the Solar Energy Research Institute in Golden, Colorado.

2. The best available source of growth figures for renewables is the Resource and Technology Management Corporation of Arlington, Virginia. These figures are taken from their *Alternative Energy Data Summary for the United States, 1975–1980*, vol. 2, 1981.

3. Edwards' statement made before the Senate Subcommittee on Appropriations for the Department of Interior and Related Agencies, March 2, 1982.

4. This definition distinguishes solar energy from the products of "ancient sun-

shine" (oil, gas, and coal), but includes direct sunshine, the wind, falling water, and plant matter—except for some century-old trees.

Not surprisingly, the lack of an established definition for solar energy has tended to obfuscate press reports regarding solar energy and its true potential in this century. For instance, a story in *New York Times* was headlined "Solar Energy Held Still Decades Away" (*New York Times*, February 1, 1979, p. A7). The *Times* story, a summary of the report by H. Ehrenreich *et al.*, *American Physical Society Study on Solar Photovoltaic Energy Conversion* (New York: American Physical Society, 1979), explained that "the group doubts that more than one percent of the nation's electricity can be generated from sunlight by the end of the century." This group's conclusions—which closely parallel our own—were actually limited to *photovoltaic* energy conversion, only one of five technologies proposed to generate electricity from the sun, and at present, certainly not the cheapest or most technically mature. As shown above, several non-electrical technologies may also be employed to obtain energy from the sun. Indeed, it is from these other technologies that the largest near- and middle-term contributions from solar energy can be expected.

5. Satellite power systems and total energy systems are sometimes also considered in a separate category. See, for instance, U.S. Department of Energy, *Solar Energy, A Status Report*, DOE/ET-0062, June 1978, p. 9, and *Appendix A, Solar Technologies*, pp. 13–39.

6. The term "on-site" derives from the limited area within which the energy produced by a system is consumed—a house, a factory, or at most, a small cluster of structures. The on-site technologies also include agricultural and process heat, small windmills, dams, and local plant matter usage. See, for instance, U.S. Congress, Office of Technology Assessment, *Application of Solar Technology to Today's Energy Needs*, vol. 1, June 1978, pp. 11 and 19.

7. For an alternative view, see, for instance, Amory B. Lovins, *Soft Energy Paths: Towards a Durable Peace* (San Francisco: Friends of the Earth, 1977). See also Lovins, "Energy Strategy: The Road Not Taken?" *Foreign Affairs*, October 1976; E. F. Schumacher, *Small Is Beautiful: Economics As If People Mattered* (New York: Harper and Row, 1975).

8. *Biomass* is short for biological matter, and is generally used as a synonym for plant matter and animal waste.

9. For a comprehensive review of the economics and the technology of conversion processes for solar electricity, see Wolfgang Palz, *Solar Electricity: An Economic Approach to Solar Energy* (London: Butterworth, 1978).

10. Though we have chosen space and hot water heating to illustrate the potential —and the problems—of the on-site technologies, the remaining on-site technologies, such as small windmills, small dams, and, especially, agricultural and process heat, also have significant short-term potential. Some analysts believe that intermediate temperature systems for agricultural and process heat may well have the greatest short-term potential for solar energy utilization. See, for example, William D. Metz, "Solar Thermal Energy: Bringing the Pieces Together," *Science*, vol. 197, August 12, 1977.

11. R. G. Stein, *Architecture and Energy* (New York: Anchor Press/Doubleday, 1977). See also Wade Greene, "Solar Refractions," *New Times*, May 25, 1978, and Bruce Anderson, *Solar Energy: Fundamentals in Building Design* (New York: McGraw-Hill, 1977).

12. Bruce Anderson, *Solar Energy*, chaps. IIA, B, C. For an excellent analysis of passive design technologies, see John I. Meyer, "The Cost of Passive Solar Energy," M.S. thesis, Massachusetts Institute of Technology, June 1977. The distinction between passive solar and conservation blurs in some cases. Some argue that the impressive strides that have been made in superinsulation and double envelope houses should be considered passive. In reality, passive is a hybrid form of technology somewhere between conservation and active solar. For an informative look at new developments in superinsulation and other passive applications, see William Schurcliff, *Superinsulated Houses and Double Envelope Houses* (Cambridge, Mass.: William A. Schurcliff, 1980).

13. The Texas house information is from *New York Times*, "Passive Approach Found to be Active Cost Saver in a Solar House in Texas," May 18, 1978, supplemented by personal communications from the owner of the house, Colonel Archie Erwin. The Maine building information is also from *New York Times*, "Solar Heated Shop in Maine is Called Most Innovative," May 9, 1978, p. A29. Field research and personal communications with Michael Corbett, builder and designer of Corbett Homes, Davis, CA. See also David Bainbridge, Judy Corbett, and John Hofacre, *Village Homes' Solar House Designs*, Rodale Press, Emmaus, PA, 1979.

On passive houses, see R. W. Bliss, "Why Not Just Build the House Right in the First Place?" *Bulletin of the Atomic Scientists*, March 1976; Owens Corning Fiberglass, *Energy-Saving Homes: The Arkansas Story*, June 1976. See also Reference 16.

For general background on active systems, see Anderson, *Solar Energy: Fundamentals in Building Design*, parts III, IV, V.

14. On Denver tour, see *Solar Times*, June 1981, p. 10. Supplemented by interview with Denis Hayes, January 1983.

15. Ralph Johnson, president of the National Association of Homebuilders Research Foundation, January 1982.

16. Data on the total number of solar installations is extremely difficult to obtain. Estimates here are based upon an examination of IRS records of residential tax credits and a survey of DOE solar installers, supplemented by personal estimates by Carlo La Porta of the Solar Lobby.

17. "Standard Oil Sells DWH Technology," *Solar Times*, November 1981, p. 1. As an indication of the future direction in this technology, Standard Oil of California abandoned its entire plate collection business—based upon a thermidiode and its thermosyphon system—and as of November 1981, hoped to sell the technology to a Japanese manufacturer.

18. "Olin Corp. Bows Out of Solar—Blames Soft Market for Departure," *Solar Times*, August 1981. In February 1981 when Exxon announced it was selling its Daystar Corporation subsidiary for $2.2 million to the American Solar King

Corporation of Waco, Texas, it created much industry speculation about its motivations. The major public statement came from Frank Kendall, Exxon's manager of Planning and Analysis for Energy and Material Ventures: "We couldn't make a profit on Daystar because it doesn't draw on our strengths— ability to be involved in high technology and capital intensive projects." See "American Solar King Purchases Exxon's Daystar Collector Business," *Solar Times,* March 1981, pp. 1-2.

19. William T. Schleyer and Donald M. Young, "Consumer Attitudes Towards Solar Energy," Harvard Business School Energy Project Unpublished Report, May 20, 1977. Four thousand questionnaires were sent out to randomly selected residents of eight states, two from each of four regions: Northeast (Massachusetts, Connecticut), South (Florida, Georgia), Southwest (Arizona, Colorado), and West (California, Nevada). About 19 percent of those polled responded.

Other surveys have borne out the five-year payback requirement for major solar retrofit. See William H. Cunningham and Sally Cook Lopreato, *Energy Use and Conservation Incentives: a Study of the Southwestern United States* (New York: Praeger, 1977), pp. 87-88.

For the sources of the estimates of solar heating system prices, see Reference 16.

20. For information on our nationwide consumer survey, see Reference 35. Also see *Massachusetts Solar Action Office Demographic Analysis of Applicants and Grant Recipients Under HUD Residential Solar Domestic Hot Water Initiative Program,* September 1977. "California's Solar Energy Tax Credit: An Analysis of Tax Returns for 1977," California Energy Commission staff report, September 1979.

The provision for incorporation of solar heating in military housing and other military construction was made by Senator Gary Hart of Colorado. See Military Construction Act of 1979, Bill No. S3079.

21. For a detailed analysis of the economics and design of an actual solar home, see Mark Hyman, "Solar Economics Comes Home," *Technology Review,* February 1978, pp. 28-35.

22. For a review of the pitfalls of simple payback analysis, see Henry H. Leck, "Pitfalls of Payback Analysis," *Solar Engineering Magazine,* September 1978, pp. 22-25.

23. Personal Interview. For the current state of solar building code legislation, see *Solar State Legislation.*

24. Robert O. Smith and Associates found that only 15 percent of the one hundred New England utilities' solar domestic water heating experimental installations functioned well during the first year of operation. In addition to reliability problems, the consultants found that twenty-seven of the systems —when operating—produced very low savings of energy, or none. The average savings of energy used for hot water heating with the *best* fifteen systems was 37 percent. A variety of problems with pipes, valves, controllers, and undersizing of the panels and controllers—*primarily installation problems*—were cited

as explanations of the poor results. The consultants concluded that the experiment had been a "learning experience" for the industry, and that with appropriate installation it was still reasonable to expect a target savings of 50 percent (in the New England area) of the energy consumed by water heating.

System Reliability	*% of Installations*
1. Functioned well	15
2. No *major* breakdowns	8
3. At least one major breakdown	57
4. Severely unreliable	20
TOTAL	100%

For further information on this subject, see Robert O. Smith and Associates, "Summary of Performance Problems of 100 Residential Solar Water Heaters installed by the New England Electric Company subsidiaries in 1976–77," Boston, 1978. For a study of how utilities could help to alleviate installation problems, see Bruce M. Smackey, "Should Electric Utilities Market Solar Energy?" *Public Utilities Fortnightly,* September 28, 1978, pp. 37–43.

For difficulties with active solar installation, and how the purchaser can deal with them, see John Rothchild, *Stop Burning Your Money: The Only Home Energy Guide You'll Ever Need* (New York: Penguin, 1982).

25. Interview with Alan Ackerman, president of Energyworks, Newton, Mass.
26. See Joyce R. Swain, Oklahoma Solar Information Office, "States Focus on Tax Incentives, Lag Behind on Sun Rights, Codes," *Solar Engineering Magazine,* April 1978, p. 22. See also *Solar State Legislation;* W. R. Harris, "Is the Right to Light a California Necessity?" Rand Corporation, Paper 5558, 1975.
27. Letter from First American Bank for Savings, Brockton, Massachusetts, to Massachusetts Action Office, November 22, 1977.
28. As an example of the skepticism of the utility industry regarding solar energy, see Lelan F. Sillin, Jr., "Overview of Issues Facing the Electric Utility Industry," Paper presented to the 55th American Assembly, November 1978, pp. 10–14. Sillin cited a Booz-Allen study: "It is necessary for Northeast Utilities to continue to rely on conventional generation technologies to meet its base load capacity requirements in the late 1980s and early 1990s." Sillin also added that "no alternative technology . . . could justify delaying the decision to install a conventional—that is, nuclear or coal—base load generating facility in the 1990 time frame."
29. For a review of the solar loan market, see "Solar Financing: Picture Brightens," *Solar Engineering Magazine,* January 1978, pp. 7–8. Some states, however, have passed laws excluding solar energy equipment from property taxes. See, for instance, *Solar State Legislation* (Rockville, Md.: National Solar Heating and Cooling Information Center, January 1978). For more detailed

description of PG&E's rebate program and a comprehensive discussion of the policy issue surrounding this program, see Margaret Curran Gardels, "Utility Financing Loans or Rebates," *Solar Law Reporter,* September–October 1981, p. 477–486.

30. Interview with Pat Harris, director of public relations, TVA, February 1982. See also Smackey, "Should Electric Utilities Market Solar Energy," *Public Utilities Fortnightly.* For an alternative view, see Joseph G. Asburg and Ronald O. Mueller, "Solar Energy and Electric Utilities: Should They Be Interfaced?" *Science,* vol. 195, no. 4277, February 1977, pp. 445–450. Eight of the major U.S. gas and electric utilities were also interviewed by one of the authors, Frank Schuller. For opposition to utility involvement, see Jane W. Stein, "Law to Force SDG&E to Stop Selling Solar Energy Systems," San Diego *Union,* December 24, 1978, p. A3. For an analysis of alternative solar-heating strategies for the utilities, see M. Maidique and B. Woo, "Solar Heating Strategies for the Electric Utilities," *Technology Review,* May 1980.

31. Should the government intervene? Most analysts of this question have come to the same general conclusion: Government intervention is justified when it helps to "bring private decisions about costs and benefits more closely in line with total cost and benefits" (J. Herbert Holloman and Michele Grenon, *U.S. Energy Research and Development Policy* [Cambridge, Mass.: Ballinger, 1975], p. 12). For instance, assume that a promising new home solar electric converter has been developed, but the cost of installing the first prototypes will be $100,000, or, say, fifty times the cost of a competitive conventional system. It may be in the interest of society to subsidize the first several users, because the knowledge gained in those first few installations can serve as a guide (to invest or not to invest) to tens of millions of potential buyers. The value of this knowledge for society will far exceed the cost of a 90 percent subsidy to a few pioneering users. Similarly, government investment in research and development can be justified when an industry, because of structural reasons and/or inappropriate incentives due to government regulation, is underinvesting in research and development. Housing, a fragmented industry, is a case in point. The housing industry is made up of many small firms, none of which is sufficiently large to carry out a major R&D program. See, for instance, Edwin Mansfield, *The Economics of Technological Change* (New York: W. W. Norton, 1968), p. 229. For an analysis of the proper role of the government in energy R&D, see Holloman and Grenon, *U.S. Energy Research and Development Policy.*

But the most compelling argument for government intervention is found in the marginal cost of energy. When the cost of a product is rising, as has been the case for energy, its *average* price is lower than the cost for the last additional BTU of energy—the marginal cost. Although a system could be arranged to reflect the marginal cost of petroleum, gas, and so on, this would be politically difficult because of the income distribution consequences. The altnerative—placing solar energy on an even basis with fossil fuels by means of subsidies—is politically much more realistic and palatable.

32. Case studies of the diffusion of a wide variety of innovations, from color TV to hybrid corn, show that market development follows a pattern characterized by an S-shaped logistic curve: Diffusion starts out very gradually, then rises rapidly, flattening off again in the last stage until the market is saturated. See, for instance, Edwin Mansfield, *Industrial Research and Technological Innovation* (New York: W. W. Norton, 1968), chaps. 7, 8, 9, pp. 133–191. For data on the actual diffusion of the color TV innovation over a twenty-year period, see, for instance, *Zenith C* (Boston: Intercollegiate Case Clearing House, 9-674-095, revised August 1977). For hybrid corn, see Zvi Grilliches, "Hybrid Corn and the Economics of Innovation," *The Economics of Technological Change*, ed. Nathan Rosenberg (Middlesex, Engl.: Penguin Books, 1971). For recent views on potential rates of diffusion of the solar energy technologies, see Dennis Schiffel, Dennis Costello, David Posner, and Robert Witholder, *The Market Penetration of Solar Energy: A Model Review Workshop Summary*, Solar Energy Research Institute, Golden, Colo., January 1978. Similar diffusion curves, called product life cycles, are found by plotting sales of most products from birth to maturity. See, for example, Theodore Levitt, "Exploit the Product Life Cycle," *Harvard Business Review*, November–December 1965, p. 81.

33. Although the actual number of installations is difficult to verify, it is generally agreed that the total number of California installations has at least doubled since the 65,000 level in 1980. These estimates were made from interviews with the Solar Cal Council, the California Energy Commission, the California Solar Energy Office, Sun Ray, and the Sun Work Institute. That California far exceeds the rest of the nation in the rate of solar installations is clear. Nearly half of the present installations are in that state. But the extent to which the state credits are responsible is a matter of debate. Other factors contributing to solar's growth in California are a favorable political climate, abundant sunshine, lifestyle amenabilities, and favorable utility disposition. See "California's 55% Solar Tax Credit Scrutinized After Three Years' Trial," *Solar Times*, November 1979, p. 1.

34. Nonetheless, there is a danger in the development of codes or standards too early in the industry's infancy, particularly if they are too restrictive. In a June 30, 1978 letter to the Division of Solar Energy, William A. Schurcliff argues that "standards should be worded in such a way that any company selling any queer kind of system, can claim it *meets* the standard unless it explicitly flunks. That is, I urge that you avoid placing a company under a dark shadow merely because you have not gotten around to writing a standard that applies to it. Write standards that are 'fail-safe,' i.e., are not condemnatory by default."

35. Nobel laureate Melvin Calvin describes the sugar cane plant as "the best, most efficient solar energy device we have today on a large scale." Melvin Calvin, "The Sunny Side of the Future," *Chemtech*, June 1977, p. 353. See also *Energy From Biological Processes*, Report of the Energy Program, Office of Technology Assessment, U.S. Congress, March 1980.

36. Denis Hayes, *Energy: The Solar Prospect*, Worldwatch Paper 11 (Washington, D.C.: Worldwatch Institute, March 1977).

37. Another 20 percent of the country's energy was derived indirectly from work animal feed. See, for instance, John C. Fisher, *Energy Crises in Perspective* (New York: John Wiley and Sons, 1974), p. 14. Only fifty years earlier, in 1850, solar energy—fuel wood, work animal feed, wind, and falling water—had accounted for 93 percent of U.S. energy consumption (Fisher, p. 13).

38. See E. L. Ellwood et al., *The Potential of Lignocellulosic Materials for the Production of Chemicals, Fuels and Energy*, National Research Council (Springfield, Va.: National Technical Information Service, 1976), p. 11. For similar estimates, including a 1970 breakdown into fuel wood and forest industry waste, see Thomas Gage, *Renewable Resources for Industrial Materials* (Washington, D.C.: National Academy of Sciences, 1976), and *Energy From Biological Processes*. For the estimates of Swedish and Finnish wood consumption, see Richard Merril and Thomas Gage, *Energy Primer, Solar, Water, Wind and Biofuels* (New York: Delta, 1978), a good basic source on biomass fuels, especially wood.

   Biomass, or plant matter, is a byproduct of photosynthesis. Light (sunshine) is absorbed by chlorophyll, which in turn produces oxygen and hydrogen. The oxygen and hydrogen fuel the photosynthesis process by which carbon is converted to carbohydrates, the principal product of most green plants. For an excellent overview of the biomass alternative, see C. C. Burwell, "Solar Biomass Energy: An Overview of U.S. Potential," *Science*, vol. 199, March 10, 1978, pp. 1041–1048. For a compact classic article on biomass possibilities and processes, see Melvin Calvin, "The Sunny Side of the Future," *Chemtech*. See also *Energy From Biological Processes*.

39. See *A New Prosperity, Building a Sustainable Energy Future*, The SERI Solar/Conservation Study, (Andover, Mass.: Brick House, 1981), p. 249. Figures on biomass use have been extremely difficult to come by as DOE did not typically include them in their monthly reports. However, in mid-1981 the Congressional Wood Caucus solicited a letter from DOE Secretary Edwards that documents this level. Interview with Steve Morgan, New England Energy Congress.

40. Alan D. Poole and Robert H. Williams, "Flower Power," *Bulletin of Atomic Scientists*, May 1976; John R. Benemann, *Biofuels: A Survey*, #ER-746-SR, Special Report (Palo Alto, Calif.: Electric Power Research Institute, June 1978).

41. Allen L. Hammond, "Alcohol: A Brazilian Answer to the Energy Crisis," *Science*, vol. 195, February 11, 1977. For more information on liquid and gaseous biomass, see Roberta Navicki, "Biomass," *Science News*, vol. 113, no. 16, April 22, 1978, p. 259. See also Warren Hodge, "Brazil is High on Alcohol Fuel," *New York Times*, June 14, 1979, p. D1. For research on new sources of biomass, see Benemann, *Biofuels: A Survey*, sec. 1.

42. "Energy From Biological Processes," p. IV-54 to 56. See also Meekhof, R. L., W. E. Tyner, and F. D. Holland, "Agricultural Policy and Gasohol," Purdue University, May 1979.

43. Although press reports have downplayed Brazil's degree of success in achieving

this goal, the results remain impressive. From 1976 when the program began until 1980, production levels of ethanol increased from 600 million liters (4 liters equals one gallon) to 3.5 billion liters. The 1985 goal is 10.7 billion liters. (Source: Dave Hallberg, president of Renewable Fuels Association.) See also "Brazil Ethanol Fuels Program a Victim of Its Own Success," *Business Week*, August 24, 1981.

44. Allen L. Hammond, "Photosynthetic Solar Energy: Rediscovering Biomass Fuels," *Science*, vol. 197, August 19, 1977, pp. 745–746.

45. James S. Trefit, "Wood Stoves Glow Warmly Again in Millions of Homes," *Smithsonian Magazine*, October 1978, pp. 54–63. Our own interviews with leading wood stove and furnace manufacturers indicate that several of the largest manufacturers are selling 100,000 or more units a year.

46. The estimates for wood, dry crop wastes, and Western coals are from Allen L. Hammond, "Photosynthetic Solar Energy: Rediscovering Biomass Fuels," *Science*. The estimate for Eastern coal energy content is from C. Duane Schaub, Guarantee Fuels, Independence, Kansas.

47. Wood's sulfur content is .1 percent, compared to .5 to 1 percent for Western coal and 2 to 4 percent for Eastern coals. Source: C. Duane Schaub, Guarantee Fuels.

48. E. A. Richards, "Alternate Energy Sources," *Brewer's Digest*, vol. 52, no. 8, August 1977, pp. 54–56, 58.

49. Hammond, "Photosynthetic Solar Energy: Rediscovering Biomass Fuels," *Science*. One firm in Canada estimates that yield of its forest land may be increased by seven times; others claim even higher yields. See "Growing Energy," *Science News*, March 11, 1978, p. 153. Claims of higher yield hybrid tree species are viewed with uneasiness by some environmentalists who are concerned with their impact on soil deterioration.

50. Burwell, "Solar Biomass Energy: An Overview of U.S. Potential," *Science*. See also Navicki, "Biomass," *Science News*. See also Stephen H. Spurr, "Silviculture," *Scientific American*, vol. 240, no. 2, February 1979, pp. 76–91.

51. Interview with Bill O'Bear, Director of Wood Commercialization Program, Mass. Energy Office; Steve Morgan, Research Assistant, New England Energy Congress, Member of Congressional Wood Caucus; Gordon Dean, New England Regional Commission.

52. Our estimate is based upon the most conservative assumptions. The Solar Energy Research Institute in *A New Prosperity*, p. 249, suggests that if the government does nothing to promote wood, this source alone will provide 1.5 to 2.5 quads. That study also indicates that "the best available analyses" project that the available sustainable biomass supply in the U.S. can conservatively be between 7 and 17 quads. in 2000.

53. *Energy From Biological Processes*, Vol. II, OTA, Washington, D.C., September 1980. Supplemented with personal conversation with Tom Bull project director of that study.

54. Interview with Ruxton Villet, Solar Energy Research Institute, Golden, Colorado, and David Baltimore, Massachusetts Institute of Technology.

55. The Energy Extension Service was created for such a purpose. See "Energy Extension Service," *Government R&D Report.*

56. Daniel Behrman, *Solar Energy: The Awakening Science* (Boston: Little, Brown, 1976), pp. 32-33, 36.

57. In fact, most of the funds under the solar thermal category are absorbed by the power-tower program. See, William D. Metz, "Solar Thermal Electricity: Power Tower Dominates Research," *Science,* July 22, 1977, p. 353.

For a summary of the U.S. power-tower program, see Department of Energy, *Solar Thermal Energy Conversion, Program Summary,* ERDA 76–159, October 1976, pp. 1–4. See also Energy Research and Development Administration, *Central Receiver Solar Thermal Power System, Phase 1, 10MW Electric Pilot Plant* (Washington, D.C.: Government Printing Office, 1976). For cost-sharing information, see "Sun Power as a Peak Source for the Electric Utilities," *Solar Engineering Magazine,* June 1978, pp. 21–22. For a popular account, see Walter Sullivan, "Solar Test Facility is Near Completion," *New York Times,* November 13, 1977, p. 59. For local attitudes toward the Barstow power tower, see Robert Lindsey, "Desert Town Puts Hopes in Solar Plant," *New York Times,* October 14, 1977, p. A.14.

Metz, "Solar Thermal Electricity: Power Tower Dominates Research," *Science,* pp. 353–356. For the original reference see Caputo, R., "An Initial Comparative Assessment of Orbital and Terrestrial Central Power Systems," Jet Propulsion Lab 77–44, March 1977. For an alternative view of power-tower economics, see Alvin F. Hildebrand and Lovin L. Vant-Hull, "Power with Heliostats," *Science,* September 16, 1977, pp. 1139–1146. For additional views, see Palz, *Solar Electricity: An Economic Approach to Solar Energy,* pp. 170–174.

58. "Barstow Receiver Successfully Tested," *Solar Times,* April 1980, p. 1.

59. Interview with Forrest Stoddard, president of Stoddard Consultants, consultant to the Wind Turbine Industry and formerly chief engineer of U.S. Windpower, Inc.

60. Interview with Russell Wolfe, cofounder of U.S. Windpower, Inc., Burlington, Mass.

61. See Christopher Flavin, *Windpower—A Turning Point,* Worldwatch Paper 45, July 1981.

62. See "Three-Machine Windfarm Starts Up—Then Shuts Down for Repairs," *Solar Times,* July 1981, p. 1, and "Experimental Wind Turbine Blows Over During Test," *Solar Times,* May 1981, p. 2.

63. For a fascinating description of the evolution of hydropower technology, see Daniel Deudrey, *Rivers of Energy,* Worldwatch Paper #44, June 1981.

64. See Essex Development Associates, Harvard Business School case by Anne Columbia. Figures supplemented by interview with Howard C. Ris, program director of the New England River Basins Study. Interview with Howard Munson.

65. 1981 DOE Authorization (Solar Ponds and Solar Material Research). Hearing before the Subcommittee on Energy Development and Application of the

Committee on Science and Technology, U.S. House of Representatives, 96 Cong., March 19, 1980, No. 154, Vol. VIII, pp. 1–3.

66. For a small classic on photovoltaic principles and technology, see Bruce Chalmers, "The Photovoltaic Generation of Electricity," *Scientific American,* October 1976, pp. 34–43. For an excellent review of the photovoltaic field, see John C. C. Fan, "Solar Cells: Plugging into the Sun," *Technology Review,* August/September 1978, pp. 14–35.

67. See, for instance, Isaac Asimov, *Isaac Asimov's Biographic Encyclopedia of Science and Technology* (New York: Avon, 1972), p. 588.

68. Allen L. Hammond, "Photovoltaics: The Semiconductor Revolution Comes to Solar," *Science,* vol. 197, July 29, 1977, pp. 445–447.

69. For a review of government's role in the civilian electronics industry (including semiconductors), see J. M. Uterback and Albert E. Murray, "The Influence of Defense Procurement and Sponsorship of Defense and Development on the Development of the Civilian Electronics Industry," M.I.T. Center for Policy Alternatives, CPA-77-5, June 30, 1977.

70. *Solar Engineering Magazine,* November 1977, p. 12, gives a range of $13 to $27 per peak watt for 1977, and estimates an average of $16. Our interviews with industry executives indicated that average prices dropped to $9 to $11 by 1981. For an overview issue on the photovoltaic industry, see "Watts Ahead for Solar Cells," *Solar Engineering Magazine,* November 1977; for price estimates, see same issue, pp. 12, 14.

71. Source: Strategies Unlimited, a marketing research firm in Mountain View, Calif.

72. Interview with Robert C. Peterson, vice-president, Operations, Solar Power Corporation, June 1977. Mr. Peterson is now a senior vice-president of Collaborative Research, Inc.

73. For the best available description of emerging photovoltaic technology, see Paul Maycock and Edward Stirewalt, *Photovoltaic: Sunlight to Electricity in One Step* (Andover, Mass.: Brick House, 1981), pp. 19–63. Personal conversation with Ron Arnault, president of Arco Solar, January 1982.

74. Interview with Paul Maycock, June 1981, and interview in *Solar Times,* April 1981, p. 12.

75. Interview with Paul Maycock.

76. In a June 1978 Department of Energy study (*Solar Energy, A Status Report,* DOE/ET-0062), the authors examined sixteen projections and found a range of from 3 to 39 quads of solar energy for the year 2000 and from 11 to 109 quads for 2020, not including hydropower.

77. For instance, to Denis Hayes the solar options are "wind, falling water, biomass and direct sunlight." Hayes includes solar heating and cooling and photovoltaics under direct sunlight; "falling water" is his term for hydropower. See Denis Hayes, *Energy: The Solar Prospect.* This is a classic primer on solar energy. For a more extensive treatment of the subject by the same author, see *Rays of Hope: The Transition to a Post-Petroleum World* (New York: W. W. Norton, 1977).

78. Council on Environmental Quality, Executive Office of the President, *Solar Energy, Progress and Promise*, April 1978.

79a. Harvey Brooks and Jack M. Hollander, "United States Energy Alternatives to 2010 and Beyond: The CONAES Study," *Ann. Rev. Energy*, 1979 4: 1–70. See especially pp. 25, 55, and 56. See also "Energy," National Academy of Sciences Newsletter, *Newsreport*, a review of *Energy in Transition, 1985–2010*. Final report, Committee on Nuclear and Alternative Energy Systems, National Research Council, *Energy in Transition, 1985–2010* (San Francisco: W. H. Freeman, 1980).

79b. Henry W. Kendall and Steven J. Nadis, editors, *Energy Strategies: Toward a Solar Future*, a report of the Union of Concerned Scientists, Ballinger Publishing Co., Cambridge, MA, 1980, p. 284.

79c. In a letter to the *New York Times*, Philip Handler and Harvey Brooks, respectively president of the National Academy of Sciences and co-chairman of CONAES, indicated that a 20-percent contribution from solar, including hydropower, by the year 2000 coincided with the "upper bound of what will be technically feasible," according to CONAES. See "When American Solar Goals Clash With Reality," *New York Times*, Letters, March 27, 1980, p. A30. For a criticism of the CONAES findings, see the earlier letter by Gus Speth, Chairman of the President's Council on Environmental Quality, "Prestigious but Wrong Price Tag for Solar Energy," *New York Times*, Letters, February 26, 1980, p. A14.

80. Division of Solar Energy, Energy Research and Development Administration, *Solar Energy in America's Future: A Preliminary Assessment* (Washington, D.C.: ERDA, March 1977). This report documents a Stanford Research Institute study.

81. Other countries have set similar goals for the year 2000. In a study by the Australian Academy of Science, a target of one quarter of the country's energy from solar was set for the year 2000. See *Report of the Committee on Solar Energy Research in Australia*, September, 1973. Plans for virtually complete solar self-efficiency by 2020 have already been developed by both Sweden and California. See, for instance, Thomas B. Johannson and Peter Steen, "Solar Sweden," *AMBIO*, vol. 7, no. 2, June 1978; Mark Christiensen *et al.*, *Distributed Energy Systems in California Energy Future: A Preliminary Report* (Springfield, Va.: National Technical Information Service, September 1977).

82. Unlike the federal tax credit program, any such program should include passive solar energy designs. A key difficulty here is qualifying the cost of the passive "system" and distinguishing it from the remainder of the structure. See also Reference 32.

The funds required for such a program and the amount of solar energy produced could vary widely depending on how much of an investment is made in conservation and which solar technology is chosen. For instance, an active system to heat a conventionally insulated residence may cost $8,000, while a passive system incorporated into a highly insulated structure may only cost a few hundred dollars. In general, the best policy is first to insulate the structure very well and only then to consider solar energy. If, as an example, an average installation cost of $3,000 is assumed (averaged over a mix of old and new homes, active and passive systems, wall-insulated and poorly insulated structures, and hot water and space heating systems) for each of 10 million installations over the next ten years, the total cost would be $30 billion. If commercial installations are included, the total could rise to perhaps $40 billion, or $4 billion yearly. With a 50 percent tax credit, this would result in a subsidy of $2 billion a year.

83. Predictions regarding total U.S. energy in the year 2000 vary widely. The projections cited in Table 7-2 vary from 32 to 70 mbd, or a 2 to 1 range. By choosing a 50 mbd scenario my aim is not to introduce an additional projection, but to emphasize that a strong conservation program, which a 45 mbd scenario would require, should be an integral part of a shift toward solar energy.

84. Relative to the remainder of the world, hydropower in the United States is highly developed. While North America includes only about 13 percent of the world's hydropower potential it produces 40 percent of the total power in the world. But according to at least one estimate, the total potential hydroelectric capacity of the United States is about three times present output, or about 170,000 megawatts. See, for instance, Federal Power Commission, *Hydroelectric Power Resources of the United States* (Washington, D.C.: Government Printing Office, November 1976), p. vii. Yet, due to environmental opposition and economic constraints, it is not likely that much of this potential will be realized. For these reasons, I have used an estimate of 1 to 2 percent growth for major hydroelectric installations, instead of the historic average of 4 percent growth, and rounded to the nearest quad. For an estimate of hydroelectric growth, see John C. Fisher, *Energy Crises in Perspective* (New York: John Wiley and Sons, 1974), p. 28.

However, the potential for low-head (*head* is the height of fall of the water) hydropower, or small installations typically under one megawatt of power, is considerable. According to the Federal Power Commission, present hydroelectric generating capacity could be doubled by developing the nation's 50,000 existing small dams. Two key advantages of the small dams are reduced environmental opposition and the speed with which they can be developed, in comparison to the decade or more required for the large nuclear or coal burning plants. The village of Lyndonville, Vermont, is an example of what is possible. It earns a profit from its beautiful 600-kilowatt plant on the Passumpsic River. For an analysis of the potential of low-head hydro, see David E. Lilienthal, "Lost Megawatts Flow Over Nation's Myriad Spillways," *Smithsonian Magazine*, vol. 8, no. 6, September 1977, pp. 83–88. Mr. Lilienthal was former chairman of the Atomic Energy Commission and Tennessee Valley Authority. See also J.R. McDonald, "Estimate of National Hydroelectric Power Potential at Existing Dams," U.S. Army Corps of Engineers, Institute for Water Resources, Mimeographed paper, July 20, 1977.

Chapter 8 | *Energy Wars*

1. Public opinion in *New York Times*, November 6, 1979; Al Richman, "The Polls: Public Attitudes Toward the Energy Crisis," *Public Opinion Quarterly* (1979): 576–85; William Schneider, "Public Opinion and the Energy Crisis," in Daniel Yergin, ed., *The Dependence Dilemma: Gasoline Consumption and America's Security* (Cambridge: Harvard Center for International Affairs, 1980); letter from Thomas J. Murray and Eric A. Abbott, Energy Information Project, University of Wisconsin, February 11, 1980.

2. U.S. Department of Energy, Energy Information Administration, *Annual Report to Congress, Volume III, 1978* (Washington, D.C.: Superintendent of Documents, May 1978), p. 33. This represents an increase, in 1979 dollars, of over $10 per barrel of the 84 billion barrels of crude oil equivalent that were in U.S. proved reserves of crude oil, natural gas, and natural gas liquids at the end of 1973, and of over $30 per barrel of the 65 billion barrels as of January 1, 1980. This estimate overstates the value, because future income was not discounted to obtain a present value. It understates the increase in value of all oil and gas in the ground because additions will be made to proved reserves. We benefitted from discussions with Kenneth Arrow on welfare economics as well as on a number of other issues in this chapter.

3. See Kenneth J. Arrow and Joseph P. Kalt, *Petroleum Price Regulation: Should We Decontrol?* (Washington: American Enterprise Institute, 1979). Also, Hans H. Landsberg, *Energy: The Next Twenty Years* (Cambridge, Mass.: Ballinger, 1979), chapter 5; and Thomas C. Schelling, *Thinking Through the Energy Problem* (New York: CED, 1979), and Thomas C. Schelling, "Energy and Poverty," discussion paper 852, September 1981 (Harvard Institute of Economic Research, Harvard University). For the very poor, Fuel Marketing Advisory Committee, *Low Income Energy Assistance Programs* (Washington, DOE, 1980).

4. See Karl Kaiser, "The Great Nuclear Debate," *Foreign Policy*, Number 30, Spring 1978, pp. 83–110.

5. The most influential public statements of the conservation views were the Ford Foundation Energy Policy Project, *A Time to Choose: America's Energy Future* (Cambridge, Mass.: Ballinger, 1974); Amory Lovins, "Energy strategy; the road not taken," *Foreign Affairs*, October 1974, pp. 65–96. On proliferation, See Nuclear Energy Policy Study Group, *Nuclear Power: Issues and Choices* (Cambridge, Mass.: Ballinger, 1977).

6. U.S. Congress, Senate, Energy Committee, *The President's Energy Program: A Compilation of Documents*, 95th Congress, 1st Session, 1977, pp. 2, 4, 5, 8, 10.

7. U.S. Congress, Senate, Energy Committee, *Executive Energy Documents*, 95th Congress, 2nd Session, pp. 379–85.

8. *National Journal*, February 11, 1978, p. 231.

9. Executive Office of the President, *The National Energy Plan* (Washington: U.S. Government Printing Office, 1977) pp. xv–xxiii, 96.

10. U.S. Central Intelligence Agency, *The International Energy Situation, the Outlook to 1985*, Washington, April 1977. David Stockman, "The Wrong War? The Case Against National Energy Policy," *Public Interest*, Fall 1978, pp. 3–44. S. Fred Singer, "OPEC's Price Reduction," *The New Republic*, January 6, 1979, pp. 11–12.

11. For the windfall tax provisions, see Chapter 2, Ref. 79.

12. Paul Ignatius, Eugene Zuchert, and Lloyd Cutler, *Washington Post*, June 10, 1979. Yergin and Hillenbrand, *Global Insecurity*, p. 109.

13. *New York Times*, June 16, 1979, p. A10.

14. "Rare bottle of wine" is from Reagan Energy Transition report, quoted in Yergin and Hillenbrand, *Global Insecurity*, p. 110.

Chapter 9 | *Conclusion: Toward a Balanced Energy Program*

1. By any measure, exploration and development activity for both oil and gas have increased substantially; the number of wells drilled, as one example, almost tripled between 1973 and 1981. But domestic production and domestic reserves of oil and gas declined. See *Monthly Energy Review* and data from American Petroleum Institute and American Gas Association.

2. These costs are a result of "market failure." For an excellent discussion of this general subject, see Francis M. Bator, "The Anatomy of Market Failure," *Quarterly Journal of Economics*, LXXII (August 1958), pp. 351–379. Authors have referred to such costs by a variety of names. For examples, see "Externalities," in Robert M. Solow, "The Economics of Resources or the Resources of Economics," *The American Economic Review*, 64 (May 1974), pp. 1–14; "side effects," in Fred Hirsch, *The Social Limits of Growth* (Cambridge, Mass.: Harvard University Press, 1977), p. 3, "uncounted costs and benefits," in Charles E. Lindblom, *Politics and Markets* (New York: Basic Books, 1977), pp. 79, 80; "byproducts" in Thomas C. Schelling, "On the Ecology of Micromotives," in Robbin Marris, ed., *The Corporate Society* (London: Macmillan, 1974), p. 39. This category of costs, together with the costs paid for directly by the users of the energy, is called "social costs"; see Robert Dorfman and Mancy S. Dorfman, *Economics of the Environment* (New York: W. W. Norton, 1977).

3. Although carbon dioxide emissions from burning hydrocarbons could eventually prove to be a large cost for future generations.

4. See Table 9-1.

5. They are discussed at greater length in Chapter 2.

6. The increased costs to the United States flowing from higher oil prices can be thought of as an externality in the sense that a user does not encounter, at the time the consumption decision is made, the subsequent higher costs resulting from his (or her) actions. Such costs are often called "pecuniary costs." This example is but one of a class of actions that causes market failure in the economic sense. See Alfred Kahn, "The Tyranny of Small Decisions:

Market Failures, Imperfections, and the Limits of Economics," *Kyklos* (1966), pp. 23–46; Thomas C. Schelling, "On the Ecology of Micromotives," pp. 19–64; and Schelling, *Micromotives and Macrobehavior* (New York: W. W. Norton, 1978).

7. For a list of methods available to correct distortions, see Schelling, "On the Ecology of Micromotives," p. 28. For an indication of the preference of business executives (as well as of the former chairman of the Council of Economic Advisors, Charles Schultz) for incentives rather than sanctions, see *Chemical Week*, September 6, 1978, p. 15.

8. The subjective nature of costs is developed at length in James M. Buchanan, *Costs and Choice* (Chicago: Markham Publishing, 1969). For a discussion of the difficulty in using the Gross National Product to assess economic welfare, see William D. Nordhaus and James Tobin, "Is Growth Obsolete?" in *Economic Growth* (New York: National Bureau of Economic Research, 1972). For an indication of the difficulty of determining the relationship of higher energy prices to GNP, see Energy Modeling Forum, *Energy and the Economy, EMF Report 1, Volume 1* (Stanford: Stanford University, Institute of Energy Studies, September 1977).

9. For general discussions, see Bator, "Anatomy of Market Failure"; Dorfman and Dorfman, *Economics of the Environment;* Kahn, "The Tyranny of Small Decisions"; and Schelling, *Micromotives and Macrobehavior.* But something is needed to force action, as volunteerism is not suited to solve inefficiencies in energy markets. Schelling's observations about conditions in which volunteerism is unlikely to work apply to energy. There is "nothing heroic in the occasion"; what is required is often a "protracted nuisance." The individual feels no particular community with many others who would benefit from his sacrifices, and he likely would suspect that large numbers of people were not cooperating. Thus, it is not surprising that President Carter discovered after he launched his "moral equivalent of war" that the nation needs quite a bit more than moral exhortation from the White House to restrain oil imports. Perhaps the classic illustration of individual actions which result in suboptimal economic results is the "tragedy of the commons," in which everyone benefits from the upkeep of the common, but no one has the motivation to tend it himself; thus, there develops the opposite and fatal incentive to overgraze it before others complete its ruin. See R. Hardin, *Collective Action* (Baltimore: The Johns Hopkins University Press, 1982), for Resources for the Future, and G. Hardin, "The Tragedy of the Commons," *Science,* December 13, 1968, pp. 1243–1248. Perhaps the most dramatic case was the killing of 20 million to 30 million buffalo within half a dozen years, just for the hides. For every penny of hide, five pounds of meat rotted. Fifteen years later, this meat could have been transported to market. This example is given in Thomas Schelling, "On the Ecology of Micromotives."

10. For estimates of price subsidies received by U.S. consumers, see Reference 1 of Chapter 3 (for natural gas). Consumers are also receiving a large price subsidy by paying much less for electricity—sometimes less than half—than

for electricity from new coal, nuclear, and hydroelectric plants. Estimates shown elsewhere, although not complete for all consuming sectors and based on different data, are consistent with the $50 billion figure. See Sant in Reference 12. In addition to price subsidies granted consumers (principally at the expense of the owners of natural gas and electrical generating plants), producers of conventional energy sources have received large subsidies from the government, and are continuing to receive subsidies. One study showed past subsidies to be $120 billion. See Battelle Memorial Institute, *An Analysis of Federal Incentives Used to Stimulate Energy Production* (Springfield, Va.: National Technical Information Service, March 1978).

We recognize that some forms of pollution could be caused by certain forms of solar energy and cogeneration, but our statement is generally correct. Of course, all oil, domestic and imported, has external costs because of environmental effects. For example, even so-called low-sulfur oils, whether found in nature or refined from crude oils containing sulfur, still have sulfur in them; thus sulfur dioxide is released into the atmosphere when the oil is burned. And burning oil (and gas), of course, also releases carbon dioxide, thereby contributing to a possible social cost for some future generation.

11. This conclusion is consistent with the so-called theory of the second best, which establishes that when the prices of some products (such as oil) are held below free-market levels, it may be economically beneficial for the nation to hold the prices of competing prices (such as conservation and solar energies) below their free-market levels. See R. G. Lipsey and Kelvin Lancaster, "The General Theory of Second Best," *Review of Economic Studies*, 24 (1956), pp. 11–32; E. J. Mishan, "Second Thoughts on Second Best," *Oxford Economic Papers*, 14 (October 1962), pp. 205–17; R. Rees, "Second-Best Rules for Public Enterprise Pricing," *Economica*, 35 (August 1968), pp. 260–73; William J. Baumol and David F. Bradford, "Optimal Departures from Marginal Cost Pricing," *American Economic Review*, 60 (June 1970), pp. 265–83.

12. In fact, there is no way of knowing for sure what the return on investment would be for the nation in giving financial incentives for conservation and renewable energy sources. But there are powerful reasons for trying fairly large payments and for believing that the nation would be justified in spending tens of billions of dollars on such a program. Certainly there are formidable political and economic constraints in providing supplies of energy from conventional sources in sufficient quantities to stop the growth of oil imports. Furthermore, although more analyses are required, it appears that a saving of the equivalent of 10 million barrels of oil per day, estimated to require an investment of some $220 billion, is cheaper than providing the equivalent of an additional 10 million barrels per day of oil from conventional energy sources—and certainly cheaper than the cost of marginal oil imports. For the comparison of conservation and conventional energy sources, see Roger Sant, "A Preliminary Assessment of the Potential to Adjust Capital Stock to Higher Energy Using Efficiencies," Paper presented at the American Association for the Advance-

ment of Science, Washington, D.C., February 14, 1978. A similar analysis is not available for solar energy, but data in Chapter 7 suggest that the cost of solar energy varies over a wide range and some forms are quite cost effective when compared with the cost of incremental supplies of conventional energy sources, as reported by Sant. Note that the analysis by Sant does not include external costs. And it apparently does not consider a possible upward bias in econometric and technological forecasts of supplies of conventional energy sources, as discussed in our Appendix.

Information in Reference 2 of Chapter 6 indicates that conservation and solar energy are more cost effective than nuclear power.

13. Ideally, it would be desirable for the cost of marginal BTUs of energy from conservation and solar to equal the cost of marginal BTUs from each of the other energy sources. No adequate information exists to fine-tune financial incentives in such a manner. But our contention is that for the next five million or so barrels of oil daily above current levels, conservation (with some solar energy, also) will be at lower cost than the main alternative: oil imports. *In addition, financial incentives for conservation and soilar have only a nominal impact on the consumer price index compared with the major impact of imported oil.*

14. Separate economic units, because of lack of risk-pooling, are more risk-averse than all economic units taken together. Reference 31, Chapter 7, contains references justifying payments to speed the diffusion of innovation. In addition, because investors do not capture all the beneficial effects of experience, there is a natural tendency for society to underinvest; see Kenneth Arrow, "The Economic Implications of Learning by Doing," *Review of Economic Studies,* 29 (June 1962), pp. 155–173. Also, learning-curve effects are greater during the early stages of an industry's life than during the later stages, the tendency to underinvest is greater during the early stages.

15. In order to partially correct such an obvious underestimation of the cost of sickness, one U.S. government study gave all housewives the value of a domestic servant. See Dorothy P. Rice, *Estimating the Cost of Illness* (Health Economics Series No. 6), U.S. Public Health Service, 1966. A more recent approach has given values to each duty a housewife performs, an approach that resulted in a value (in 1972) of about $6,000 yearly. The psychic value of a housewife to her family or society was not considered. Also, pain and suffering are not included in the cost of illness. See Barbara S. Cooper and Dorothy P. Rice, "The Economic Cost of Illness Revisited," Social Security Administration, DHEW Publication No. (55A) 76-11703, reprinted from the *Social Security Bulletin,* February 1976, U.S. Department of Health, Education, and Welfare. Also see Lester B. Lave and Eugene P. Seskin, *Air Pollution and Human Health* (Baltimore: Johns Hopkins University Press, 1977), pp. 225, 348, 349. Another complicating factor in estimating the cost of pollution is the impossibility of proving empirically that it causes illness. There is controversy surrounding, especially, the issue of air pollution, but two leading investigators conclude that it does. See Lester B. Lave and Eugene P. Seskin, "Does

Air Pollution Cause Mortality?" *Statistics and the Environment,* Proceedings of the Fourth Symposium, March 3–5, 1976 (Washington, D.C.: American Statistical Association). Their conclusion is supported by other observations. For example, more than 4,000 citizens of London died from an extended period of severe air pollution there in 1952; see *Resources* (Washington, D.C.: Resources for the Future, April–July 1978), p. 1.

For an example of an oil-company publication that ignores the fact that conservation and solar energy are competing against oil and gas priced below their economic values, see *Our Energy Dilemma . . . Fact and Commentary,* Report by Marathon Oil Company, Findlay, Ohio, July 1977.

16. These estimates of 36 and 42 mbd, respectively, include the 0.9 mbd of biomass consumed in 1981 but not reported in the statistics published by the Department of Energy, Energy Information Administration.

17. Various projections can be found in: U.S. Department of Energy, Energy Information Administration, *1981 Annual Report to Congress,* Volume 3, Energy Projections, February 1981, DOE/EIA-0173(81)/3; U.S. Department of Energy, *Securing America's Future—The National Energy Policy Plan,* a report to the Congress (Washington, D.C.: U.S. Government Printing Office, July 1981); U.S. Department of Energy, Office of Policy, Planning and Analysis, *Energy Projections to the Year 2000—A Supplement to the National Energy Policy Plan Required by Title VIII of the U.S. Department of Energy Organization Act (Public Law 95-91)* (National Technical Information Service (NTIS), U.S. Department of Commerce, Springfield, Va., July 1981); a report prepared by the Congressional Research Service for the Use of the Committee on Energy and Commerce of the U.S. House of Representatives, *U.S. Energy Outlook: A Demand Perspective for the Eighties* (Washington, D.C.: Government Printing Office, July 1981); Conoco Inc., Coordinating and Planning Department, *World Energy Outlook Through 2000,* January 1982; The MITRE Corporation, *U.S. Energy Strategies: Some Options for Eliminating Oil Imports by the Year 2000* (McLean, Va.: The MITRE Corporation, April 1981); and Exxon Company, U.S.A., *Exxon Company, U.S.A.'s Energy Outlook 1980–2000* (Houston, Texas: Exxon Company, U.S.A., December 1980).

18. American Telephone and Telegraph, "Energy Conservation at AT&T" (1979).

Appendix: | *Limits to Models*

This Appendix is based heavily on the analyses in Sergio Koreisha, "A Survey on the Limitations of Three Energy Policy Models," Working paper, Energy Project at the Harvard Business School, 1979. We wish to express our appreciation to William W. Hogan, Hendrik Houthakker, and Henry Jacoby for their efforts in facilitating our review of their work, and to Hogan in particular for general discussions on the roles of models and the importance of lags. We, of course, bear full responsibility for this appendix.

1. "Rear-view mirror" analogy from Arthur Schlaifer, Jr., professor at Harvard Business School, to whom we express appreciation for reviewing the manuscript. Of course, in some cases econometric models are used to forecast *new* energy sources, and technological models are used to forecast *existing* energy sources. The use of judgment represents the use of an "implicit mental model," a term used by William W. Hogan, "Energy Modeling: Building Understanding for Better Use," Paper presented at the Second Lawrence Symposium on the Systems and Decision Sciences, Berkeley, California, October 3, 1978. In using their judgment, modelers sometimes change the results directly and sometimes change the assumptions in the model in order to obtain different results.

2. "The Economic Modelers Vie for Washington's Ear," *Fortune,* November 20, 1978; quote on "public officials," p. 105, and "when the history," p. 102. Some authors have cited examples in which U.S. political leaders have ceded "large tracts of traditionally political territory to the custody of experts"; Martin Greenberger *et al., Models in the Policy Process* (New York: Russell Sage Foundation, 1976), p. 28. Also see Robert E. Lance, "The Decline of Politics and Ideology in a Knowledgeable Society," *American Journal of Sociology* 31 (1968), pp. 657–658. In addition to the information in this appendix, see especially Chapters 2, 3, and 6 for support of this conclusion. For further discussion of problems in using models, see Lester C. Thurow, "Economics 1977," *Daedalus,* 106 (Fall 1977), pp. 79–94. For an essay on the misuse of macroeconomic models by economists, see James B. Ramsey, *Economic Forecasting—Models or Markets* (London: The Institute of Economic Affairs, 1977). Also see "The Economist as Prophet," *Morgan Guaranty Survey,* August 1978, pp. 9–14; and Leonard Silk, "The Highly Inexact Science of Economics," *New York Times,* December 8, 1977, p. 65. Our judgment is that reliance on economic and technology studies is more likely by the executive branch than by members of Congress, who are elected by constituents, who in turn feel little need for such studies to form an opinion about their interests.

3. *New York Times,* November 13, 1974, p. 1; *Business Week,* January 13, 1975, p. 67. For information about oil prices in 1974, see Reference 26.

4. See article by Assistant Secretary of State Thomas O. Enders about the need for a floor price in the industrial nations, in "OPEC and the Industrial Countries: The Next Ten Years," *Foreign Affairs,* July 1975, pp. 625–637. Of course, a floor price was never instituted.

5. "A Conversation with Henry Ford," Los Angeles *Times,* January 21, 1979.

6. For an excellent example of a model builder's description of limitations, see the writings by William W. Hogan in Energy Modeling Forum, *Energy and the Economy, EMF Report 1,* vol. 1 (Stanford: Stanford University, Institute for Energy Studies, September 1977), p. iv. Within the model-building profession, there has been concern for some time about the use and misuse of models; see Hogan, "Energy Modeling: Building Understanding for Better Use." For a recent review of energy models, see Alan S. Manne, Richard G.

Richels, and John P. Weyant, "Energy Policy Modeling: A Survey," *Operations Research,* forthcoming. Also, in recent years much greater emphasis has been placed on assessing models; the Energy Modeling Forum at Stanford has an active program underway. For an example of their work, see Energy Modeling Forum, *Coal in Transition: 1980–2000, EMF Report* 2, vol. 1 (Stanford: Stanford University, Energy Modeling Forum, July 1978). A group at MIT also has been active in this field: for example, see MIT Energy Laboratory Policy Study Group, "The FEA Project Independence Report: An Analytical Review and Evaluation," Energy Laboratory Report MIT-EL-75-017, Mimeographed paper, May 1975.

7. With reference to the principle of *exclusion,* omitting a significant variable from the equation biases the estimates of the coefficients associated with the variables actually used in the model. See G. S. Maddala, *Econometrics* (McGraw-Hill, New York, 1977), p. 156. The requirement of relevant historical experience, of course, has been recognized. In January 1974, for example, William Fellner, then a member of the President's Council of Economic Advisors, stated that "it is definitely impossible" to specify what the price elasticity of demand for gasoline would be with the drastically higher gasoline prices; quoted in *New York Times,* January 11, 1974, pp. 41, 48. Quotes by others in this article reflect the same sentiment.

The problem of extrapolating far outside the range of prior experience often is compounded by the assumption (for convenience) that one elasticity equation exists over the entire range. For example, for convenience and because of lack of a more precise theory, model builders often assume that over the entire range of forecasts, quantity and price have either a linear relationship or constant elasticity. If one assumes a linear relationship, then a change in price from $10.000 to $11.00 is assumed to have the same effect on quantity demanded (or supplied) as a change in price from $1.00 to $2.00; in other words, a 10-percent price increase at the upper level would have the same effect on quantity as a 100-percent price increase at the lower level. Thus, at high price levels, demand and supply are assumed to be very responsive to price changes; so, as the price rises, demand is forecast to decrease very rapidly and supply to increase very rapidly. Therefore, with upward price movements, demand and supply are forecast to come into equilibrium very quickly. This condition existed with the Kennedy-Houthakker model, which used linear equations for demand and supply. (The demand equations were linear approximations of the double-logarithmic equations used to estimate the demand function; see Reference 9.)

But what if the model builder assumes a constant elasticity over the entire range? The practical implication of this is that if the price elasticity of demand is less than one—as was the case for OPEC oil in 1974 and likely still is the case in 1979—then the higher the price, the greater the income of the suppliers (see Adelman in Reference 45); thus, in this formulation, there is no practical cut-off in price increases. Therefore, using a constant elasticity over a very broad range has the potential to create unrealistic results.

8. Gary C. Hufbauer, *Synthetic Materials and the Theory of International Trade* (Cambridge: Harvard University Press, 1966), pp. 46–57, and Robert B. Stobaugh and Phillip L. Townsend, "Price Forecasting and Strategic Planning: The Case of Petrochemicals," *Journal of Marketing Research,* XII (February 1975), pp. 19–29.

9. For a description of the model, which has been documented more than most models, see Michael Kennedy, "An Economic Model of the World Oil Market," *The Bell Journal of Economics and Management Science,* 5 (Autumn 1974), pp. 540–577. For more detailed descriptions of the model, see Michael Kennedy, "A World Oil Model," in Dale Jorgenson, ed., *Econometric Studies of U.S. Energy Policy* (Amsterdam: North-Holland, 1976), pp. 95–175, and Michael Kennedy, "An Economic Model of the World Oil Market," Ph.D. thesis, Harvard University, November 1974. Also, an important contribution of this model is its solution algorithm, which is much more efficient than most models. For an earlier paper on a similar subject, see H. S. Houthakker, "The Capacity Method of Quadratic Programming," *Econometrica,* 28 (January 1960), pp. 62–87.

10. The host-government "revenue" officially is a combination of royalty and income tax, but often is referred to as a royalty or export duty—the terminology of Kennedy and Houthakker. For convenience, we refer to it as a host-government tax. What the U.S. government officially deems it to be—royalty or income tax—could make a substantial difference in U.S. taxation of U.S. companies.

11. Parts of the World Oil Model have been incorporated into a new model, the World Energy Model, that is, a dynamic long-run model that contains natural gas, coal, nuclear, hydro, and electrical power, in addition to oil. For the results of the model, see H. S. Houthakker and Michael Kennedy, "Long-Range Energy Prospects," in Ragaei El Mallakh and Dorothea H. El Mallakh, *Energy Options and Conservation* (Boulder, Colo.: The International Research Center for Energy and Economic Development, 1978), pp. 11–41. For a description of the methodology, see Houthakker and Kennedy, "A Long-Run Model of World Energy Demands, Supplies and Prices," Mimeographed paper, prepared in 1978.

12. "The equation for gasoline demand was run on pooled time series observations from 12 countries (Portugal, Italy, Austria, Belgium, Denmark, France, West Germany, Netherlands, Norway, Sweden, United Kingdom, an United States) which covered the years 1962–1972. The remaining equations (kerosene, distillate fuel, residual oil fuel) were fitted over a smaller sample of 9 countries (Japan, Italy, Belgium, Denmark, France, West Germany, Netherlands, Sweden, and United Kingdom), for the years 1965–1970. The U.S. was not included due to data deficiency"; Kennedy, "An Economic Model," Ph.D. thesis, pp. IV–11 and IV–12.

13. Some of the standard errors for the regression coefficients for certain product-demand equations were larger or as large as the coefficients themselves; Kennedy, "An Economic Model," *Bell Journal.* It is quite common for model

builders to modify their elasticities in order to ensure that the models produce what the modelers consider to be reasonable results. "The Economic Modelers Vie for Washington's Ear," *Fortune*, November 20, 1978, p. 105. At times, modelers handle some of the potential problems raised by our "red flags" by running several scenarios and choosing one that reflects their judgment. It is desirable, of course, to show estimates obtained with elasticities based upon data and those obtained with elasticities based upon judgment.

14. Kennedy, "An Economic Model," *Bell Journal*, p. 571. See Reference 26 for a discussion of world oil prices in 1974. They assumed, of course, that U.S. price controls on oil would be removed, but even with controls the average prices paid by U.S. refiners and prices paid for new oil were higher than some of the equilibrium prices estimated by Kennedy and Houthakker. See discussion later in text about possible nonmonetary effects of price controls. Effective January 1, 1979, the OPEC price for market crude had been raised to $13.34 and the host-government tax is a little lower, generally 10 to 30 cents, depending on operating costs, whether the company operated the oil fields, and the reinvestment rate of the companies within the host-nation; *Wall Street Journal*, December 18, 1978, p. 2.

15. Kennedy and Houthakker used a nonlinear model, which made it difficult to calculate likely boundaries; see Reference 9.

16. For information about world oil prices during 1974, see Reference 26.

17. First quote from Hendrik S. Houthakker, "The Oil Problem and the International Monetary System," Talk before the Conference Board on United States —Japanese Economic Policy, Tokyo, Japan, April 1, 1974, p. 10. Other quotes by Vermont Royster, a writer for *Wall Street Journal*, in reporting on a conference on the world oil situation at the American Enterprise Institute, in "Glimmer Amid the Gloom," *Wall Street Journal*, October 9, 1974, p. 26.

18. Quote from Hendrik S. Houthakker, *The World Price of Oil: A Medium-Term Analysis* (Washington, D.C.: American Enterprise Institute for Public Policy Research, 1976), p. 27. This publication also contains estimates for 1985. Information about reason for using judgment in estimating output of Middle East and North Africa, from interview with Houthakker.

19. The Policy Study Group of the MIT Energy Laboratory, "Energy Self-Sufficiency: An Economic Evaluation," *Technology Review*, May 1974, pp. 23–58; quote is from p. 24. Note that this was an *assumption* used for analytical purposes, not a *prediction*. For their economic models, they used long-term elasticities and assumed that they applied for 1980.

20. The group recognized the explicit problem of aggregating onshore and off-shore drilling activity; "Energy Self-Sufficiency," p. 34 (quote is on p. 29). In fact, U.S. production of crude oil in 1980 almost surely will not be as high as that indicated by the MIT econometric study for the prices actually received for newly found oil. But also see later discussion in text about possible non-monetary effects of price controls.

21. The group's report explicitly recognized these two problems: "Energy Self-Sufficiency," p. 34.

22. See Chapter 2, Reference 69.
23. The Department of Energy estimate was $24 in 1975 dollars; *Chemical Week*, November 8, 1978, p. 36.
24. For example, refer to the shale-oil story in Chapter 2.
25. For starts toward developing a conceptual model describing the progress of new technologies, see John Diffenbach, "New Energy Technologies: Evolution and Cross-Impact," Harvard Business School doctoral thesis, and David Bodde, "The Influence of Regulation on Technical Evolution of the Electric Generating Industry," Harvard Business School doctoral thesis, 1976.
26. The estimates of natural gas supply in the MIT study seem especially high, presumably because of the elasticities in the MacAvoy-Pindyck model used by MIT. See Chapter 3 of this book for prices of newly found natural gas. In addition to assuming price decontrol of oil in all cases and gas in some cases, the MIT group also assumed that offshore territories would be leased. The price of OPEC oil at the time of the MIT study was not clear to anyone, not even the oil companies. The OPEC members had agreed on a host-government tax of $7.00, effective January 1, 1974. But demand for oil continued strong and in March 1974, the oil companies in anticipation of retroactive tax action by OPEC members began transferring crude oil from their producing subsidiaries to their other subsidiaries at about $9.50 per barrel, which would imply a government tax of about $9.00. By the end of 1974, through retroactive action and OPEC "participation," that is, the OPEC members' takeover of all or part of the operating properties from the companies, the government tax on market crude was raised to $10.12 a barrel, effective January 1, 1975. See Edith Penrose, "The Development of Crisis," in Raymond Vernon, ed., *The Oil Crisis* (New York: W. W. Norton, 1976), p. 52; and "Energy Self-Sufficiency," pp. 48–49. For more details on oil prices during 1974, see Reference 32, Chapter 2. We interpret a host-government tax of $7.00 a barrel to be the basis for the MIT group's world capacity estimates as well as to be the "current" level from which they based their prediction that price was more likely to fall than rise. After describing the uncertainty surrounding OPEC price at that particular time, they state, "Our assumption at other points in this study has been that the average payment will converge in the short run on a figure close to $7.00 per barrel"; "Energy Self-Sufficiency," p. 49. They mention a $9.00 level delivered to the United States, which equates to about $7.00 host-government tax; see p. 54.

    Because of the limitations inherent in using a single econometric model to predict world oil supplies, the Supply Analysis Group of the MIT World Oil Project is developing a forecasting method that incorporates explicit representations of the different steps in the oil-supply process for different major oil fields. See Paul L. Eckbo, Henry D. Jacoby, and James L. Smith, "Oil Supply Forecasting: A Disaggregated Process Approach," *The Bell Journal of Economics*, 9 (Spring 1978), pp. 218–235; and M. A. Adelman and H. D. Jacoby, "Alternative Methods of Oil Supply Forecasting," in Robert S. Pindyck, ed., *Advances in the Economics of Energy Resources, Volume II: The*

Production and Pricing of Energy Resources (Greenwich, Conn.: J.A.I. Press, forthcoming).

27. "Energy Self-Sufficiency," pp. 28–30.

28. "Energy Self-Sufficiency," p. 28.

29. The National Petroleum Council studies on which the MIT group relied heavily for their judgmental supply forecasts consist of a series of reports published in 1972 and 1973 on the U.S. energy outlook from then until the end of the century. The studies' participants included energy experts not only from the oil and gas industries, but also from government and the coal, nuclear, and electric utilities industries. The NPC supply forecasts were relatively insensitive to price, being 38.4, 39.3, and 39.4 million barrels of oil equivalent per day, respectively, at the three price levels ($7, $9, and $11 in 1973 dollars). "Energy Self-Sufficiency," p. 28. The MIT group's judgmental demand estimates relied most heavily on the NPC studies and a study by the National Economic Research Associates; p. 30. We made no attempt to evaluate the judgmental forecasts. First, evaluating such forecasts is more difficult than evaluating econometric estimates—a factor that makes econometric models easier to criticize than judgmental forecasts—for the assumptions underlying judgmental assessments are seldom as clearly identified. Second, we are not in a position to question the expertise of those making the assessments. In fact, we know personally a number of the experts who participated in the National Petroleum Council work used by MIT and doubt whether it would have been possible to obtain a better qualified panel. But the ability of any expert to make accurate predictions of supply-and-demand relationships under conditions quite different from any historical experience is very limited. See Reference 30, this chapter, about the disadvantage of considering energy as one homogeneous source.

30. Federal Energy Administration, *Project Independence Report* (Washington, D.C.: Government Printing Office, November 1974), app. AII. The demand forecasts do not reflect economic and resource restrictions, such as levels of domestic supplies of energy sources, financial ability to build new facilities, or import levels of energy products. These restrictions are incorporated into the model at a later stage. The demand forecasts, however, do reflect effects of non-price initiatives taken to conserve energy. Regional forecasts were obtained by disaggregating the national forecasts according to census regions. Note that there obviously is an important advantage in a model that determines demand by fuel type and allows substitution of one fuel for another only when this is possible. In contrast, relatively simple energy models in which energy is considered as one homogeneous product can be misleading. For example, GNP affects electricity demand, which in turn affects the demand for coal. Thus, as long as coal is available, a rise in energy usage caused by a rise in GNP would not be met entirely by imported oil. In two computer runs done by the PIES-74 group, for example, GNP was reduced, thereby lowering demand for energy by 10 quads, but oil imports were reduced only 2 quads; this example from interview with William Hogan.

31. If the prices derived by the linear program were not significantly different from the ones estimated by the econometric model, then the linear program prices and quantities were considered to be the equilibrium solution. If the prices were significantly different, then trial and error was used until there was a convergence of the prices from the linear program and econometric model.

32. A good critique is J. A. Hausman, "Project Independence Report: An Appraisal of U.S. Energy Needs up to 1985," *Bell Journal of Economics*, 6 (Autumn 1975), pp. 517–551; and a related study, MIT Energy Laboratory Policy Study Group, "The FEA Project Independence Report." Also see U.S. General Accounting Office, *Review of the 1974 Project Independence Evaluation System*, OPA-76-20, Washington, D.C., April 1976. A later version of PIES was critiqued in Hans Landsberg, "Review of the Federal Energy Administration *National Energy Outlook, 1976,*" Report to the National Science Foundation, Resources for the Future, Washington, D.C., March, 1977.

33. Federal Energy Administration, *Project Independence Report*, pp. 414–416.

34. Martin Greenberger *et. al.*, *Models in the Policy Process*, p. 45.

35. For another example, see Reference 6, this appendix.

36. In technical terms, substitute goods theoretically should have a positive cross elasticity, whereas the PIES authors obtained a number of negative cross elasticities; *Project Independence Report*, app. A-11, p. 62.

37. U.S. Comptroller General Report to Congress, *Review of the 1974 Project Independence Evaluation System* (Washington, D.C.: Government Printing Office, November 1974), p. 38.

38. *Project Independence Report*, pp. 82–83.

39. *Project Independence Report*, p. 49.

40. Hogan, "Energy Modeling: Building Understanding for Better Use"; and "The Economist as Prophet," *The Morgan Guaranty Survey*, August 1978, p. 13.

41. Hogan, "Energy Modeling," and A. M. Geoffrion, "The Purpose of Mathematical Programming Is Insight, Not Numbers," *Interface*, November 1976, pp. 81–92. Some model builders, however, disagree with this.

42. This is even ignoring the deliberate misuse of model results for political purposes. In this appendix, we are not suggesting that there is something better than models, but that sometimes formal models are not adequate to provide predictions within a range sufficiently narrow to be useful. Neither are judgmental models, sometimes.

43. Robert Pindyck, "The Economics of Oil Pricing," *Wall Street Journal*, December 20, 1977, p. 16. Also, see his "OPEC's Threat to the West," *Foreign Policy*, Spring 1978, pp. 36–52, and "Gains to Producers from the Cartelization of Exhaustible Resources," in *Review of Economics and Statistics*, LX (May 1978), pp. 238–251.

44. Pindyck, "The Economics of Oil Pricing."

45. M. A. Adelman, "Need for Caution over Prices," *Petroleum Economist*, September 1977, p. 359.

46. Hogan, "Energy Modeling."

47. Note that on models linking energy consumption to GNP, the elasticity can be 1.0 and the ratio of energy to GNP can change. For evidence on the conclusion that too much attention was focused on the potential of traditional energy sources at the expense of conservation and solar energy, see especially Chapters 6 and 7, this book.

48. *Chemical Week*, November 8, 1978, p. 36.

49. "Energy Self-Sufficiency," p. 24.

INDEX

ABOUT THE AUTHORS

ROBERT STOBAUGH is a professor of business administration at the Harvard Business School and director of the Energy Project. A graduate of Louisiana State University with a degree in chemical engineering, he spent eighteen years in the oil and petrochemical industries in the U.S. and abroad before earning his doctorate at the Harvard Business School. Author or coauthor of eight books, he is a past president of the Academy of International Business, a member of the American Economics Association, and has been a consultant to a number of companies, cabinet-level departments and congressional committees, and to the United Nations and several foreign countries. He recently completed the basic energy balances to the year 2000 for the new study, *Global Insecurity: A Strategy for Energy and Economic Renewal.*

DANIEL YERGIN is a lecturer at the Kennedy School of Government at Harvard, a member of its Energy and Environmental Policy Center, and chairman of the Harvard International Energy and Security Seminar. He was formerly a lecturer at the Harvard Business School. A Yale graduate, he received his Ph.D. in international relationship from Cambridge University. He is author of *Shattered Peace: the Origins of the Cold War,* and senior author of *Global Insecurity: a Strategy for Energy and Economic Renewal.*

He has been a consultant to the Energy Directorate of the European Community, the U.S. Senate Foreign Relations Committee, and the U.S. Departments of Energy, State, and Transportation.

I. C. BUPP is an associate professor at the Harvard Business School, where he has done extensive research and course-development work on the utilities and natural gas industries. After graduating from Swarthmore College, he worked for the Atomic Energy Commission and later received his Ph.D. from the Harvard Government Department. He is co-author of *Light Water: How the Nuclear Dream Dissolved.*

MEL HORWITCH is an assistant professor at the Sloan School of Management at M.I.T. He received his B.A. from Princeton and his M.B.A. and doctorate from the Harvard Business School, where he specialized in coporate planning. Formerly a member of the Harvard Business School faculty, he is the author of the book, *Clipped Wings: The American SST Conflict.*

SERGIO KOREISHA is an assistant professor of business administration at the University of Oregon. He has bachelor's and master's degrees in engineering from the University of California and received his doctorate in mathematical analysis and managerial decision from the Harvard Business School.

MODESTO A. MAIDIQUE is a specialist in the management of technological innovation. Formerly an assistant professor at the Harvard Business School, he is now an associate professor at Stanford's School of Industrial Engineering. He holds B.S. and Ph.D. degrees in physics from M.I.T. He was a founder and for seven years a vice-president of an electronics firm and holds several patents.

FRANK SCHULLER a graduate of the University of Texas, has an M.B.A. degree and a Doctor of Business Administration degree (on technological innovation in international business) from the Harvard Business School. He has also had extensive experience in the oil and gas industries.